Field Manual
No. 3-05.130

Department of the Army
Washington, DC, 30 September 2008

Army Special Operations Forces Unconventional Warfare

Contents

		Page
	PREFACE	iv
Chapter 1	INTRODUCTION	1-1
	Overview	1-1
	Unconventional Warfare	1-2
	Conventional Warfare	1-4
	Irregular Warfare	1-5
Chapter 2	UNITED STATES NATIONAL POWER	2-1
	The International Environment	2-1
	Instruments of United States National Power	2-1
	The Effectiveness of Integrated National Power	2-14
Chapter 3	POLICY AND DOCTRINE	3-1
	National Policy	3-1
	Conventional Warfare and Major Combat Operations	3-15
	Irregular Warfare	3-21
Chapter 4	PLANNING CONSIDERATIONS	4-1
	Unconventional Warfare Planning	4-1
	Seven Phases of Unconventional Warfare	4-5
	Unconventional Warfare Termination of Operations	4-12
	Army Special Operations Forces	4-14
	Supporting Elements and Activities	4-20
	Interagency Activities	4-20

Distribution Restriction: Distribution authorized to U.S. Government agencies and their contractors only to protect technical or operational information from automatic dissemination under the International Exchange Program or by other means. This determination was made on 28 August 2008. Other requests for this document must be referred to Commander, United States Army John F. Kennedy Special Warfare Center and School, ATTN: AOJK-DTD-JA, Fort Bragg, NC 28310-9610, or by e-mail to JAComments@soc.mil.

Destruction Notice: Destroy by any method that will prevent disclosure of contents or reconstruction of the document.

Foreign Disclosure Restriction (FD 6): This publication has been reviewed by the product developers in coordination with the United States Army John F. Kennedy Special Warfare Center and School foreign disclosure authority. This product is releasable to students from foreign countries on a case-by-case basis only.

Contents

Chapter 5	**SPECIAL FORCES OPERATIONS** **5-1**
	Introduction 5-1
	Phase I: Preparation 5-1
	Phase II: Initial Contact 5-2
	Phase III: Infiltration 5-2
	Phase IV: Organization 5-3
	Phase V: Buildup 5-6
	Phase VI: Employment 5-7
	Phase VII: Transition 5-8
Chapter 6	**PSYCHOLOGICAL OPERATIONS** **6-1**
	Introduction 6-1
	Phase I: Preparation 6-1
	Phase II: Initial Contact 6-4
	Phase III: Infiltration 6-5
	Phase IV: Organization 6-6
	Phase V: Buildup 6-9
	Phase VI: Employment 6-11
	Phase VII: Transition 6-12
Chapter 7	**CIVIL AFFAIRS OPERATIONS** **7-1**
	Introduction 7-1
	Phase I: Preparation 7-1
	Phase II: Initial Contact 7-3
	Phase III: Infiltration 7-4
	Phase IV: Organization 7-5
	Phase V: Buildup 7-6
	Phase VI: Employment 7-6
	Phase VII: Transition 7-10
Chapter 8	**SUPPORTING ELEMENTS AND ACTIVITIES** **8-1**
	Introduction 8-1
	Communications Support 8-1
	Logistics Support 8-5
	Force Health Protection 8-8
	Aviation Support 8-11
Appendix A	THE DIPLOMATIC INSTRUMENT OF NATIONAL POWER A-1
Appendix B	THE INFORMATIONAL INSTRUMENT OF NATIONAL POWER B-1
Appendix C	THE INTELLIGENCE INSTRUMENT OF NATIONAL POWER C-1
Appendix D	THE ECONOMIC INSTRUMENT OF NATIONAL POWER D-1
Appendix E	THE FINANCIAL INSTRUMENT OF NATIONAL POWER E-1
Appendix F	THE LAW ENFORCEMENT INSTRUMENT OF NATIONAL POWER F-1
Appendix G	THE MILITARY INSTRUMENT OF NATIONAL POWER G-1
Appendix H	THE ROLE OF HISTORY AND CULTURE H-1
Appendix I	A HISTORICAL SURVEY OF UNCONVENTIONAL WARFARE I-1
Appendix J	AN OUTLINE HISTORY OF THE UNCONVENTIONAL WARFARE DEFINITION J-1

Contents

GLOSSARY Glossary-1
REFERENCES References-1
INDEX Index-1

Figures

Figure 1-1. Contrasting conventional and irregular warfare 1-7
Figure 1-2. Principles of major combat operations 1-8
Figure 1-3. Joint operating concept relationships 1-9
Figure 2-1. The intelligence process 2-5
Figure 4-1. Classic components of an insurgency in an unconventional warfare operational area 4-8
Figure 6-1. Psychological Operations and Special Forces Soldiers building rapport with an unconventional warfare force in Afghanistan 6-6
Figure 6-2. Afghan village elder addressing population on Psychological Operations loudspeaker 6-8
Figure 7-1. Civil-military lines of operation in support of unconventional warfare 7-2
Figure 7-2. Active Army Civil Affairs battalion operational structure 7-3
Figure 7-3. Civil Affairs core tasks in support of civil-military operations 7-4
Figure 7-4. Sample checklist for transition planning 7-11
Figure A-1. Organizations grouping almost all countries in their respective continents A-7
Figure A-2. Several smaller regional organizations with nonoverlapping memberships A-8
Figure A-3. Several nonoverlapping large alliances A-8
Figure B-1. The information environment B-2
Figure B-2. Information quality criteria B-2

Tables

Table B-1. Information operations integration into joint operations B-20

Preface

Field Manual (FM) 3-05.130, *Army Special Operations Forces Unconventional Warfare*, establishes keystone doctrine for Army special operations forces (ARSOF) operations in unconventional warfare (UW). It is based on lessons learned from both historical and contemporary UW operations. It is also based on existing, long-standing Army Special Forces (SF) UW doctrine; recently developed doctrine, such as counterinsurgency (COIN); and emerging affiliated concepts, such as irregular warfare (IW).

PURPOSE

Since 11 September 2001 and the onset of the War on Terrorism (WOT), existing UW doctrinal publications have undergone intense scrutiny and timely revision. A majority of existing ARSOF manuals have incorporated recent lessons learned and updated tactics, techniques, and procedures (TTP) of immediate utility to the conduct of war. For this reason, the Army has classified most of these revised manuals. UW remains an enduring and effective means of warfighting and is recognized as a central effort in the WOT. Although the classification of existing doctrine is prudent for operational security, it limits the distribution of concepts necessary for an effective joint, interagency, and multinational effort. ARSOF and other audiences require an unclassified conceptual manual useful to understanding the nature of UW and its role in the nation's application of power. This manual provides that unclassified conceptual treatment.

SCOPE

ARSOF execute and are the functional proponent for UW under United States Special Operations Command (USSOCOM) Directive 10-1, *Terms of Reference for Component Commanders*, and other authorities. Currently, there exists no authoritative interagency or joint doctrine specifically for UW—although sufficient joint doctrine does exist for general campaign design and execution of joint and Army operations. This manual is the overarching doctrinal reference that specifically addresses UW as conducted by ARSOF. Detailed TTP for UW can be found in FM 3-05.201, *(S/NF) Special Forces Unconventional Warfare (U)*.

The first chapter establishes what UW is and includes a comparison of traditional and emerging concepts with which UW is sometimes confused. Chapter 2 discusses the international environment and United States (U.S.) instruments of national power within which all military operations—including UW—occur. Chapter 3 addresses policy and doctrine that define, enable, and constrain UW. Chapter 4 outlines planning considerations for UW. The next three chapters provide a more focused operational discussion of ARSOF's three main component disciplines: SF operations, Psychological Operations (PSYOP), and Civil Affairs operations (CAO). Chapter 8, which concerns supporting elements and activities of UW, concludes the basic manual. The appendixes contain useful supplemental information. The first seven appendixes (A–G) provide expanded and detailed information on U.S. instruments of national power within the broader context of the international environment. Appendix H is a survey of definitions and current academic considerations concerning historical and cultural concepts useful to the assessment of human environments. Appendix I provides a historical survey of UW. Appendix J contains an outline sketch of change and constancy in the definition of UW. Current doctrinal references and an expanded bibliography provide a guide for further reading and mature understanding of UW within the endeavor of war.

Both the text and the Glossary identify terms that have joint or Army definitions. FM 3-05.130 is the proponent field manual (the authority) for UW, but is not the proponent for any other Army term.

APPLICABILITY

The primary audience for this manual is leaders and planners at all levels of ARSOF. The manual is useful to a joint, interagency, and multinational audience that may collaborate with ARSOF in the conduct of UW. This publication applies to the Active Army, Army National Guard (ARNG)/Army National Guard of the United States, and United States Army Reserve (USAR) unless otherwise stated.

ADMINISTRATIVE INFORMATION

Unless this publication states otherwise, masculine nouns and pronouns do not refer exclusively to men. The proponent of this manual is the United States Army John F. Kennedy Special Warfare Center and School (USAJFKSWCS). Submit comments and recommended changes to Commander, USAJFKSWCS, ATTN: AOJK-DTD-JA, Fort Bragg, NC 28310-9610, or by e-mail to JAComments@soc.mil.

This page intentionally left blank.

Chapter 1
Introduction

OVERVIEW

1-1. Competition between contending groups using all their means of power has always characterized the international environment. In the modern era since the Treaty of Westphalia (1648), this competition has generally been conceived as occurring between nation-states. Such competition involved all instruments of state power: diplomatic, informational, military, and economic (DIME) expanded in some recent policy documents to diplomatic, informational, military, economic, financial, intelligence, and law enforcement (DIMEFIL). The overwhelming majority of these competitions were peaceful. Most often, nation-states used the military instrument of power peacefully for static defense, as a force-in-being that enabled diplomatic posturing or a credible deterrent, or for essentially nonmilitary purposes, such as engineering projects or disaster relief. Only when other instruments of national power were exhausted or proved inadequate was the military instrument of power wielded to settle international differences. Claus von Clausewitz famously characterized such use of state military power as, "an act of violence to compel the enemy to do our will." This assertion has been profoundly influential. However, it is too constrained of a vision for applying national power in today's world. The ancient Sun Tzu is more relevant today; although battles should be won, "winning 100 victories in 100 battles is not the acme of skill; defeating the enemy without fighting is the acme of skill." There is more than one way to compel an enemy.

1-2. Following the conventions of the time, the United States established a standing Continental Army of uniformed regulars who, in combination with guerrilla raiders and a rebellious population, won American independence. In the 19th century, the United States further developed its military power sufficient to expand and defend a young continental nation. In the 20th century, the United States used its unparalleled military power to successfully conclude two world wars and provide the credibility required to win a third (albeit "Cold") war. The late 20th century understood the fullest manifestation of actual (or potential) war thus defined as the large-scale mobilization and total commitment of massive organizations wielding immense destructive power.

1-3. The international environment in the 21st century, however, presents new challenges. The United States possesses overwhelming conventional military superiority, and other nation-states recognize that a direct military threat to the United States is a losing proposition. Therefore, large-scale and direct conventional war against the United States is increasingly unlikely. Competition in the international environment using all instruments of power, however, remains timeless and continuous. Competitors now concentrate on the nonmilitary instruments of power in the natural intercourse between nations. Most such intercourse remains peaceful and routine. Enemy competitors, however, use the instruments of power as weapons. Moreover, not all modern enemy competitors are synonymous with nation-states.

1-4. International actors in the current era have awakened to the potential of such "unconventional" methods for compelling an enemy to do one's will. Avoiding the advantages of U.S. military power, these international actors seek to erode the ability of the United States to employ that comparative advantage. Using the other instruments of power—especially the informational—they seek to employ what is variably referred to as "irregular," "asymmetric," or "unrestricted" warfare. Even when violence is joined, direct methods are generally avoided for the classic techniques of guerrilla warfare, terrorism, sabotage, subversion, and insurgency.

1-5. Such indirect methods are not unprecedented. Since ancient times, kingdoms and empires have employed psychological warfare to terrorize, demoralize, and subvert their opponents. Guerrillas have attacked and sabotaged where possible to weaken a superior contending power. Combined with political purpose, such guerrillas and political warriors have sought to resist the occupier, or subvert and overthrow the oppressor. The postcolonial, modern era especially saw the widespread expansion of such unconventional methods.

Chapter 1

1-6. The United States is not unpracticed in using many of these methods. It is accustomed to wielding all instruments of national power. It has effectively done so in the past. At the dawn of the 21st century, the United States still enjoys the largest economy in the world and continues to wield enormous economic and financial influence. The tangible and cultural products produced by the United States are spread across the planet. In addition to its military power, the combined weight and multifaceted appeal of this national output enhances the influence of the diplomatic and informational message of the United States. U.S. military power guarantees and significantly enhances the rule of law in the international system. The reach of all these instruments is paralleled by intelligence and law-enforcement instruments that provide constant feedback of information and respect for international codes of behavior.

1-7. Failing a peaceful resolution of international competition, the United States has a tested military capability to use UW. Although such special operations (SO) are inherently joint missions of the USSOCOM, the capability has traditionally and primarily resided in ARSOF. The spiritual forbearers of American UW can be traced to the colonial period. ARSOF has a direct military lineage of conducting UW, which dates back more than 50 years to the World War II (WWII) Office of Strategic Services (OSS). The United States has conducted UW in support of resistance movements, insurgencies, and ongoing or pending conventional military operations. It has operated by, with, or through irregular forces against a variety of state and nonstate opponents. Such sensitive operations are a high-value component and a specific application of the military instrument of national power. ARSOF UW—properly employed within the context of all such power effectively integrated—is more relevant than ever in the 21st century international environment.

UNCONVENTIONAL WARFARE

1-8. The definition of UW has evolved over time. The initial doctrinal concept for the United States to conduct UW originated with the creation of the OSS during WWII. In that classic context, UW was generally defined in terms of guerrilla and covert operations in enemy-held or -influenced territory. The first official Army definition that touched upon aspects of UW appeared in 1950 as "partisan warfare." In 1951, the Army's UW assets were consolidated under the Office of Psychological Warfare, and the Army published the first two field manuals for the conduct of SO (with an emphasis on UW). By 1955, the first historical manual that specifically linked Army SF to UW (FM 31-20, *Special Forces Group*) declared, "UW consists of the three interrelated fields of guerrilla warfare (GW), escape and evasion, and subversion against hostile states."

1-9. In the subsequent Cold War decades, the definition expanded and contracted, verbiage changed, and missions conceived as a part of this unconventional enterprise were added or subtracted. The common conceptual core has nevertheless remained as working by, with, or through irregular surrogates in a clandestine and/or covert manner against opposing actors. It is common for definitions to evolve, and ARSOF have distilled the definition below to highlight the essentials of UW and eliminate the nonessential. In this era of definitional and conceptual change, ARSOF—and its joint, interagency, and multinational partners—must be unified with a clear and concise understanding of the UW core mission.

1-10. The current definition of UW is as follows:

> *Operations conducted by, with, or through irregular forces in support of a resistance movement, an insurgency, or conventional military operations.*
>
> FM 3-05.201, *(S/NF) Special Forces Unconventional Warfare (U)*
> 28 September 2007

This definition reflects two essential criteria: UW must be conducted by, with, or through surrogates; and such surrogates must be irregular forces. Moreover, this definition is consistent with the historical reasons that the United States has conducted UW. UW has been conducted in support of both an insurgency, such as the Contras in 1980s Nicaragua, and resistance movements to defeat an occupying power, such as the Mujahideen in 1980s Afghanistan. UW has also been conducted in support of pending or ongoing conventional military operations; for example, OSS/Jedburgh activities in France and OSS/Detachment 101 activities in the Pacific in WWII and, more recently, SF operations in Operation ENDURING FREEDOM (OEF)/Afghanistan in 2001 and Operation IRAQI FREEDOM (OIF)/Iraq in 2003. Finally and in keeping with the clandestine and/or covert nature of historical UW operations, it has involved the conduct of classified surrogate operations. Details of classified operations are in FM 3-05.20, *(C) Special Forces Operations (U)*, and FM 3-05.201.

1-11. The definition establishes a "litmus test" for clearly differentiating UW from other activities and clearly establishes the purpose for conducting UW. Including the idea of "by, with, or through surrogates" eliminates any confusion with unilateral direct action (DA), special reconnaissance (SR), or counterterrorism (CT) missions. Identifying the historically demonstrated use of irregular forces as surrogates in the definition eliminates any confusion with foreign internal defense (FID) or coalition activities using regular forces. The clearly stated purpose of UW to support insurgencies, resistance movements, and conventional military operations not only eliminates the possibility of incorrectly characterizing UW as solely an IW activity but also articulates UW's relevance to the Army and joint force by specifying support to other operations.

> Personnel should not confuse UW with other operations that involve indigenous personnel, such as FID. The United States characterizes FID as an *overt, direct* method of assistance to free and protect a host nation (HN) government from insurgency or lawlessness. Forces conduct FID with recognized HN *regular* forces. These forces are armed individuals or groups of individuals who are members of the regular armed force, police force, or other internal security force of that nation. There may be instances in which the United States or the HN overtly employs civilian personnel to enhance operational effectiveness; however, those personnel are openly recognized as an augmentation to the regular forces of the HN.
>
> Army and joint doctrine currently do not define *regulars*, or *regular forces*. For use in this manual, these forces are defined as being opposite of irregular forces. Regulars are armed individuals or groups of individuals who are members of a regular armed force, police, or other internal security force. Once a nation charters or sponsors a force to provide internal security, that force is considered to be a regular force. Regardless of its appearance or naming convention, if the force operates under governmental control, it is a regular force.
>
> *Irregulars,* or *irregular forces,* are individuals or groups of individuals who are not members of a regular armed force, police, or other internal security force. They are usually nonstate-sponsored and unconstrained by sovereign nation legalities and boundaries. These forces may include, but are not limited to, specific paramilitary forces, contractors, individuals, businesses, foreign political organizations, resistance or insurgent organizations, expatriates, transnational terrorism adversaries, disillusioned transnational terrorism members, black marketers, and other social or political "undesirables."

1-12. However, the definition of UW is not simply a list of essential criteria and rationales connected end-to-end. It is the most concise definition possible that allows for the essential UW criteria and rationales, and explicitly or implicitly answers the "who, what, when, where, and why" questions of a military definition. For example, working "by, with, or through" is having one act on the behalf of another so the commonly used concept of "surrogate" is implied. Moreover, the one on whose behalf action is taken implies the "who" and is likewise unnecessary. The "what and why" questions are explicitly answered by UW's purpose as stated above, and the "when and where" are implicit in the times and spaces the purpose is being pursued.

1-13. Given the ongoing utility of UW in the WOT era, and in the context of the emerging IW effort, it is equally important to highlight what UW is not. It is not simply a catchall phrase for anything that is not conventional, regular, or traditional. It is synonymous neither with the emerging term "irregular warfare" nor with the currently influential (but nondoctrinal) terms "asymmetric warfare," "unrestricted warfare," or "fourth-generation warfare" (although there are conceptual similarities). Moreover, and despite widespread confusion outside of ARSOF, UW is not synonymous with either "special operations" or "guerrilla warfare." All UW operations are special operations, but not all special operations are UW. Although GW is a classic inherent component of UW and is featured in many historical definitions, UW is an operation, whereas GW is a technique.

CONVENTIONAL WARFARE

1-14. The traditional meaning of UW and how it differs from conventional warfare has been clear to ARSOF for more than a half-century. Commentators outside the ARSOF community, however, have often misused the term. One reason for this conceptual confusion is that conventional warfare is not defined in either Joint Publication (JP) 1-02, *Department of Defense Dictionary of Military and Associated Terms*, or FM 1-02, *Operational Terms and Graphics*.

1-15. The Irregular Warfare Joint Operating Concept (IW JOC), Version 1.0, dated 11 September 2007, describes conventional or "traditional" warfare as:

> *A form of warfare between states that employs direct military confrontation to defeat an adversary's armed forces, destroy an adversary's war-making capacity, or seize or retain territory in order to force a change in an adversary's government or policies. The focus of conventional military operations is normally an adversary's armed forces with the objective of influencing the adversary's government. It generally assumes that the indigenous populations within the operational area are nonbelligerents and will accept whatever political outcome the belligerent governments impose, arbitrate, or negotiate. A fundamental military objective in conventional military operations is to minimize civilian interference in those operations.*

1-16. UW is a specific military operation and is not merely the inverse of conventional war as defined above. UW can be employed against either state or nonstate actors. The directness or indirectness of UW varies according to the situation, the level of warfare, and over time. Although it usually seeks to destroy or weaken an opponent's war-making capability, this effort may or may not involve direct military confrontation. When UW does involve such confrontation, forces take special care to attempt engagement only during circumstances advantageous to the resistance or insurgent force. Seizure and retention of terrain is rarely achieved directly and only achieved decisively as a result of overall victory in the larger strategic campaign. The focus of UW is the leveraging of others, who may or may not then focus on the adversary's armed forces. UW generally assumes that some portion of the indigenous populations—sometimes a majority of that population—are either belligerents or in support of the UW operation. UW is specifically focused on leveraging the unwillingness of some portion of the indigenous population to accept the status quo or "whatever political outcome the belligerent governments impose, arbitrate, or negotiate." A fundamental military objective in UW is the deliberate involvement and leveraging of civilian interference in the unconventional warfare operational area (UWOA).

IRREGULAR WARFARE

1-17. For some, the emerging concept of IW risks adding further confusion to what is unconventional in warfare. Along with many other operations, UW is now considered a component part of IW. It is first necessary to understand how IW differs from conventional warfare, followed by a clarification of how IW relates to UW. Just as UW is a special operation but not all special operations are UW, UW is an IW activity but not all IW activities are UW.

1-18. The 9/11 terrorist attack on the United States highlighted the increased danger of warfare conducted by other-than-state enemies. Recognizing that such irregular threats by nonstate actors would be a likely and even dominant pattern throughout the 21st century, national policy makers dictated that planners must analyze and prepare for such irregular threats. It was clear that previous assumptions about the terms "conventional," "traditional," or "regular" warfare, and reliance solely on a "regular" or "conventional warfare" doctrine were inadequate. IW was a significant theme in the 2006 Quadrennial Defense Review Report. In April 2006, the Pentagon drafted the execution roadmap for IW as a means of combating this growing threat from actions beyond conventional state-to-state military conflict.

1-19. JP 1-02 defines IW as "a violent struggle among state and nonstate actors for legitimacy and influence over the relevant populations. IW favors indirect and asymmetric approaches, though it may employ the full range of military and other capacities in order to erode an adversary's power, influence, and will." IW is inherently a protracted conflict that will test the resolve of the United States and its partners. Adversaries will pursue IW strategies, employing a hybrid of irregular, disruptive, traditional, and catastrophic capabilities to undermine and erode the influence and will of the United States and its strategic partners. Meeting these challenges and combating this approach will require the concerted efforts of all instruments of U.S. national power.

1-20. IW is about people, not platforms. IW does not depend on military prowess alone. It also relies on the understanding of such social dynamics as tribal politics, social networks, religious influences, and cultural mores. Although IW is a violent struggle, not all participating irregulars or irregular forces are necessarily armed. People, more so than weaponry, platforms, and advanced technology, will be the key to success in IW. Successful IW relies on building relationships and partnerships at the local level. It takes patient, persistent, and culturally savvy people within the joint force to execute IW.

1-21. Waging protracted IW depends on building global capability and capacity. IW will not be won by the United States alone but rather through combined efforts with multinational partners. Combined IW will require the joint force to establish a long-term sustained presence in numerous countries to build partner capability and capacity. This capability and capacity extends U.S. operational reach, multiplies forces available, and provides increased options for defeating adversaries. The constituent activities of IW are—

- Insurgency.
- COIN.
- UW.
- Terrorism.
- CT.
- FID.
- Stability, security, transition, and reconstruction (SSTR) operations.
- Strategic communication (SC).
- PSYOP.
- Civil-military operations (CMO).
- Information operations (IO).
- Intelligence and counterintelligence (CI) activities.
- Transnational criminal activities, including narco-trafficking, illicit arms dealing, and illegal financial transactions that support or sustain IW.
- Law enforcement activities focused on countering irregular adversaries.

1-22. The above list of operations and activities can be conducted within IW; however, they are not new and most are addressed in current joint and Service doctrine. What is new is their application within the IW conceptual construct. The list of activities considered together is also useful in characterizing how IW is distinct from conventional warfare and its emphasis on major combat operations (MCO). Particularly noteworthy is that UW (including support for insurgencies), CT, FID, PSYOP, and CMO/CAO are ARSOF core tasks; thus, ARSOF are well-suited to be major practitioners of IW.

1-23. The working definition for conventional warfare provides an appropriate starting point from which to contrast IW. The terms "conventional," "regular," and "traditional" warfare are essentially synonymous. Conventional warfare is focused on the direct military confrontation between nation-states, in which the desired effect is to influence an adversary's government through the defeat of the adversary's military. Moreover, conventional warfare attempts to isolate the population from conflict and to minimize civilian interference (Figure 1-1, page 1-6). The definition agrees with the JP-1, *Doctrine for the Armed Forces of the United States,* discussion of traditional warfare as a confrontation between nation-states or coalitions/alliances of nation-states. The contrasting definitions also agree with the Army's understanding of MCO within the spectrum of conflict, and that MCO are distinct from IW (Figure 1-2, page 1-6).

Chapter 1

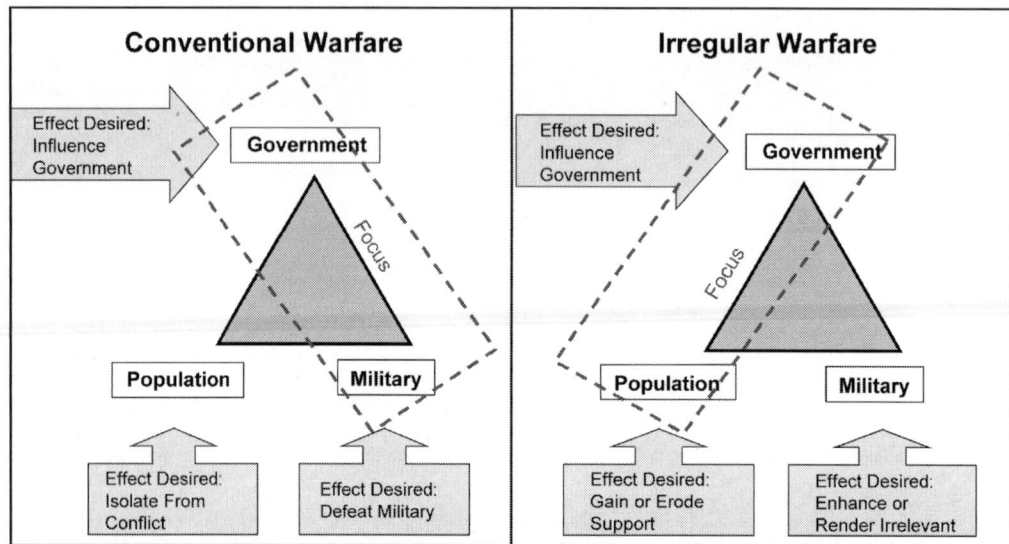

Figure 1-1. Contrasting conventional and irregular warfare

> Joint Doctrine: (MCO JOC v.2.0, December 2006)
> - Focused on seizing the initiative and dominating the adversary.
> - Inherently military actions taken directly or indirectly to defeat an adversary's military (however, they can be directed against other hostile forces presenting any one—or a combination—of the four challenges described in the National Military Strategy).
>
> Army: (FM 3-0, *Operations*)
> - An operational theme that describes general characteristics of the major operation.
> - Takes place in circumstances usually characterized as war.
> - Full-spectrum dominance over an organized and capable adversary.
> - High tempo, high resource consumption, high casualty rates.
> - Significant national or coalition interests are threatened.
> - Often waged between uniformed armed forces of nation-states.
> - Seek to defeat enemy's armed forces and seize terrain.
> - Offensive and defensive operations predominate.
> - Doctrine and principles of war originally derived from MCO.
>
> Comments:
> - MCO are not defined in JP 1-02 or in FM 1-02.
> - The characterization listed above is an appropriate description of MCO (however, the Army's characteristics do not include purpose or end state, unlike the definition of IW proposed in the IW JOC).

Figure 1-2. Principles of major combat operations

1-24. IW is integral to the conduct of both MCO and military support to SSTR operations (Figure 1-3, page 1-7). It complements the conduct of deterrence operations and shaping operations. It also offers both complementary and competing ideas for ways and means to address strategic and operational challenges. The IW JOC addresses aspects of IW that other current JOCs do not:

- Theater strategy for IW.
- IW campaign design, planning, and execution.
- Global scale of IW operations.

- Protracted time frame of IW.
- Offensive applications of IW, particularly against hostile armed groups operating in nonbelligerent states.

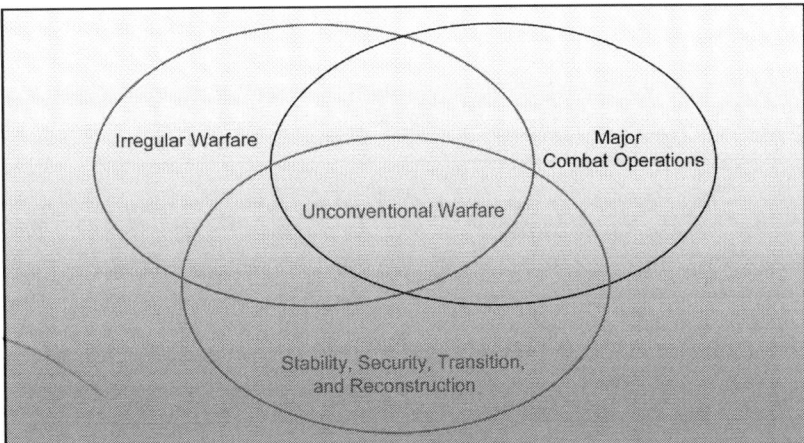

Figure 1-3. Joint operating concept relationships

1-25. The MCO JOC includes a general description of IW that focuses on cases where IW is integral to large-scale combat operations. The IW JOC provides a more robust discussion of IW, both in combination with conventional military operations and also as part of a protracted regional or global IW campaign that may not include significant conventional military operations.

1-26. The SSTR JOC focuses on the full range of military support across the continuum from peace to crisis and conflict to assist a state or region that is under severe stress. IW occurs primarily during crisis or conflict. In both IW and SSTR operations, a primary focus is on gaining the support of the population. In both concepts, the joint force normally plays an enabling role to the efforts of other government agencies (OGAs) rather than a lead role. SSTR operations are a vital component of most IW operations and campaigns, but SSTR operations also occur outside the scope of IW. In some operations, IW may contrast with SSTR operations, such as supporting an insurgency or conducting UW where the goal is not to support the host government but rather to undermine stability and security to erode an adversary's control over its territory or population. As with IW, many SSTR tasks are best performed by indigenous institutions, intergovernmental organizations (IGOs), nongovernmental organizations (NGOs), and OGAs. Nonetheless, both concepts envision the requirement for joint forces to perform all tasks necessary to establish or maintain civil order when civilian agencies cannot do so.

1-27. Much of what the IW concept offers, however, aligns with traditional ARSOF doctrine, practice, and conceptualization. What makes IW different from conventional warfare is the focus of its operations—a relevant population—and its strategic purpose to gain or maintain control or influence over the population and to support that population through political, psychological, and economic methods. ARSOF practitioners of UW have long understood the importance of focusing on the population and that a campaign's logical lines of operation could include not only combat operations but also information, intelligence, and developing capability. JP-1 states that IW is marked by a struggle among state and nonstate actors for legitimacy and influence over the relevant population; that it primarily involves an indirect approach to erode power, influence, and will; and that it is determined by the characteristics of the adversary and is not, as such, a new or independent type of warfare. These are all familiar UW insights for ARSOF.

1-28. UW is a component and method of prosecuting IW, but UW and IW are each distinct. Both IW and UW focus on influencing relevant populations. However, whereas IW does not necessarily require operations with irregular forces, UW is always conducted by, with, or through irregular forces. UW may be a central effort in a holistic IW campaign in which conventional military operations are not used, or it may be conducted as an IW element in support of what is predominantly a conventional military operation. The emerging IW concept borrows heavily from traditional ARSOF concepts, but they are not synonymous.

> **Doctrinal Terms and Definitions**
>
> *Conventional or traditional warfare*: A form of warfare between states that employs direct military confrontation to defeat an adversary's armed forces, destroy an adversary's war-making capacity, or seize or retain territory in order to force a change in an adversary's government or policies. The focus of conventional military operations is normally an adversary's armed forces with the objective of influencing the adversary's government. It generally assumes that the indigenous populations within the operational area are nonbelligerents and will accept whatever political outcome the belligerent governments impose, arbitrate, or negotiate. A fundamental military objective in conventional military operations is to minimize civilian interference in those operations. (IW JOC, V1.0)
>
> *Irregular warfare*: A violent struggle among state and nonstate actors for legitimacy and influence over the relevant populations. (JP 1, Doctrine for the Armed Forces of the United States)
>
> *Unconventional warfare*: Operations conducted by, with, or through irregular forces in support of a resistance movement, an insurgency, or conventional military operations. (FM 3-05.201)
>
> *Foreign internal defense*: Participation by civilian and military agencies of a government in any of the action programs taken by another government or other designated organization to free and protect its society from subversion, lawlessness, and insurgency. (JP 1-02; FM 3-05.137, *Army Special Operations Forces Foreign Internal Defense*)
>
> *Counterinsurgency*: Those political, economic, military, paramilitary, psychological, and civil actions taken by a government to defeat an insurgency. (JP 1-02; FM 3-24, *Counterinsurgency*)

Chapter 2
United States National Power

THE INTERNATIONAL ENVIRONMENT

2-1. The different types of power with which international players—chiefly sovereign nation-states—contend are all interconnected. This is one of the reasons it is difficult to separate them into distinct categories. It is also the single greatest reason that the ideas of UW, IW, COIN, and so on present such a challenge both conceptually and practically. Every time a serious commentator exhorts the need for interagency coordination to solve an international problem or calls for a "holistic" approach to its prosecution, it is this natural and man-made interconnectedness of power to which he refers.

2-2. The instruments of national power as codified in U.S. policy and doctrine include DIME and DIMEFIL. The listing order of the identified instruments does not matter. This chapter and its supporting appendixes list the instruments in an order that allows for the smoothest transition between interrelated concepts. This chapter addresses the military instrument last. Readers should refer to each supporting appendix (A through G) for a broad overview of the global environment in which each instrument of U.S. national power operates.

INSTRUMENTS OF UNITED STATES NATIONAL POWER

2-3. The ability of the United States to achieve its national strategic objectives depends in large measure on the effectiveness of the United States Government (USG) in employing the instruments of national power. The appropriate executive branch officials, often with National Security Council (NSC) direction, normally coordinate these DIMEFIL instruments. The USG uses DIMEFIL instruments to apply its sources of power; power founded in human potential, economy, industry, science and technology, academic institutions, geography, and national will. The President and the Secretary of Defense (SecDef) establish the rules for military power and integrate it with the other instruments of national power to advance and defend U.S. values, interests, and objectives. To accomplish this integration, the armed forces interact with the other responsible agencies to ensure mutual understanding of the capabilities, limitations, and consequences of military and civilian actions and to identify the ways in which military and nonmilitary capabilities best complement each other.

DIPLOMATIC INSTRUMENT OF NATIONAL POWER

2-4. The diplomatic instrument of national power is the principal instrument for engaging with other states and foreign groups to advance U.S. values, interests, and objectives. However, without the credible threat of force, diplomacy is inadequate against a determined adversary. Leaders of the U.S. armed forces have a responsibility to understand U.S. foreign policy and to assure that those responsible for U.S. diplomacy have a clear understanding of the capabilities, limitations, and consequences of military action.

Role of Geographic Combatant Commanders

2-5. Geographic combatant commanders (GCCs) are responsible for integrating military activities with diplomatic activities in their area of responsibility (AOR). The U.S. Ambassador and the corresponding Country Team are normally in charge of diplomatic-military activities in countries abroad. When directed by the President or SecDef, the GCC employs military forces in concert with the other instruments of national power. In these circumstances, the U.S. Ambassador and the Country Team may have complementary activities (employing the diplomatic instrument) that do not entail control of military forces, which remain under command authority of the GCC. (Appendix A includes further information on the diplomatic instrument of national power.)

Diplomatic Instrument of United States National Power and Unconventional Warfare

2-6. The United States avoids resorting to military force, preferring to wield all other instruments of power in the pursuit of national objectives and in the context of international competition and conflict. Therefore, diplomacy routinely blocks the need for the application of the military instrument of power. However, when the President decides to employ the specific military application of UW, the Department of State (DOS) plays a crucial role. Regardless of whether the United States conducts the UW operation in support of resistance, insurgency, or conventional military operations, close coordination between ARSOF and DOS elements is required. For example—

- All UW missions involve diplomatic facilitation with foreign audiences, both external and indigenous to the UWOA. DOS channels may prove valuable for third-nation or surrogate support, and DOS liaison abilities may be the adhesive that allows diverse coalitions to persevere in a long-term effort.
- The sensitivity of missions involving covert and clandestine activities requires DOS elements to effect coordination of foreign support from friendly governments and the diplomatic compliance or misdirection of adversary governments.
- The United States may conduct some ARSOF UW operations in states that are not belligerents. The U.S. Ambassador and his Country Team may in fact have complete or significant control over ARSOF inside the ambassador's host country of responsibility. In such cases, the relationship between ARSOF conducting UW and the Country Team requires the best possible coordination to be effective and appropriate.
- Even when UW is conducted in third-party states, much of the mission preparation and support may be conducted in or transit other states. Most states have U.S. diplomatic representation, and coordination with DOS personnel will be a key task for effective execution of UW operations.
- Like ARSOF, DOS personnel spend a majority of their careers in foreign countries. Many DOS personnel have expert knowledge, cultural and language abilities, current situational awareness, and a network of HN contacts at their disposal. It is imperative that ARSOF access these valuable resources, when appropriate, in the conduct of UW.

INFORMATIONAL INSTRUMENT OF NATIONAL POWER

2-7. The informational instrument of national power has a diffuse and complex set of components with no single center of control. In the United States, individuals exchange information freely with minimal government control. Information itself is a strategic resource vital to national security. This reality applies to all instruments, entities, and activities of national power and extends to the armed forces at all levels. Military operations in particular are dependent upon many simultaneous and integrated activities that, in turn, depend on information and information systems. Information and information-based technologies are vital elements throughout the spectrum of conflict. Normally, the USG only imposes constraints on public access to USG information for national security and individual privacy reasons. Information readily available from multiple sources influences domestic and foreign audiences, including citizens, adversaries, and governments.

Role of the Media

2-8. It is important for the official agencies of government, including the armed forces, to recognize the fundamental role of the media as a conduit of information. The USG uses SC to provide top-down guidance for using the informational instrument of national power through coordinated information, themes, messages, and products synchronized with the other instruments of national power. The armed forces support SC themes and messages through IO, public affairs (PA), and defense support to public diplomacy (DSPD). The armed forces must assure media access consistent with classification requirements, operations security, legal restrictions, and individual privacy. The armed forces must also provide timely and accurate information to the public. Success in military operations depends on acquiring and integrating essential information and denying it to the adversary. The armed forces are responsible for conducting IO, protecting what should not be disclosed, and aggressively attacking adversary information systems. IO may involve complex legal and policy issues that require approval, review, and coordination at the national level.

2-9. By definition, UW consists of operations conducted by, with, or through irregular forces. Such engagement with the "human terrain" is fundamentally a conflict of ideas. It is essential that ARSOF understand the informational environment within which forces execute UW and how informational instruments of power wielded by the United States and other actors can shape the human terrain. (Appendix B includes further details on the informational instrument of national power.)

Informational Instrument of United States National Power and Unconventional Warfare

2-10. Informational power consists of both the universe of diffuse influences—most of which are beyond the control of the USG—shaping the international and domestic environments and USG-controlled specific instruments that can be deliberately employed against tailored target audiences (TAs) for specific ends.

2-11. For ARSOF practitioners of UW, the essential task with those influences that shape international and domestic environments is to understand the operational environment in its complex entirety and identify the sources of informational influence that contribute to that complexity. This is a difficult undertaking because cultural worldviews and assumptions underlay the reception and interpretation of ideas. A substitute does not exist for a persistent, detailed, and accurate understanding of the UW human terrain in which ARSOF must operate. Most of this larger information environment will remain beyond USG control or influence. Therefore, the best that practitioners of UW can achieve is to recognize the variety of information present within the human terrain of a UWOA, "navigate" along its conceptual contours, and leverage such cultural awareness to U.S. goals whenever possible. ARSOF UW is only partly a science; it is fundamentally an "art" of human interaction.

2-12. By contrast, USG-controlled specific instruments of informational power, while narrower in scope, can achieve specific and measurable results useful to prosecuting UW. ARSOF can work with DOS counterparts to identify and engage select TAs that are able to influence behavior within a UWOA. Such TAs may be inside the UWOA itself or outside but able to influence the UWOA. The USG can then subject these TAs, directly or indirectly, to a DOS public diplomacy (PD) campaign coordinated to support the UW effort. Similarly, since UW may be a long-duration or politically sensitive effort, ARSOF and its DOS partner, the Bureau of Public Affairs, can craft a PA campaign intended to keep the U.S. domestic audience informed of the truth in a manner supportive of USG goals and the effective prosecution of UW.

2-13. In both the foreign and domestic arenas, ARSOF UW planners should continuously monitor adversary attempts to deliberately mislead foreign and domestic audiences. Planners must employ responsive friendly information foreign adversaries to counteract foreign misinformation. Domestically, "misinformation" is a politically contentious concept. ARSOF UW planners must work closely with IO and legal professionals to identify domestic misinformation and provide evidence of such attempts to joint task force (JTF) commanders charged with prosecuting a UW campaign. Senior ARSOF leaders must then keep the Department of Defense (DOD) and other civilian leadership informed as a DSPD responsibility.

2-14. PSYOP are one of the core tasks of ARSOF and a component discipline of UW. In some cases, an entire ARSOF UW effort may involve only PSYOP forces and may never include the employment of SF or Civil Affairs (CA) forces. This is an acknowledgement of the power and centrality of ideas in warfare, including UW. Regardless of the scale or degree of ARSOF commitment in a UW effort, PSYOP are an initial and continuous, integral, and fundamentally central activity of ARSOF UW.

INTELLIGENCE INSTRUMENT OF NATIONAL POWER

2-15. Intelligence, as an instrument of national power, provides the national leadership with the information needed to realize national goals and objectives while providing military leadership with the information needed to accomplish missions and implement the national security strategy (NSS). Planners use intelligence to identify the adversary's capabilities and centers of gravity, project probable courses of action (COAs), and assist in planning friendly force employment. Intelligence also provides assessments that help the joint force commander (JFC) decide which forces to deploy; when, how, and where to deploy them; and how to employ them in a manner that accomplishes the mission at the lowest human and political cost.

2-16. The traditional "DIME" construct of national power incorporated intelligence into the informational instrument. This was appropriate because all intelligence is a form of information. In the post-9/11 world, however, the DIMEFIL construct separates the two into related but distinct instruments." Informational

Chapter 2

power conveys themes to selected TAs whether or not the USG deliberately focuses or even controls those themes. Intelligence as a national instrument of power is a more specific tool with a deliberate focus controlled by the USG. Whereas informational power projects information to shape an environment, intelligence seeks to gather information to understand the environment and inform USG decision making. The USG usually crafts intelligence to answer specific questions.

Interagency Intelligence Process

2-17. Intelligence supports joint operations by providing critical information and finished intelligence products to the combatant command (COCOM), the subordinate service and functional component commands, and subordinate joint forces. Commanders at all levels depend on timely, accurate information and intelligence on an adversary's dispositions, strategies, tactics, intents, objectives, strengths, weaknesses, values, capabilities, and critical vulnerabilities. The intelligence process is comprised of a wide variety of interrelated intelligence operations. These intelligence operations (planning and direction, collection, processing and exploitation, analysis and production, dissemination and integration, and evaluation and feedback) must focus on the commander's mission and concept of operations (Figure 2-1).

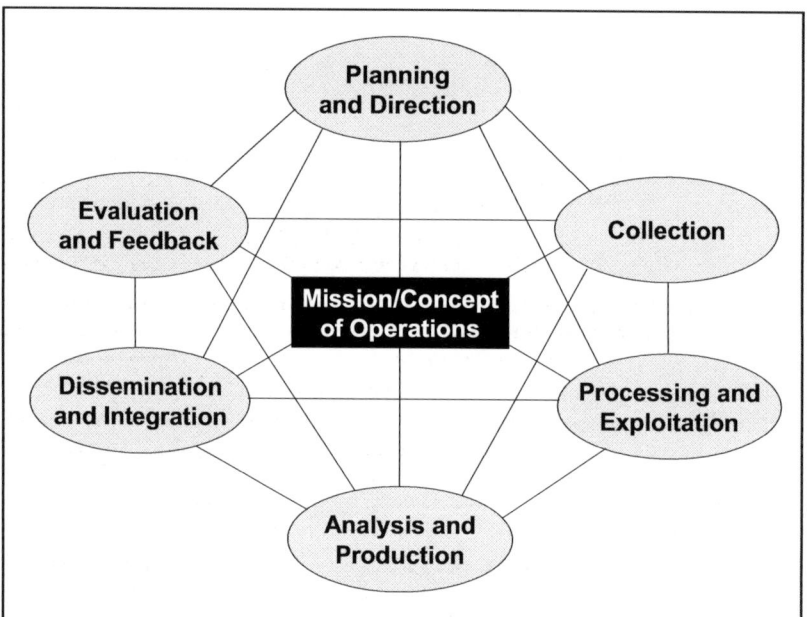

Figure 2-1. The intelligence process

2-18. The intelligence process describes how the various types of intelligence operations interact to meet the commander's intelligence needs. The intelligence process provides a useful model that, albeit simplistic, nevertheless facilitates understanding the wide variety of intelligence operations and their interrelationships. There are no firm boundaries outlining where each operation within the modern intelligence process begins or ends. Intelligence operations are not sequential; rather, they are nearly simultaneous. In addition, not all operations necessarily continue throughout the entire intelligence process.

2-19. The increased tempo of military operations requires an unimpeded flow of automatically processed and exploited data that is both timely and relevant to the commander's needs. This unanalyzed combat information must be simultaneously available to both the commander (for time-critical decision making) and to the intelligence analyst (for the production of current intelligence assessments).

2-20. Examples of uses for such unanalyzed combat information include, but are not limited to, time-sensitive targeting, personnel recovery operations, and threat warning alerts. Likewise, those conducting the analysis, production, and dissemination of intelligence products must do so in time to support the commander's decision-making needs.

2-21. Joint intelligence operations begin with the identification of a need for intelligence regarding all relevant aspects of the operational environment, especially the adversary. The commander and all joint force staff elements identify these intelligence needs, and the J-2 formalizes these needs as intelligence requirements early in the planning process. The commander identifies those critical pieces of intelligence that he must know by a particular time to plan and execute a successful mission as his priority intelligence requirements (PIRs). Commanders identify PIRs at every level and base them on guidance obtained from the mission statement, the commander's intent, and the end-state objectives.

2-22. Intelligence requirements are the basis for current and future intelligence operations and are prioritized based on consumer inputs during the planning and direction portion of the intelligence process. The J-2 provides the focus and direction for collection requirements to support the COCOM or subordinate joint force.

2-23. The collection portion of the intelligence process involves tasking appropriate collection assets and resources to acquire the data and information required to satisfy collection objectives. Collection includes the identification, coordination, and positioning of assets and resources to satisfy collection objectives.

2-24. Once the data that might satisfy the requirement is collected, it undergoes processing and exploitation. Processing and exploitation transforms the collected raw data into information that intelligence analysts can use to produce and disseminate multidiscipline intelligence products. Relevant, critical information should also be disseminated to the commander and joint force staff to facilitate time-sensitive decision making. Processing and exploitation time varies depending on the characteristics of specific collection assets. For example, some intelligence, surveillance, and reconnaissance (ISR) systems accomplish processing and exploitation automatically and nearly simultaneously with collection, while other collection assets, such as human intelligence (HUMINT) teams, may require substantially more time. Personnel prioritize and synchronize processing and exploitation requirements with the commander's PIRs.

2-25. The analysis and production portion of the intelligence process involves integrating, evaluating, analyzing, and interpreting information from single or multiple sources into a finished intelligence product. The demands of the modern operational environment require intelligence products that anticipate the needs of the commander and are timely, accurate, usable, complete, relevant, objective, and available.

2-26. Personnel disseminate intelligence products to the requester, who integrates the intelligence into the decision-making and planning processes. In the case of threat warning alerts essential to the preservation of life or vital resources, such information must be immediately communicated directly to those forces, platforms, or personnel identified at risk so the appropriate responsive action can be taken once such notification has been acknowledged.

2-27. Evaluation of intelligence operations, activities, and products is continuous. Based on these evaluations and the resulting feedback, remedial actions should be initiated, as required, to improve the performance of intelligence operations and the overall functioning of the intelligence process. (Appendix C contains further information on the intelligence instrument of national power.)

Intelligence Instrument of United States National Power and Unconventional Warfare

2-28. Good intelligence is central to good decision making by national leaders throughout the spectrum of conflict. When the USG employs ARSOF in UW, good intelligence is likewise a prerequisite for its effective prosecution. Just as ARSOF must understand the information environment that shapes the human terrain in a UWOA, commanders prosecuting UW must receive timely and accurate intelligence on specific, pertinent aspects of the UWOA.

2-29. UW is conducted by, with, or through irregular forces. Knowledge of the values, motivations, capabilities, and limitations of such populations is usually difficult to acquire and even more difficult to accurately assess. Typically, ARSOF UW elements will be introduced to resistance or insurgent forces by OGAs—usually a USG intelligence agency. Such intelligence preparation will normally be the result of discrete and persistent efforts over many years. It is clear that effective intelligence preparation must

Chapter 2

precede ARSOF UW efforts. Therefore, ARSOF cultivate a close working relationship with U.S. intelligence agencies.

2-30. Forces predominately conduct UW—directly or indirectly—in hostile, nonpermissive, or denied territory. Such operations are both physically and often politically high-risk activities. Small U.S. units and their surrogates operating in denied territory are usually beyond the reach of most friendly support. The margin for error in such conditions is very small. Good intelligence preparation before deployment and continuously updated, accurate, and timely intelligence during employment are critical.

2-31. The purpose of UW is to support resistance, insurgency, or conventional military operations. Political control and legitimacy of regimes are the issues. Therefore, UW has strategic utility that can alter the balance of power between sovereign states. Such high stakes carry the highest political risk in both the international and domestic political arenas and necessarily require sensitive execution. The necessity to operate with clandestine and covert means and sometimes a varying mix of clandestine and covert ways and ends places a premium on excellent intelligence of the UWOA. As in all conflict scenarios short of large-scale, state-to-state warfare, the DOS, intelligence providers, and ARSOF must closely coordinate their activities to enable and safeguard sensitive UW operations.

2-32. Finally, when the USG employs UW in support of conventional military operations, the end state of friendly conventional victory is typically overt. Intelligence requirements of conventional forces will focus on traditional warfighting information, such as enemy order of battle, adversary state infrastructure, or terrain and weather. Consideration of human factors is secondary. Human factors are primarily addressed for how they may affect the progress of conventional operations. Despite the UW role of ARSOF in support of a conventional main effort in this case, the intelligence requirements of the UW operation itself remain specialized; they necessarily focus on the human terrain. Intelligence providers and conventional force JTF commanders must understand the differing requirements of intelligence for MCO and UW.

ECONOMIC INSTRUMENT OF NATIONAL POWER

2-33. Governmental agencies only partially control the economic instrument of national power. In keeping with U.S. values and constitutional imperatives, individuals and entities have broad freedom of action worldwide. The responsibility of the USG lies with facilitating the production, distribution, and consumption of goods and services worldwide that promote U.S. fundamental objectives, such as promoting general welfare and supporting security interests and objectives.

Role of the United States Economy

2-34. A strong U.S. economy with free access to global markets and resources is a fundamental engine of the general welfare, the guarantor of a strong national defense, and an influence for economic expansion by U.S. trade partners worldwide. The armed forces must coordinate with USG agencies responsible for employing the economic instrument to facilitate unified action. The NSC has primary responsibility for the integration of the economic and military instruments of national power abroad. (Appendix D contains further information on the economic instrument of national power.)

Economic Instrument of United States National Power and Unconventional Warfare

2-35. Economic intercourse, great and small, is a natural human activity and—along with information exchange and the spectrum of conflict—is a timeless characteristic of the international environment. Nation-states, human groups, and individuals all respond to economic activity. Most such exchange is unmanaged, routine, and peaceful. However, entities can use economic inputs and flows as a "weapon" in times of conflict up to and including large-scale general war. ARSOF understand that properly integrated manipulation of economic power can and should be a component of UW.

2-36. The United States can use managed access to U.S. economic inputs to leverage the policies and cooperation of state governments. Economic incentive and disincentives—real, implied, or simply identified—can build and sustain international coalitions waging or supporting U.S. UW campaigns. As part of an interagency effort, the U.S. Department of Commerce (DOC) can recommend changes to U.S. policy that can provide such incentives to state governments and others at the national strategic policy level.

2-37. If properly authorized and coordinated, ARSOF can use measured and focused economic incentives and disincentives to persuade adversaries, allies, and surrogates to modify their behavior at the theater strategic, operational, and tactical levels. Such application of economic power must be part of a circumspect, integrated, and consistent UW plan.

2-38. Like all other instruments of U.S. national power, the use and effects of economic "weapons" are interrelated and they must be coordinated carefully. Once again, ARSOF must work carefully with the DOS and intelligence community (IC) to determine which elements of the human terrain in the UWOA are most susceptible to economic engagement and what second- and third-order effects are likely from such engagement. The United States Agency for International Development's (USAID's) placement abroad and its mission to engage human groups provide one channel for leveraging economic incentives. The DOC's can similarly leverage its routine influence with U.S. corporations active abroad. Moreover, the IO effects of economic promises kept (or ignored) can prove critical to the legitimacy of U.S. UW efforts. UW practitioners must plan for these effects.

2-39. CA units in ARSOF are the natural lead planners for focusing JTF commanders' planning on the use of the economic weapon in UW. ARSOF understand the importance of not assuming that CMO in UW are somehow an adjunct to the "real fight." The role of CA in wielding the economic weapon is an important element in ARSOF UW operations.

FINANCIAL INSTRUMENT OF NATIONAL POWER

2-40. The financial instrument of national power promotes the conditions for prosperity and stability in the United States and encourages prosperity and stability in the rest of the world. The Department of the Treasury (Treasury) is the primary federal agency responsible for the economic and financial prosperity and security of the United States and as such is responsible for a wide range of activities, including advising the President on economic and financial issues, promoting the President's growth agenda, and enhancing corporate governance in financial institutions. In the international arena, the Treasury works with other federal agencies, the governments of other nations, and the international financial institutions to encourage economic growth; raise standards of living; and predict and prevent, to the extent possible, economic and financial crises.

International Financial System

2-41. The functions attached to any good or token that operate in trade as a medium of exchange, store of value, and unit of account commonly defines money. In common usage, money refers more specifically to currency, particularly the many circulating currencies with legal tender status conferred by a national state. More recently, deposit accounts denominated in such currencies are also considered part of the money supply. Money may also serve as a means of rationing access to scarce resources and as a quantitative measure that provides a common standard for the comparison and valuation of both quality and quantity of goods and services.

2-42. The use of money provides an easier alternative to the ancient technique of barter, which, in a modern, complex economy, is inefficient because it requires a coincidence of wants between traders and an agreement that these needs are of equal value before a transaction can occur. The use of money creates efficiency gains that encourage trade and the division of labor, which in turn increases productivity and wealth.

2-43. Like language, money is a social organization and civilizing force that provides a means and incentive for human beings to relate to one another economically by exchanging goods and services for mutual benefit. The capacity to convert perishable commodities and nonstorable human labor into money provides a powerful incentive for people to produce more than they need for present personal consumption and to convert the surplus value into money so that it can be stored to meet future needs. Thus, the invention of money has stimulated the development of society by fostering hard work, higher productivity, and continuous innovation. (Appendix E includes further information on the financial instrument of national power.)

Chapter 2

Financial Instrument of U.S. National Power and Unconventional Warfare

2-44. The agent controlling the creation, flow, and access to "stores of value" wields power. Although finance is generally an operation of real and virtual currency, anything that can serve as a "medium of exchange" provides those who accept the medium with a method of financial transaction. For both reasons, ARSOF understand that they can and should exploit the active and analytical capabilities existing in the financial instrument of U.S. power in the conduct of UW.

2-45. Like the economic activity, which all nation-states, human groups, and individuals respond to, ARSOF can use financial power as a weapon in times of conflict up to and including large-scale general war. Like the economic activity that it is related to, most financial power is unmanaged, routine, and peaceful. However, manipulation of U.S. financial strength can leverage the policies and cooperation of state governments. Financial incentives and disincentives can build and sustain international coalitions waging or supporting U.S. UW campaigns. As part of an interagency effort, the U.S. Treasury can recommend changes to U.S. policy that can provide such incentives to state governments and others at the national strategic policy level. Participation in international financial organizations, such as the World Bank (WB), International Monetary Fund (IMF), Organization for Economic Cooperation and Development (OECD), and the Bank for International Settlements (BIS), offers the U.S. diplomatic-financial venues to accomplish such coalitions.

2-46. State manipulation of tax and interest rates and other legal and bureaucratic measures can apply unilateral U.S. financial action to open, modify, or close financial flows. Government can apply unilateral and indirect financial power through persuasive influence to international and domestic financial institutions regarding availability and terms of loans, grants, or other financial assistance to foreign state and nonstate actors.

2-47. If properly authorized and coordinated, ARSOF can use—or coordinate for other agencies to use—measured and focused financial incentives or disincentives to persuade adversaries, allies, and surrogates to modify their behavior at the theater strategic, operational, and tactical levels. Such application of financial power must be part of a circumspect, integrated, and consistent UW plan.

2-48. Like all other instruments of U.S. national power, the use and effects of financial weapons are interrelated and they must be coordinated carefully. Once again, ARSOF must work with the DOS and IC to determine which elements of the human terrain in the UWOA are most susceptible to financial engagement and what second- and third-order effects are likely from such engagement. The Treasury's Office of International Affairs and Office of Terrorism and Financial Intelligence (TFI) (and its components), together with the Financial Crimes Enforcement Network (FinCEN), provide financially mission-focused channels for identifying opportunities to employ the financial weapon. In addition to intelligence and policy changes that may provide active incentive or disincentive leverage, the Office of Foreign Assets Control (OFAC) has a long history of conducting economic warfare valuable to any ARSOF UW campaign.

LAW ENFORCEMENT INSTRUMENT OF NATIONAL POWER

2-49. Through the law enforcement instrument of national power, the USG is accountable to its people and can govern its territory effectively. The USG has the capability and capacity to—
- Enforce the law and defend the interests of the United States according to the law.
- Ensure public safety against threats foreign and domestic.
- Provide federal leadership in preventing and controlling crime.
- Seek just punishment for those guilty of unlawful behavior.
- Ensure fair and impartial administration of justice for all Americans.

2-50. As globalization increases world integration, the scope of threats to U.S. security and public safety becomes more global. The law enforcement instrument increasingly and necessarily works outside of U.S. borders to combat these threats.

International Law Enforcement Environment

2-51. Most nation-states have some means of enforcing national and subordinate law. The quality and effectiveness of state law enforcement instruments vary greatly, however, and represent a paradox. In liberal democracies, citizens enjoy enforcement entities bound by legal guarantees of citizen rights and due process under the rule of deliberative law. However, the very liberty protected by such safeguards sometimes frustrates crime and terror prevention because common and political criminals use that relative freedom to perpetrate crimes. By contrast, people subject to dictatorial regimes are likely to suffer too much law enforcement because cruel and severe entities of state internal security limit individual freedom. With less liberty, criminals experience more difficulty in achieving their ends.

2-52. At a minimum, all governments oppose threats to their existence. However, the apparatus of government represents only a small portion of a citizenry and directly controls only a small portion of its subject territory. Regardless of its desire to do so, no government can control everything within its jurisdiction or prevent all violations of law all of the time. The attitude of the population, degree of control provided by competing (nonstate government) enforcers of law, and traditions of civic order—or lack thereof—are key components of the overall law enforcement environment. All of these varying conditions will contribute to the degree of lawlessness in any given society. These conditions and the political willingness of other states to cooperate in such efforts affects the ability of the United States to use the law enforcement instrument of power abroad. (Appendix F includes further information on the law enforcement instrument of national power.)

Law Enforcement Instrument of United States National Power and Unconventional Warfare

2-53. ARSOF recognize several similarities of law enforcement activities with military operations and potentially useful applications of the law enforcement instrument of U.S. power to the conduct of UW. Although UW is not a direct task for law enforcement, nonmilitary law enforcement agencies conduct routine operations that parallel or support other ARSOF operations. Such agencies may also play a supporting role in an ARSOF UW effort.

2-54. For example, reasonable opinions continue to differ whether a long-term CT effort is essentially a military or law enforcement challenge. One reason this issue remains contentious is that many of the activities required to successfully conduct CT are identical, regardless of which institutions are tasked to do them. CT requires excellent intelligence, painstaking attention to detail in assessing human terrain, sharply focused target discrimination, sensitivity to deadly threats, and a persistent USG presence abroad for effective target surveillance, information sharing, and combined operations with allied partners. Terrorist adversaries also seek to avoid the scrutiny of all government entities that seek them out.

2-55. The conduct of UW requires similar activities. Effective UW is based on intelligence involving a painstaking attention to detail in assessing human terrain and sharply focusing on target discrimination. U.S. law enforcement agencies routinely and necessarily conduct and share such intelligence with their foreign counterparts and the U.S. IC. Some friendly and adversary actors in the UWOA may be persons or groups of interest to U.S. law enforcement agencies. Within the boundaries of by law, ARSOF understand the importance of coordinating law enforcement intelligence efforts and data sharing with UW planning and operations.

2-56. Actors engaged in supporting elements in the UWOA may rely on criminal activities, such as smuggling, narcotics, or human trafficking. Political and military adversaries in the UWOA will exhibit the same sensitivity to official exposure and engagement because criminal entities routinely seek to avoid law enforcement. Sometimes, political and military adversaries are simultaneously criminal adversaries, which ARSOF UW planners must consider a threat. At other times, the methods and networks of real or perceived criminal entities can be useful as supporting elements of a U.S.-sponsored UW effort. In either case, ARSOF understand the importance of coordinating military intelligence preparation of the battlefield (IPB) for specific UW campaigns with the routine intelligence activities conducted by U.S. law enforcement agencies.

Chapter 2

MILITARY INSTRUMENT OF NATIONAL POWER

2-57. In wielding the military instrument of national power, the armed forces must ensure their adherence to U.S. values, constitutional principles, and standards for the profession of arms. While responsibility for wielding the other instruments of power rests outside the military establishment, U.S. military leaders are responsible for providing the advice and recommendations necessary for the overall U.S. effort to properly incorporate the military instrument with the other instruments of national power. Unified action within the military instrument supports the national strategic unity of effort through close coordination with the other instruments of national power.

International Security Environment

2-58. Sovereign nation-states, each of which pursues what it perceives to be in its national interest, is traditionally the focus in the modern era. Where those interests come into conflict, nation-states use all of the instruments of national power at their disposal in the attempt to resolve conflicts in their favor.

2-59. Occasionally, nation-states employ the military instrument when conflicting interests are otherwise irreconcilable by other means. This use of the military instrument may range from peaceful use of military assets in support of other instruments of national power through the commitment of massive military power in global total war.

Instruments of United States Military Power

2-60. The U.S. military, officially known as the U.S. armed forces, consists of five uniformed branches, the United States Army (USA), United States Navy (USN), United States Marine Corps (USMC), United States Air Force (USAF), and the United States Coast Guard (USCG). These branches are under civilian control, with the U.S. President serving as commander in chief. All branches except the USCG are part of the DOD, which is under the authority of the SecDef, who is also a civilian. The USCG falls under the authority of the Department of Homeland Security (DHS). During wartime, the SecDef may place the USCG under the DOD in the Department of the Navy (DN).

2-61. The USA, USN, and USAF are the primary instruments of U.S. military power on land, on sea, and in aerospace respectively. The USMC is a specialized land power, with a traditional focus on projecting land power from the sea. The USCG is a specialized sea power, with a traditional focus on enforcing maritime law and defense of U.S. shore areas. The U.S. armed forces have global responsibilities and are routinely stationed or deployed throughout the world. Although the primary function of the armed services is warfighting, much of U.S. military capability is necessarily involved in logistics and transportation, which enable rapid buildup of forces as needed. The USAF maintains a large fleet of combat, transportation and aerial refueling aircraft. The USMC maintains Marine Expeditionary Units (MEUs) at sea with the USN's Atlantic and Pacific fleets. The USN's fleet of active aircraft carriers, combined with a military doctrine of power projection, enables a flexible response to potential threats. Traditionally, the USA has not been used as much as the USMC as an expeditionary force. However, the USA is reorganizing its active-duty units into brigade combat teams with an emphasis on rapid power projection. These are some of the reasons that the U.S. military is universally considered the most powerful in the world. (Appendix G includes further information on the military instrument of national power.)

Military Instrument of United States National Power and Unconventional Warfare

2-62. The U.S. armed forces excel at conducting conventional warfare; most observers would admit that they are the most powerful and successful conventional armed forces in human history. However, UW is not an enterprise rooted in the direct application of missiles, air wings, naval fleets, and combat brigades. Most assets of the military instrument of U.S. national power are inappropriate—even counterproductive— to UW. The strengths of conventional forces (seizing terrain, destroying property, and winning battles against other conventional armed forces) are largely irrelevant and seldom effective in a UW effort. UW is a fundamentally indirect application of power that leverages human groups to act in concert with U.S. national objectives. Persuading human actors requires specially trained personnel and techniques to act on the full range of human motivation beyond mere narrowly defined actual or threatened physical coercion.

2-63. ARSOF UW operations are specialized (military) operations. However, even some military special operations forces (SOF) assets are inappropriate and counterproductive to effective UW. Regardless of the specialized capabilities of some other elite units, the primary military assets for conducting UW reside in SF, PSYOP, and CA units of ARSOF. Similarly, ARSOF UW operations are inherently joint operations, and UWOAs are JSOAs. However, the inherently political nature, typically protracted time frame, usually discreet execution, and expected involvement of non-DOD interagency and multinational partners in UW conceptually set the UWOA apart from all other JSOAs. UW operations are unique military operations in which most USG involvement may be outside direct military control. Finally, and by contrast, the application of all USG DIMEFIL instruments in the most effective conduct of UW is the ideal. By the nature of UW, ARSOF Soldiers may often find themselves the sole USG representative in their assigned sector of a UWOA. At those times and places, USG efforts will be "integrated" in the creative and flexible ARSOF warrior.

THE EFFECTIVENESS OF INTEGRATED NATIONAL POWER

2-64. The supporting appendixes for this chapter (Appendixes A through G) provide a broader treatment of the global environment within which each U.S. instrument of national power is employed. While unusual in scope for an FM, this explanatory technique is both appropriate and necessary. UW is difficult to conceptualize and even more difficult to effectively execute, because it does not easily conform to simple definitions, narrowly conceived and separated bureaucratic responsibilities, or direct and simplistic application of brute power.

2-65. The military strength of a 12-man Special Forces operational detachment A (SFODA) in direct combat with enemy infantry is slight. However, the ability of that same SFODA—properly employed in UW—to persuade other human actors to conduct activities in concert with U.S. national objectives can have strategic consequences. UW permits the leveraging of actors to conduct operations beyond the normal range of direct U.S. power. It permits a relatively small (but focused) U.S. investment to multiply effects in the UWOA thereby indirectly multiplying such U.S. power. The ways in which ARSOF achieve these effects are based on the range of possible human motivations. Therefore, ARSOF must consider and plan for all media of human interaction, and the most effective ARSOF UW operation will integrate all U.S. instruments to achieve the desired end state.

2-66. All carefully planned UW operations require timely and accurate intelligence. ARSOF must properly understand the human terrain to effectively negotiate the currents of human interaction. The U.S. IC is obviously chartered to gather such information. However, every instrument of U.S. national power likewise requires access to timely and accurate information for its own effectiveness. ARSOF understand the necessity of tapping into the data that all other agencies routinely acquire and use such information in the conduct of UW. For example, ARSOF must exploit the inherent expertise of the DOS in understanding foreign environments and audiences before and during the prosecution of a UW effort. The routine foreign presence of other agencies, such as the Drug Enforcement Administration (DEA), Federal Bureau of Investigation (FBI), or commercial sections of the DOC, can each provide valuable insights into the human terrain and motivations of the UWOA.

2-67. ARSOF do not use information solely for understanding. The manipulation of information can be an effective weapon that can shape TAs' perceptions. The calculated and integrated use of specific messages is a component of ARSOF attempts to persuade or dissuade certain behaviors in the context of a UW campaign. PSYOP units are specifically designed to execute such efforts. However, the variety of information capable of affecting human perception is enormous; only a tiny percentage of such information sources resides within the military's direct ability to wield. The activities of all U.S. instruments of national power carry informational messages (intended and unintended). ARSOF UW planners must work with their interagency partners to improve the messages that each U.S. activity carries. The most effective information plan for a UW campaign will attempt to ensure that the correct message is delivered to—and perceived by—the correct TA, as intended, at the right time, and in the context of an integrated plan of desired effects. The value of an integrated coordination of themes and products of the DOS's Bureau of International Information Programs (IIP), the federal agency International Broadcasting Bureau (IBB), and military PSYOP units in the conduct of UW is obvious. However, other nonintuitive media of information have significant military importance. For example, U.S. economic and financial promises made and kept

Chapter 2

(or ignored), the perception of justice (or injustice or ineffectiveness) of U.S. or allied law enforcement, or the inherent cultural values carried by non-USG-controlled popular culture have the ability to shape the attitudes and behaviors of human groups in the UWOA.

2-68. The application of economic or financial incentives is among the most powerful ideas in the U.S. arsenal of power. Although some U.S. adversaries are irreconcilable to accommodation with U.S. interests and must be engaged in other ways, many declared or potential adversaries can be persuaded or dissuaded by economic or financial means to become declared or potential allies (or at least neutralized). CA units are specifically designed, in part, to create desired effects from the manipulation of material inputs in their assigned area of operations (AO). Like the information environment, varied economic intercourse is a universal and mostly unmanaged human activity. However, the ability of the USG to affect the economic environment is enormous, and it has economic weapons at its disposal. ARSOF UW planners must carefully coordinate the introduction and withholding of economic and financial assets into the UWOA with their interagency partners. For example, direct application of USAID grants to specific human groups can alter negative behaviors or cement positive affiliations. The direct activities of the DOC's U.S. and Foreign Commercial Service to promote export expansion for U.S. and other multinational corporations (MNCs) can have similar (albeit indirect) effects. At the highest levels of diplomatic and financial interaction, the USG's ability to influence international financial institutions—with corresponding effects to exchange rates, interest rates, credit availability, and money supplies—can cement multinational coalitions for UW campaigns or dissuade adversary nation-state governments from supporting specific actors in the UWOA.

2-69. The ability of the United States to achieve its national strategic objectives depends in large measure on the effectiveness of the USG in employing the instruments of national power in a coordinated manner. All competition and conflict between states and other states (or nonstate actors) reflect a mix of the DIMEFIL instruments. UW, as one specific military operation, conducted by a few specially dedicated (primarily ARSOF) units within the military instrument, is not exempt from this truth. UW is fundamentally about influencing human groups within a specific area (usually beyond the reach of unilateral U.S. military power). Every means of influencing human behavior applies to UW.

2-70. It is the responsibility of the President and the SecDef to establish the rules for and integration of military power with the other instruments of national power. To accomplish this integration, the armed forces interact with the other responsible agencies to ensure mutual understanding of the capabilities, limitations, and consequences of military and civilian actions and to identify the ways in which military and nonmilitary capabilities can best complement each other. ARSOF understand that the most effective UW effort will coordinate all instruments of U.S. national power into an integrated and circumspect whole.

Chapter 3
Policy and Doctrine

NATIONAL POLICY

3-1. The President and his NSC ultimately determine authoritative U.S. UW policy. Further, the departments and institutions of the USG executive branch develop UW policy into doctrine and implement it. The legislative and judicial branches of the USG both support and constrain U.S. policy. In addition, the U.S. democratic system provides for an orderly transfer of power between individuals and parties on a routine basis. One strength of this system is that it allows for changes of policy direction that reflect changing U.S. understanding of the international environment. However, since the conduct of UW typically requires long-term effort, relatively short-term changes of administration and changes in the makeup of legislative and judicial bodies can result in policy changes that frustrate consistent and persistent effort. Moreover, changes in the international environment and international law can affect such policy. National-level strategies applicable to UW are therefore necessarily a snapshot in time.

NATIONAL SECURITY STRATEGY OF THE UNITED STATES (2006)

3-2. It is the policy of the United States to seek and support democratic movements and institutions in every nation and culture, with the ultimate goal of ending tyranny in the world. The fundamental character of regimes is as important as the distribution of power among them. The goal of U.S. statecraft is to help create a world of democratic, well-governed states that can meet citizens' needs and act responsibly in the international system. This is the best way to provide enduring security for the American people.

3-3. Achieving this goal is the work of generations. The United States is in the early years of a long struggle, similar to what the country faced in the early years of the Cold War. In the 20th century, freedom triumphed over the threats of fascism and communism. Yet a new totalitarian ideology now threatens—an ideology grounded not in secular philosophy but in the perversion of a religion. Its content may be different from the ideologies of the last century, but its means are similar: intolerance, murder, terror, enslavement, and repression. As in the past, today the United States must lay the foundations and build the institutions that the country needs to meet these challenges. Therefore, the United States must—

- Champion aspirations for human dignity.
- Strengthen alliances to defeat global terrorism and work to prevent attacks against the United States and its allies.
- Work with others to defuse regional conflicts.
- Prevent enemies from threatening the United States and its allies with weapons of mass destruction (WMD).
- Ignite a new era of global economic growth through free markets and free trade.
- Expand the circle of development by opening societies and building the infrastructure of democracy.
- Develop agendas for cooperative action with other main centers of global power.
- Transform America's national security institutions to meet the challenges and opportunities of the 21st century.
- Engage the opportunities and confront the challenges of globalization.

NATIONAL DEFENSE STRATEGY OF THE UNITED STATES (2005)

3-4. The national defense strategy (NDS) outlines an active, multilayer approach to the defense of the nation and its interests. The NDS seeks to create conditions that bring about a respect for national sovereignty and a secure international order favorable to freedom, democracy, and economic opportunity.

Chapter 3

This strategy promotes close cooperation with other nation around the world and commitment to these goals. It addresses mature and emerging threats. The strategic objectives of the NDS are to—

- *Secure the United States from direct attack.* The DOD gives top priority to dissuading, deterring, and defeating those who seek to harm the United States directly, especially extremist enemies with WMD.
- *Secure strategic access and retain global freedom of action.* The DOD will promote security, prosperity, and freedom of action of the United States and its partners by securing access to key regions, lines of communication, and the global commons.
- *Strengthen alliances and partnerships.* The DOD will expand the community of nations that share principles and interests with the United States. The DOD will help partners increase their capacity to defend themselves and collectively meet challenges to interests in common with those of the United States.
- *Establish favorable security conditions.* Working with others in the USG, the DOD will create conditions for a favorable international system by honoring U.S. security commitments and working with other nations to bring about a common appreciation of threats; a broad, secure, and lasting peace; and the steps required to protect against these threats. The DOD will accomplish these objectives with the following activities:
    - *By assuring allies and friends.* The DOD will provide assurance by demonstrating U.S. resolve to fulfill alliance and other defense commitments and help protect common interests.
    - *By dissuading potential adversaries.* The DOD will work to dissuade potential adversaries from adopting threatening capabilities, methods, and ambitions, particularly by developing key U.S. military advantages.
    - *By deterring aggression and countering coercion.* The DOD will deter aggression and counter coercion by maintaining capable and rapidly deployable military forces and, when necessary, demonstrating the will to resolve conflicts decisively on favorable terms.
    - *By defeating adversaries.* At the direction of the President, the DOD will defeat adversaries at the time, place, and in the manner of U.S. choosing, setting the conditions for future security.

3-5. The four NDS guidelines that structure DOD strategic planning and decision making are—

- *Conducting active, layered defense.* The DOD will focus military planning, posture, operations, and capabilities on the active, forward, and layered defense of the United States, its interests, and its partners.
- *Conducting continuous transformation.* The DOD will continually adapt how it approaches and confronts challenges, conducts business, and works with others.
- *Conducting a capabilities-based approach.* The DOD will operationalize the NDS to address mature and emerging challenges by setting priorities among competing capabilities.
- *Managing risks.* The DOD will consider the full range of risks associated with resources and operations and manage clear trade-offs across the department.

NATIONAL MILITARY STRATEGY OF THE UNITED STATES (2004)

3-6. The military challenge is to stay the course in the WOT while transforming the armed forces to conduct future joint operations. To meet this challenge, the armed forces will continue to focus on three priorities: winning the WOT, enhancing joint warfighting, and transforming for the future. The national military strategy (NMS) provides focus for military activities by defining a set of interrelated military objectives from which the Service chiefs and combatant commanders (CCDRs) identify desired capabilities and against which the Chairman of the Joint Chiefs of Staff (CJCS) assesses risk.

Military Objectives

3-7. The NMS establishes three military objectives that support the NDS. These are to—

- Protect the United States against external attacks and aggression.
- Prevent conflict and surprise attack.
- Prevail against adversaries.

Joint Vision for Future Warfighting

3-8. Sustaining and increasing the qualitative military advantages the United States enjoys today will require transformation—a transformation achieved by combining technological, intellectual, and cultural changes across the joint community. The goal is full-spectrum dominance—the ability to control any situation or defeat any adversary across the range of military operations.

3-9. The United States faces a number of dangerous and pervasive threats. Traditional, irregular, catastrophic, and disruptive challenges will require the armed forces to adjust quickly and decisively to change and anticipate emerging threats:

- States employing recognized military capabilities and forces in well-understood forms of military competition and conflict pose traditional challenges.
- States employing unconventional methods to counter the traditional advantages of stronger opponents pose irregular challenges.
- Adversaries acquiring, possessing, and using WMD or methods producing WMD-like effects pose catastrophic challenges.
- Adversaries developing and using breakthrough technologies to negate current U.S. advantages in key operational domains pose disruptive challenges.

3-10. Three key aspects of the security environment have unique implications for executing this military strategy. These aspects will drive the development of concepts and capabilities that ensure success in future operations:

- A wider range of adversaries.
- A more complex and distributed operational environment.
- An increase in technology diffusion and access.

A Wider Range of Adversaries

3-11. The range of adversaries capable of threatening the United States, its allies, and its interests include states, nonstate organizations, and individuals. Some states with traditional military forces and advanced systems, including cruise and ballistic missiles, could seek to control key regions of the world. A few of these states are "rogues" that violate treaties, secretly pursue and proliferate WMD, reject peaceful resolution of disputes, and display callous disregard for their citizens. Some of these states sponsor terrorists, providing them financial support, sanctuary, and access to dangerous capabilities. Some nonstate actors, such as terrorist networks, international criminal organizations, and illegal armed groups, menace stability and security. Even some individuals may have the means and will to disrupt international order. Some of these adversaries are not politically constrained. This makes these adversaries, particularly nonstate actors, less susceptible to traditional means of deterrence. Adversaries are increasingly seeking asymmetric capabilities and are using them in innovative ways. They avoid U.S. strengths, such as precision strikes, and seek to counter U.S. power projection capabilities by creating antiaccess environments. Such adversaries will target civilian populations, economic centers, and symbolic locations as a way to attack U.S. political will and resolve.

3-12. This volatile mix of challenges requires new methods of deterrence and operational approaches to defeat these threats should deterrence fail. Intelligence systems must allow commanders to understand enemy intent, predict threat actions, and detect adversary movements. This understanding provides them the time necessary to take preventive measures. Long before conflicts occur, these intelligence systems must provide a more thorough understanding of adversaries' motivations, goals, and organizations to determine effective deterrent COAs. However, there may be adversaries that remain undeterred. Should they acquire WMD or dangerous asymmetric capabilities or demonstrate the intent to mount a surprise attack, the United States must be prepared to prevent them from striking.

A More Complex and Distributed Operational Environment

3-13. Adversaries threaten the United States throughout a complex operational environment, extending from critical regions overseas to the homeland and spanning the global commons of international airspace, waters, space, and cyberspace. An "arc of instability" exists, stretching from the western hemisphere, through Africa and the Middle East and extending to Asia. There are areas in this arc that serve as breeding grounds for threats to U.S. interests. Within these areas, rogue states provide sanctuary to terrorists, protecting them from surveillance and attack. Other adversaries take advantage of ungoverned space and undergoverned territories from which they prepare plans, train forces, and launch attacks. These ungoverned areas often coincide with locations of illicit activities; such coincidence creates opportunities for hostile coalitions of criminal elements and ideological extremists.

3-14. The United States will conduct operations in widely diverse locations—from densely populated urban areas located in shore regions to remote, inhospitable, and austere locations. Military operations in this complex environment may be dramatically different from the high-intensity combat missions for which U.S. forces routinely train. While U.S. armed forces will continue to emphasize precision, speed, lethality, and distributed operations, commanders must expect and plan for the possibility that their operations will produce unintended second- and third-order effects. For example, U.S. forces can precisely locate, track, and destroy discrete targets to reduce collateral damage and conclude operations as quickly as possible. Operations that rely on precision may result in large elements of an adversary's military remaining intact and segments of the population unaffected. Commanders must prepare to operate in regions where pockets of resistance remain and the potential exists for continued combat operations amid a large number of noncombatants.

3-15. This operational environment places unique demands on military organizations and interagency partners and requires more detailed coordination and synchronization of activities both overseas and at home. U.S. experiences in Afghanistan and Iraq highlight the need for a comprehensive strategy to achieve longer-term national goals and objectives. The United States must adopt an "active defense-in-depth" that merges joint force, interagency, international NGOs and multinational capabilities in a synergistic manner. This defense does not solely rely on passive measures. The United States must enhance security at home while actively patrolling strategic approaches and extending defensive capabilities well beyond U.S. borders. An effective defense-in-depth must also include the capability to strike swiftly at any target around the globe using forces at home as well as forward-based, forward-deployed, and rotational forces.

An Increase in Technology Diffusion and Access

3-16. Global proliferation of a wide range of technology and weaponry will affect the character of future conflict. Dual-use civilian technologies, especially information technologies, high-resolution imagery, and global positioning systems are widely available. These relatively low-cost, commercially available technologies will improve the disruptive and destructive capabilities of a wide range of state and nonstate actors. Advances in automation and information processing will allow some adversaries to locate and attack targets both overseas and in the United States. Software tools for network attack, intrusion, and disruption are globally available over the Internet, providing almost any interested adversary a basic computer network exploitation or attack capability. Access to advanced weapons systems and innovative delivery systems could fundamentally change warfighting and dramatically increase an adversary's ability to threaten the United States.

3-17. Technology diffusion and access to advanced weapons and delivery systems have significant implications for military capabilities. The United States must have the ability to deny adversaries such disruptive technologies and weapons. However, the armed forces cannot solely focus on these threats and cannot assume there are no other challenges on the horizon. Ensuring current readiness while continuing to transform and maintain unchallenged military superiority will require investment. These are not mutually exclusive goals. The armed forces must remain ready to fight even as they transform and transform even as they fight.

Applicability of National Policy to Army Special Operations Forces Unconventional Warfare

3-18. The key components of these national policy documents have direct implications for the conduct of ARSOF UW. The NSS states that U.S. policy is "to seek and support democratic movements and institutions in every nation and culture" and identifies that this bold and noble policy is "the work of generations." This deliberately stated American support for democracy is consistent with the SF motto "to free the oppressed." The seeking out and supporting of democratic movements—even within nondemocratic state regimes—imply the utility of ARSOF UW in denied, hostile, and sensitive areas. The focused persistence required for a generational effort is consistent with the long-term shaping, political work, and partner organization-building fundamental to understanding UW.

3-19. Likewise, the strategic objectives of the NDS represent imperatives for the ARSOF execution of and strengths for the conduct of UW. ARSOF are a military asset whose role in UW contributes to dissuading, deterring, and defeating adversaries (especially extremists); securing strategic access to key regions; strengthening alliances and partnerships; and working with others in the USG to achieve these goals.

3-20. Finally, although the military objectives related in the NMS—protect the United States, prevent conflict, and prevail against adversaries—are essentially timeless imperatives for all U.S. armed forces (not just ARSOF), the key aspects of the security environment reflect the specific utility of ARSOF UW. ARSOF are adept at operating against a wider range of adversaries, in part, because of regional orientation and expertise in remote global areas. The more complex and distributed battlespace includes many of these same remote, unusual, and hostile areas. Moreover, one implication of technology diffusion and access means that adversarial conflict is no longer the prerogative of nation-state standing armed forces; modern adversaries empowered by 21st century technologies are now more likely to be prevalent in the same remote and unusual operational environments in which ARSOF thrive and ARSOF UW is often conducted.

3-21. The following paragraphs highlight special attributes and strengths that ARSOF bring to the conduct of UW. As stated earlier, ARSOF predominantly conduct UW. However, the USA does not train, assess and equip all ARSOF to conduct UW. SF, PSYOP, and CA elements primarily conduct ARSOF UW, while other ARSOF units, such as Rangers, engage in other SO. FM 3-05, *Army Special Operations Forces*, provides a general coverage of all ARSOF SO.

MILITARY CONCEPTS AND DOCTRINE

3-22. Since UW is defined as "operations conducted by, with, or through irregular forces to support insurgency, resistance, and conventional military operations," not all UW is a component of the WOT. Nevertheless, the WOT is a national priority that can involve significant use of ARSOF to conduct UW against adversarial states, supporters of terrorists, and a wide variety of nonstate actors.

3-23. ARSOF are the executors of and functional proponent for UW under the authority of Commander, USSOCOM. Currently, there is no authoritative interagency or joint doctrine specifically for UW—although sufficient joint doctrine exists for general campaign design and execution of joint and Army operations. This manual is the overarching doctrinal reference that specifically addresses UW as conducted by ARSOF. FM 3-05.201 contains detailed TTP for UW. The spectrum of likely operations describes a need for ARSOF in joint, combined, and multinational formations for a variety of missions including UW.

ARMY SPECIAL OPERATIONS FORCES IN SUPPORT OF THE WAR ON TERRORISM

3-24. ARSOF are continuously engaged in the WOT. USSOCOM is the lead COCOM for planning, synchronizing, and, as directed, executing global operations against terrorist networks in coordination with (ICW) other CCDRs. The Commander, USSOCOM, leads a global collaborative planning process leveraging other COCOM capabilities and expertise that results in decentralized execution by both USSOCOM and other COCOMs against terrorist networks. Internally, USSOCOM considers its role in the process of synchronizing DOD efforts in the WOT to be a core task of its headquarters (HQ), with specific responsibilities including—

- Integrating DOD strategy, plans, intelligence priorities, and operations against terrorist networks, as designated by the SecDef.
- Planning campaigns against terrorist networks and exercising command and control (C2) of operations in support of selected campaigns, as directed.
- Prioritizing and synchronizing theater security cooperation activities, deployments, and capabilities supporting campaigns against designated terrorist networks ICW the GCCs.
- Providing military representation to U.S. national and international agencies for matters related to U.S. and multinational campaigns against designated terrorist networks, as directed by the SecDef.
- Planning, executing, or synchronizing the execution of shaping operations ICW the GCCs.

Chapter 3

3-25. ARSOF support the WOT by providing forces trained and equipped to support the USSOCOM effort. ARSOF support USSOCOM's strategy for winning the WOT by conducting SO (including UW) to find, fix, and finish terrorists globally. ARSOF employ their forces to shape the global informational and geographic operational environment by conducting SO (including UW) to influence, deter, locate, isolate, and destroy terrorists and their support systems.

3-26. ARSOF face the four persistent and emerging challenges in this new, more uncertain era: traditional, irregular, catastrophic, and disruptive. Often, no hard boundaries distinguish one challenge from another. Indeed, the most dangerous circumstances are those where ARSOF face, or will face, multiple challenges simultaneously.

3-27. ARSOF are a key enabler in the WOT by conducting SO (including UW) that obtain actionable intelligence. Such intelligence assists commanders in determining the appropriate force package and in preparing the force to destroy terrorist networks. In UW, ARSOF combine with irregular forces acting alone or in combination with joint conventional force operations. ARSOF conducting UW can operate in hostile, denied, or sensitive environments to collect, monitor, or verify information of strategic or operational significance, often requiring low-visibility techniques. ARSOF can feed the results of these activities directly to a commander or Country Team or input them into the intelligence process for processing, analyzing, and disseminating to military and OGAs.

Range of Military Operations

3-28. The United States employs ARSOF capabilities at home and abroad in support of U.S. national security goals in a variety of operations. ARSOF conduct UW in support of major operations and campaigns when necessary. However, ARSOF conduct the majority of UW below the threshold of armed conflict between nation-states. Such relatively discrete and indirect activities allow the United States to engage partners and adversaries in a manner that helps shape the global operational environment and keep the day-to-day tensions between nations or groups below the threshold of armed conflict while maintaining U.S. global influence. Such UW operations provide a wide range of support to irregular forces conducive to furthering U.S. interests. Although SF are designed to support such irregular forces in a combat role if necessary, a majority of ARSOF UW involves SF, PSYOP, and CA activities that do not involve combat.

Global Nature of Operations

3-29. ARSOF have global reach and are capable of engaging threats and influencing potential adversaries with a variety of capabilities (including UW). The conduct of UW by ARSOF provides national decision makers a tool for engaging adversarial states controlling hostile or denied territory, which may otherwise be beyond the reach of U.S. influence. However, global reach and influence are not just the purview of nation-states. Globalization and emerging technologies allow small groups to use asymmetric approaches, to include criminal activity, terrorism, or armed aggression on a transnational scale, with relative ease and with little cost. The conduct of UW by ARSOF allows discrete and effective engagement of these adversarial nonstate actors as well.

3-30. Adversaries understand that direct challenges to U.S. power are likely to be a losing proposition. Therefore, adversaries often place greater emphasis on developing capabilities to threaten the United States indirectly. Increased interdependence of national economies and rapid movement of information around the world create significant challenges in the defense of U.S. interests. Identifying potential threats (both state and nonstate actors) operating independently or in loose coalitions, determining their intent, and determining the best COA to counter their actions are interagency and multinational challenges for the United States. In conjunction with the other instruments of power, the military use of ARSOF in UW provides a means of addressing such indirect threats.

3-31. The elusive nature of adversaries and the ever-increasing speed of global communications and the media demand greater adaptability and networking from ARSOF, particularly communications and intelligence resources. Consequently, ARSOF conduct operations on a global scale as part of the NSS. ARSOF conducts UW operations in depth, focusing on the threat source across geographical regions. ARSOF Soldiers' routine employment in forward regions, developed expertise in dealing with foreign

Policy and Doctrine

irregular forces and peoples, discretion, and versatility make the conduct of UW an effective tool for seeking out such elusive opponents.

Military Engagement, Security Cooperation, and Deterrence

3-32. These ongoing and specialized activities establish, shape, maintain, and refine relations with other nations and domestic civil authorities. Security cooperation involves all DOD interactions with foreign defense establishments to build defense relationships that promote specific U.S. security interests, develop allied and friendly military capabilities for self-defense and multinational operations, and provide ARSOF with peacetime and contingency access to an HN. An HN internal defense and development (IDAD) program may include nation assistance, FID, security assistance, humanitarian and civic assistance, antiterrorism, DOD support to counterdrug operations, show-of-force operations, arms control, and so on. In addition to ARSOF participation in these missions, ARSOF may also conduct UW that supports the WOT within the context of military engagement, security coordination, and deterrence. UW capabilities developed within an HN may give capable irregular forces the ability to defeat terrorist threats within their sovereign borders.

Limited Contingency Operations

3-33. The United States often uses ARSOF to respond to a crisis that does not require large-scale combat operations to resolve. A limited contingency operation can be a single small-scale, limited-duration operation or a significant part of a major operation of extended duration involving combat. The associated general strategic and operational objectives are to protect U.S. interests and to prevent surprise attack or further conflict. The levels of complexity, duration, and resources depend on the circumstances. Included are operations to ensure the safety of American citizens and U.S. interests while maintaining and improving U.S. ability to operate with multinational partners in deterring the hostile ambitions of potential aggressors. Many of these operations involve a combination of conventional and unconventional forces and capabilities in close cooperation with OGAs and NGOs. ARSOF conduct of UW in these cases is likely to be a supporting effort to other SO or conventional operations.

Major Operations and Campaigns

3-34. When required to achieve national strategic objectives or to protect national interests, the U.S. national leadership may decide to conduct a major operation or campaign involving large-scale combat, placing the United States in a wartime state. In such cases, the general goal is to prevail against the enemy as quickly as possible; to conclude hostilities; and to establish conditions favorable to the HN, the United States, and its multinational partners. ARSOF conduct UW in support of such major combat operations either directly or indirectly.

Types of Military Operations

3-35. Army doctrine addresses the range of full-spectrum operations across the spectrum of conflict, as described in FM 1, *The Army*. Army commanders at all echelons may combine different types of operations simultaneously and sequentially to accomplish missions. For each mission, the JFC and Army component commander determine the emphasis Army forces place on each type of operation.

Army Full-Spectrum Operations

3-36. Missions in any environment require ARSOF to be prepared to conduct any combination of offensive, defensive, stability, and civil-support operations described below. However, the conduct of UW by ARSOF has particular strengths and weaknesses within the context of each operation:

- *Offensive operations destroy or defeat an enemy.* Their purpose is to impose U.S. will on the enemy and to achieve decisive victory. ARSOF elements conducting UW are typically small and therefore of limited direct offensive value to a JFC. However, ARSOF Soldiers' particular excellence in serving as a force multiplier of irregular combat forces in UW makes ARSOF a potentially valuable indirect element of offensive power. Moreover, since ARSOF conduct of UW frequently occurs in an adversary's rear area, the coordinated application of ARSOF-led

Chapter 3

irregular forces to the JFC's operational plan can provide offensive advantages in surprise, maneuver, and economy of force.

- *Defensive operations defeat an enemy attack, buy time, economize forces, or develop conditions favorable for offensive operations.* Defensive operations alone normally cannot achieve a decision. As with offensive operations, ARSOF conducting UW are of limited direct defensive value because of their small element size and typically isolated and unsupported positioning. However, when ARSOF use UW to leverage irregular forces into larger combat formations, they can play a significant indirect defensive role. Moreover, whereas the JFC may be conducting a defensive mission at the strategic, operational, or tactical levels, ARSOF Soldiers' typical positioning in the adversary's rear area and in support of irregular forces place ARSOF UW elements in position to conduct offensive missions with strategic, operational, and tactical significance to the JFC's conduct of the defense.

- *Stability operations promote and protect U.S. national interests by influencing the threat, political, and information dimensions of the operational environment through a combination of peacetime developmental, cooperative activities and coercive actions in response to crises.* The United States can employ ARSOF to assist civil authorities (foreign or domestic) in responding to crises and in relieving suffering. As part of a larger USG interagency strategy, ARSOF UW activities can be useful in supporting the conduct of stability operations. (More information on these often classified activities can be found in FM 3-05.201.)

- *Civil support operations address the consequences of man-made or natural accidents and incidents beyond the capabilities of civilian authorities.* Army forces do not conduct stability operations within the United States—under U.S. law, the federal and state governments are responsible for those tasks. Instead, Army forces conduct civil-support operations when requested, providing Army expertise and capabilities to lead agency authorities. ARSOF does not conduct UW within the United States.

3-37. When commanders conduct full-spectrum operations as part of an overseas joint campaign, they combine and sequence offensive, defensive, and stability operations to accomplish the mission. The JFC and the SO component commander for a particular mission determine the emphasis ARSOF place on each type of operation (including UW). Throughout the campaign, offensive, defensive, and stability operations occur simultaneously. As missions change from promoting peace to deterring war and from resolving conflict to war itself, the combinations of and transitions between these operations require skillful assessment, planning, preparation, and execution. Moreover, ARSOF may sometimes conduct a continuous UW effort throughout the entire duration of an overseas joint campaign regardless of any changing emphasis of the conventional force mission, and regardless of joint forces' location within the spectrum of conflict.

3-38. ARSOF can conduct UW in support of the JFC at all levels:

- *Strategic.* The strategic level concerns the broadest aspects of national and theater policy. Decisions at this level reflect national and multinational goals, integrate all the instruments of national power, provide forces, and determine constraints on their use. The President or the SecDef and the GCCs determine the strategic-national and strategic-theater objectives and the manner of use of military means to achieve them. The President or the SecDef and the GCCs may directly or indirectly (through subordinate commanders) employ ARSOF in pursuit of these objectives. ARSOF conduct of UW provides a national-level ability to affect strategic U.S. interests, and the most effective use of ARSOF UW requires a deliberate and comprehensive use of all instruments of national power. In fact, although ARSOF are the military weapon of choice to conduct UW, the other (nonmilitary) instruments of U.S. national power at the strategic level may make up a majority of a successful UW campaign force.

- *Operational.* The operational level focuses on theater campaigns and major operations. JFCs determine operational objectives that lead to the attainment of strategic-theater objectives. The design, organization, and conduct of campaigns and major operations attain these objectives and, in turn, guide tactical events. A GCC, subordinate unified command commander, JTF commander, Service component commander, or functional component commander may employ ARSOF as part of a joint force to attain these operational objectives. ARSOF UW can be an

integral part of theater campaigns and major operations. The feasibility of UW should be considered in any campaign.
- *Tactical.* The tactical level focuses on battles and engagements. Decisions at this level apply combat power to create advantages while in contact with or close to the enemy. ARSOF may support tactical actions (offense, defense, and stability actions) designed to have significant effect in attaining operational objectives. Tactical actions may directly attain tactical, operational, and strategic objectives simultaneously, which is especially true in the conduct of ARSOF SO (including UW). The typical sensitivity of ARSOF UW activities can magnify the positive or negative consequences of tactical success or failure.

Principles of War

3-39. ARSOF missions may require unorthodox approaches, but these approaches do not negate the nine traditional principles of war. Rather, they place a different emphasis on their combination or relative importance. In some SO missions, surprise achieved through speed, stealth, audacity, deception, and new tactics or techniques can be far more effective and efficient than traditional conventional tactics based on massed firepower and tactical maneuvers. The following discussion of the principles of war highlights their application to ARSOF when conducting UW:

- *Objective.* Direct every military operation toward a clearly defined, decisive, and attainable objective. ARSOF objectives are as much political, economic, and informational as they are military in nature. This fact is highlighted in UW because the fundamental objective of UW is to accomplish activities by, with, or through irregular forces as U.S. surrogates. The objective of UW is always inherently political. JFCs and ARSOF UW planners must avoid mistaking secondary objectives (such as employing lethal force against an adversary) for the primary objective of persuading the irregular surrogate to take action in concert with U.S. objectives.
- *Offensive.* Seize, retain, and exploit the initiative. ARSOF are inherently offensive in nature because they seek to strike or engage the enemy to compel, deter, or counter enemy actions. In UW, such initiative is conducted by, with, or through an irregular surrogate. In ARSOF UW, "offensive" is not necessarily synonymous with the application of lethal force. It is imperative that SF, PSYOP, and CA forces conducting UW exploit the initiative by proactively persuading, advising, and gaining the support of irregular forces and the civilians in the UWOA as part of a comprehensive UW campaign plan.
- *Mass.* Concentrate the effects of combat power at the decisive place and time. Commanders mass the effects of overwhelming combat power at the decisive time and place to overwhelm the enemy or to gain control of the situation. ARSOF concentrate the effects of combat power at critical times and discriminate selected targets to produce decisive results that accomplish the commander's objectives. The truth of this principle is unchangeable, but what constitutes overwhelming power is relative. Referring to guerrilla warfare, Mao Tse-tung famously said "The strategy is one to ten, the tactics are ten to one." The correlation of forces that an ARSOF element may represent to an adversary in UW may be a distinct numerical U.S. disadvantage. However, a small force may achieve success if massed at the right time and place, and in the context of a well-conceived plan. Moreover, combat power must not be misunderstood to mean only lethal force. Chapter 2 of this manual and FM 3-24, for example, observe that some of the best weapons do not shoot. Massing the effects of a properly executed PSYOP or CA plan can have decisive results for ARSOF UW.
- *Economy of force.* Allocate minimum essential combat power to secondary efforts and employ all combat power available in the most effective way possible. ARSOF provide an essential economy of force when military objectives are subordinate to political, economic, and informational objectives. This is particularly true when ARSOF conduct UW. By definition, small ARSOF cadres are often able to leverage huge efforts by indigenous populations, irregular forces, and other surrogates through carefully crafted psychological appeals, political interaction, and other trust-building activities. In the context of a well-orchestrated UW campaign plan, the effect of such activities can prove decisive.
- *Maneuver.* Place the enemy in a disadvantageous position through the flexible application of combat power. As military units conducting SO, ARSOF elements do conduct maneuver in the

traditional sense in strategic, operational, and tactical environments and possess tremendous capability to gain positions of advantage for the GCC. When conducting UW, ARSOF Soldiers' ability to leverage segments of the population resident in the UWOA can be particularly useful to the campaign plan when ARSOF-supported irregular forces can apply combat power in the adversary's secure operating environment. Once again, combat power in ARSOF UW does not automatically denote lethal force. The properly timed and positioned interdiction of lines of communication, popular uprisings, or sabotaged adversary infrastructure, for example, can be flexible applications of combat power that place the enemy in a disadvantageous position.

- *Unity of command.* Ensure unity of effort under one responsible commander for every objective. Theater special operations command (TSOC) commanders under the COCOM of the GCC can either tailor the C2 architecture for ARSOF operations under the direct control of the TSOC or recommend subordinate JFC relationships to ensure unity of effort of SOF. Therefore, integration, synchronization, and unity of effort for these forces are incumbent upon commanders and staffs at every level. To the extent SF, PSYOP, and CA work together in an ARSOF UW campaign, it is imperative that these forces integrate and coordinate their efforts throughout the duration of the mission.

- *Security.* Prohibit the enemy from acquiring an unexpected advantage. ARSOF can provide security to the JFC by denying the enemy the ability to use his expected advantages. ARSOF provide security through various intelligence-collection methods, force protection (FP), and force applications. The irregular forces and populations indigenous to a UWOA and engaged by ARSOF can multiply friendly intelligence and greatly enhance friendly security.

- *Surprise.* Strike the enemy at a time and place or in a manner for which he is unprepared. ARSOF can deceive the enemy, inhibit the enemy's decision making, or restrict the enemy's capability to react to the commander's operations or campaign. As irregular forces and target populations engaged by ARSOF multiply friendly intelligence and enhance security in UW, that same enhanced situational awareness multiplies opportunities to identify adversary weaknesses. Moreover, the discrete building of a UW organization itself in an adversary's territory—and judicious revelation of that organization's abilities—has the greatest potential for surprise. The calculated use of such surprise can have vital psychological effects in an ARSOF UW campaign.

- *Simplicity.* Prepare clear, uncomplicated plans and concise orders to ensure a thorough understanding. ARSOF use unorthodox and sophisticated methods and equipment. The plans and procedures the force employs must be simple and direct to facilitate understanding, to withstand the stress of operational environments, and to allow for rapid adaptation to changing situations. This principle is as valid in UW as it is to other ARSOF SO. However, the fundamental activity of ARSOF UW is a political activity of small-scale human interaction; persuading and leading irregular forces to act in concert with U.S. objectives. As Clausewitz famously noted, "In war everything is simple, but the simplest thing is difficult." U.S. political interaction with irregular surrogates is inherently difficult and only properly selected and trained ARSOF personnel should conduct UW.

Other Principles

3-40. UW is inherently a joint activity, and JP 3-0, *Joint Operations*, identifies three additional principles ARSOF must consider: restraint, perseverance, and legitimacy. The following paragraphs address each of these principles.

Restraint

3-41. The purpose of restraint is to limit collateral damage and to prevent the unnecessary or unlawful use of force. A single act could cause significant military and political consequences; therefore, judicious use of force is necessary. Restraint requires the careful and disciplined balancing of the need for security, the conduct of military operations, and the national strategic end state. For example, the exposure of intelligence-gathering activities could have significant political and military repercussions. Because of this, Soldiers should exercise sound judgment when conducting intelligence gathering. Excessive force antagonizes other parties involved, thereby damaging the legitimacy of the organization using excessive force and potentially enhancing the legitimacy of the opposing party.

3-42. ARSOF commanders at all levels must take proactive steps to ensure their personnel are properly trained in the rules of engagement (ROE) and are quickly informed of any changes. In multinational operations, use of force may be dictated by coalition or allied force ROE. Failure to understand and comply with established ROE can result in fratricide, mission failure, or national embarrassment.

3-43. The use of ARSOF in UW has several special considerations regarding restraint. At a national strategic level, the use of discrete ARSOF UW operations can itself be a measure of U.S. restraint. Small, highly trained ARSOF elements working by, with, or through irregular surrogates in UW can sometimes eliminate the need for large-scale U.S. military operations. This indirect use of military power through ARSOF UW can provide significant strategic results supporting U.S. objectives while providing a perception of USG restraint. However, the very sensitivity of some ARSOF UW operations can magnify USG embarrassment if exposed. Therefore, use of ARSOF UW in highly sensitive situations requires careful consideration of risk.

3-44. An additional restraint complexity in ARSOF UW involves the inherent nature of working by, with, or through irregular surrogates. Although a successful ARSOF UW operation may not require U.S. forces to apply any lethal force whatsoever, persuading and leading irregular surrogates to act in concert with U.S. objectives is a human political interaction that is inherently difficult to control. ARSOF personnel conducting UW must impart a notion of restraint to their irregular counterparts. Unrestrained actions by irregular forces working with ARSOF may reflect badly on the United States, may provoke adversary force retaliation or international political condemnation, and may result in counterproductive popular resistance within the UWOA, all of which may jeopardize the mission.

3-45. The foreign, often hostile, and sometimes remote locations that ARSOF typically executes UW in make the maintenance of restraint more difficult. JTF commanders and ARSOF elements must thoroughly understand the cultural and legal customs of the UWOA. Traditional regard for life and rule of law (or lack thereof) may differ greatly from conventional battlefields and international standards of behavior. ARSOF must understand and anticipate such differences before infiltrating the UWOA. Since ARSOF personnel conducting UW will typically be part of small U.S. elements within a large foreign environment and often beyond rapid U.S. support, the selection, preparation, and judgment of the ARSOF personnel are crucial considerations. If U.S. irregular surrogates continuously behave in a manner that jeopardizes U.S. interests, the maintenance of U.S. restraint may require ending the UW mission.

Perseverance

3-46. The purpose of perseverance is to ensure the commitment necessary to attain the national strategic end state. Some joint operations may require years to reach the termination criteria, and ARSOF must anticipate operations that are both measured and protracted. The underlying causes of the crisis may be elusive, making the achievement of decisive resolution difficult. The patient, resolute, and persistent pursuit of national goals and objectives is often a requirement for success. This effort frequently involves measures from all instruments of U.S. national power to supplement military efforts.

3-47. Perseverance in pursuit of U.S. objectives is fundamental to the conduct of ARSOF UW. If the seeking out and support of democratic elements in every nation and culture as outlined in the NSS is "the work of generations" and ARSOF UW is a central tool to achieve this policy, ARSOF UW requires a persistence of USG effort far beyond most other enterprises of government. One appeal of most SO (such as direct action) to policy makers and commanders is that SO are of relatively short duration and often promise dramatic and easily quantifiable results. Most ARSOF UW, by contrast, may take years or decades to develop properly, and clear results may not be dramatic, easily measured, or readily gratified. Perhaps more than any other military operation, ARSOF UW requires patient effort.

Legitimacy

3-48. The purpose of legitimacy is to develop and maintain the will necessary to attain the national strategic end state. The basis for legitimacy is the legality, morality, and rightness of the actions undertaken, as well as the will of the U.S. public to support the actions. Legitimacy is frequently a decisive element. The perception of legitimacy by the U.S. public is strengthened if obvious national or humanitarian interests are at stake and American lives are not being needlessly or carelessly placed at risk.

Other interested audiences may include foreign nations, civil populations in the UWOA, and participating forces.

3-49. ARSOF committed to a UW operation must sustain the legitimacy of the operation and of irregular surrogates with which they work, where applicable. The USG must balance legitimacy concerns with actions by U.S.-sponsored irregular forces. The USG must consider all actions in the light of potentially competing strategic and tactical requirements and must exhibit fairness in dealing with competing factions, where appropriate. In some cases of ARSOF UW, the use of force is both appropriate and necessary. However, judicious restraint in the use of force by U.S. and U.S.-sponsored irregular forces will likely reinforce legitimacy.

3-50. Legitimacy may depend on adherence to objectives agreed to by the international community, ensuring the action is appropriate to the situation, and fairness in dealing with various factions. However, since ARSOF UW is particularly useful in sensitive environments, U.S. legitimacy may depend on the UW operation itself not being exposed. By contrast, exposure of or creating the perception of an adversary's illegitimacy is a common PSYOP theme in ARSOF UW.

CONVENTIONAL WARFARE AND MAJOR COMBAT OPERATIONS

3-51. Although conventional forces, SOF, and the interagency force can all play some role in any type of warfare, each of these forces plays either a leading or supporting role. Conventional warfare, which has historically been typified by MCO, is characterized by the predominant role of conventional forces with SOF and the interagency force in support.

CONVENTIONAL FORCES

3-52. The Capstone Concept for Joint Operations and MCO describes how the future joint force intends to conduct combat operations in support of national military objectives. Future major combat operations will—

- Provide the combat contribution to the larger projection of all instruments of available national power in a tight, seamless, and organically integrated fashion to achieve political objectives.
- Emphasize disintegration as the principal mechanism used to defeat an adversary's military system.
- Engulf the adversary through comprehensive engagement in every domain and dimension.
- Be more distributed and interdependently joint.
- Derive strength from and contribute to continuous global shaping.
- Utilize both the informational and cognitive domains to create a sense of relentless pressure on and absolute dominance over an adversary.
- Create and exploit opportunities, many of which are fleeting, while simultaneously denying or spoiling opportunities for the adversary.
- Reduce, by synergistic joint operations, harmful seams, gaps, and vulnerabilities that heretofore limited rapid, interdependent, distributed, and decisive application of joint combat power.

3-53. Personnel must consider MCO, IW, and military support to SSTR operations holistically as complementary concepts working together during crises with an end view of restoration of the rule of law and a sustainable peace under civil policing. Commanders and their interagency and multinational partners should assess the potential integration requirements and opportunities of these operations.

3-54. The U.S. military will fight an uncertain and unpredictable enemy or, even more demanding, multiple enemy forces simultaneously in widely dispersed joint operations areas (JOAs). The future environment will be characterized by—

- Globalization.
- Complex terrain.
- Dynamic coalitions, alliances, and partnerships.

3-55. The joint force will face a range of adaptive, thinking adversaries with access to militarily useful capabilities. These adversaries will sometimes pose complex combinations of traditional, irregular, catastrophic, and disruptive challenges.

The Military Problem

3-56. Adversaries with capable militaries, including access denial, IO, advanced conventional, WMD, and IW capabilities may creatively use them in new ways to coerce or attack U.S. friends or allies, threaten regional stability, or take other actions that pose an unacceptable threat to the United States. The U.S. military must be capable of defeating such adversaries while minimizing the prospects for unintended escalation and considering the burdens of postwar transition and reconstruction.

3-57. The military problem describes the enemy and its behavior using a systems approach. Disintegration of the enemy system through integrated destruction and dislocation will be the defeat mechanism used to compel the enemy to accede to U.S. will.

The Military Solution

3-58. The joint force, supported by other instruments of national power, will conduct synergistic, high-tempo actions in multiple domains to shatter the coherence of the adversary's plans and dispositions and render him unable or unwilling to militarily oppose the achievement of U.S. strategic objectives.

3-59. Should the failure of peaceful preventive measures dictate the use of force, the United States, preferably with multinational partners but unilaterally if required, will conduct MCO to overmatch and overwhelm the enemy and deny the use of and contain enemy-held WMD.

3-60. Combat operations are those inherently military actions taken directly or indirectly to defeat an adversary's military. Under the long-standing principle of self-defense, commanders may be required to conduct offensive operations against undeterred adversaries that pose an unmistakable threat of grave harm to national security interests. In any case, once the commander decides to respond with the use of force, the U.S. military rapidly conducts joint offensive and defensive combat operations to defeat the enemy. Moreover, the JFC must anticipate setting the conditions for stability in the crisis area. To do this, the joint force aims to see first, understand first, decide first, and act first in a cyclic process and ultimately finish decisively.

SPECIAL OPERATIONS FORCES

3-61. Five basic criteria facilitate the employment of ARSOF in support of the joint force campaign or operation plan (OPLAN). These criteria provide guidelines for conventional and ARSOF commanders and planners to use when considering the employment of ARSOF:

- *Is the mission appropriate?* Commander use ARSOF to achieve effects that require their unique skills and capabilities. If the effects do not require those skills and capabilities, commanders should not assign ARSOF to the operation. Commander should not use ARSOF as a substitute for other forces.
- *Does the mission support the campaign plan?* If the mission does not support the JFC's campaign or major OPLAN, the JFC should consider ARSOF for more appropriate missions available.
- *Is the mission operationally feasible?* ARSOF are not structured for attrition or force-on-force warfare. As such, commanders should not assign them to missions beyond their capabilities. ARSOF commanders and their staffs must consider the vulnerability of ARSOF units to larger, more heavily armed or mobile forces in hostile territory.
- *Are required resources available for the mission?* Some ARSOF missions require support from other forces for success. Support involves aiding, protecting, complementing, and sustaining employed ARSOF. Support can include airlift, intelligence, communications, IO, medical, logistics, space, weather, and numerous other types of support. Although a target may be

vulnerable to ARSOF, deficiencies in supportability may affect the likelihood for success or may entirely invalidate the feasibility of employing ARSOF.
- *Will the outcome of the mission justify the risk?* ARSOF have high value and limited resources. Commanders must make sure the benefits of successful mission execution are measurable and in balance with the risks inherent in the mission assessment. Some operations that ARSOF can execute make only a marginal contribution to the JFC's campaign plan and present great risk to personnel and materiel. Commanders should recognize the high value and limited resources of ARSOF. Risk management considers not only the potential loss of ARSOF units and equipment but also the risk of adverse effects on U.S. diplomatic and political interests if the mission fails.

Army Special Operations Forces Capabilities

3-62. The unique capabilities of ARSOF (including those pertinent to UW) are a function of the quality of ARSOF Soldiers, the training and education of those Soldiers, and the mission profiles the Soldiers must execute. The competitive ARSOF selection process, coupled with technological training and education, produces an ARSOF Soldier who is adaptable, mature, innovative, culturally aware, self-assured, and self-reliant. Thus, policy decision makers use ARSOF as a force to expand the range of available options.

3-63. ARSOF are specially organized, trained, and equipped military forces. They conduct SO (including UW) to achieve military, political, economic, or informational objectives by generally unconventional means in hostile, denied, or politically sensitive areas. Decision makers may choose the ARSOF option because ARSOF provide the broadest range of capabilities that have direct applicability in an increasing number of environments. Political-military requirements frequently cast ARSOF into clandestine or low-visibility environments that require oversight at the national level. ARSOF operations differ from conventional force operations by their degree of acceptable physical and political risk, their modes of employment, and their operational techniques. ARSOF allow the unified commander or JFC to perform critical small-unit missions that directly or indirectly support the objective of his operational mission.

3-64. Early use of ARSOF in an operation may prevent or limit conflict and conserve national resources. When conflict is imminent, the USG may use ARSOF in a variety of prehostility missions to signal determination, to demonstrate support to allies, and to begin the complicated processes of positioning forces for combat and shaping the AO.

3-65. During conflict, ARSOF may be most effective in conducting strategic or operational economy-of-force operations (including UW) that generate military and diplomatic advantages disproportionate to the resources they represent. ARSOF—or the irregular forces they support when conducting UW—can locate, seize, or destroy strategic or operational targets and obtain critical intelligence. They can analyze an enemy's defenses and diminish enemy morale. ARSOF can disorganize, disrupt, and demoralize enemy troops. They can also divert the enemy's important resources.

3-66. ARSOF expand the options of the President, the SecDef, and GCCs, particularly in crises and contingencies that fall between wholly diplomatic initiatives and the overt use of large conventional forces. The small size, rapid reaction, and self-sufficient nature of ARSOF elements provide military options that do not involve the risk of escalation normally associated with larger, more visible conventional forces. The use of ARSOF enables decision makers to prevent a conflict or to limit its scope. Therefore, decision makers can better control committed U.S. forces and resources. When conducting UW in support of conventional operations, ARSOF can support irregular surrogates acting in concert with U.S. objectives, further limiting the scope of involvement by U.S. forces.

3-67. ARSOF are adept at using lethal force. However, ARSOF conducting UW need not always use lethal force in a mission. Language skills, cross-cultural training, regional orientation, and understanding of the political context of operational areas make ARSOF unparalleled when operating in complex environments. ARSOF skills enable them to work as effectively with civilian populations as with other military forces to favorably influence situations toward U.S. national interests. This ability to apply discreet leverage is a very important ARSOF contribution to the NMS.

Characteristics

3-68. To ensure UW missions in support of conventional operations selected for ARSOF are compatible with their capabilities, commanders must be familiar with the following SO characteristics:

- ARSOF personnel undergo careful selection processes or mission-specific training beyond basic military skills to achieve entry-level SO skills. Being proficient in these skills makes rapid replacement or generation of personnel or capabilities highly unlikely.
- Mature, experienced personnel make up ARSOF. Many maintain a high level of competency in more than one military specialty.
- Most ARSOF are regionally oriented for employment. Cross-cultural communication skills are a routine part of their training and represent a fundamental characteristic of their utility in UW.
- ARSOF conduct specific tactical operations by small units with unique talents that directly strike or engage strategic and operational aims or objectives. More importantly for UW, ARSOF are able to persuade and provide support for irregular forces to make such engagements. These direct tactical engagements often represent indirect operational and strategic approaches for the JFC.
- Planning for SO may begin at the unified, joint, or interagency level for execution that requires extensive, rigorous rehearsal. Protracted UW campaigns usually require early interagency coordination.
- SO are frequently clandestine or low-visibility operations, or they may be combined with overt operations. SO can be covert but require a declaration of war or a specific finding approved by the President or the SecDef. ARSOF can deploy at relatively low cost, with a low profile less intrusive than that of larger conventional forces.
- Selected ARSOF units often conduct SO at great distances from operational bases. These units employ sophisticated communications systems and means of insertion, support, and extraction to penetrate and return from hostile, denied, or politically sensitive areas.
- SO occur throughout the range of military operations.
- SO influence the will of foreign leadership to create conditions favorable to U.S. strategic aims and objectives.
- SO are often high-risk operations that have limited windows of execution and require first-time success. However, although UW will often be a high-risk special operation, it typically involves a longer time frame of activities and a long-term USG commitment. Also, the results of UW operations may take years or decades to materialize. ARSOF SF, PSYOP, and CA units are ideally suited to perform SO with, through, or by indigenous personnel.
- SO require theater- and, frequently, national-level intelligence support.
- Selected SO (especially UW) require a detailed knowledge of the cultural nuances and languages of a country or region where employed.
- SO are inherently joint and sometimes multinational, requiring interagency and international coordination. The contribution of ARSOF to national security is greatest when the JFC fully integrates ARSOF into his plan at the earliest stages of planning.
- ARSOF can be task-organized quickly and deployed rapidly to provide tailored responses to many different situations. However, while Soldiers can conduct UW in quick reaction to events, such as OEF/Afghanistan, this quick-reaction use of UW is atypical.
- Selected ARSOF can gain access to hostile and denied areas.
- ARSOF can provide limited security and medical support for themselves.
- Selected ARSOF can live in austere, harsh environments without extensive support. For long-duration operations, ARSOF require support from the Army Service component command (ASCC).
- Selected ARSOF can survey and assess local situations and rapidly report these assessments.
- Selected ARSOF can work closely with regional military and civilian authorities and populations.

3-69. ARSOF are not a substitute for conventional forces. They are, however, a necessary adjunct to the capabilities of existing conventional forces. ARSOF characteristics and ability to conduct UW can contribute significantly to conventional forces and MCO.

INTERAGENCY ACTIVITIES

3-70. Multinational and interagency partners have special capabilities that contribute to achieving dominant effects in support of unified action, as well as achieving military and political objectives and end states. The United States routinely integrates and executes multinational and interagency actions rapidly and coherently in support of the JFC. As the JFC integrates interagency capabilities into his plan, he similarly integrates ARSOF SF, PSYOP, and CA elements conducting UW in support of the conventional plan with the interagency.

3-71. The JFC integrates multinational capabilities and collaborates with interagency and international partner leaders during planning and throughout the campaign to achieve synergies, further isolate, and deny sanctuary to the enemy. The U.S. military uses day-to-day interactions, frequent preconflict engagement venues, periodic joint C2 training exercises, an extensive and vigorous liaison program, and an expanded collaborative information environment to build favorable and practiced relationships with these partners. The U.S. military fosters the development of interoperable and well-trained alliance and coalition capabilities that can readily plug into plans and operations. The U.S. military uses forward basing and security cooperation to build strong, mutually supporting relationships with these partners. Conceivably, more permanent U.S.-led multinational force (MNF) HQ will emerge at the operational level in the future when mutually beneficial to the U.S. and other supportive governments. The JFC combines and exploits joint warfighting doctrine, organizations, training, technology, and leadership with special contributions from other partners to achieve desired operational-level objectives.

3-72. The JFC will also use automated synchronization and coordination tools to align and coordinate military activities with diplomatic, informational, economic, and other activities within the context of coalition planning and execution environments. Autonomous synchronization tools will provide traceability of allocated resources and shared responsibilities to effects generated. This synchronization record will allow national governments, international organizations, and certain NGO partners to trace their contributions to achieving common strategic objectives, as well as specific organizational objectives.

3-73. The interagency has a vital role in gaining and maintaining dominance in the information environment. Strategic-level information and influence strategies are critical to addressing traditional, irregular, disruptive, and catastrophic challenges and extend beyond the purview of the military commander alone. Therefore, the JFC information and influence plans must contribute to and be consistent with the higher-level strategy. Accordingly, well-conceived, well-coordinated, and well-executed operational-level information and influence plans are critical prerequisites when dealing with future operational challenges. To decisively influence an adversary, it is critical that the United States understands their decision-making process and their perceptions. "One-size-fits-all" information campaigns or influence strategies cannot overcome the unique problems each adversary presents, especially when fanaticism is a primary motivator for an irregular adversary. With concise strategic-level guidance and interagency and multinational participation, a comprehensive information and influence campaign embraces strategic-level intent and supports achievement of both military and political objectives.

3-74. In the early stages of conflict, the adversary is likely to possess the initiative in the information environment. To wrest the initiative from the adversary, a comprehensive set of offensive and defensive actions must occur. The innovative combination of electronic weapons platforms, networking systems, and strategic- and operational-level PSYOP, enabled by the net-centric operational environment, creates significant opportunities to seize the initiative and dominate an enemy. The solution set varies depending on, for example, whether the adversary employs traditional or irregular and asymmetric methods and whether the center of gravity is a military entity or a noncombatant population. Essentially, each operation and campaign requires a customized approach within the strategic information strategy to gain and maintain the initiative in the information environment.

3-75. Communication of the threat to use lethal force may be sufficient to influence and pressure an adversary or an equivocating actor to yield. If not, the actual measured use of lethal force is obviously a viable method to force an actor to give in to U.S. will. In either case, the JFC attacks the adversary's information networks and messages to limit the adversary's ability to counter the JFC's IO and influence activities. The JFC understands that his options are situation-dependent and a matter of his operational art.

3-76. How and what the media report can affect the political and public support necessary for the achievement of military objectives. Commanders must understand and work continuously with the media to gain and maintain an information environment advantage. Here, a civilian-military media operations center is the JFC's focal point. A comprehensive and coherent media plan is necessary to influence populations and senior decision makers while countering adversary propaganda efforts. In this regard, the JFC may be wise to implement a plan designed to expose affected populations to multinational force values, customs, beliefs, and intentions. This plan is critical for managing expectations, allaying fears and suspicions, explaining legitimacy, and generating support for the operation, thus minimizing public unrest and possible interference. To unhinge the adversary's information strategy, the JFC promotes a counter ideology as part of his influence and IO strategies that is feasible, practical, and believable by the affected civilian populations. Implementing such strategies may involve the early provision of emergency local communications that demonstrate coalition support to the reestablishment of essential services.

3-77. The JFC continuously assesses the effectiveness of ongoing IO and influence activities to ensure that these operations support the overall campaign plan. A trusted feedback mechanism must exist to measure the degree of success; otherwise, the JFC may subsequently make critical decisions that are exactly wrong. Here, the intelligence system, culturally adept "global scouts," U.S. interagency staff members, trusted foreign governments, and transnational corporations may provide valuable feedback and recommendations. Potentially, the adversary—traditional or irregular—or other TAs may be unresponsive to ongoing JFC IO and influence activities. Simultaneously, an intelligent and shrewd adversary may attempt to exploit the information environment to his advantage. Here, the adversary attempts to nullify or at least degrade U.S. efforts in the information environment. The commander must understand how his own, as well as his adversary's, IO and influence activities are actually proceeding—sensing and understanding ground truth in a timely manner are invaluable.

IRREGULAR WARFARE

3-78. The purpose of IW, like any other form of warfare, is to win—to achieve the strategic purpose of the war. Winning wars and campaigns involves the control of forces, populations, and territory. Conventional or "traditional" warfare is a form of warfare between states that employs direct military confrontation to defeat an adversary's armed forces, destroy an adversary's war-making capacity, or seize or retain territory to force a change in an adversary's government or policies. The focus of conventional military operations is normally an adversary's armed forces with the objective of influencing the adversary's government. It generally assumes that the indigenous populations within the operational area are nonbelligerents and will accept whatever political outcome the belligerent governments impose, arbitrate, or negotiate. A fundamental military objective in conventional military operations is to minimize civilian interference in those operations.

3-79. In contrast, IW focuses on the control or influence of populations, not on the control of an adversary's forces or territory. Ultimately, IW is a political struggle with violent and nonviolent components. The struggle is for control or influence over and the support of a relevant population. The foundation for IW is the centrality of the relevant populations to the nature of the conflict. The parties to an IW conflict, whether states or armed groups, seek to undermine their adversaries' legitimacy and credibility. They seek to physically and psychologically isolate their adversaries from the relevant populations and their external supporters. At the same time, they also seek to bolster their own legitimacy and credibility to exercise authority over that same population.

3-80. IW operations also employ subversion, coercion, attrition, and exhaustion to undermine and erode an adversary's power, influence, and will to exercise political authority over a relevant population. What makes IW "irregular" is the focus of its operations (a relevant population), its strategic purpose (to gain or maintain control or influence over), and the support of that relevant population through political, psychological, and economic methods. Creating and maintaining an enduring, functioning state requires the government to be legitimate in the eyes of the population. On the other extreme, although a brutal dictatorship may control a population, an irregular adversary can exploit the frustration and dissatisfaction

Chapter 3

that this type of government creates. Warfare that has the population as its focus of operations requires a different mind-set and different capabilities than warfare that focuses on defeating an adversary militarily.

INTERAGENCY RESPONSIBILITIES

3-81. The military cannot conduct IW operations indefinitely without eventually needing responsive support from the interagency. This interagency support can come from a variety of sources; for example, United States, coalition, or multinational. Interagency support provided not only must have the right skill sets and capabilities but also must meet capacity requirements of the conflict. Once interagency support becomes available, the military must be prepared to transition from a supported role to a supporting role. Starting with the initial design of an IW campaign, planners must consider the relationship between military forces conducting IW and the responsibilities and roles of the interagency in IW. Examples of these considerations include—

- What interagency support is required for successful IW operations?
- What interagency activities can enhance military IW operations?
- What military planning could be done better by an interagency partner?
- What are the implications related to the military performing security, diplomatic, information, economic, nation-building, rule of law, and governance functions in the absence of robust interagency involvement?
- How long should the military be prepared to accomplish these functions before the interagency arrives in force?
- What conditions need to be set to allow the military to transition these nontraditional military support roles to the interagency?

SPECIAL OPERATIONS FORCES

3-82. IW includes a wide variety of indirect operations and activities that occur in isolation or within traditional interstate combat operations. Half of the 14 component activities of IW are current core tasks for ARSOF. Therefore, ARSOF usually play a central and leading role in IW. Moreover, UW is one of the IW activities, and three others—(support for) insurgencies, PSYOP, and CMO (as conducted by ARSOF through CAO)—are the central components of the ARSOF UW mission.

3-83. Some IW activities, such as terrorism and transnational crime, violate international law. U.S. law and national policy prohibit U.S. military forces or OGAs from engaging in or supporting such activities. However, since adversaries employ terrorism and transnational criminal activities against the interests of the United States and its partners, these activities are included below as examples of the range of operations and activities that can be conducted as part of IW:

- Insurgency (support for which is the purpose of UW).
- COIN.
- UW (ARSOF core task).
- Terrorism.
- CT (ARSOF core task).
- FID (ARSOF core task).
- SSTR operations.
- SC.
- PSYOP (ARSOF core task and a central component of the ARSOF UW mission).
- IO (ARSOF support to IO).
- CMO (as conducted through the ARSOF core task of CAO, is a central component of the ARSOF UW mission).
- Intelligence and CI activities.
- Transnational criminal activities, including narco-trafficking, illicit arms dealing, and illegal financial transactions, that support or sustain IW.
- Law enforcement activities focused on countering irregular adversaries.

3-84. At the core of IW are insurgency and COIN. The purpose of insurgency is to overthrow and replace an established government or societal structure. Terrorism and CT are activities conducted as part of IW and are frequently subactivities of insurgency and COIN. However, terrorism may also stand alone when its purpose is to coerce or intimidate governments or societies without overthrowing them. FID refers to the participation of the agencies of one government in the programs of another government to free and protect its society from subversion, lawlessness, and insurgency. FID is thus the external support component of COIN.

3-85. UW most frequently refers to the military and paramilitary aspects of an insurgency designed to resist, overthrow, or gain political autonomy from an established government, or used to resist or expel a foreign occupying power. However, UW can also refer to military and paramilitary support to an irregular armed group seeking increased power and influence relative to its political rivals without overthrowing the central government and in the absence of a foreign occupying power. SSTR operations are an essential component of COIN campaigns, but SSTR operations, such as foreign disaster relief or foreign humanitarian assistance (FHA), can also occur outside the context of IW or armed conflict.

3-86. PSYOP, CMO, IO, and intelligence and law enforcement activities can occur in MCO, IW, or SSTR operations. They are listed above because their role in IW is often proportionally greater than is the case in MCO. They all directly affect the operational focus of IW—the relevant populations—in ways that combat operations do not.

3-87. In practice, most wars and campaigns are hybrids of conventional and IW operations. The balance or primary focus of operations gives a war, campaign, or major operation its predominant character.

CONVENTIONAL FORCES

3-88. Campaign planning for support of IW operations in a long war is different than planning for shorter conventional operations against an adversary during MCO. The adversary faced during IW operations usually operates without space and time limits. He may be a state or a nonstate actor and he often employs asymmetric tactics in a complex environment. The population is important, as is a thorough understanding of religious, cultural, and economic influences. In this regard, the JFC and his staff must be able to effectively accomplish responsive operational planning using techniques that effectively respond to the IW threat. Operational command techniques that will work best for the conduct of IW campaigns and operations during the long war are still evolving. Conventional forces are likely to play a supporting role in most IW efforts.

UNCONVENTIONAL WARFARE WITHIN IRREGULAR WARFARE

3-89. While conventional forces most often play the leading role in conventional warfare, and the interagency can be expected to take the leading role in IW (with or without a supporting UW effort), UW is most often led by SOF. A SOF-led UW campaign will usually require some interagency support and may occasionally involve support by conventional forces.

Special Operations Forces

3-90. The application of UW envisioned by joint IW planners differs from the more traditional uses of UW and requires further analysis. The characteristics of how ARSOF conduct UW are unchanged regardless of declared adversary; ARSOF operations (including UW) and ARSOF units are flexible. However, joint IW planners properly identify that UW conducted within IW during the 21st century WOT has nontraditional threat characteristics:

- First, nonstate actors do not have the same centers of gravity or the traditional infrastructure that have been the critical nodes for planning traditional UW operations.
- Second, unlike more typical UW campaigns against hostile states or occupying powers, future campaigns will be conducted against nonstate actors operating either within or behind the laws of nonbelligerent states with which the United States is not at war. Whereas this is normally the purview of OGAs, analysis of potential support that the joint force may be required to provide to

Chapter 3

support those agencies in that operational area must be done to accurately determine a true picture of the scope of global IW support requirements.
- Finally, UW campaigns also will be conducted against nonstate actors existing outside of the normal institutions of a state (such as ungoverned or undergoverned areas) or within a hostile state that harbors, either wittingly or unwittingly, these nonstate actors within its borders.

Interagency Responsibilities

3-91. Just as the global environment of the 21st century and the challenges of the WOT have caused military operations to become more innovative and flexible, so too must the interagency adopt new approaches to wielding U.S. national power in combating adversaries. Political authorities must find innovative ways to manipulate all instruments of U.S. national power against elusive opponents and their supporters. The interagency can apply economic and financial incentives and disincentives to interdict adversary financing, support partners and allies, and dissuade adversary supporters. U.S. law enforcement entities must cooperate with each other, international partners, and the DOD to maximize intelligence and legitimacy and to constrain adversary freedom of movement. The legitimacy of IW efforts must be a central and persistent theme of any holistic and coordinated information operation. Any UW effort within an IW campaign should integrate the interagency.

Conventional Forces

3-92. The JFC and his staff must be able to effectively accomplish responsive operational planning using techniques that effectively respond to the IW threat. In some cases, such as OEF/Afghanistan or OIF, the JFC will conduct MCO and IW with UW operations simultaneously. In other cases, such as OEF/Philippines or OEF/Colombia, IW (possibly with UW operations) will be the main effort, with conventional forces playing a much smaller and supporting role.

Chapter 4
Planning Considerations

UNCONVENTIONAL WARFARE PLANNING

4-1. UW planning begins at the theater and national levels, typically using classified channels. In most cases, ARSOF personnel expand the planning effort to provide subject-matter expertise and additional planning manpower. The plan incorporates interagency participation and the contributions of other DOD elements.

4-2. The actual planning of a UW effort—whether it is deliberate or crisis-action planning—utilizes the standard joint operation planning process or military decision-making process described in JP 5-0, *Joint Operation Planning*; FM 5.0, *Army Planning and Orders Production*; and FM 3-05. As any UW effort will include more than just the military instrument of a national power, an effects-based approach to planning may be especially useful.

4-3. The following paragraphs discuss the ARSOF imperatives and their applicability to UW. Although the imperatives may not equally apply to all specific UW situations, ARSOF commanders must consider each during mission planning and execution.

UNDERSTAND THE OPERATIONAL ENVIRONMENT

4-4. The most important ARSOF planning consideration is to understand the environment where the unit will operate. This consideration may be divided into two factors—internal and external.

Internal Factors

4-5. The civilian population is the critical internal factor. ARSOF planners must understand the demography, culture, taboos, beliefs, customs, history, goals, ethnic composition, and expectations of the civilian population. Most importantly, planners must recognize the dynamics of the many correlations among the various aspects of a society. Planners must be aware of who the agents of influence are, who they target, and how that influence may be achieved and exercised. They must also be aware of any incidental effect that the actions with any one factor might have upon another.

External Factors

4-6. Planners must understand the U.S. military command relationships (Service and joint, military and interagency) that may affect ARSOF elements and supported irregular forces. In addition, planners must understand the—

- Scope and limitations of each agency's influence and programs.
- Legal and political restrictions on ARSOF activities.
- Sources and assistance available to ARSOF to further assure mission accomplishment.
- Role of the U.S. media and the international press.
- Intent and goals of the USG.
- Intent and goals of NGOs, humanitarian relief organizations, and other key civilian agencies in the UWOA.
- Command relationships of international agencies and NGOs with representatives of the USG.
- Intent and goals of international agencies (such as the United Nations [UN] or North Atlantic Treaty Organization [NATO]).
- Applicable ROE, to include their intent and the specifically enumerated provisions.

Chapter 4

VISUALIZE UNFORESEEN CIRCUMSTANCES

4-7. Commanders and their planners must be able to visualize and act upon unforeseen circumstances. To accomplish this, they must have a clear understanding of the charter and goals of the total U.S. effort. Although it is impossible to predict every situation and write specific ROE or COAs to address them, an executing element that understands the commander's intent can respond with rapid flexibility to unforeseen and unplanned circumstances.

RECOGNIZE POLITICAL IMPLICATIONS

4-8. UW has a political end state. Every act, from advising military activities to an informal conversation, carries with it the potential for political impact. ARSOF planners should not anticipate a conventional environment that is dominated by traditional military concerns that are separate from a political context. Whether conducting UW as an independent ARSOF operation or in conjunction with conventional forces, ARSOF planners must consider both the short- and long-term political implications of proposed action.

FACILITATE INTERAGENCY ACTIVITIES

4-9. UW, both by definition and actual implementation, is an interagency effort in which military operations represent only one part—and not always the most important part—of the overall U.S. program. ARSOF must be aware of all agencies comprising the UW effort. ARSOF may also act as the liaison between the irregular organizations, U.S. agencies, and other DOD components to ensure the achievement of synergy. When participating in an interagency (and often joint) effort, ARSOF must strive for unity of effort and recognize the difficulty in achieving it. ARSOF must also anticipate ambiguous missions, conflicting interests and goals, and a disunity of effort.

ENGAGE THE THREAT DISCRIMINATELY

4-10. The ARSOF commander must know when, where, and how to employ assets based upon short- and long-term objectives. During UW efforts, this imperative contains three key components for the ARSOF planner: selection and distribution of resources; training, advice, and assistance; and tactical considerations.

Selection and Distribution of Resources

4-11. The first component of engaging threats discriminately involves the selection and distribution of resources for both personnel and materiel. Appropriateness, not mass, is the standard. ARSOF commanders must ensure that units selected for the mission are capable, qualified, trained, and necessary for the effort. The desired outcome is to minimize the U.S. presence while maximizing the U.S. impact in realizing objectives.

Training, Advice, and Assistance

4-12. The second component of engaging threats discriminately is selecting what training, advice, and assistance to provide. Because resources are normally limited in a UW environment, ARSOF must use them wisely for best effect. Based upon ARSOF understanding of the operational environment and its complex internal dynamics, ARSOF must carefully select which particular training to provide and advice to offer. Commanders must consider the impact that training and advice will have against the threat, as well as the political implications of the type of assistance provided to foreign nationals.

Tactical Considerations

4-13. The third component of engaging threats discriminately deals with tactical considerations. ARSOF must carefully target tactical operations in UW to ensure success and avoid alienating the civilian population.

Consider the Long-Term Effects

4-14. UW efforts are typically long-term affairs; however, such operations can also result in a dramatic regime change in a relatively short period. Planners must analyze conditions in the UWOA and the irregular forces involved, and they must understand higher HQ's intent and the overall operational scheme. This analysis enables planners to effectively determine the anticipated duration of operations and to adequately plan for linkup operations and the transition of irregular elements. ARSOF units must recognize that the operational scheme may be nonmilitary in nature.

4-15. Planners should consider each problem in its broader political, military, and psychological context. ARSOF units often must allow for legal and political constraints to avoid strategic failure while achieving tactical success. They must not jeopardize the success of long-term theater goals with the desire for immediate, short-term success. Policies, plans, and operations must be consistent with U.S. national and theater priorities and the objectives that they support.

Ensure Legitimacy and Credibility of Special Operations

4-16. Significant moral and legal considerations often exist in a UW effort. Legitimacy is the most crucial factor in developing and maintaining international and internal support. Without this support, the United States cannot sustain assistance to an irregular force. Without recognized legitimacy and credibility, military operations do not receive the support of the indigenous population, the U.S. population, or the international community.

Anticipate and Control Psychological Effects

4-17. All operations and activities in a UW environment have significant psychological effects. Combat operations and civic action programs are two examples of the type of operations or activities with obvious psychological effects. ARSOF may conduct some operations and activities specifically to produce a desired psychological effect. A negative psychological impact may overshadow or negate a tactical victory. Recognizing that perceptions may be more important than reality in the UW arena, ARSOF must strive to ensure that all audiences understand operations. Losing control of perceptions may result in a distortion of facts and may even diminish or destroy the gains of even superbly planned and executed missions.

Apply Capabilities Indirectly

4-18. The role of ARSOF in UW is to advise, train, and aid irregular forces. The area commander typically assumes primary authority and responsibility for the success or failure of this combined effort. Successful U.S.-advised operations reinforce and enhance the legitimacy and credibility of the area command and irregular forces. UW is fundamentally a political activity to persuade surrogates to act in concert with U.S. objectives, which is an indirect application of U.S. power.

Develop Multiple Options

4-19. ARSOF elements engaged in a UW operation must recognize and prepare for possible contingencies and follow-on missions. ARSOF personnel must plan to use their range of expertise, even if not specifically tasked to do so. A change of operational environment may dictate a change of mission or ROE. ARSOF maintains operational flexibility by visualizing and developing a broad range of options and concept plans, thereby enabling personnel to shift from one option to another before and during mission execution.

Ensure Long-Term Sustainment

4-20. ARSOF involved in a UW effort must avoid advising or training the irregular forces in techniques and procedures that extend beyond the forces' sustainment capabilities. For example, planners may modify U.S. TTP (including tactical communications, demolitions, weapons systems, and logistics) to negate the threat and allow for training programs and equipment that are durable, consistent, and sustainable by the irregular forces.

Chapter 4

PROVIDE SUFFICIENT INTELLIGENCE

4-21. Intelligence forms the basis for all UW activities and programs. UW operations depend upon detailed and comprehensive intelligence on all aspects of the operational environment and its internal dynamics. Commanders establish the priority of effort when they identify intelligence requirements. ARSOF in a UW environment often use classified techniques to acquire intelligence that identifies the enemy's locations and intentions for future operations. However, not all threats may come from an identifiable enemy. ARSOF should consider the nonmilitary threats posed by the civil sector, such as criminal activities, hazardous materials, civil unrest, and disease. The knowledge gained through intelligence collection activities enables ARSOF to effectively advise, train, and employ the irregular force. Effective operations security (OPSEC) requires an alert organization that can assess the hostile threat, warn the unit, and take timely action to penetrate and neutralize the hostile effort.

BALANCE SECURITY AND SYNCHRONIZATION

4-22. ARSOF elements performing a UW mission can often provide significant help to other SOF and conventional forces in accomplishing their missions. In order to address security concerns, SO often operate in a compartmentalized manner; however, compartmentalization must allow for key personnel to participate in the planning process. Although insufficient security may certainly compromise a mission, excessive security will usually cause the mission to fail (primarily because of inadequate face-to-face coordination). Leaders must constantly strive to achieve an effective balance of security and mission-planning synchronization.

MAINTAIN FORCE PROTECTION

4-23. FP during UW is similar to that during any other operation or deployment; FP is a mission enhancer—not a mission. The ARSOF commander's FP plan normally includes all actions—ranging from standard antiterrorism items to medical and sanitation issues to tactics used in the field—that ensure the forces' ability to achieve mission success. ARSOF leaders, however, usually face a unique challenge in maintaining FP because of the operational environment and the (typically) small size of the element conducting UW. USSOCOM Directive 525-4, *Antiterrorism (FOUO)*, and United States Army Special Operations Command (USASOC) Directive 525-13, *Plans and Operations—Force Protection (FOUO)*, provide an outline of FP requirements. The size of the ARSOF element, mission requirements, and guidance from higher HQ dictate the methods and techniques used to ensure adequate FP while achieving mission success. Some of these TTP are classified. FM 3-05.220, *(S/NF) Special Forces Advanced Special Operations (U)*, provides a detailed explanation of these TTP.

SEVEN PHASES OF UNCONVENTIONAL WARFARE

4-24. Each application of UW is unique, particularly when applied against nonstate actors. However, U.S.-sponsored UW efforts generally pass through the following seven distinct phases:

- Preparation.
- Initial contact.
- Infiltration.
- Organization.
- Buildup.
- Employment.
- Transition.

4-25. Some of the phases may occur simultaneously or—in certain situations—not at all. For example, a large and effective resistance movement may require only logistical support, thereby bypassing the organization phase. The phases may also occur out of sequence, with each receiving varying degrees of emphasis. One example of this is when members of an irregular force are exfiltrated to a partner nation (PN) to be trained and organized before infiltrating back into the UWOA, either with or without the ARSOF unit. In this case, the typical order of the phases would change.

PHASE I: PREPARATION

4-26. USG activities that deliberately alter or shape the potential operational environment enhance the GCC's war plans, OPLANs, and contingency plans. Every UW situation is unique, but all instruments of U.S. national power can potentially play a role in influencing and shaping the UWOA as part of a UW campaign. Much of the ARSOF role in such shaping activities is classified. (FM 3-05.201 contains further information on this subject.) Integrated USG UW "preparation of the environment" (PE) activities can create or affect local, regional, and global conditions that are beneficial to future UW operations. PE happens globally and continuously (outside of and before a UWOA is officially designated). Once the USG designates an area as a UWOA, PE may expand.

4-27. The preparation phase for UW is part of a three-step process that consists of intelligence preparation of the operational environment (IPOE), war planning, and shaping activities. First, IPOE attempts to graphically represent the current reality and predict probable enemy COAs in the UWOA. Second, war planning describes future military operations. Third, shaping activities work to modify the UWOA to make it more conducive to all types of future operations.

4-28. The preparation phase must begin with a complete IPOE. This phase includes a thorough analysis of the local populace and, if applicable, the irregular force's strengths, weaknesses, logistic concerns, levels of training and experience, political or military agendas, factional relationships, and external political ties. ARSOF units must consider the roles of DIMEFIL elements—the instruments of U.S. national power—when planning the employment of UW. Developing a systems perspective of the AO through a systems analysis can facilitate understanding of complex environments in which UW occurs. In addition to this data, analysts should complete a thorough area study of the AO. This area study should include (but is not limited to) issues regarding politics, religion, economics, weather, living standards, medicine, education, government services, and so on. Once planners initially assess the UWOA, participating ARSOF elements ensure that the joint force commander (JFC) is aware of ARSOF capabilities to shape the UWOA, and they recommend interagency participation in the effort as appropriate.

PHASE II: INITIAL CONTACT

4-29. Ideally, a pilot team should make initial contact with an established or potential irregular element. However, there may be occasions when the infiltrating ARSOF unit makes initial contact. A pilot team is typically a preplanned, ad hoc, interagency element composed of individuals possessing specialized skills. During contact, pilot team personnel begin the assessment of the potential to conduct UW in the UWOA and the compatibility of U.S. and local interests and objectives with the UWOA. This procedure not only allows for an accurate assessment of UW capability in the UWOA but also arranges for the reception and initial assistance of additional ARSOF elements, typically an SF unit. If deemed necessary, the theater special operations command (TSOC) may arrange to exfiltrate an asset from the UWOA to brief the ARSOF elements during planning. Once the theater command or TSOC determines the feasibility of developing the area, the President or SecDef may direct the infiltration of additional ARSOF elements. The pilot team may then remain with these follow-on units or may exfiltrate.

PHASE III: INFILTRATION

4-30. During this phase, the ARSOF units infiltrate the UWOA. Infiltration may be as overt as using a chartered civilian flight or as discreet as a clandestine insertion. Mission requirements—along with mission, enemy, terrain and weather, troops and support available–time available and civil considerations (METT-TC)—determine the most desirable method of infiltration. After infiltration, the ARSOF unit links up with the pilot team or irregular force. Because the infiltration phase is not complete until the initial entry report is sent to the unit's higher HQ, the ARSOF unit must submit this report as soon as possible upon infiltration—even if they fail to contact the irregular force. Immediately upon infiltration, the ARSOF unit continues the area assessment initiated by the pilot team to confirm or refute the previously received information. The ARSOF unit must continue to report all relevant operational information to higher HQ.

Chapter 4

PHASE IV: ORGANIZATION

4-31. During the organization phase, the ARSOF unit begins to develop the capability of the irregular force. Depending on the size and scope of the ARSOF effort, the size of this force can range from one individual to a resistance element of potentially any size. Planners traditionally conceive UW with an emphasis on guerrilla warfare. Such efforts may entail the organization of large guerrilla units to conduct combat operations, and SF are specially designed to organize such elements. However, resistance or insurgency is not solely a guerrilla warfare effort. The organization of resistance or insurgent elements may involve other ARSOF personnel with PSYOP, CA, or other skill sets. Although each irregular force or organization in UW is unique, the traditional ARSOF practice of conceiving UW as U.S. support to an insurgency or resistance movement provides a unifying general concept for irregular force organizational structure. Although support for classic insurgency or resistance against state opponents may be less common in the 21st century, ARSOF retain this capability and use this traditional unifying concept as a reference template against which ARSOF Soldiers are assessed, trained, and employed in UW.

The Components of an Insurgency

4-32. ARSOF units subdivide an insurgency into three components—guerrillas, underground, and the auxiliary. These elements are designed to be—
- Self-sufficient and self-contained.
- Capable of centralized command but decentralized execution.
- Redundant, in the event that the enemy destroys a portion of the element.

4-33. The insurgency support mechanisms need to remain hidden in order to survive. For this reason, they remain partially compartmentalized, dispersed, and fluid. The organization must constantly adapt to the changing security environment and avoid establishing predictable patterns. Elements are organized—not according to any template—based upon the needs of the region.

4-34. The overall insurgent organization or resistance group is not referred to as a military unit; rather, the element is titled an "area command." This label indicates the focus of organizational upon an area or region and—unlike traditional military units—is not based upon a specific number of personnel. For this reason, the overall indigenous commander is doctrinally referred to as the area commander. Subordinate commands within an area command are known as sector commands. These subordinate commands encompass all elements within their respective areas. This decentralization allows the sector commands to control all of the functions required to operate independently while maintaining the ability (rather than the necessity) to centralize or coordinate operations with the area command.

4-35. The area command is not a separate physical node like the three standard components of the insurgency (Figure 4-1, page 4-7). The area command is instead integrated throughout these components at all levels of the irregular organization. The area command is made up from the leadership cells of the underground, auxiliary, and guerrillas, as well as members of ARSOF (most typically SF) when present in the UWOA. Many of these leaders may function as deliberate or de facto leaders of a shadow government within the UWOA or as a government in exile if it exists. Key movement leaders who provide strategic political direction may also be identifiable in the shadow government or government in exile.

4-36. The three components of the insurgency do not necessarily represent three distinct groups or units; they more accurately describe three types of individuals within the organization. All three components provide different functions that support the overall goals of the organization. The size of the components will vary according to the unique conditions present in each UWOA. For example, in urban environments the ratio of underground and auxiliary personnel to guerrillas may be much higher than is true in rural environments.

The Guerrillas

4-37. Guerrillas represent the most commonly recognized portion of the insurgency. They are a group of irregular, predominantly indigenous personnel organized along military lines to conduct paramilitary operations in enemy-held, hostile, or denied territory. Guerrillas carry out most of the armed conflict that openly challenges the regional authority.

Planning Considerations

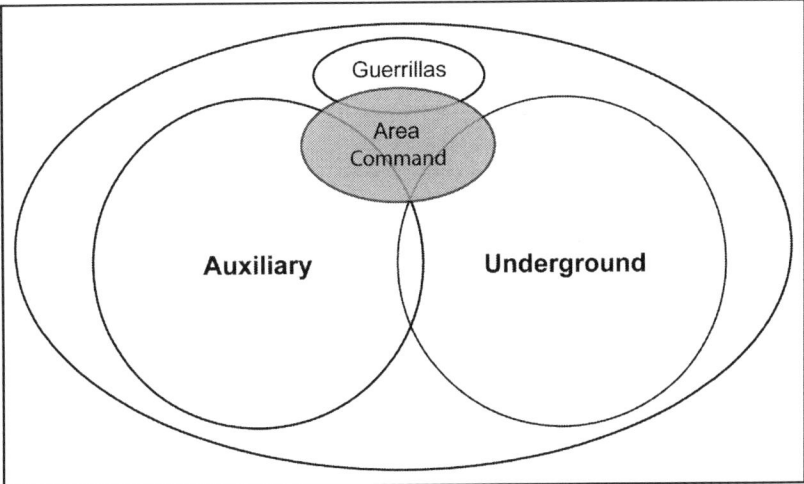

Figure 4-1. Classic components of an insurgency
in an unconventional warfare operational area

The Underground

4-38. The underground is a cellular organization within the irregular movement that is responsible for subversion, sabotage, intelligence collection, and other compartmentalized activities. Most underground operations are required to take place in and around population centers. As such, the underground must have the ability to conduct operations in areas that are usually inaccessible to the guerrillas, such as areas under government military control. Underground members often fill leadership positions, overseeing specific functions that auxiliary workers carry out. The underground and auxiliary—although technically separate units—are, in reality, loosely connected elements that provide coordinated capabilities for the irregular movement. The key distinction between them is that the underground is the element of the irregular organization that operates in areas denied to the guerrilla force. Specific functions of the underground and auxiliary include the following:

- Control of intelligence and CI networks.
- Control of clandestine movement networks.
- Direction and coordination of PSYOP and IO against the government, the population, and the international community.
- Direction and coordination of urban cells used to conduct acts of sabotage.
- Operation of the command structure or shadow government, if present.
- Control of cells used to neutralize informants and collaborators. The underground and auxiliary typically conduct this activity to meet the tactical necessity, as well as to serve as a deterrent to other members of the population that may be considering collaboration with the enemy. Such activities are normally coordinated with the CI and PSYOP cells.

4-39. Underground members are sometimes considered the "professional revolutionaries" of an irregular movement. They may be indigenous or professionals from another country. The underground members sometimes operate using a false identity and are less likely to be active members of the community, whereas auxiliary members most often tend to live "double lives" by providing part-time support and still acting as actual members of the community. Government suspicion often forces auxiliary workers to abandon their normal lives within the community. These individuals are typically well suited to become part of the guerrilla force or to serve as underground members in charge of other auxiliary workers who can still function within the community.

4-40. Undergrounds are more likely in urban environments where the proximity and concentration of adversary forces make overt irregular operations more dangerous. The underground performs its functions in urban environments by operating in small, compartmentalized cells and by utilizing "safe houses," apparently innocent houses or premises established by an organization for the purposes of conducting clandestine or covert activity in relative security. Members conduct activities with a minimum of contact between personnel and in such a manner as to not draw attention to unusual activity. The core underground cadre members survive by maintaining secrecy, compartmentalizing information, and having their auxiliary workers assume the majority of the risk.

The Auxiliary

4-41. The auxiliary is the primary support element of the irregular organization whose organization and operations are clandestine in nature and whose members do not openly indicate their sympathy or involvement with the irregular movement. This support enables the guerrilla force—and often the underground—to survive and function. This support can take the form of logistics, labor, or intelligence. Although many functions of the auxiliary and underground overlap, auxiliaries are more likely in rural environments where the relative distance and dispersion of adversary forces permit operations by guerrilla or other armed irregular forces. Members of the auxiliary are sometimes characterized as "part-time members" of the irregular organization, continuing to participate in the life of their community—to all appearances concerned only with their normal occupations—and at the same time engaging in irregular operations to varying degrees. Local cell or element leaders organize and coordinate all efforts, which the area or sector command directs. These various elements may serve as support cells within compartmentalized support networks. Specific functions of the auxiliary include—

- Managing logistics.
- Providing security and early warning (rural and urban).
- Conducting CI.
- Conducting intelligence gathering.
- Recruiting personnel.
- Conducting PSYOP (to include subversion).
- Running safe houses or portions of networks.

The Mass Base

4-42. Finally, although not traditionally considered a component of a U.S.-sponsored insurgent or resistance movement, the larger indigenous population from which the irregular forces are drawn must be an organizational consideration. UW is an elemental IW activity; as such, influence over a relevant population is critical. Communist insurgents of the 20th century referred to the general population (in a UWOA) as the "mass base." Insurgent leaders tasked elements of the underground with infiltrating civil institutions and manipulating popular grievances and overt indigenous political activities to support insurgent objectives. Many of these activities, such as strikes, labor unrest, food riots, and so on may be effective methods of combating and weakening the adversary government, without being directly associated with the insurgent effort. The participants in such mass-popular activities may be unaware that of their manipulation by and for the insurgent movement. Therefore, practitioners of UW cannot consider these participants a direct part of the insurgent organization. However, practitioners should take the insurgency's use of these participants in a U.S.-sponsored UW effort into account as an adjunct organizational factor. Therefore, UW leaders must continuously emphasize the maintenance of influence over this group.

Other Organizational Considerations

4-43. ARSOF personnel establish rapport with the local leadership by demonstrating an understanding of, a confidence in and a concern for the group and its cause. If necessary, ARSOF units explain their capabilities and limitations and begin the development of the organization. During subsequent operations, the ARSOF unit may have to prove its value in actual operations. Building rapport is a difficult and complicated process that is based largely on mutual trust, confidence, and understanding; it is rarely accomplished overnight.

4-44. During the organization phase, larger irregular organizations require more detailed work than smaller groups. Before a larger irregular organization can successfully engage in operations, the leadership must organize an infrastructure that can sustain itself and withstand the anticipated hostile reaction by opposing forces. During this phase, the leadership may identify a cadre that will serve as the organizational nucleus during the buildup phase. The ARSOF units assist the leadership in conducting the cadre training program to prepare for the eventual buildup of the organization.

4-45. When working with an irregular element, the local leader and ARSOF unit commander must agree upon C2 arrangements. ARSOF personnel normally advise and assist counterpart irregular leaders. In some situations, ARSOF members may actually direct some activities.

4-46. The specifics of the irregular organization depend upon local conditions and USG requirements. UW requires centralized direction and decentralized execution under conditions that place great demands on the organization and its leadership. No two irregular organizations will require the same degree or level of organization. The ARSOF unit commander should consider the following factors when advising any irregular leadership regarding organization:

- Effectiveness of the existing organization.
- Extent of cooperation between the organization and the local populace.
- Hostile activity and security measures.
- Political boundaries, natural terrain features, potential targets, population density, and other characteristics of the UWOA.
- Religious, ethnic, political, and ideological differences among elements of the population and competing organizations.
- Proposed type and scope of UW operations.
- Degree of U.S. influence with the irregular organization.

4-47. Although the classic and unifying conceptual template of ARSOF UW remains support to insurgency, resistance, or conventional military operations, not all instances of UW operations fit neatly into this concept. In the 21st century, UW conducted by, with, or through irregular forces, such as the Northern Alliance in Afghanistan or the united Kurdish forces in northern Iraq, still fits the classic concept well. Other UW operations, however, such as those conducted in support of FID, COIN, or other IW activities (as mentioned in Chapter 1), or those conducted in nonbelligerent states or ungoverned territories are more organizationally counterintuitive. Just because ARSOF have the capability to train, advise, and assist sizeable irregular forces and organizations in hostile or denied areas, does not mean that ARSOF UW must be conducted only in such areas and only with large elements. Especially in the context of combating global terrorism, a UWOA may be large and not entirely inside hostile or denied territory, and UW organizations can be very small or diffuse.

4-48. Circumstances may dictate that certain members of the irregular force be exfiltrated from the immediate UWOA to a designated safe haven or PN. Once there, they may organize, train, and coordinate with other elements before reinsertion. This trained cadre may more effectively form the core for the established infrastructure.

PHASE V: BUILDUP

4-49. The buildup phase involves the expanding of the irregular elements and their capabilities to meet mission objectives. ARSOF unit tasks include infiltration or procurement of equipment and supplies to support this expansion and subsequent operations. During the buildup phase, the ARSOF unit assists the cadre in expanding into an effective organization that is capable of conducting operations. Because successful missions lead to increases in recruitment, leaders should initially select confidence targets—those with a high probability of success and low risk to the irregular force. Irregular force missions and tactics normally dictate a simple, mobile, and flexible organization that is capable of rapid dispersion and reconsolidation in response to the tactical situation. Each unit is normally self-contained, with its own intelligence, communications, and logistics systems.

4-50. UW planners need to consider the appropriate level of capability and then balance the intended size of irregular forces against the requirement for a reduced signature. This focus should be on the capability required for the mission, not on the size of the force. As an organization grows, it creates a larger signature, thereby degrading the ability to conduct clandestine operations. If the irregular force begins noticeable operations too early, opposition forces may concentrate efforts on the irregular force and diminish their chances of mission success.

4-51. In some instances, such as with the Northern Alliance in Afghanistan in 2001, this phase may be relatively short. In such cases, the buildup phase mainly consists of coordinating with the preexisting resistance organization, developing combined standing operating procedures (SOPs) and fire control measures, and then moving directly to the sixth phase—employment.

PHASE VI: EMPLOYMENT

4-52. During the employment phase, indigenous or other irregular forces increasingly operate in a combat or hostile environment. These operations build in scope and size to support the objectives of the area command (if applicable) and the theater commander. The ARSOF unit ensures that effects of the activities continue to support the goals of the theater commander. These operations range from interdiction with guerrilla forces designed to drain the hostile power's morale and resources through combat to active intelligence collection with an indigenous informant network. Regardless of the type of operation, the overall purpose is to achieve strategic political-military objectives. Even when the UW operation involves combat actions, such combat employment does not necessarily require ARSOF units to be physically engaged in combat. It involves the conduct of operations in a combat or hostile environment. In addition, planners may use irregular forces to achieve objectives without direct U.S. participation.

4-53. When UW operations are in support of MCO of conventional forces, ARSOF must give careful attention to the capabilities of irregular forces and to coordination and deconfliction of such UW operations with theater objectives. UW forces can indirectly support conventional operations through interdictions and diversions throughout their UWOA or more directly support conventional movement by providing security of routes, drop zones (DZs), beach landing sites, and so on. Planners must carefully coordinate any subsequent linkup between irregular and conventional forces. Following successful linkup, UW forces may potentially continue to support conventional MCO through such activities as reconnaissance, rear area security, or support to CMO.

PHASE VII: TRANSITION

4-54. Transition is the final, most difficult, and most sensitive phase of UW operations. The planning for transition begins when the USG decides to sponsor an irregular organization and ends in the UWOA upon cessation of hostilities or operations. Transition does not necessarily mean demobilization or the commencement of FID operations. However, it usually requires some form of stability operations. Some SF units may focus continuing UW efforts on providing security with their irregular counterparts to begin conducting FID operations. Other ARSOF units may also continue to conduct UW activities in support of a larger FID mission. CA will usually play a leading role in transition by facilitating assistance from nonmilitary organizations. Preplanned PSYOP themes will explain HN (and, directly or indirectly, U.S.) goals and enhance compliance by population groups in the UWOA.

4-55. Civilian USG agencies, along with international organizations and agencies, such as the UN, normally assist in the transition of any organized military groups. ARSOF units may help these agencies conduct transition, using their knowledge of both the terrain and the forces within the UWOA. The manner in which transition occurs affects the postwar attitudes of the people and the government toward the United States. The greatest transition danger is the possibility that former resistance members may resort to subversion of the new government, factional disputes, or banditry. The new government brings arms and ammunition under its control to ensure public security and to return to a functional civil structure based on the rule of law. The government helps former resistance forces integrate into the newly reconstituted national army, police forces, or other security forces or assists their return to previous occupations. The new government must make every effort to reorient former resistance members to a peaceful society and to gain their trust.

UNCONVENTIONAL WARFARE TERMINATION OF OPERATIONS

4-56. The nature of the termination will shape the futures of the contesting nations or groups. It is essential to understand that termination of operations is an essential link between national security strategy, national defense strategy, national military strategy, and the national strategic end state. Furthermore, other military operations and USG activities will normally continue after the conclusion of any UW combat operations. An extended U.S. presence is required to conduct stability operations to enable legitimate civil authority and to attain the national strategic end state. Planners must address the consideration of stability operations at the initiation of UW planning and must continually update the UW plan during execution. Historically, stability operations have required extended U.S. presence and assistance. Planners should consider this contingency during the initial COA development and execution recommendation.

TERMINATION APPROACHES

4-57. There are three approaches for achieving national strategic objectives by military force. The first is to force an imposed settlement by the threat to occupy—or the actual occupation of—an enemy's territory and domination of his land, resources, and people. The threat or actual occupation of the territory can be supported by destruction of critical functions and assets (such as C2 or infrastructure), which makes the adversary unable to resist the imposition of U.S. will.

4-58. The second approach seeks a negotiated settlement through coordinated political, diplomatic, military, and economic actions that convince an adversary that yielding will be less painful than continuing to resist. Negotiating power in armed conflict springs from three sources: national resolve, military success, and military potential. History has demonstrated that U.S. national resolve is the most important source of negotiating power when impressing upon an adversary the need to negotiate a conclusion to conflict. Military success provides military, geographic, political, psychological, or economic advantage and sets the stage for negotiations. Military potential may compel the opposing nation or group to consider a negotiated conclusion. Negotiating an advantageous conclusion to operations requires time, power, and the demonstrated will to use both. In addition to imposed and negotiated termination, there may be an armistice or truce, which is a negotiated intermission in operations, not a peace. In effect, it is a device to buy time pending negotiation of a permanent settlement or resumption of operations.

4-59. The third approach for achieving national security objectives in relation to the irregular challenges posed by nonstate actors is an indirect approach that erodes an adversary's power, influence, and will; undermines the credibility and legitimacy of its political authority; and undermines the adversary's influence with, control over, and support by the indigenous population.

4-60. Even when pursuing an imposed termination, the USG requires some means of communication with the adversary. Declarations of intentions, requirements, and minor concessions may speed conflict termination, as the adversary considers the advantages of early termination versus extended resistance.

4-61. An adversary's will and freedom of action affects termination. Once the adversary's strategic objective shifts from maintaining or extending gains to reducing losses, the possibilities for negotiating an advantageous termination improve. The USG needs to coordinate the efforts of all the instruments of national power toward causing and exploiting such a shift. The USG must consider termination of operations from the outset of planning. Termination should be a coordinated interagency, IGO, NGO, and multinational effort that is refined as operations move toward advantageous termination.

THE NATIONAL STRATEGIC END STATE

4-62. The first political task regarding termination is determining an achievable national strategic end state based on clear national strategic objectives. For situations that require the employment of military capabilities (particularly for anticipated major operations), the President and SecDef will establish a set of national strategic objectives. Achieving these objectives is necessary to attain the national strategic end state—the broadly expressed DIME conditions that should exist after the campaign or operation. The supported CCDR must work closely with the civilian leadership to ensure a clearly defined national strategic end state is determined. Thinking of this "end state" as an integrated set of aims is useful because national strategic objectives usually are closely related rather than independent. The supported CCDR often has a role in achieving more than one national strategic objective. Some national strategic objectives will be the primary responsibility of the supported CCDR, while others will require a more balanced use of all instruments of national power, with the CCDR in support of other agencies. Therefore, considering all of the objectives necessary to reach the national strategic end state will help the supported CCDR formulate

Chapter 4

proposed termination criteria—the specified standards approved by the President or SecDef that must be met before a joint operation can be concluded. Commanders and their staffs must understand that many factors can affect national strategic objectives, possibly causing the national strategic end state to change even as military operations unfold.

MILITARY CONSIDERATIONS

4-63. In its strategic context, the measure of military success is in the attainment of military objectives supporting the national strategic end state and associated termination criteria. Termination criteria for a negotiated settlement will differ significantly from those of an imposed settlement. Planners should review military strategic advice to civilian leadership regarding termination criteria for military feasibility, adequacy, and acceptability, as well as estimates of the time, costs, and military forces required to reach the criteria. Implementing military commanders should request clarification of the national strategic end state and termination criteria from higher authority when necessary. An essential consideration is ensuring that the longer-term stabilization and enabling of civil authority needed to achieve national strategic objectives continues upon the conclusion of sustained operations. Stability operations that support SSTR efforts primarily support OGAs, IGOs, and NGOs to restore civil authority; rebuild the infrastructure; and reestablish commerce, education, and public utilities. Leaders should initiate planning for these operations when the joint operation planning process begins. The JFC and staff should consider conducting early collaborative planning with interagency and multinational members, harmonizing the civil and military effort and establishing the appropriate organization to conduct operations during the "stabilize" and "enable civil authority" phases of stability operations.

ARMY SPECIAL OPERATIONS FORCES

4-64. USASOC is the Army Service component command of USSOCOM. The term ARSOF refers to the United States Army Special Forces Command (Airborne) (USASFC[A]), which consists of five Active Army SF groups and two ARNG groups, the 75th Ranger Regiment, the 160th Special Operations Aviation Regiment (SOAR), the 4th Psychological Operations Group (Airborne) (4th POG[A]), the 95th Civil Affairs Brigade (Airborne) (95th CA BDE[A]), and the Sustainment Brigade (Special Operations) (Airborne) (SB[SO][A]).

4-65. SF, the 4th POG(A), and the 95th CA BDE(A) are uniquely trained within the DOD to work with irregular forces against a hostile government or nonstate actor. Therefore, SF, the 4th POG(A), and the 95th CA BDE(A) are the ARSOF that conduct UW, while the SOAR and SB(SO)(A) support UW operations. The 75th Ranger Regiment does not conduct UW but may support UW indirectly as part of the JFC's overall campaign plan. FM 3-05.20 and FM 3-05 contain more information on SF. FM 3-05.30, *Psychological Operations*, and JP 3-53, *Doctrine for Joint Psychological Operations*, contain more information on PSYOP. FM 3-05.40, *Civil Affairs Operations*, and JP 3-57, *Civil-Military Operations*, contain more information on CAO.

SPECIAL FORCES

4-66. SF is the ARSOF element traditionally and most closely associated with the execution of UW. SF Soldiers and units at all echelons of C2 contribute to the ARSOF UW effort.

Special Forces Operational Detachment A

4-67. Although it is capable of a wide range of ARSOF core and supporting missions, the U.S. Army designed the SFODA to organize, equip, train, advise or direct, and support irregular forces engaged in UW activities. The SFODA is the classic signature element in the conduct of ARSOF UW. While the SFODA typically conducts the majority of direct interface with irregular forces within the UWOA, it represents only the "tip of the iceberg." Only after significant and detailed planning, coordination, and approval at all levels of military and civilian decision making, is the SFODA actually employed in UW. After infiltration and throughout the conduct of UW, the SFODA benefits from the collective UW expertise from the SF command structure employed in support of the operation. This usually includes, at a minimum, an SF battalion operating as a special operations task force (SOTF), an SF group operating as a JSOTF, and a TSOC operating as a joint force special operations component command.

> ### ARSOF UW in Afghanistan
> The joint special operations task force (JSOTF) UW campaign to topple the Taliban regime in Afghanistan was led by ARSOF. Combat operations on the ground were primarily dominated by 5th Special Forces Group SFODAs supporting the anti-Taliban leaders in the north, northeast, and south. PSYOP teams prepared leaflets, broadcasts, and a boots-on-the-ground video presented nationwide, and CA teams coordinated humanitarian relief to the Afghan population. As the cities fell to anti-Taliban forces, tactical PSYOP teams and CA teams were attached to SFODAs. The 160th SOAR aircrews supported these UW operations by inserting teams, guarding insertions, and conducting surgical air raids that required multiple aerial and ground refuels in extremely bad weather. Precursor elements of the SB(SO)(A) supported all ARSOF elements in the conduct of their UW operations. The 75th Ranger Regiment supported the overall campaign by assaulting airstrips for use in follow-on operations. JSOTF-North at K2 Uzbekistan, which was commanded by an SF colonel, developed the UW campaign plan, daily directed offensives in a constantly evolving operation, orchestrated Army and Air Force SOF assets into combat multipliers, and successfully fought the war to overthrow the Taliban in less than two months.
>
> *Weapon of Choice: ARSOF in Afghanistan*

4-68. The time-tested composition of the SFODA remains as viable and relevant to UW today as it has been throughout the history of SF. The commander of an SFODA is a captain. His two primary assistants are an assistant detachment commander (an SF warrant officer) and an operations sergeant (a master sergeant). The SFODA has one intelligence sergeant and two noncommissioned officers (NCOs) specializing in each of the four primary SF functional areas (weapons, engineer, medical, and communications). This structure represents a highly capable SO unit with significant expertise and redundancy.

4-69. The SFODA has many functions pertinent to UW. It can—
- Plan and conduct SF operations separately or as part of a larger force.
- Conduct operations in remote areas and hostile environments for extended periods with a minimum of external direction and support.
- Infiltrate and exfiltrate specified operational areas by air, land, and sea. Each SFODA trains in an additional specialty, such as underwater operations, military free-fall parachuting, SF military mountaineering, surface maritime operations, and vehicle operations. These specializations provide varied means of infiltration into denied or sensitive areas.
- Develop, organize, equip, train, and advise or direct irregular forces up to battalion size. Although the primary focus is on developing the irregular force's combat capability, members are also capable of training selected individuals in unit staff functions.
- Train, advise, and assist other U.S. and multinational forces and agencies.
- Plan and conduct unilateral SF operations or other SO activities as directed.

4-70. The SFODA provides the majority of effort within the UWOA. During UW against a standing government, the SFODA will often train and advise existing irregular organizations, as well as conduct combat operations with such groups. Examples of such efforts include OEF, which resulted in the overthrow of the Taliban regime in Afghanistan in 2001–02, and the UW efforts with the Kurds in northern Iraq during OIF in 2003. In other cases, members of SFODAs can conduct shaping operations to prepare an area for future UW efforts against adversary states and nonstate actors, such as terrorist organizations. Many of these shaping TTP are classified. FM 3-05.201 addresses these TTP in detail.

Special Forces Company

4-71. When the UW operation expands beyond the capability of the employed force to synchronize the overall effort or involves more elements than can be effectively controlled, the SF company HQ (or Special Forces operational detachment B [SFODB]) can serve as a C2 or operational element. As an area C2 element, it commands and coordinates the effort of SFODAs and other assets in the area. The company can also function in a manner similar to that of an SFODA—training, advising, and conducting combat operations with a larger UW organization, especially when the experience and rank of the company-level personnel are required.

Special Forces Battalion

4-72. The SF battalion, also known as the SOTF, provides the employed forces with the functions of a standing staff, sustainment assets, and C2 capability to both support and direct UW operations. The battalion provides a significant capability to collect, analyze, and disseminate intelligence; coordinate and direct operations and operational support; coordinate and execute logistics; and provide signal support. The commander and his staff use their extensive experience and expanded situational awareness to execute battle command specific to UW the SFODA or company cannot match. In unique situations, the battalion staff may act as a separate operating element with the C2 of subordinate SFODAs and SFODBs retained with the battalion rear element.

Special Forces Group

4-73. The SF group constitutes the largest combat element of ARSOF. The SF group is an extremely flexible organization designed to have self-contained C2 and support elements for long-duration missions. SF groups and their subordinate elements are regionally oriented, experienced, language-qualified, and specifically organized and trained to command and control UW. The group staff officers represent an integrated mix of Army branches. These officers are predominately senior SF officers with theater expertise. They are uniquely suited to conduct and provide oversight for the operations process for UW. When tasked by the TSOC, the SF group can form the core for a JSOTF. The commander of the JSOTF is a JFC. He exercises the authority and responsibility assigned by the establishing TSOC. The SF group that is assigned the role of JSOTF synchronizes the actions of the joint, interagency, intergovernmental, and military elements involved in a UW operation in support of the JFC's campaign.

PSYCHOLOGICAL OPERATIONS

4-74. JP 1-02 defines PSYOP as "planned operations to convey selected information and indicators to foreign audiences to influence their emotions, motives, objective reasoning, and ultimately the behavior of foreign governments, organizations, groups, and individuals." The mission of PSYOP is to influence the behavior of foreign TAs to support U.S. national objectives.

4-75. In the full range of military operations, PSYOP take on an added significance. Modern conflict is often a protracted political-military struggle between political systems. It often encompasses all spheres of national activity—political, military, economic, social, and cultural. In protracted operations (including most UW campaigns), noncombat activities can be as decisive as combat operations are decisive in conventional warfare. Sometimes, failure to achieve PSYOP objectives can mean defeat, regardless of the outcome of combat operations.

4-76. In modern conflict, emphasis on the psychological or informational objective places PSYOP in a unique position. During stability operations, the USG can use PSYOP unilaterally or with economic, social, and political activities to limit or preclude the use of military force. In some cases, the military objective may be relevant only in terms of the psychological effect. History has shown that conflict is a battle of wills in which the intangible nature of morale and willpower can be defeated more in psychological terms than in physical terms.

4-77. PSYOP forces are a critical component of UW operations. The USG begins PSYOP as far in advance as possible. When commanders properly employ, coordinate, and integrate PSYOP units, these units can significantly enhance the combat power of resistance forces during UW operations directed against a state or nonstate entity and support the overall U.S. effort during each phase of UW employment. PSYOP units help prepare the resistance organization and the civilian population to accept U.S. sponsorship.

4-78. Leaders must identify, request, and integrate PSYOP requirements during the initial planning phase of the UW operation. PSYOP requirements will vary according to the specific UW situation; the security classification of the product or act, the status of the PSYOP as overt or covert, the types of media used, and so on. One of the most important roles of PSYOP forces during preparation for a UW campaign is aiding in the analysis of the UWOA from a PSYOP perspective and conducting detailed analysis of potential TAs, to include potential allies and enemy forces. The target audience analysis (TAA) may aid in the identification of potential leaders in the irregular force and identify lines of persuasion to bolster support for the movement among sympathizers and the uncommitted populace. The TAA also identifies lines of persuasion that create a desired behavior change among hostile forces and their sympathizers. TAAs identify key leaders, communicators, and groups, as well as their vulnerability and accessibility to future PSYOP products.

4-79. The following PSYOP events take place during UW campaign planning:
- PSYOP objectives are developed to support the commander's objectives.
- Product approval processes are designed and approved.
- PSYOP programs are approved by the President or SecDef.
- Supporting PSYOP products are developed.

4-80. PSYOP objectives are typically oriented around the following general topics:
- Creating popular support for the resistance movement.
- Developing support of the populace to allow the friendly forces freedom of movement.
- Promoting the recruitment of others into the resistance movement.
- Discrediting the existing government or hostile nonstate actor.
- Discrediting external supporters of adversary governments or nonstate actors.
- Maintaining support of the indigenous populace for the U.S. presence.
- Dividing and inducing defection among hostile forces.
- Winning the support of uncommitted population groups and key individuals.
- Preserving and strengthening friendly civilian support.
- Developing unity within the irregular force.
- Maintaining motivation within the irregular force.

4-81. Once the President or SecDef approves the operation's execution, forces execute the planned PSYOP UW operations. PSYOP forces immediately begin monitoring the program. In a UW environment, psychological actions may have a greater impact than at other times simply by harnessing and building upon preexisting feelings of frustration within the populace toward the existing government or nonstate actor. Potential psychological actions must undergo detailed, deliberate planning and assessment for effectiveness and risk to U.S. objectives. However, judicious use of PSYOP in UW can prove decisive.

CIVIL AFFAIRS

4-82. CAO are conducted by forces organized, trained, and equipped to provide specialized support to commanders conducting CMO. CMO are operations that involve the interaction of military forces with the civilian populace. In all operations, commanders must consider not only military forces but also the nonmilitary environment in which they operate. ARSOF conduct UW within and rely on foreign populations, which greatly magnifies the importance of ARSOF CAO in UW. CAO typically assist SF in the establishment and running of infrastructure, which provides important support services to the irregular organization. This human environment includes a civil populace that may be supportive, neutral, or antagonistic to the presence of military forces, both friendly and opposing. A supportive populace (and auxiliaries) can provide material resources that facilitate friendly operations, as well as a positive moral climate that confers advantages on the military and diplomatic activities ARSOF pursue in achieving foreign policy objectives through UW. A hostile populace threatens the immediate operations of deployed ARSOF. It also often undermines public support at home for U.S. policy objectives.

4-83. ARSOF CA conduct CAO to establish, maintain, influence, or exploit relations between military forces and civil authorities (government and nongovernment) and the civilian populace in a friendly, neutral, or hostile AO to facilitate military operations and to consolidate operational objectives. Judicious use of CA as part of an integrated UW campaign can thus have psychological impact, which can improve the effectiveness of other UW activities. For example, the psychological perception by selected targeted audiences in the UWOA that U.S.-sponsored irregular organizations are responsive to their needs can be decisive in winning popular support. CA forces may assist in the performance of shadow government activities and functions by military forces that would normally be the responsibility of a legitimate local government. They may also occur, if directed, in the absence of other military operations.

4-84. Although CAO may support all phases of UW, in situations where irregular organizations transition into a new government, the most important role of CAO is usually facilitating the swift transition of power from the resistance forces to a legitimate government after the cessation of hostilities.

4-85. CAO are an integral part of ARSOF UW campaign planning from the beginning; they are not an afterthought. CA forces may also assist SF units in planning and executing UW operations by—

- Advising ARSOF units in cultural, political, and economic considerations within the UWOA.
- Assessing the impact of proposed missions upon the local populace.
- Advising ARSOF units on the development of irregular organizations and the expansion of the UWOA by gaining and maintaining popular support.
- Assisting irregular forces to develop infrastructure and conduct populace and resources shaping (PRS) operations.
- Assisting ARSOF units in integrating with OGAs (DOS and USAID, for example).
- Advising and assisting in planning, coordinating, and establishing of dislocated civilian camps.
- Advising ARSOF units in planning measures to gain support of the civilian populace.
- Planning mobilization of popular support to UW operations.
- Analyzing the impact of irregular organizations on indigenous populations and institutions (IPI) and centers of gravity through CA input to the IPB.
- Providing the supported commander with critical elements of civil information to support effects-based approaches and to improve situational awareness and understanding within the battlefield.
- Advising ARSOF units and irregular forces on the development of civil administration within the UWOA as a legitimate government begins to operate.
- Gaining access for development into otherwise restricted or denied areas.

SUPPORTING ELEMENTS AND ACTIVITIES

4-86. Other ARSOF elements can perform vital roles during the conduct of UW. The situation and unique requirements during each UW operation dictate the participants and their required contributions. However, almost all SO (including UW) require communications, logistics, health, and (usually) aviation support. ARSOF have organic units that routinely support these requirements. (Chapter 8 includes an expanded discussion of ARSOF supporting elements and activities for UW.)

INTERAGENCY ACTIVITIES

4-87. OGA, both within and outside of the USG, may perform vital roles during the conduct of UW. The situation and unique requirements during each UW operation dictate the participants and their required contributions.

4-88. During the conduct of UW, ARSOF units often work in conjunction with (or in close proximity to) personnel from other USG agencies. This relationship is normally nondoctrinal; the two elements generally provide mutual support without any formal tactical control (TACON) or operational control (OPCON) relationship. Mission planning at the TSOC or JSOTF typically establishes the details of this cooperation.

4-89. Interagency coordination occurs between agencies of the USG to accomplish an objective. Military operations must be coordinated with the activities of OGAs, IGOs, NGOs, regional organizations, foreign forces, and various HN/PN agencies.

4-90. The JFC may choose to draw on the capabilities of other organizations, provide the joint force capabilities to other organizations, or merely deconflict the joint force activities with those of other agencies. Interagency coordination forges the vital link between the military and other U.S. instruments of national power. Successful interagency, IGO, and NGO coordination enables the USG to build international support, conserve resources, and conduct coherent operations that efficiently achieve shared goals.

4-91. When deliberate or crisis-action planning is required, the degree to which military and civilian components can be integrated and harmonized bears directly on the efficiency and success of the collective UW effort. Because a solution to a problem seldom resides within the capability of a single agency, campaign plans and OPLANs must be crafted to recognize the core competencies of many agencies. The military activities and resources should be coordinated with their counterparts in other agencies to achieve the desired end state.

4-92. Relationships between the armed forces and OGAs, IGOs, and NGOs do not equate to C2 of a military operation. Military operations depend upon a command structure that is different from that of civilian organizations. These differences may present significant challenges to coordination efforts. The different—and sometimes conflicting—goals, policies, procedures, and decision-making techniques of the various USG agencies make unity of effort a challenge.

4-93. In addition to extensive USG agency coordination, commanders must also fully integrate operations into local efforts when appropriate. Such integration requires close coordination with local government agencies and bureaus; local military, paramilitary, or police forces; and multinational partners. A structure, such as a mixed military working group, made up of senior officials of the military and other agencies may assist such an effort. If appropriate, these working groups may also incorporate belligerent parties.

The Nature of Interagency Bureaucracy

4-94. Each agency has core values and legal requirements that it may not compromise. In any interaction, all participants must be constantly aware that each agency will continuously cultivate and create external sources of support and maneuver to protect its core values. Individual agency perspectives and agendas complicate policy development. Protection of institutional prerogatives may often drive the various USG agencies' positions. These positions may not always coincide with a common approach to UW.

4-95. As uncertainty increases during a crisis, so does the likelihood of compromise. Compromise may bring the sacrifice of power, security, or prestige. Uncertainty allows for the coexistence of varying views about the likely outcomes of a given action; these differences in viewpoint often lead to conflicting interests. An organization will seek to reduce uncertainty and lessen the threat to its own stability. Information can reduce uncertainty and increase an organization's power. Thus, information equals power in interagency coordination, because it provides those who possess it a decided advantage in the decision-making process. Maintaining unity of effort in complex, sometimes contentious, and often long-term UW interagency campaign planning is a coordination challenge for ARSOF execution of UW.

United States Government Interagency Planning for Unconventional Warfare

4-96. USG support to a UW campaign will include the complete range of DIMEFIL functions to strengthen the legitimacy and effectiveness of irregular forces and those actors who support them directly or indirectly. The appropriate balance among the functions will vary depending on the situation. The leadership should thoroughly assess the environment before planning and continuously evaluate the environment throughout the course of the UW effort to determine the balance of functions. Agencies' and departments' day-to-day reporting, assessments, evaluations, and other activities support the decision-making process leading to the conduct of a joint, interagency analysis.

4-97. A "whole-of-government" approach to a UW engagement begins with a strategic-level joint and interagency analysis of the manifesting or escalating conflict through USG support for irregular forces engaged in insurgency, resistance, or otherwise supporting U.S. conventional operations. ARSOF need to participate in this strategic-level joint analysis by all other relevant members of the interagency to ensure an integrated response. Dynamics that drive and mitigate conflict are complex and interrelated. Diplomatic, development, or military action alone cannot address these dynamics. Independent analyses by individual agencies are likely to identify only the symptoms of conflict that the individual agency can address outside the whole-of-government context and without concern for the prioritization and sequencing of efforts by other agencies.

4-98. Policy-level/strategic planning can use conflict assessments that utilize tools and modeling, such as the Interagency Methodology for Analyzing Instability and Conflict and Political Instability Modeling, to develop situation-specific information. This first step provides a mechanism for prioritizing a whole-of-government engagement. Conflict assessments using tools such as USAID's Conflict Assessment Framework, Tactical Conflict Assessment Framework, and other agency and department assessment and modeling tools can then inform programmatic, operational- and tactical-level design and planning.

4-99. When the USG decides to use ARSOF to conduct UW, ARSOF facilitate interagency understanding of ARSOF capabilities and solicit support from the interagency to achieve the mission. Any interagency conflict assessment must analyze the entire conflict. General steps in the performance of an interagency conflict assessment include—

- Articulation of the purpose, audience, and deliverers of the assessment. For example, an interagency group may conduct the assessment to establish a basis for interagency strategic planning in support of U.S.-sponsored and ARSOF-executed UW.
- Collection of data (through field-based activities or secondary sources resident in or accessible to each USG department and agency). This data will regard the UWOA and other actors capable of influencing the UWOA and will include background factors and underlying risks, stakeholders' interests and needs, opinion leaders' motivations and means, and potential action triggers in an integrated UW campaign plan. If a preexisting irregular force is present, data collection should specify links between the above categories and the supported irregular force.
- Description of the dynamics present within the context of the observed background factors—stakeholders' needs, opinion leaders' motivations and means, political causes, demographic trends, and so on that contribute to the existence and potential utility of the irregular force to U.S.-sponsored UW.
- Identification of the adversary's local and regional capacity and resilience to combat the U.S.-sponsored irregular force. For example, the legitimacy of the adversary state and the effectiveness of its political, social, economic, and security institutions; attitudes of the civil society by subgroup; and international and regional factors.

4-100. Once interagency planners make these assessments, they can identify the ability—or lack thereof—of U.S. instruments of national power to shape conditions in the UWOA. While ARSOF execute UW as part of the U.S. military instrument, it is important that the interagency assist the JFC in identifying which other U.S. instruments of power he can use as weapons in a holistic UW campaign plan.

Chapter 5
Special Forces Operations

INTRODUCTION

5-1. Although each application of UW is unique and a wide range of efforts can make up UW as a whole—including nonlethal or even nonmilitary activities, the classic centerpiece is the introduction of military advisors into hostile and denied territory to organize, train, equip, and advise armed irregulars. The U.S. military specifically designed SF groups, battalions, companies, and SFODAs to conduct these operations. However, a large body of traditional and updated TTP already exists for SF conduct of UW. Consistent with the conceptual purpose of this unclassified manual, this chapter is deliberately brief. FM 3-05.201 contains more information on SF conduct of UW.

> **NOTE:** Some of the following phases may occur simultaneously or—in certain situations—not at all.

PHASE I: PREPARATION

5-2. The preparation phase for UW is part of a three-step process that consists of IPOE, war planning, and shaping activities. First, IPOE attempts to graphically represent the current reality and predict probable enemy COAs in the UWOA. Second, war planning describes future military operations. Third, shaping activities work to modify the UWOA to make it more conducive to all types of future operations.

5-3. The preparation phase must begin with a complete IPOE. When directed to prepare for UW, the SF group staff, supported by higher ARSOF echelons and the resources of the IC, conducts a thorough analysis of the local populace and, if applicable, the irregular force's strengths, weaknesses, logistic concerns, levels of training and experience, political or military agendas, factional relationships, and external political ties. Depending on projected authorities, scope of employment, support requirements, and designated timelines for execution, the SF group may assign focused preparation responsibilities to its subordinate battalions and companies. SF units at all echelons must consider the roles of DIMEFIL elements when planning the employment of UW. Development of a systems perspective of the AO, through a system of systems analysis, can facilitate understanding of complex UW environments. In addition to this data, the SFODAs complete a thorough area study of the projected UWOA. This area study should include (but is not limited to) issues regarding politics, religion, economics, weather, living standards, medicine, education, and government services.

5-4. As war planning proceeds to preparation for execution of UW, SF groups and battalions take all operational steps for predeployment, deployment, employment, operational sustainment, survivability, C2, and redeployment of themselves, their subordinate staff elements, SF companies, and SFODAs.

5-5. Once preparers complete the initial UWOA assessment, participating SF elements apprise the JFC of SF capabilities to shape the UWOA and recommend interagency participation in the effort as appropriate. Much of the SF role in such shaping activities is classified. (FM 3-05.201 includes further information.) Integrated USG UW preparation activities can create or affect local, regional, and global conditions that are beneficial to future UW operations.

PHASE II: INITIAL CONTACT

5-6. Ideally, a pilot team makes initial contact with an established or potential irregular element. The intent of pilot teams is to make initial liaison with irregular elements within the UWOA to coordinate and establish plans and procedures for subsequent friendly infiltration and the conduct of future UW activities. Since most UWOAs are in denied and hostile territory, the presence and activities of the pilot team usually

Chapter 5

represent a hazardous and often politically sensitive mission. A standard SFODA can function as a pilot team when directed. However, since each UW mission will have unique characteristics specific to the situation, SF groups commonly establish temporary ad hoc pilot teams from group personnel. This arrangement is often desirable because it allows the SF group to use the broad range of skills, experience, and language and theater expertise resident in the regionally oriented SF group. SF Soldiers typically lead such teams. However, the team may include PSYOP, CA, intelligence, or other Soldiers with relevant expertise. Teams can also expect to have participants from OGAs. Moreover, given the interagency nature of ARSOF UW, it is equally common for SF Soldiers to augment pilot teams led by and primarily constituted of OGA personnel.

5-7. The pilot team assesses the potential of the UWOA and gains rapport with the irregular force. The time needed to accomplish these tasks depends on the operational environment, the maturity and numbers of irregular forces, and the tactical situation. Once approved by the TSOC for further development, the pilot team plans and coordinates for the reception, staging, onward movement, and integration of all follow-on detachments infiltrating the UWOA.

PHASE III: INFILTRATION

5-8. The success of an SFODA's infiltration of a designated UWOA depends primarily on detailed planning and preparation. Procedures and techniques for employing any one of the four general methods of infiltration will be dependent on certain factors being present that will enhance the success of the mission. Depending upon the situation, the SFODA may need to use a number of these methods concurrently.

AIR INFILTRATION

5-9. Air delivery by parachute is one of the principle means available for the infiltration of SFODAs. In most instances, standard troop carrier aircraft are well equipped and satisfy airdrop requirements. Some situations may dictate a requirement for aircraft capable of parachute delivery of personnel and equipment from high altitudes using free-fall parachute techniques or static-line stabilization chute descent to low altitude. In addition, assault-type aircraft, as well as amphibious and utility types, used by several Services may be available in varying numbers. Some situations may require that these aircraft be able to use relatively short, unprepared airstrips and to conduct air-landing operations during infiltration. Under certain circumstances, longer-range tactical aircraft may be used.

WATER INFILTRATION

5-10. ARSOF may frequently employ water infiltration by either undersea craft or surface craft in UWOAs with exposed coastlines, coastal river junctions, and harbors. Water infiltration using seaplane landings on large bodies of water, rivers, or coastal waters may be possible. In such cases, planning by the commander considers the ship-to-shore movement and subsequent land-movement characteristics of a normal water-infiltration operation.

LAND INFILTRATION

5-11. ARSOF may conduct land infiltration similar to that of a long-range tactical patrol into enemy territory. Generally, units utilize guides during land infiltration. If guides are not available, the unit must have detailed intelligence of the route—particularly if borders are to be crossed. The unit selects routes that take maximum advantage of cover and concealment and avoid enemy outposts, patrols, and installations. Units may also conduct infiltration through an intricate irregular support mechanism. Planners will provide the unit with the location and means of contacting selected individuals who will furnish assistance. These individuals may be used as local guides and provide information, food, transportation, and shelter. Commanders may restrict equipment and supplies to individual arms and communication equipment. However, the situation may allow the use of additional transportation options from indigenous pack animals and low-visibility vehicles to various tactical vehicles in the SF inventory. Their utilization will allow the infiltration of additional operational equipment with the detachment.

STAY-BEHIND INFILTRATION

5-12. Stay-behind infiltration is the easiest method to accomplish and one of the most valuable when the adversary has the potential of occupying the area with armed forces. Stay-behind infiltration involves the positioning of SFODAs within the proposed UWOA before the initiation of enemy advances through or occupation of the general area. This technique enables the SF elements to organize a nucleus of resistance forces or to pre-position themselves for employment in a unilateral role. Planners should consider stay-behind operations when the attitude of the civil populace indicates it will support stay-behind operations.

PHASE IV: ORGANIZATION

5-13. Although each irregular force or organization in UW is unique, the traditional SF practice of conceiving UW as U.S. support to an insurgency or resistance movement provides a unifying general concept for irregular force organizational structure. SF traditionally conceive UW with an emphasis on the conduct of guerrilla warfare. Such efforts may entail the organization of large guerrilla units to conduct combat operations, and the U.S. military designed SF units to organize such elements. However, resistance or insurgency is not solely a guerrilla warfare effort. The organization of resistance or insurgent elements may involve other ARSOF personnel with PSYOP, CA, or other skill sets. FM 3-05.201 contains detailed information on SF UW.

5-14. The SFODA's initial requirement is the establishment of a good working relationship between SF and the irregular elements in the UWOA. A sound working and command relationship helps to develop a high degree of cooperation and some degree of control over the irregular force. SF abilities to build trust and to carefully persuade the irregulars to act in concert with U.S. objectives strengthen relative control over the irregular force. SF Soldiers further build trust and relative control by providing organizational leadership skills and assets that help the irregular organization to meet its objectives in a manner that supports the overall plan.

SPECIAL FORCES ORGANIZATION OF THE AREA COMPLEX

5-15. Developing the command structure and the physical organization of the UWOA are priority tasks of SF units. In some situations, the organization of the UWOA may be well established. In others, organization and C2 may be incomplete or absent. In all cases, some improvement in physical area organization will probably be necessary. SF units are adept at being flexible and creative in developing such irregular organizations. A number of requirements dictate the organization of the UWOA, but the organization depends more on local conditions and U.S. political-military objectives than on any fixed set of rules. Major factors to be considered include—

- The effectiveness of the area command.
- The degree of irregular organization overall effectiveness.
- The degree of guerrilla or armed irregular force organization and effectiveness.
- The extent of cooperation between the irregular organization and the larger civilian populace.
- The activities and effectiveness of the enemy or adversary.
- The degree of development desired and achievable in the context of U.S. objectives.
- The limitations and opportunities present in the human and physical environments.

5-16. All of these factors in combination will influence in varying degrees the shape, size, and ultimate organization of the UWOA. Regardless of the size of the area or extent of U.S. efforts, SF units conducting UW assist the area command in organizing its operational elements to achieve dispersion, control, and flexibility.

5-17. SF organization of the area complex consists of both the physical and human components of the irregular organization. Physical components of the area complex typically include guerrilla operational base safe areas, security and intelligence systems, communication systems, mission support sites (MSSs), supply installations, training areas, DZs, landing zones, reception sites, and evasion and escape mechanisms, as required. The area complex is not primarily a continuous pattern of tangible installations, but a series of intangible lines of communication connected to all other irregular elements in a clandestine manner.

Chapter 5

5-18. SF units also have capabilities to support the organization of the area complex's human components, especially in conjunction with ARSOF PSYOP and CA units. ARSOF may direct considerable activity during this period toward creating a political and psychological climate that encourages irregular participants (or potential participants) to accept personal risks in support of the irregular force's cause. With discriminating SF support of proper area command leadership, the real or potential elements of the irregular organization will grow larger, become better trained and equipped, and will cooperate more effectively in achieving the organization's objectives. Organizational growth occurs when natural leaders—such as former military personnel, clergy, local office holders, educators, and neighborhood representatives—emerge, providing the area command with a potential cadre resource on which to plan the growth and expansion of the irregular organization, armed forces, and operational environment.

5-19. Regardless of how developed or underdeveloped the irregular organization is initially, primary consideration should be given to ensuring that certain basic functions and operations exist. If they do, ARSOF should improve upon and organize them as needed. If they do not exist, ARSOF should put them into effect immediately. These functions are not established separately, but may be established concurrently and developed as required. The organization established to perform them directly affects the following functions:

- Performing unit or element organization.
- Providing security and intelligence systems.
- Operating communications systems.
- Operating administrative systems.
- Operating logistical support systems.
- Providing training programs.
- Planning and executing combat operations (violent activities).
- Planning and executing political activities.
- Expanding the irregular organization and its constituent elements.

SPECIAL FORCES ORGANIZATION AND THE COMPONENTS OF AN INSURGENCY

5-20. As discussed in Chapter 4, the classic template for conducting UW as support for resistance movements or insurgencies—whether for their own objectives or in support of conventional military operations—remains a pertinent and unifying concept for how SF can begin to organize any irregular organization.

The Area Command

5-21. Working through the irregular force's area command and subordinate sector commands (as detailed in Chapter 4), SF Soldiers organize and develop the various components of an insurgency (or similar irregular organization). SF Soldiers' special attributes, training, experience, and preparation make them particularly well suited for the persuasive human interaction required for this task. The larger the UWOA and the more expansive the UW effort, the more likely that higher echelons of SF will participate in developing and advising the area command, potentially involving SF companies, battalions, or groups.

The Guerrillas

5-22. Guerrillas, or similar armed forces, represent the most commonly recognized portion of an insurgency and the portion most commonly associated with the warrior skills of participating SF Soldiers. They are a group of irregular, predominantly indigenous personnel that organize along military lines to conduct paramilitary operations in enemy-held, hostile, or denied territory. Guerrillas carry out most of the armed conflict that openly challenges the regional authority.

5-23. In classic guerrilla scenarios, armed units could be formed into squad, platoon, company, battalion, and even regiment size. Once again, the more expansive the UW effort, the more likely that more SFODAs will be employed and that SF companies, battalions, or even groups will participate in advising and leading larger irregular armed forces. SF Soldiers have traditionally been able to impart military training to these elements appropriate to the situation. The unique structure and capabilities of the SFODA provide a training cadre capable of unit development from basic individual training up to and including advanced and combined tactical training at the battalion level. Since SF members are professional combat Soldiers comprised predominantly of senior enlisted leaders, they can not only train irregular units but also advise and lead them in tactical operations.

The Underground

5-24. There is more SF participation in developing and advising underground elements than is widely understood or acknowledged. Most such participation is classified and inappropriate for inclusion in this manual.

The Auxiliary

5-25. There is more SF participation in developing and advising auxiliary elements than is widely understood or acknowledged. Most such participation is classified and inappropriate for inclusion in this manual.

The Mass Base

5-26. SF participation in the creation of effects within the mass base to shape the operation environment is done indirectly and primarily through the underground and auxiliary. Most such participation is classified and inappropriate for inclusion in this manual.

5-27. Organization of the larger indigenous population from which the irregular forces are drawn—the mass base—must likewise be conducted primarily by the irregular organization itself under indirect guidance of SF. The primary value of the mass base to UW operations is less a matter of formal organization than of marshalling population groups to act in specific ways that support the overall UW campaign. The mass base, or general population and society at large, is recognized as an operational rather than a structural effort for ARSOF in UW. Elements of the mass base are divided into three distinct groups in relation to the cause or movement—pro, anti/con, and those who are uncommitted, undecided, or ambivalent. ARSOF, the underground, and the auxiliary then conduct irregular activities to influence or leverage these groups. These groups may be witting or unwitting of the UW nature of the operations or activities in which they are utilized.

PHASE V: BUILDUP

5-28. The buildup of forces is counterproductive if the irregular force does not obtain enough resources to support and sustain the buildup. These resources include weapons, munitions, medical supplies and services, internal and external support for rations, as well as an expanded intelligence apparatus to ensure force protection and targeting abilities. The buildup phase involves SF units assisting the irregular organization to expand the capabilities of its component elements as required for mission objectives. SF unit tasks include infiltration or procurement of equipment and supplies to support this expansion and subsequent operations. During the buildup phase, the SF unit assists the irregular force cadre in expanding into an effective organization that is capable of conducting operations. Because successful missions lead to increases in recruitment, leaders should initially select confidence targets—those with a high probability of success and low risk to the irregular force. Irregular force missions and tactics normally dictate a simple, mobile, and flexible organization that is capable of rapid dispersion and reconsolidation in response to the tactical situation. Each unit is normally self-contained, with its own intelligence, communications, and logistics systems.

5-29. UW planners need to consider the appropriate level of capability and balance the intended size of irregular forces against the requirement for a reduced signature. This focus should be on the capability required for the mission, not on the size of the force. As an organization grows, it creates a larger signature, thereby degrading the ability to conduct clandestine operations. If the irregular force begins noticeable operations too early, opposition forces may concentrate efforts on the irregular force and diminish their chances of mission success.

5-30. The traditional SF standard for building an insurgent organization is that one SFODA can raise, train, equip, and advise one guerrilla battalion. The redundancy provided by an SFODA's manning structure can allow small elements to conduct split-team or smaller subelement SF placement with widely dispersed irregular forces. However, when the UWOA is large or larger irregular forces are present (or needed) and appropriate or when complex operations, such as modern urban underground operations are involved, SF manpower requirements may increase. SF companies, battalions, and groups are all deployable and capable of providing training, advice, and assistance to large irregular organizations as needed. The U. S. military may infiltrate additional SF units during the buildup phase and may attempt to further "force multiply" by selecting and training additional indigenous cadres capable of supporting a growing irregular force. Sustainable buildup of an irregular organization may take a long time to achieve when conducted under effective pressure from adversary forces or may be relatively short if the irregular organization and its forces are already well developed.

PHASE VI: EMPLOYMENT

5-31. During the employment phase, SF units support indigenous or other irregular forces conducting operations against the common adversaries of irregular organizations and the United States. Such operations may involve any or all components of the irregular organization. The classic conception of UW employment is SF Soldiers advising and assisting guerrilla forces to raid, ambush, sabotage, and otherwise interdict the adversary in ways designed to drain that hostile power's morale and resources through military activities up to and including combat.

5-32. Not all SF employment of irregular elements necessarily involves direct combat, however. SF Soldiers are adept at leveraging active intelligence collection with an indigenous informant network. The intelligence thus collected can support SF's conduct of the UW effort itself, and it can sometimes be of strategic value to a holistic USG effort against state or nonstate adversaries. SF units, usually in conjunction with irregular elements, can also establish safe areas, sites, and procedures as part of an unconventional, assisted-recovery mechanism useful to the evasion and recovery of SOF or conventional personnel, such as downed pilots. SF can also employ classified TTP by, with, and through the clandestine and covert capabilities of the underground and auxiliary to conduct holistic warfare against a wide range of hostile state and nonstate actors.

5-33. Regardless of the type of operation employed, the overall purpose is to achieve strategic political-military objectives. The U.S. Army specially selects, trains, equips, and prepares SF Soldiers to persuade irregular forces to act in concert with such U.S. strategic political-military objectives. Even when the UW operation involves combat actions, such combat employment does not necessarily require the SF units to be physically engaged in combat. It involves the conduct of operations in a combat or hostile environment. In addition, the USG may use irregular forces achieve objectives without direct U.S. participation.

5-34. When forces conduct UW operations in support of MCO of conventional forces, SF groups, battalions, companies, and SFODAs ensure that UW forces properly integrate into the conventional JFC's campaign plan. Since SF units understand both the capabilities of U.S. forces and irregular forces within the specific conditions of a unique UWOA, these SF echelons are uniquely positioned to coordinate and deconflict irregular force operations with theater objectives. SF units conduct UW operations by, with, or through irregular forces to indirectly support conventional operations through interdictions and diversions of adversaries throughout the UWOA. SF units train, advise, and assist irregular forces to directly support conventional movement by providing security of routes, DZs, beach landing sites, and similar missions. When appropriate, SF companies can establish a special operations C2 element attached to conventional division or corps HQ to further assist in coordinating and deconflicting UW operations with those of conventional forces.

5-35. Link-up operations are particularly hazardous, even among elements of the same army. Linkup between foreign irregular forces and conventional forces are even more difficult. SF units' familiarity with the UWOA and expertise with irregular forces attempting linkup greatly mitigate the risks of any such subsequent linkup between irregular and conventional forces. Following successful linkup, UW forces may potentially continue to support conventional MCO through such activities as reconnaissance, rear area security, or support to CMO. SF units' continuing support of such irregular force conduct of these activities provides enhanced cross-cultural communication, intelligence-gathering opportunities, effective coordination of assets, and reduces the risk of fratricide.

PHASE VII: TRANSITION

5-36. Transition does not necessarily mean the end of hostilities or SF operations in the UWOA. Some SF units may focus continuing UW efforts by providing security with their irregular counterparts to support stabilization efforts and the beginning of FID operations. SF units will also likely assist civilian USG agencies, international organizations and agencies, and any new government with integrating the remaining irregular forces into the newly reconstituted national army, police forces, or other security forces or assisting with their return to previous occupations. Depending on the quality of rapport built with irregular forces in earlier phases, this relationship uniquely situates SF units to assist OGA and HN civil authorities in transitioning these irregular forces.

This page intentionally left blank.

Chapter 6
Psychological Operations

INTRODUCTION

6-1. PSYOP support of UW should begin as early as possible. Typically, the psychological battle will begin before commitment of U.S. military PSYOP forces. Before commitment of U.S. PSYOP support to the UW operation, elements of the guerrilla forces or the underground may have begun an embryonic PSYOP program or at least begun to examine the psychological effects they wish to generate. In some cases, such irregular forces may have a more developed PSYOP program than they have combat capacity. In other cases, the situation facing ARSOF PSYOP personnel may be one of guerrilla forces or the underground having no PSYOP program whatsoever. In addition, they may have already made mistakes in attempts at conducting PSYOP or they may even have conducted military or other operations that have alienated potential supporters. All ARSOF personnel must begin UW operations mindful of the ARSOF imperative that anticipating and controlling the psychological effects are going to be either a key enabler or a critical shortfall.

> **NOTE:** Some of the following phases may occur simultaneously or—in certain situations—not at all.

PHASE I: PREPARATION

6-2. It is important that planners identify, request, and integrate requirements for PSYOP forces during the planning phase of an operation. PSYOP forces and the supported unit must embrace the concept that no matter what type of operation PSYOP support, the PSYOP process does not change. What changes from operation to operation is the security classification of support, the overtness or covertness of the PSYOP, and potentially, and the types of media used. PSYOP forces' most important role during the preparation phase of the operation is aiding in the analysis of the environment from a psychological perspective and conducting detailed analysis of potential TAs, to include potential allies as well as enemy forces. TAA can aid in the identification of potential leaders of the insurgent force and identify PSYOP arguments that will help bolster support for the insurgency among sympathizers and the uncommitted populace. TAA also identifies PSYOP arguments that will aid in creating a desired behavior change among enemy forces and enemy sympathizers. TAA will identify the vulnerabilities of key leaders and communicators and groups and their accessibility to future PSYOP series.

6-3. It is during this phase that Psychological Operations objectives (POs) are developed to support the commander's objectives, product approval processes are designed and approved, supporting PSYOP documents are developed (estimates, annexes, and tabs), and PSYOP programs are approved by the President or SecDef. POs may be oriented around the following general topics:

- Creating popular support for the insurgency movement.
- Developing support of the populace to allow the insurgents to avoid detection and move freely.
- Promoting the recruitment of others into the resistance movement.
- Discrediting the existing government and its programs.
- Introducing or delineating a shadow government or government in exile.
- Maintaining support of the indigenous populace for U.S. support and presence.
- Dividing and inducing defection among enemy forces.
- Winning the support of the uncommitted.
- Preserving and strengthening friendly civilian support.

Chapter 6

- Developing unity among the UW force.
- Maintaining motivation in the UW force.

6-4. Once PSYOP are authorized, PSYOP forces will execute and monitor planned programs and series supporting PE. In a UW environment, Psychological Operations actions (PSYACTs) can have a greater impact than at other times simply by harnessing and building upon preexisting feelings of overall frustration of the populace with regard to the existing government. PSYACTs incorporated into a PSYOP series must undergo detailed, deliberate planning to war game potential outcomes of the activity. For example, a planned demonstration can easily turn into a riot when emotions run high. Whether this occurs deliberately or spontaneously can affect the potential outcome. War gaming allows forces to plan for different outcomes, protect the appropriate parties, and achieve the desired objective from the goal.

FORMAL LAUNCH

6-5. Typically, the movement sponsored by the United States in a UW effort is already in existence. However, the movement may be highly generalized and perhaps conducted by several different organizations. If the effort to oppose an adversary during UW has some sort of benchmark date or event, such as the anniversary of a general strike or an excess crackdown by the government, this date may be of psychological value in formally launching an insurgency.

6-6. In addition, if two or more groups join in common cause and form a united front, the date of this event may be exploitable. Formation of a united front may include the formal declaration of a government in exile or some form of early shadow government organization. These organizations may or may not have been in existence before a formal launch and therefore may have preexisting conditions or may be a blank slate. The former may present considerable challenges to overcoming perceptions of inertia or even incompetence. The latter may present challenges of establishing the a government in exile that is viable and credible. PSYOP forces may disseminate series in support of this government in exile as early as Phase I or may merely conduct research for later use. Typically, forces would do this in Phase IV as the UW effort becomes increasingly viable militarily.

6-7. The declaration of a movement or escalation of resistance (particularly if the government has not yet faced armed resistance) by a key communicator can provide psychological incentive to the UW effort. Planners must base any formal launch of a new movement or a reinvented movement on careful analysis of the key TAs. A formal launch of the UW effort with PSYOP series can be counterproductive if they will generate unrealistic expectations in TAs. Therefore, ARSOF forces may need to caution irregular forces against such a COA.

Example of Forming a United Front

The example of the Patriotic Union of Kurdistan (PUK) and the Kurdistan Democratic Party (KDP) in Iraq points out both the benefits and pitfalls of a formal launch of a new "united front" of formerly combative groups. Before OIF, the PUK and KDP had a long history of conflict. In May 1994, supporters of the PUK clashed with supporters of the KDP leaving 300 people dead. Relations among the groups further soured in March 1995 when the KDP backed out of an attack on Saddam's front lines led by the Iraqi National Congress. Over the next year, the PUK and KDP fought several more times, eventually devolving into a state of civil war. At the start of OIF, both the KDP and PUK worked alongside ARSOF units in northern Iraq against what had always been a common enemy in Saddam Hussein. PSYOP and public diplomacy supported the unification of the former rivals.

In 2004, the KDP and PUK, along with several smaller Kurdish and one ethnic Turkoman party, united to form a joint political coalition, the Democratic Patriotic Alliance of Kurdistan (DPAK). This alliance clearly constituted a formal launch of the latter stages of a UW effort. Initially, this formal launch bore political fruit with the winning of 75 seats in the Iraqi Council of Representatives. In addition, the KDP and

> PUK were able to secure the selection of Jalal Talabani (the PUK leader) as President of Iraq, while Massoud Barzani (the KDP leader) became President of Iraqi Kurdistan. In May 2006, the KDP formed an alliance with the PUK to run Irbil as a unified party.
>
> However, relations have since soured again, with northern Iraq effectively divided into KDP-controlled territory and PUK-controlled territory (centered on Suleymaniya). In 2006, a reconstituted DPAK that still contained both the PUK and KDP tempered this deterioration.
>
> This particular case highlights the inherent challenge in UW of persuading human actors to operate in concert with U.S. objectives. The breakdown of a union that was earlier launched and championed through PSYOP and public diplomacy was useful despite later complications; the union contributed to the overall success of the UW effort in northern Iraq. Moreover, as ARSOF efforts transition more to FID operations, this breakdown can be couched in PSYOP and public diplomacy terms as the normal functioning of a democratic process in which parties do not always agree.

CONSTANT COURSE

6-8. In UW, the forces battling an adversary frequently emerge from debates and issues that have degenerated into armed conflict. In most cases, certain themes and symbols will already resonate with current and potential sympathizers, supporters, or recruits. If so, rather than any change in themes or any new formal launch of a resistance movement, the most effective approach may be to "stay on message" and continue to use the themes and symbols that have resonated before the escalation to a UW effort. In addition, a careful PSYOP assessment may reveal gaps in knowledge of the vulnerabilities or accessibility of TAs that require further study of the type of PSYOP programs or inadvertent PSYOP that any antigovernment organizations or key communicators have put out. If the impact of prior PSYOP is immeasurable during initial TAA, the initial COA for U.S. or insurgent PSYOP efforts may be silence during the preparation phase or may be limited to face-to-face PSYOP during initial contact.

MILITARY DECEPTION SCENARIOS

6-9. In preparing for UW operations, the potential to conduct military deception (MILDEC) operations exists. For example, commanders may consider PSYOP support to MILDEC operations that obscure and misdirect government efforts to discern the intent and strength of preparations and then to accurately assess later phases (such as initial contact and infiltration of irregular and U.S. forces). Commanders may use MILDEC operations in later phases as well. The same caveats and cautions that apply to use of MILDEC in other operations apply in UW as well. ARSOF personnel may have to dissuade insurgent forces from improperly using PSYOP series intent on perpetrating deception. Of particular concern is irregular forces inflating their capability, thereby damaging their credibility their credibility with supporters and with government forces. Another concern is any proposed deception of supporters or sympathizers. Educating insurgent PSYOP cadre on the pitfalls of unrealistic and potentially damaging support to MILDEC should take place as the phases of UW evolve. In addition, careful planning of U.S. PSYOP support to MILDEC operations is necessary.

PHASE II: INITIAL CONTACT

6-10. During the initial contact phase of an operation, PSYOP support continues by executing PSYOP series (products and PSYACTs) that support the preparation of the environment. This phase includes preparing the civilian population to receive allied forces and actively assist in the UW mission to follow. PSYOP forces should identify requirements for information that the pilot team can gather during its assessments. This information can range from media availability and transmission technical data to validating psychological assessments of key individuals and communicators to identifying personnel and equipment requirements for establishing irregular PSYOP forces. The burden is on PSYOP forces to stay

Chapter 6

abreast of all activities during each phase of the operation and meet suspenses for turning in information requirements.

EXPATRIATES

6-11. During the initial contact phase and possibly extending back into the preparation phase, expatriates from the nations in the UWOA may be a valuable asset. ARSOF must assess expatriates on an individual basis because both their motivations and willingness to accept risk may vary greatly. Expatriates who support a resistance can vary from mildly supportive and only ideologically sympathetic to willing to support initial contact and even take part in armed resistance. Some expatriates may be former members of TAs. These expatriates can help with both TAA and product pretesting. Some key communicators can come from the expatriate community. Symbolic or active leaders of UW operations may emerge from the expatriate community.

INDIGENOUS POPULATION

6-12. Rank-and-file members of the population at remote locations, such as villages away from major population centers, typically make initial contact in UW. When evaluating these individuals for potential training as dedicated PSYOP cadre, or even for basic awareness of the psychological impact of UW operations, ARSOF may encounter a wide range of education and comprehension levels. In addition, during initial contact, necessity may dictate expending PSYOP resources on TAs that eventually will not be the focus of effort. Initial contact in terms of PSYOP may be with TAs that in the early stages of resistance may be critical to UW operations, such as rural villagers. As a UW operation matures, the focus of resources may shift to other TAs.

KEY COMMUNICATORS

6-13. Reaching and recruiting key communicators may be the focus of initial contact efforts. Like many UW efforts, the initial key communicators may be much more localized in the early stages of a UW operation. The village elder who is a key communicator in initial contact may eventually become simply a member of a wider TA, such as village elders in a given province or other subnational area. Conversely, major political dissidents or other key communicators typically have relevancy over the entire course of a UW operation.

PHASE III: INFILTRATION

6-14. PSYOP forces may infiltrate with SF units complete or in part or may follow on at a later time. Many factors contribute to this, including the tactical situation; connectivity to development, production and dissemination assets; and location of the irregular force. PSYOP series may transition to another phase or program at this time depending on the plan that was developed during Phase I. When this occurs, PSYOP series products designed to elicit support and assistance for the UW organization and U.S. forces must be carefully monitored. Evaluation criteria not only provide feedback for the evaluation of a series of products and/or PSYOP program but may provide indicators that aid in FP measures and OPSEC as well.

RANK-AND-FILE PSYCHOLOGICAL OPERATIONS AWARENESS

6-15. Developing awareness of the psychological impact of their activities begins when ARSOF infiltrate to begin assisting irregular forces. ARSOF should make the rank-and-file armed members, undergrounds, and auxiliaries aware of PSYOP program objectives and any themes they should stress or avoid. In addition, ARSOF personnel need to begin communicating ideas and actual planned face-to-face PSYOP products that conform to the U.S. PSYOP program. If the infiltration plan includes transporting preapproved PSYOP products for dissemination by irregular forces in an overt manner that will bring them in contact with the intended TA, they should have a sufficient understanding of the product to (at a minimum) not detract from or contradict the product. Ideally, such dissemination plans should include supporting face-to-face PSYOP products as part of the series. Joint, interagency, intergovernmental, and multinational (JIIM) partners should also be sufficiently cognizant of the PSYOP program to do no harm to the overall effort. Adequate intelligence sharing must take place so that ARSOF Soldiers are aware of any PSYOP executed by JIIM partners.

DEDICATED CADRE

6-16. During the infiltration phase, the segregation of dedicated PSYOP cadre in any arm of the irregular movement may be impractical or represent an unacceptable drain on limited personnel in the early phases of UW. In addition, resources in terms of media as well as a lack of comprehensive knowledge of PSYOP may prohibit irregulars' production of PSYOP series. However, during infiltration ARSOF can identify personnel within the resistance who can become the nucleus of a dedicated PSYOP force. As they develop, the underground and auxiliaries may be the first source of a practical, dedicated PSYOP arm.

PHASE IV: ORGANIZATION

6-17. During organization, the focus of the ARSOF units is developing the capability of the required irregular force. PSYOP forces may need to develop an organic PSYOP capability within the force. PSYOP forces should carefully consider the organization, role, and techniques the irregular force will use. The insurgent force can use PSYOP forces as a neutral sounding board. In this capacity, PSYOP Soldiers can form relationships with irregulars through informal contact during and after training. From these conversations, PSYOP Soldiers can help SF personnel gauge the morale of the insurgents and help ensure that the training provided the irregulars is accomplished using the most culturally relevant techniques available (Figure 6-1). For example, some irregulars may initially feel homesick or miss family members and support groups from their local village while in training. This situation was a common occurrence while training Afghan personnel. Since Afghan culture and society are tribally based, members of different tribes who trained together often felt more of a sense of belonging to their own tribe or village instead of to the group they were training with. If ARSOF leave this situation unchecked, high potential exists for desertion. PSYOP Soldiers help identify factors that might cause desertion from training and create communication techniques and messages that reinforce the greater good of sacrificing for the irregular effort. Themes of patriotism and nationalism are of particular use when properly employed in this situation.

Figure 6-1. Psychological Operations and Special Forces Soldiers building rapport with an unconventional warfare force in Afghanistan

> **Supporting Unity and Cohesion in a Developing UW Organization**
>
> In Afghanistan, PSYOP Soldiers developed a recruiting and retention video that highlighted the pain one new Afghan soldier felt when separated from his family and village support system while training with other Afghans he regarded as strangers. The video acknowledged the new recruit's pain but then also portrayed him speaking the words he was writing to his father—telling of his hardships in training and the loneliness he felt at times, while also feeling the tremendous pride of serving in the new Afghan National Army with his compatriots.
>
> The video portrayed the soldier writing in the letter to his father that, despite his discomfort with his surroundings and training, he remained committed to the security and safety of his family and tribe that the new army would afford them in the coming months. He ended the letter stating that for the sake of the honor of his family and their long-term safety he remained committed to the new army and his training.

6-18. It is natural to want to design the force similar to a U.S. organization. However, this may not be the most appropriate organization to accomplish the immediate tasks facing the irregular force. Likewise, techniques taught must follow the legal guidelines that PSYOP forces follow to avoid potential legal fallout for the USG when training an irregular force. In addition, PSYOP forces can educate irregular force personnel on psychological aspects of the enemy force if they are not familiar with them. During Phase IV, PSYOP forces should support the development of the UW organization by capitalizing on U.S. rapport-building activities and multiplying their effects. PSYOP forces should take advantage of the situation during the organization phase to capture images (whether still or video) and interview the UW force to capture information for use in future products.

GRASSROOTS PSYCHOLOGICAL OPERATIONS

6-19. Whether members of the irregular force are dedicated specifically to a PSYOP mission or are doing so as an additional duty, lack of equipment or support in this stage may limit them to basic PSYOP media. They may conduct what might best be termed grassroots PSYOP that utilize whatever media they can use independently (Figure 6-2, page 6-7). The inability to receive either indirect or direct support from U.S. or other allied forces may necessitate grassroots PSYOP. If executed using sound methodology and sufficient research, multiple low-cost, high-reward avenues exist to reach select TAs. When tactically feasible, face-to-face PSYOP and other in-person products, such as guerrilla theater, can resonate with TAs. Members of the underground or auxiliaries can pursue limited-risk covert media. This media can range from graffiti to simple alternative newsletters and handbills. Recent experience has shown that some electronic media have passed into the realm of grassroots PSYOP. Various electronic formats, such as digital video discs (DVDs), can provide a degree of security for irregular personnel located in adversary-controlled areas. These formats have had significant impact. U.S. personnel supporting and advising such activities must keep an open mind on what might be an unusual form of media. However, U.S. personnel must also analyze proposed products that may be counterproductive, offensive, or may violate any of the basic tenets and historical truths of successful PSYOP.

DEDICATED FORCES

6-20. In the organization phase, it may prove useful and practical to encourage the formation of dedicated PSYOP cadre and to train them for later stages. The goal is to build a skeletal structure that forces can flesh out during buildup as recruitment grows. However, it can unacceptably drain limited combat power by overbuilding an indigenous PSYOP force. In addition, such a force in the underground or auxiliaries could expose it to a level of adversary scrutiny that is unacceptable. Therefore, in Phase IV (just as in Phase III) it may be necessary to limit the number of specifically tasked PSYOP personnel and continue to build databases of potential personnel with skill sets that might warrant a transfer of function at a later date.

Psychological Operations

Figure 6-2. Afghan village elder addressing population
on Psychological Operations loudspeaker

RELATIONSHIP WITH OTHER ORGANIZATIONS

6-21. It is likely that relationships between ad hoc or dedicated PSYOP cadre will become an important consideration at this time. Organizations paralleling U.S. military and OGA structures will increasingly form in Phase IV, even if it is in embryonic form. Organizations among the guerrillas paralleling U.S. organizations that typically would work or deconflict with DOD PSYOP personnel should begin to work with dedicated military PSYOP cadre. At this stage, military PSYOP cadre and government-in-exile or shadow-government civilian PSYOP cadre may be the same organization. It is foreseeable that this task organization may continue even through the success of the insurgency. PSYOP cadre should attempt to establish bonds, boundaries, and communications with their relevant counterparts within the armed wing of the insurgency, as well as any relevant civilian government-in-exile organizations.

TRANSREGIONAL AND GLOBAL REACH

6-22. With the advent of multiple avenues of instant or near-real-time transfers of information and data, UW operator can assume that the UW operation has primarily a local or U.S. domestic audience. U.S. PSYOP forces are always aware of the potential for any action to quickly have an impact across the region in which the UW operation is being conducted and, quite often, across the globe. Irregular forces may or may not appreciate this fact and may require training and advising from ARSOF personnel. Conversely, they may from early stages plan for and use asymmetric capacity to reach wider audiences. Although such efforts may only begin in later phases, only a small group of trained individuals is necessary for an irregular force to utilize the Internet and global media outlets to promote PSYOP programs. When the underground or auxiliary must emphasize concealing their involvement, the global media can sometimes provide additional anonymity because of the difficulty of tracing through multiple servers and routers. Overt supporters of either a U.S.-sponsored irregular organization or its opponents can use the reach of global media quite openly and overtly. ARSOF Soldiers must be aware of all such efforts by the U.S.-sponsored irregular, allied, competitor, or antagonistic groups. In most instances, control of these types of asymmetric approaches used by an adversary may be impossible. The focus then must switch to counterpropaganda efforts.

PHASE V: BUILDUP

6-23. During Phases IV and V, PSYOP forces may focus on recruiting and building external support for the force. Depending on the duration of Phase V, ARSOF may focus on, increase the number of, or maintain the previous level of capitulation programs during this phase. PSYOP forces may or may not begin more emphasis on preparing the populace for introduction of the UW force. In general, ARSOF must ensure that no party compromises the covert nature of the operation. All operators at every level must safeguard the force. Although it is generally easy for forces supporting or conducting tactical-level support to keep this foremost in their minds, forces conducting strategic- or operational-level PSYOP may forget or be unaware of the potential compromising effects of products on the force—whether they come unintentionally while disseminating talking points or unconsciously in a newspaper article.

RECRUITMENT

6-24. Typically during buildup, some active PSYOP programs to produce series on recruitment can be pursued. Although recruitment of members of the underground or auxiliary remains either covert or clandestine, motivating TAs susceptible to joining these organizations can be pursued by highlighting the successes of the organization. In addition, recruitment series for the armed force may have an effect on recruitment in other areas as well. No PSYOP support to recruitment should make unrealistic or unfulfillable promises. ARSOF Soldiers must caution irregular fighters and organizations from making these promises as well. Although potential recruits may be accustomed to strong-arm tactics or coercion from the government, ARSOF Soldiers should discourage this avenue in face-to-face encounters and avoid it as a PSYOP approach.

DOMESTIC SUPPORT

6-25. Although not necessarily the primary effort in PSYOP programs, some PSYOP series typically target supporters of the irregular effort. The behavior desired in such groups is often to increase efforts, donations, and recruitment. In the buildup phase, this may entail attempting to move supporters from nominal agreement to active participation. During buildup, some supporters have unrealistically short time spans for success. Common themes during UW are often perseverance and the tactical necessity of a "long war." Themes may need to discourage abortive, disorganized efforts as well. In many UW efforts, uniting several dissimilar organizations into a single front is useful. During buildup, ARSOF advisors may frequently need to advise against COAs that might alienate supporters.

6-26. In any insurgency, even those initiated with support from a large portion of the population, sizeable portions of the population will be uncommitted to either the adversary or the forces backed in the UW effort. In a UW operation where the government maintains large blocks of tacit support through coercion, violence, or bribery, that support may disappear when the government loses power. In addition to supporting desired behaviors in committed supporters, U.S.-directed PSYOP support and irregular force PSYOP programs will typically target the uncommitted in UW efforts. An irony of UW is that every person remaining uncommitted rather than supporting the adversary is a partial success. Typically, this behavior is not actively encouraged. However, ARSOF should not ignore the reality that antiadversary PSYOP may produce this effect. In the long-term PSYOP plan, this may be a necessary stage before garnering active support for the UW effort. However, the focus of programs should usually be on moving fence-sitters into passive or active support of the irregular organization's efforts.

6-27. Supporters of an adversary government can vary greatly in their degree of commitment. Early TAA will reveal the likelihood that government supporters will be susceptible to abandoning the government, moving against it, or metaphorically or literally "dying in place" for it. Hard-core government supporters may be unreachable no matter how impossible their tactical situation becomes. History has shown, however, that authoritarian regimes (the typical target in UW) do not enjoy deep ideological commitment beyond the upper levels of the regime and those completely dependent upon it. Even powerful backers, such as major corporations, may well be swayed if they perceive no threat from the irregular organization. During buildup, susceptible TAs within the ranks of government supporters may be a lucrative target. In addition, inevitability and capitulation themes and symbols may be useful during buildup. However, if buildup is progressing well and OPSEC allows release of some figures, government supporters may not believe the actual level of support for the UW effort and such series may be counterproductive.

EXTERNAL SUPPORT

6-28. Although not as critical to success in UW as is internal support, external support for an irregular effort is for the most part beneficial. An exception is always external support that may be viewed in a negative way by domestic TAs. For instance, the assistance of regional nations or organizations can be seen as interventionist or self-serving. ARSOF may need to downplay U.S. support for this reason as well. Typically, the opposite is true—external support for the insurgency legitimizes it and increases the psychological effects of the irregular's cause. U.S. PSYOP support may attempt to build greater external support for an irregular effort or leave this function to irregular PSYOP organizations. Surrogate PSYOP forces and the irregular force should be cautioned not to inflate claims of external support.

INCREASING MEDIA OPERATIONS

6-29. During buildup, the security situation in limited areas may shift sufficiently to allow for committal of more U.S. PSYOP assets, as well as the operation of new types of media by the underground or the auxiliary. The projection of new media types from external sites may become practical as the irregular organization grows. In addition, more sophisticated types of media may have been deliberately held back until sufficient levels were reached during buildup. This situation can be particularly true if TAs would not find U.S.-produced media credible.

PHASE VI: EMPLOYMENT

6-30. Combat operations may not directly involve U.S. forces, but this does not preclude PSYOP forces from supporting the UW force. During the employment phase, widely varying mixtures of unilateral U.S. combined and unilateral irregular force PSYOP are possible. In all cases, however, PSYOP forces' primary role is not that of a shooter in direct action roles. PSYOP forces should be careful not to misuse their skills. PSYOP forces support SFODAs by communicating messages designed to elicit desired behaviors from local people that support the activities of the SF units and the irregular organization. PSYOP programs can capitalize on the actions of the UW force to support capitulation of individuals, groups, and units. PSYOP forces continue their role as a force multiplier by eliciting support for the operation in and around combat operation areas. Sympathizers may be much more susceptible to recruitment PSYOP arguments once action has started. In addition, rewards for information programs can provide information that may prove invaluable to the operation.

6-31. Another means of bolstering the fighting spirit and morale of insurgent forces is to mitigate or minimize any tactical setbacks. Doing so may entail mitigating the mistakes of individual irregular force or shadow government leaders and stressing the competence of leadership in general. Highlighting tactical or operational successes also mitigates any failures by the irregular force. Regardless of the type of support they are providing, however, PSYOP forces must not get caught up in the excitement of long-awaited action. PSYOP forces should—

- Continue to update TAA.
- Capture and analyze feedback from ongoing and previously executed programs and series.
- Analyze government and other adversary propaganda.
- Update plans for supporting the next phase of the operation.

> **PSYOP Support to the UW Force in Afghanistan**
> During combat operations in Afghanistan, ARSOF provided support to the Northern Alliance. The Northern Alliance was having offensive success and had driven the enemy forces to the town of Kunduz. Anticoalition militias moving into the town forced the people of Kunduz to support them. This fact was known to the commanding officer of the Northern Alliance, and he requested that PSYOP forces assist in reducing collateral damage and unwanted civilian casualties during the capture of the town. The objective was to reduce the number of civilian casualties and win the support of the town's people for the Northern Alliance. PSYOP forces broadcast radio messages from the EC-130, COMMANDO SOLO, and dropped leaflets that let the people know if they opened their gates to the Northern Alliance there would be no retribution taken against them, and the Northern Alliance would safeguard them. The people of Kunduz took this message as credible and opened the town's gates to the Northern Alliance. The Northern Alliance took the town and gained the support of the local populace.

6-32. During the employment phase, PSYOP forces typically direct products toward eliciting behaviors that degrade the support for the adversary forces and their standing government. Generally during the employment phase, some degree or even a high degree of vilification of the government and standing military forces is useful. PSYOP forces may need to caution the irregular force against using overly divisive series that may make their own consolidation of power and any national reconciliation more difficult. PSYOP series at this point typically share the UWOA with PA messages and DOS products communicating the USG position on the standing government. PSYOP series may inform select TAs of USG positions as well, but this is secondary to eliciting specific behaviors, such as defections, to the irregular force. ARSOF personnel during this time may also have to caution irregular forces from inflating claims of success or making unachievable promises.

PHASE VII: TRANSITION

6-33. The transition phase marks the end of hostilities and the start of stability operations. Depending on the situation, rewards for information programs may continue. Generally, however, transition phase marks the introduction of legitimacy and professionalism programs. Regardless of whether or not U.S. military forces begin FID operations, PSYOP forces can work with OGAs and embassy teams to support DOS and national objectives. If PSYOP forces transition from supporting DOD operations to DOS missions, they must ensure that programs do not lapse and that PSYOP execution remains seamless.

LEGITIMIZATION

6-34. Legitimization of any new government, military, and other institutions formed by or radically reorganized by a successful UW effort is often central to transition PSYOP. U.S. PSYOP forces may not accomplish this legitimization. Instead, former irregular force PSYOP personnel may conduct postconflict programs. Part of the legitimization of a new government may entail advising the new government and military against reprisals of any kind. PSYOP programs supporting amnesties, new freedoms, or enforcement of long-denied civil rights; domestic disarmament programs; and humanitarian measures not only provide practical benefits but also legitimize or create a better climate in which the new government can be legitimized. A major focus of DOD PSYOP and DOS public information efforts may center on new constitutions, national laws, or elections. ARSOF personnel may promote the need for a national self-determining vote from the beginning to support a successful irregular movement's new government. At this stage, however, ARSOF personnel may need to discourage the same sort of behaviors the outgoing military and government conducted, including voting irregularities.

SHIFT OF FOCUS

6-35. During transition, previously untargeted TAs may become more important to the peacetime PSYOP program. For instance, UW efforts rarely result in the immediate halt of armed opposition. Typically, a hard-core element of the former government and military begins an insurgency of its own at this time. Although small in number, it may have secured large amounts of resources before abandoning previous bases and sites. As underdogs, these elements may be more susceptible to PSYOP.

6-36. Other TAs and new desired behaviors typically emerge in transition operations, regardless of the level of resistance the new government faces. Even if the old adversary government's supporters do begin an insurgency, the new government established by the UW effort should focus on promoting its agenda rather than reacting to an insurgency. Domestic PSYOP programs may instead focus on economic and governance issues and, thereby, minimize an insurgency. In addition, PSYOP in the transition phase may focus some resources on regional or international issues, such as reassuring bordering nations or traditional trade partners. In the early days of transition, this and other issues not typically the purview of U.S. PSYOP may of necessity be done by members of the former irregular force until the new government can form a civilian international information program and a diplomatic corps.

STANDING DOWN FORCES

6-37. After a successful UW operation, the new military may expand any existing military PSYOP force they had during earlier phases or release personnel from other duties to join or start such a force. Typically, a new government will also ask for more U.S. PSYOP support in transition rather than less. However, the sociopolitical realities in the country may make domestic PSYOP impossible, especially if the former government had propaganda units associated with excesses or civil rights violations. Although needed, political realities may force the immediate redeployment of most or all ARSOF PSYOP personnel. In a society expecting a smaller military or less military participation in the life of the nation, one of the last endeavors for domestic or U.S. PSYOP personnel may be to focus attention and support from select TAs for a stand-down of forces.

EXTENDED ARMY SPECIAL OPERATIONS FORCES PSYCHOLOGICAL OPERATIONS PRESENCE

6-38. Regardless of whether large-scale FID operations become necessary, PSYOP personnel may have an extended presence in what can now be termed an HN. Whether the new government creates, expands, or stands down its own PSYOP force, the U.S. Ambassador may request the deployment of a military information support team. A larger U.S. PSYOP presence may also tackle other problem areas even if they do not train, advise, or support HN PSYOP personnel. In the wake of the changes brought about by UW, other threat elements may emerge that also affect U.S. national interests. These can include narcotics production and trafficking, maritime or intellectual piracy, and, because of new freedoms and openness in society, terrorism. Much as the UW effort is a long-term process, the consolidation of the advantages gained by a new government may take years to achieve. It may take years to stabilize the new government and establish its viability against any armed resistance. This process may involve frequent rotations of PSYOP personnel or the long-term deployment of a military information support team.

This page intentionally left blank.

Chapter 7

Civil Affairs Operations

INTRODUCTION

7-1. During the past century, most internal resistance movements have failed. Standing governments crushed most internal resistance movements before they developed a critical mass of skill and support or were simply incapable of attaining such a critical mass. Successful movements possessed sufficient FP and CI capabilities to prevent the government, whether an indigenous regime or outside partner, from pushing the conflict to decision in the military realm until the power balance shifted in favor of the irregular force. They did this either by making the political and psychological realms decisive (since it was much easier for them to attain parity with the government in this sphere) or by postponing decisive military encounters until they weakened the controlling force through guerrilla, political, CA, and psychological operations.

7-2. For the irregular efforts to succeed, they must attain the pivotal concept of legitimacy. This concept assumes the people of a country will decide whether the government or the insurgents can offer them the "best alternative" in terms of goods and services and then will support that organization. Following this line of thought, the basis of ARSOF UW activity is the irregular forces identifying the genuine grievances of its people and taking political, economic, and social actions to redress them. The integration of CA forces in the seven phases of UW enhances the ARSOF planner's margin for success.

> **NOTE:** Some of the following phases may occur simultaneously or—in certain situations—not at all.

PHASE I: PREPARATION

7-3. ARSOF and irregular force leaders must consider not only the military forces but also the operational environment in which those forces operate. To see first, understand first, act first, and finish decisively in the operational environment, irregular forces must consider civilian component political, military, economic, social, informational, and infrastructure factors. In other words, they must consider civil areas, structures, capabilities, organizations, people, and events (ASCOPE) aspects and their impact on the mission of irregular forces. CA forces support the ARSOF commander in CMO by focusing on CA core tasks when conducting CAO. It is imperative that CA personnel are included in all phases of the operation from planning to transition and are capable of performing CMO in support of UW (Figure 7-1, page 7-2).

AREA STUDY AND AREA ASSESSMENT

7-4. The U.S. military orients CA units toward a specific region of the world. This orientation helps CA units focus their personnel and training. Examples include language, cultural norms, and operational requirements unique to the assigned region. The initiating process of prime importance in preparation for operations is the area study. Area study files contain information on a designated area. General areas of information include history, public administration, cultural relations, and supply, among others. This information supports contingency and SO planning in areas assigned to operational forces. CA personnel obtain, analyze, and record information in advance of a need. Although an area study has no set format, information acquired through the study supports the area assessment.

7-5. The CA area assessment begins with the receipt of a mission. The CA area assessment supports SO. This assessment should supplement, not repeat, the basic area study. The area study and assessment ensure all functional areas of the AOR are covered.

Chapter 7

UW Phase	I Preparation	II Initial Contact	III Infiltration	IV Organization	V Buildup	VI CBT Employment	VII Transition
Who	CAPT/LNO	CAPT/CAT/LNO	CAPT/LNO	CAPT/LNO	CAPT/LNO	CAPT/LNO	CAPT/LNO
Where	CONUS	JSOTF/SOTF/AOB	SOTF/AOB	SOTF/AOB	SOTF/AOB	SOTF/AOB	SOTF/AOB
Three lines of operation							
IPB — Continuous and simultaneous throughout the UW phases	ASCOPE — Continuous assessments, validations, refinements of CA inputs to IPB (area, structures, capabilities, organizations, people, events)						
	• Isolate • POL/MIL • End state • CDR's intent for CMO • ID MOEs	• Integrate w/ pilot team planning cell • ID FHA sources	• Confirm or deny CA inputs to IPB	• Refine CA inputs to IPB	• Revalidate MOEs		• Track MOEs
Enabling operations — Must facilitate the ability to "surge" any CA operation at any point in any UW phase	Conduct CA operations ISO SF CDR's UW objectives; o/o establish CMOC						
	• Procure funding • ID CERP funds • ID OHDACA follow-on funds	• May insert w/pilot team POL/MIL • Analyze pilot team's assessments	• May insert w/SFOD • Contact key players • ID CMO influencers	• Facilitate G-Force Build • Surge FHA • NA • ID CMO influencers	• Surge FHA • Monitor effects • DC operations PRC • NA	• Monitor/ mitigate impacts • Advise SF CDR • Surge FHA • DC operations PRC	• RSOI USAR • Liaison • Support to civil administration
Transitions operations — Facilitates transitions to stability operations and to follow-on CA forces, USG, international organizations, NGOs, HN	Identify, set, and continually develop conditions for transition to stability operations; o/o establish CMOC						
	• Disengagement concept • CMO end state	• Exploit pilot team's assessment • Identify quick, high impact projects	• Define post-hostilities infrastructure	• Surge FHA • NA • PRC	• Revalidate MOEs • Surge FHA • NA • PRC	• Surge FHA • Revalidate MOEs • Deconflict international organizations/ NGO operations • PRC	• Legitimate posthostilities institutions • Support to civil administration

Figure 7-1. Civil-military lines of operation in support of unconventional warfare

SYSTEM ANALYSIS OF THE UNCONVENTIONAL WARFARE OPERATIONS AREA

7-6. The culmination of the area study and area assessment effort is a system analysis of the operational area. This analysis equips ARSOF CA forces with unique information requirements (IRs). IRs contained in the analysis target specific areas, people, source materials, and agencies relevant to the operation and essential to mission preparation and execution. Such IRs might include but are not limited to—

- Typography, hydrography, climate, weather, and terrain, including landforms, drainage, vegetation, and soils.
- Census, location, ethnic composition, and health factors of the population.
- Attitude of the population, including ideological, religious, and cultural aspects.
- Government structure, including forms, personalities, existing laws, and political heritage.
- Educational standards and facilities and important cultural activities and repositories.
- Communications, transportation, utility, power, and natural resources.
- Labor potential, including availability by type and skill, practices, and organizations.
- Economic development, including principal industries, scientific and technical capabilities, commercial processes, banking structure, monetary system, price and commodity controls, extent and nature of agricultural production, and accustomed population dietary habits.
- Leadership and cadres of resistance movements.
- Organization and operation of guerrilla forces in and the extent and degree of volition involved in local support.
- Irregular activities, including espionage, sabotage, and other factors of subversion and disaffection from the indigenous population.

PHASE II: INITIAL CONTACT

7-7. CA support during Phase II is mission dependent. It may include integration and deployment to the UWOA with the pilot team. Other initial contact activities may occur outside the UWOA through coordination with shadow government and auxiliary personnel, whether conducted during Phase II or a later phase. An initial assessment based on the area study begins when the first CA personnel arrive in the

UWOA. Information contained in this assessment clarifies what support is available to both the irregular forces and the local population and what support needs to be provided. During this period the assessment team will identify or confirm the leaders, centers of gravity, and influential persons. The CA battalion (Figure 7-2), through one of its four CA companies, will then begin providing tactical CA support, to include assessment, planning, and coordination with the civil component and IGOs, NGOs, and IPI, in areas where military forces are present.

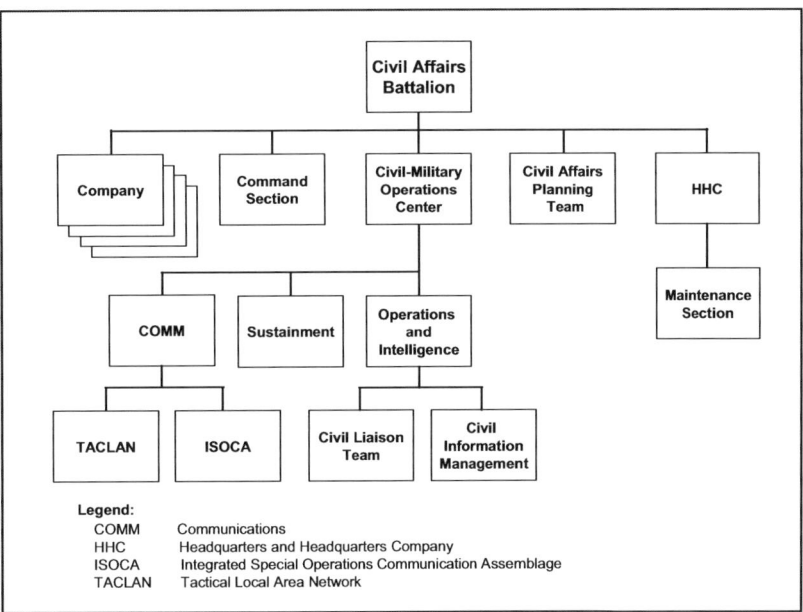

Figure 7-2. Active Army Civil Affairs battalion operational structure

7-8. Functions of the CA battalion support the core tasks of CMO (Figure 7-3, page 7-4). These functions include the following:

- Promote U.S. policy objectives before, during, and after combat operations by influencing the civil component of the operational area.
- Reduce demands on the supply system by facilitating the coordination of indigenous resources and supplies, where appropriate.
- Fulfill responsibilities of the SOF under U.S. domestic and international laws relevant to civilian populations. These responsibilities may become evident when considering the safety and protection of local government personnel, religious leaders, and others considered centers of gravity that may be targeted for reprisal.
- Minimize civilian interference with irregular operations and the impact of these operations on the civilian populace. Control measures may include curfews, movement restrictions, travel permits, registration cards, and relocation of the population.
- Coordinate ARSOF operations with other irregular forces, agencies, IPI, IGOs, and NGOs.
- Exercise civil administration in occupied or liberated areas until civilian or non-U.S. military authority can retake control of this function.
- Support civilian efforts to meet the life-sustaining needs of the civilian population; provide direct assistance in areas where civilian operators are not present and according to internationally accepted standards and principles.

- Provide expertise in civil-sector functions normally the responsibility of civilian authorities, applied to implement U.S. policy to advise or assist in rehabilitating or restoring civil-sector functions.
- Provide guidance to prevent collateral damage or destruction to HN strategic infrastructure (for example, government offices, power plants, and water treatment facilities). Identifying cultural centers of gravity (churches, mosques, village meeting halls, historic monuments, and so on) that require protection or coordinated rehabilitation is equally important.

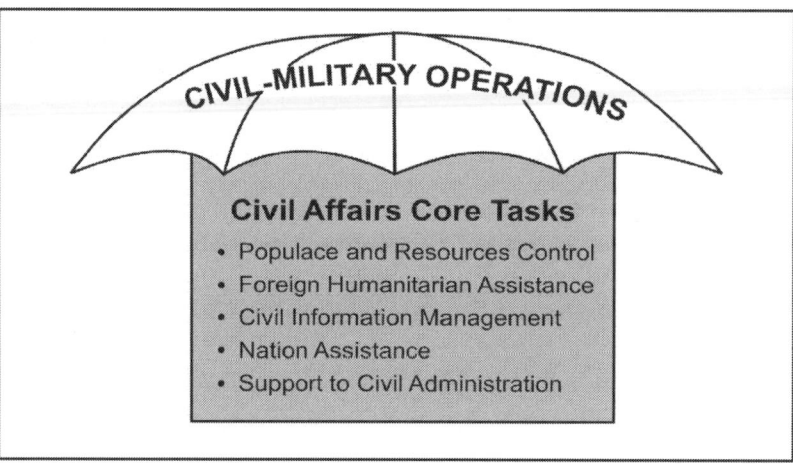

Figure 7-3. Civil Affairs core tasks in support of civil-military operations

PHASE III: INFILTRATION

7-9. As most Active Army CA personnel assigned to tactical units are CA generalists, their initial assessment will advise commanders on the application of the six functional specialty areas of CA. Normally, the USG alerts the USAR functional specialty cell during the infiltration phase.

7-10. The Active Army CA battalion rapidly deploys as the initial-entry CA force with Civil Affairs planning teams (CAPTs), civil-military operations centers (CMOCs), CA companies, and Civil Affairs teams (CATs). The CA force plans, enables, shapes, and conducts CAO to support the commander's situational understanding of the civil component and improve overall decision superiority. Active Army CA capabilities include the following:
- Provide the CAPT at the tactical level and operational level with CA planning, and regionally aligned, rapidly deployable, plug-and-play capabilities that support the JSOTF or the division HQ.
- Provide the CMOC with tactical-level management, coordination, and synchronization of key CMO within the supported commander's AO. CA personnel will operate away from the supported unit as required.
- Provide the civil liaison team with local-level to provincial-level interface and liaison capability between civil-military, HN, and humanitarian elements within the AO; serve as the "storefront" for the Active Army CA battalion where the military meets with the civil populace, the HN, and the humanitarian community.
- Provide the civil information management cell with the tactical-level collation and analysis of civil information. The CA battalion develops tactical-level civil inputs to the common operational picture. The CA battalion provides civil information input to the appropriate military and civil systems via geospatially referenced data.

PHASE IV: ORGANIZATION

7-11. Sustaining operations at any echelon can enable shaping and decisive operations by providing logistics support, rear-area and base security, movement control, terrain management, and infrastructure development. CAO and CMO normally support sustaining operations through their planning abilities in movement control and infrastructure development. CAO and CMO support sustaining operations working with IPI and local authorities to protect local sources of essential supplies and services. CA forces support sustaining operations by—

- Providing liaison to local agencies and civilian authorities.
- Identifying the local resources, facilities, and support available for insurgency operations.
- Coordinating the use by irregular forces of local resources, facilities, and support, such as civilian labor, transportation, communications, medical facilities, and miscellaneous services and supplies.
- Facilitating irregular efforts to develop and implement plans for using local resources, as well as supporting civil information programs and coordinating these efforts with those of IGOs, NGOs, and IPI.
- Minimizing the impact of UW operations on civilians through IO and by planning for possible population displacements.
- Managing civilian access to areas of ongoing operations using ARSOF advisors and local auxiliaries.
- Facilitating the passage of civilian humanitarian assistance and providers when possible.
- Advising the ARSOF command on cultural and moral considerations.

PHASE V: BUILDUP

7-12. During buildup, CA forces will assist the ARSOF commander in an expanding operational area through shaping operations. Shaping operations at any echelon create and preserve conditions for the success of the decisive operation. In UW operations, shaping operations often convert temporary gains into long-term political success. Shaping operations can aim to keep newly gained stability from being undone. Shaping operations may focus on identifying and cooling potential flash points that can occur after initial stabilization efforts. The main effort during shaping operations is military-to-civilian contact. The secondary effort is civilian-to-civilian contact by OGAs. CA forces conduct CAO, and CMO planners plan CMO to deter a potential crisis, reinforce or regain public support of the transitional government and U.S. forces, and mitigate conditions that lead toward irregular safe havens. CMO are shaping operations that gain favor with the IPI and influence positive attitudes and perceptions. CMO directly support the ARSOF commander's ability to conduct shaping operations in his UWOA by facilitating the transfer of responsibilities to IPI.

PHASE VI: EMPLOYMENT

7-13. Normally, CAO and CMO support offensive or defensive operations by enabling maneuver, mainly through planning populace and resources control (PRC) and providing critical civil information to increase the ARSOF commander's situational awareness and understanding. All CA core tasks support CMO. CMO support UW operations and normally prevent or mitigate the effects of natural or man-made disasters. Normally, CAO and CMO support UW operations through stability operations by assisting in the establishment of order in the UWOA. CMO planners and CA forces support the irregular force operations by—

- Coordinating the use by irregular forces of local resources, facilities, and support, such as civilian labor, transportation, communications, maintenance or medical facilities, and miscellaneous services and supplies through, with, and by IPI.
- Planning for possible population displacements and working with civilian organizations (IPI, and IGOs to include UN organizations) to minimize local populace interference with UW operations.
- Coordinating with civilian organizations to identify the local resources, facilities, and support available for UW operations.

- Providing liaison and coordinating CMO with local IPI, OGAs, IGOs, and NGOs, as applicable.
- Predicting movement of civilians and establishing procedures and processes to minimize their interference with operations.
- Estimating the availability of resources.
- Preparing area studies of the assigned area, as required, to support the mission.
- Providing civil information and CMO plans to U.S. and other agencies on the political, economic, social, and cultural characteristics of the local populace in support of U.S. and resistance objectives.
- Recommending policy for FHA, civil assistance, and civil administration activities and missions.
- Acting as the focal point for cultural considerations.
- Providing technical expertise in all civil functions.
- Providing timely civil information for the development of the supported ARSOF commander's common operational picture.

STABILITY OPERATIONS

7-14. Forces conduct CAO and CMO during offensive and defensive operations to set the conditions for stability operations. CMO are the major effort of stability operations. CA support to stability operations depends on the condition of the affected IPI. The CMO staff continually monitors the condition of the transitional governing body during the operation, applies available resources to affect the civilian component, and recommends functional skills required to support this critical phase. CAO support conventional forces, SOF, USG agencies, and the local civil administration in transitioning the power to the new administration.

7-15. Conflict termination marks the start of new challenges for CA forces and CMO planners. These may include encounters with the local populace as it responds to a new or significantly changed government and to a new way of life. Problems may involve the unrealized hopes and aspirations of the local populace, as well as local leaders' desire for recognition as the legitimate power. The need to maintain and restore law and order, as well as basic life services (food, water, electricity), is critical early in stability operations. During stability operations, the main effort shifts from military-to-military to military-to-civilian contacts.

7-16. Insurgency forces, if any, also present unique challenges for the commander. The ultimate goal is the complete demobilization of the irregular force and the return of those forces to civilian pursuits. Demobilization involves, among other things, the collection of weapons. The demobilization effort may be difficult unless the irregular force receives assurances of security, transition assistance, jobs, and proper resettlement.

7-17. The goals of stability operations may not be achievable in the short term. Success often requires perseverance and a long-term commitment to resolving the source of the conflict. The achievement of these goals may take years. Conversely, daily operations may require rapid responses to changing conditions based on unanticipated localized conflict among competing groups. Civil considerations are especially critical in stability operations. The civil population, new government, NGOs, and IGOs can greatly affect achieving stability.

7-18. Stability operations are usually nonlinear and noncontiguous. ARSOF and indigenous leaders tailor the application of the operational framework, elements of operational design, and METT-TC to fit each situation. During stability operations, identifying centers of gravity, decisive points—and even the desired end state—can be more complex and unorthodox than in offensive and defensive operations. In stability operations, the adversary is often disease, hunger, or the consequences of disaster. CMO and CA planners are integral players in the successful execution of stability operation missions. Forces may conduct stability operations in any operational environment.

7-19. The CA supporting tasks in CMO are of support to the ARSOF commander's operational function in UW. Generally, CA Soldier tasks include—
- Assessing and assisting in the restoration of essential government services.
- Assisting in the protection of public health and safety (within the limits of Federal law and the United States Code [USC]).
- Assisting in the provision of emergency relief to the new government, businesses, and individuals.
- Identifying and assessing the threat posed by hazardous materials (civil considerations).
- Providing consultation through the defense coordinating officer to decision makers.
- Participating in interagency assessment, planning, and synchronizing of domestic stability operations.
- Participating in the execution of selected CMO activities, as needed or directed.

7-20. It is during this stability phase that CA personnel provide the greatest support to the indigenous populace and new or transitional government, which requires the employment of CA functional specialists from the USAR. The following paragraphs discuss CA personnel specialty areas.

Rule of Law

7-21. The purpose of rule-of-law operations is to create security and stability for the civilian population. Rule-of-law operations provide legitimacy to the new or transitional government by restoring and enhancing the effective and fair administration and enforcement of justice through impartial legal institutions and competent safety systems. Rule-of-law operations are of great importance in stability operations. Rule-of-law operations are particularly significant in the immediate aftermath of major ground combat operations when it is imperative to restore order to the civilian population in the vacuum that inevitably results when combat disrupts the routine administration of the society. Close coordination between the rule-of-law section and the governance section to achieve synchronization and synergy between efforts to restore, reform, and assist the court and legal system and the public safety system is critical. A judicial system is powerless without an effective public safety system, whereas a public safety system is not legitimate without a fair and efficient judicial system.

Infrastructure

7-22. The infrastructure section consists of functional specialists in public works, transportation, utilities, and communications. It provides technical expertise, staff advice, and planning assistance to the supported command. The section assesses the indigenous public infrastructure and systems. Using its assessments and civilian skills, the team determines methods to design, build, and maintain the organizations, architecture, and systems required to support transportation, water, communications, and power. The infrastructure section provides recommendations and, when appropriate, direction to maintain, sustain, and improve indigenous public systems and services, such as transportation, utilities, and postal systems.

Governance

7-23. The governance section consists of functional specialists in public administration and services (excluding public health and welfare), cultural relations, and education. It provides technical expertise, staff advice, and planning assistance to the supported command in creating, resourcing, managing, and sustaining the institutions and processes that govern and protect a society. Personnel in this section include public administrators, public safety administrators and managers, environmental administrators and managers, and other administrators whose civilian duties include upper-level management of public institutions at various levels (city, county, local, state, and federal).

Public Health and Welfare

7-24. The public health and welfare section consists of functional specialists in public health and medical services. It provides technical expertise, staff advice, and planning assistance to the supported command in creating, resourcing, managing, and sustaining the institutions and processes through which a society maintains the physical, mental, and social health of its people. Some skills required in this section include doctors, dentists, hospital administrators, nurses, public health specialists, environmental scientists and specialists, museum curators, archivists, and others whose civilian duties include health and welfare management in addition to arts, monuments, and archives.

Economic Stability

7-25. The economic stability section consists of functional specialists in economic fields and business administration. It provides technical expertise, staff advice, and planning assistance to the supported command. The section assesses government, corporate, and private resources and systems. Using these assessments, based on their civilian skills, the team determines how to assist in the efficient management of resources, goods, and services to enhance the viability of the society's economic system. The economic stability section provides recommendations and, when appropriate, directions to maintain, sustain, and improve economic systems and services. Some skills found in this section include economists, bankers, supply technicians, business administrators, entrepreneurs, agriculturalists, farmers, food specialists and technicians, marketing and distribution specialists, and other officer and enlisted personnel whose civilian skills make them suitable for improving a nation's economic system.

Public Education and Information

7-26. The public education and information section consists of functional specialists in education and information services. It provides technical expertise, staff advice, and planning assistance to the supported command in designing, resourcing, and implementing public education and information programs and systems through media and formal education institutions. Some skills required in this section include educators at all levels, education specialists, school administrators, public relations personnel, media specialists, and others whose civilian duties include education and information management.

LOCAL DEFENSE TRAINING

7-27. Internal defense training is an umbrella concept that covers a broad range of activities. Its primary intent is to help address internal threats and their underlying causes. Commensurate with U.S. policy goals, the focus of all U.S. efforts is to support internal defense and development. Civil defense training is not restricted to times of conflict. It can also take place in the form of training exercises and other activities that show irregular-force resolve to and for the region.

7-28. Of primary importance to the irregular forces is the security and welfare of the population that supports the movement. Without this support, the insurgency is doomed to fail. CA forces support local security through local defense training. Local defense training protects the society from subversion, lawlessness, hostile government retaliation, and the effects of man-made and natural disasters.

7-29. The proper use of ARSOF CA assets in UW is essential during all phases of an insurgency to counter retaliation by the hostile government. When used to its full potential, CMO can be crucial to solidify the position of the transitional government and improve security conditions for the people. CAO vary with the capabilities of the new administration and with the level of hostile activity. The economic, social, and political situations are also major influences. CA elements supporting local security—

- Review U.S. security assistance program goals to support the insurgent security plan.
- Plan CMO based on the seven phases of insurgency.
- Train irregular forces to plan, train for, and conduct nation assistance, PRS, and other CAO appropriate to the needs of its region.
- Train on TTP required to protect the populace from lawlessness and retaliation and develop indigenous individual, leader, and organizational skills to isolate hostile personnel and protect the civil population.
- Establish and maintain contact with nonmilitary agencies and local authorities.
- Identify specific CMO missions the new leadership can and should conduct.

PHASE VII: TRANSITION

7-30. CMO planners, usually CA-trained personnel, play a major role in transition planning. Based on their expertise, these personnel may be the best group to perform this function. For these planners to accomplish this task, a clearly identifiable end state and transition or termination criteria for the operation must be developed (JP 3-57 includes further information). Termination or transition occurs when either the mission has been accomplished or when the President or SecDef so directs. Planners may base criteria for termination or transition on events, measures of effectiveness (MOEs) and success, availability of resources, or a specific date. A successful harvest or restorations of critical facilities in the crisis area are examples of events that might trigger termination of the mission. An acceptable drop in mortality rates, a certain percentage of dislocated civilians returned to their homes, or a given decrease in threat activity against the operation are examples of MOEs that may prompt the end of ARSOF involvement.

7-31. The transition plan is vital if stability operations are to be a success. It prioritizes and plans for the successful handover of missions to a follow-on agency or force. It is either military or civil in nature or a blending of the two. Examples of these organizations are peacekeeping entities under a UN mandate, IGOs, NGOs, or IPI. CA forces and CMO planners are uniquely qualified to advise the commander on activities that reduce turmoil and stabilize the situation until international relief organizations or IPI assume control.

7-32. Transition may occur between U.S. military forces, another military force (for example, multinational or forces from the affected country), regional organizations, the UN, or indigenous civilian organizations. A detailed plan addressing the various civil functions and to whom they will transition greatly reduces the turmoil typically associated with transition. The CMO staff should periodically review the transition plan with all participating organizations. This review will ensure that planning assumptions are still valid and determine if changes in the situation require changes in the transition plan.

7-33. For CAO planners to accomplish this task, a clearly identifiable end state and transition or termination criteria for the operation must be developed (Figure 7-4). Transition planning must start during the initial phases of operation planning to ensure that planners pay adequate attention to this critical area. ARSOF plan for transition when they plan for intervention.

- Has the end state been achieved?
- Can forces be safely withdrawn from the operational area?
- Has consideration been given as to when USAR forces will be released?
- Has coordination for redeployment of the force been conducted with appropriate commands, agencies, and other organizations?
- Has the commander identified postconflict requirements?
- Has transition planning been accomplished in the event that operations are transitioning to another military force, regional organization, UN, or civilian organization?
- Have stated operational objectives been accomplished?
- Have the underlying causes of the conflict been considered, and how do they influence termination planning?
- What additional support will be required for redeployment?
- What are the FP requirements?
- What arrangements have been made with other organizations to accomplish the postconflict activities? For example, will there be humanitarian, governmental, and infrastructure assistance requirements?
- What is the policy for evacuation of equipment used by the force?
- What is the policy for redeployment?
- How will postconflict requirements impact the timeline for redeployment of the force?
- Will the force be expected to support these types of activities?

Figure 7-4. Sample checklist for transition planning

7-34. Historically, the international community has undertaken stabilization and reconstruction operations in an ad hoc fashion, recreating the tools and relationships each time a crisis arises. If the United States is to ensure that countries are set on a sustainable path toward peace, democracy, and a market economy, it needs new, institutionalized foreign-policy tools—tools that can influence the choices countries and people make about the nature of their economies, their political systems, their security, and in some cases, the very social fabric of a nation. In July 2004, Congress created the State Department's Office of the Coordinator for Reconstruction and Stabilization (S/CRS). The mission of the S/CRS is to integrate military expertise and best practices into the civilian world, while preserving the flexibility and agility necessary to respond to the highly fluid environments of conflict transformation. There is a tremendous asymmetry in the resources that the military and civilian worlds bring to bear on planning. S/CRS considers it a priority to develop a cadre of civilian planners for reconstruction, stabilization, and conflict transformation. C/SRS core objectives include—

- *Monitor and plan.* Develop clear policy options concerning states and regions of greatest risk and importance and lead U.S. planning focused on these priorities to avert crises, when possible, and to prepare for them when necessary.
- *Mobilize and deploy.* Coordinate the deployment of U.S. resources and implementation of programs in cooperation with international and local partners to accelerate transitions from conflict to peace.
- *Prepare skills and resources.* Establish and manage an interagency capability to deploy personnel and resources in an immediate surge response and the capacity to sustain assistance until traditional support mechanisms can operate effectively.
- *Learn from experience.* Incorporate best practices and lessons learned into functional changes in training, planning, exercises, and operational capabilities that support improved performance.
- *Coordinate with international partners.* Work with international and multilateral organizations, individual states, and NGOs to plan and accelerate deployment and increase interoperability of personnel and equipment in multilateral operations.

7-35. When ARSOF conduct UW, CA forces must coordinate CAO with this relatively new USG C/SRS asset from the earliest practical moment in the preparation phase through the UW operation to transition or the final ARSOF efforts in the UWOA.

Chapter 8
Supporting Elements and Activities

INTRODUCTION

8-1. ARSOF communications, logistics, medical, and aviation elements conduct activities to support SO, including support to UW. Most SO are politically sensitive, high-risk and high-reward strategic operations, and these characteristics of support to ARSOF SO will remain constant regardless of the specific operation. Nevertheless, ARSOF supporting units must consider the often-protracted nature of UW (typically within a hostile and denied territory), the fundamental UW quality of supporting (directly or indirectly) an irregular TA, and the degree of relative self-sufficiency within which ARSOF and supported irregular organizations must operate. UW is fundamentally an effort to persuade and assist others to act in concert with U.S. national strategic objectives. The focus is primarily on the behavior of relevant TAs, and the application of firepower and the conduct of combat operations is usually a secondary concern. Moreover, tactical SO characterized by time-sensitive, direct, and specifically limited application of SO capabilities—while important—will often be subordinate supporting efforts to a protracted, essentially indirect, and mutable UW campaign.

COMMUNICATIONS SUPPORT

8-2. To enable its assigned forces to perform the ARSOF core tasks, USSOCOM developed doctrinal communications principles and architectural tenets. These principles and tenets guide ARSOF communications support of SO, including support of UW. Communications systems support to ARSOF must be—

- *Global.* SOF communications systems span the full range of diverse SO missions worldwide. SOF communications make maximum use of existing national capabilities and commercial, tactical, and HN assets. Access to the infosphere is available at the lowest possible tactical level. In UW, some use of and interoperability with HN or irregular organizations' indigenous assets should be expected.
- *Secure.* Employment of SOF communications systems involves the use of the latest technology procedures and National Security Agency (NSA)-approved encryption and devices that prevent exploitation by the enemy. Use of HN or irregular assets makes adhering to this principle more challenging.
- *Mission-tailored.* SOF communications systems deploy relative to the projected operational environment, information transfer requirements, threat, and mission analysis.
- *Value-added.* SOF communications systems never compromise a unit on the ground, in the air, or at sea. Flexibility and interoperability of communications systems substantially increase the fighting effectiveness of the SOF warrior.
- *Jointly interoperable.* SOF communications systems are interoperable by design, adapting to varying C2 structures. They support operations with joint, multinational, and interagency forces. In UW, this principle implies combined interoperability with foreign irregular forces.

ARCHITECTURAL TENETS

8-3. ARSOF must be able to communicate worldwide and at any time by using national, theater, and SOF communications assets. Doctrinal principles and planning considerations are the building blocks for an operational architecture that guides communications systems strategy. The architectural tenets for SOF communications systems provide SOF elements seamless, robust, protected, and automated communications systems, using the full-frequency spectrum while making sure the systems comply with established standards.

Chapter 8

8-4. Implementation of these tenets eliminates traditional geographical, procedural, and technical boundaries. The infosphere allows SOF elements to operate with any force combination in multiple environments. SOF architectural tenets are:

- *Seamless*. Digital SOF communications systems are transparent to the warrior and support every phase of the mission profile—in garrison, in transit, and while deployed. Multiple entry points into the infosphere, high-speed networks, and worldwide Global Information Grid (GIG) connectivity are critical elements of this tenet.
- *Robust*. Robust networks feature multiple routing, alternative sources of connectivity, bandwidth on demand, modularity, and scalability. Multiple routing and alternative sources of connectivity prevent single points of failure and site isolation. Bandwidth on demand, providing automatic network reconfiguration, is available for garrison locations via secure commercial means and via the SCAMPI entry points for tactical SOF.
- *Protected*. SOF C2 nodes are lucrative targets for all types of adversaries ranging from foreign governments to hackers. A thorough information assurance (IA) plan protects SOF communications architectures and critical resources from attack and intrusion. Creating and maintaining sound communications security, computer security, and information security programs are necessary to protect the network.
- *Automated*. SOF communications systems must facilitate the exchange of digital data and implement advanced automation techniques to reduce operator manning and to exploit unattended operation. Full automation facilitates the exchange of information with all Soldiers in the mission, including elements of a multinational joint force, other SOF components, a wide range of intelligence sources, and national information sources. Networking technology of the local area network and the wide area network is the cornerstone of a digital, seamless nodal architecture that provides transparent connectivity at all echelons.
- *Full spectrum*. SOF communications systems must not be limited in the use of the entire frequency spectrum for information transfer. SOF have been at the forefront of exploiting new technology to take advantage of more of the frequency spectrum. In addition, blending in available HN assets can enhance many SO missions. ARSOF must be in a position to use not only emerging technology but also technology outside traditional high-frequency (HF) and man-portable satellite systems.
- *Standards compliant*. SOF communications systems must adhere to commercial, international, federal, and DOD hardware and software standards. Adherence to DOD communications standards ensures a capability to interchange hardware and software products. Adherence also permits the interface and exchange of data, through the infosphere and GIG, with all organizations that support or require SOF.

8-5. These tenets should be realized between ARSOF units deployed in the UWOA and U.S. stations external to it. However, combined communications between ARSOF units and the irregular organizations they support in the UWOA will make these tenets more difficult to achieve. ARSOF must consider and plan for the limitations of irregular communications capabilities.

8-6. The mission of the ARSOF 112th Signal Battalion (A) is to provide strategic, operational, and tactical communications for joint and Army SO commanders in support of deliberate plans (including UW), crisis action operations, and the WOT. It is the only Army signal unit specifically dedicated to support deployed SO. The 112th Signal Battalion (A) can provide signal force packages as directed or as available. Additional tasks include providing communications for standing JTFs in USASOC and USSOCOM as well as being the home station operations center to manage all USASOC satellite systems. The 112th Signal Battalion (A) provides required coordination between the five Theater Network Operations and Security Centers, Defense Information Systems Agency, Defense Intelligence Agency (DIA), and USSOCOM.

8-7. The 112th Signal Battalion (A) is a unique organization in its structure and its mission to support SO, including ARSOF conduct of UW. Because of its mission, the 112th Signal Battalion (A) is uniquely equipped to provide enhanced communications capabilities in support of UW. No other Army signal battalion is equipped or has the capabilities of this unique element. When deployed into the often multinational 21st century UW environment, ARSOF may have a need to give limited voice and data access to supporting HN or coalition armed forces within or adjacent to the UWOA. The 112th Signal

Battalion (A) can establish classified or unclassified coalitionwide area networks to provide an information network through which coalition forces supporting UW can coordinate with ARSOF.

COMMUNICATIONS SUPPORT TO SPECIAL FORCES

8-8. When a Special Forces group (airborne) (SFG[A]) deploys, it establishes a SOTF or, when augmented by joint SO assets, a JSOTF. The JSOTF or SOTF can have numerous subordinate SOTFs consisting of SF battalions or Ranger regiment or smaller SO elements and could even have attached conventional forces for specific missions.

8-9. The JSOTF or SOTF establishes a C2 and support base, operated with organic and attached resources, primarily for planning and coordinating SOF under its control. The JSOTF or SOTF provides C2 to subordinate SOTFs, advanced operational bases (AOBs), and selected independent SFODAs for extremely sensitive or compartmented missions. In addition to reachback and internal communications, the JSOTF or SOTF must integrate and synchronize its operations with other SOF and theater conventional operations. SF battalions can also establish JSOTFs or SOTFs and provide similar C2 support. When the U.S. military employs SFODBs as AOBs, they can serve as terminating base stations for C2 of deployed SFODAs.

8-10. In UW, the U.S. military typically deploys SFODAs in areas that are hostile or denied. This makes communication requirements more challenging because of the need to operate in a clandestine, covert, or low-visibility manner. Since UW, by definition, will involve support of irregulars, SF can use innovative combinations of U.S. and irregular communication methods. FM 3-05.201 contains more information on special communications.

COMMUNICATIONS SUPPORT TO CIVIL AFFAIRS

8-11. CA forces normally operate from several primary and secondary sites, such as—
- A G-9/S-9 staff within or near the main command post. It coordinates current operations, plans, and technical support.
- A G-9/S-9 staff within or near the rear command post. It coordinates foreign nation support, dislocated civilian operations, and transition planning.
- One or more CMOCs. These centers coordinate requests for assistance from government organizations, NGOs, international organizations, and civilians.
- Various nonmilitary locations where CA liaison duties or planning expertise are required.

8-12. In UW, communicators must anticipate the requirements for both interoperability of U.S. communications with non-U.S., nonstandard systems (which may be seriously degraded) and the likelihood of rendering advice and support on rehabilitation of indigenous communication infrastructure in the UWOA as part of the CAO plan.

COMMUNICATIONS SUPPORT TO PSYCHOLOGICAL OPERATIONS

8-13. Army signal doctrine dictates that communications responsibilities go from "higher to lower," from "left to right," and from supporting to supported unit. However, PSYOP communications requirements are inherently joint and interagency in nature and, as an echelon-above-corps unit, PSYOP units will require connectivity from the deployed location back to the sustaining base. This requirement may place extraordinary communications demands upon an undeveloped theater in a time of crisis. Therefore, commanders should adhere to the following principles when planning PSYOP in a theater. There are three distinct functions that must be supported by communications for PSYOP forces to be successful:
- C2.
- Intelligence.
- Distribution.

8-14. When elements from the 4th POG(A) are employed, these forces possess their own organic equipment and communications personnel. However, PSYOP forces may require additional augmentation

Chapter 8

and assistance from the supported GCC, SOC, JTF, or the 112th Signal Battalion (A). Because of these support requirements, it is often necessary to collocate part of the PSYOP force with the supported HQ.

8-15. For C2 and intelligence, PSYOP forces will normally operate or coordinate for periodic access of the following systems and networks:
- Local area network of the supported command.
- SECRET Internet Protocol Router Network and Non-Secure Internet Protocol Router Network of the Defense Information Systems Network.

8-16. PSYOP forces have the capability to integrate their tactical communications devices into future and legacy Army communications networks. PSYOP forces will always bring their own video distribution network to the JOA or AOR. Some networks used and planned for use by PSYOP forces include the following:
- Single-channel TACSAT.
- International maritime satellite.
- Global Broadcast System/Joint Intratheater Injection System.
- Product distribution system (PDS).
- C-, X-, and Ku-band satellite communications (SATCOM).

8-17. PSYOP forces may depend upon the communications capabilities of other Service component commands to support the PSYOP mission. For example, if USN transportable amplitude modulation and frequency modulation radio broadcast system dissemination capabilities are used, the Naval Component Command must provide organic compatible communications to receive audio products for dissemination. However, should SOF aviation units, such as the 193d Special Operations Wing (SOW), EC-130E/J COMMANDO SOLO, deploy to an undeveloped intermediate staging base, PSYOP forces will provide required distribution communications for the 193d SOW to receive and disseminate audio and video PSYOP products.

8-18. PSYOP forces coordinate bandwidth requirements with the J-6 of the supported GCC, not the supported JTF. This early coordination ensures support throughout the AOR and deconflicts PSYOP communications requirements early during contingency planning.

8-19. PSYOP communicators must coordinate and manage the frequency spectrum under the direction of the J-6 of the supported GCC and JTF. PSYOP communicators participate in the joint-restricted frequency-list coordination process with the supported command's J-6, like any other functional or Service component command. This process assigns C2 frequencies. However, the coordination between the electronic warfare officer, the primary electronic support planner of the IO cell, the J-2, the primary electronic surveillance planner of the CCDR or JTF, and the PSYOP communicator must be fully integrated to ensure capabilities are maximized and priorities are established. Allocation of targeted frequencies for dissemination must be coordinated as part of the electronic countermeasures support to the targeting process, in conjunction with the intelligence, operations, and fire support communities.

8-20. The PDS provides PSYOP forces with an organic, high-bandwidth-capable, secure/nonsecure, fully interoperable, MC SATCOM system for product distribution. This SATCOM system links all PSYOP elements on a near-real-time basis. The PDS enables commanders to receive timely, situation-specific PSYOP products. The PDS also enables video production units to produce required products and disseminators to quickly receive and relay commercial broadcast-quality products to the intended audience.

8-21. In UW, communications support to PSYOP may include utilization and manipulation of non-U.S., nonstandard media. The area assessment should include detailed consideration of communications capabilities and coverage indigenous to or capable of influencing the UWOA.

LOGISTICS SUPPORT

8-22. Logistics during UW presents unique challenges for ARSOF units. Careful planning and coordination—both with normal supply channels and other available government agencies—help to diminish these challenges and sustain the force. The SB(SO)(A) serves as the primary logistics operator and advisor to the USASOC commander and primarily focuses on operational to tactical logistical support. When deployed, the SB(SO)(A) acts as the single logistics command element for a JSOTF.

8-23. As soon as practical, the Theater Sustainment Command (TSC) or Expeditionary Sustainment Command (ESC) will release the SB(SO)(A) making it available for redeployment to the continental United States or to another theater. An ARSOF support cell will remain in-theater and embed itself within the TSC or ESC Distribution Management Center and become the forward SB(SO)(A) logistical element for ARSOF, synchronizing logistic support for JSOTF operations. ARSOF liaison elements are assigned to the SB(SO)(A) in direct support of the TSOC, with duty at the ASCC, coordinating logistic plans for Army-provided common-user logistics support for deployed ARSOF and joint SOF where the Army is the executive agent. This coordination chain will typically not be collocated with ARSOF elements within the UWOA.

8-24. In UW, ARSOF and joint force commanders responsible for a designated UWOA cannot assume that logistical requirements will be met entirely through standard U.S. procedures. The SB(SO)(A) is required to anticipate, coordinate, facilitate, and execute unorthodox logistical procedures as needed through JIIM partners, both inside and outside of the UWOA. Such nonstandard logistical requirements must be identified early in the planning process, assume close interagency cooperation, and require flexibility and ingenuity.

THE AUXILIARY

8-25. The auxiliary is the clandestine support element of the guerrilla force. As with the underground, the auxiliary is often a cellular organization that can be either rural- or urban-based. Functions of the auxiliary include the following:

- Security and early warning.
- Intelligence collection.
- CI operations.
- Recruitment of new personnel.
- Air or maritime reception support.
- Communications.
- PSYOP.
- PRS.
- Support of evasion and escape mechanisms.
- Internal logistics and medical support.
- Fund-raising.
- Augmentation.

SUPPLY

8-26. Supply requirements—whether for a resistance element or a surrogate force for UW against nonstate actors—should be established during initial planning. Regulatory requirements limit the types of supplies (specifically, lethal aid) that the DOD can provide to a resistance organization or a foreign surrogate force. Coordination with other agencies of the USG is required to procure lethal aid supplies, which DOD can then transport and deliver.

8-27. Local procurement of supplies generally provides a more favorable OPSEC posture. Local procurement includes coordination through the auxiliary to leverage its internal logistic system of barter, purchase, levy, or seizure. All elements of the UW force can accomplish battlefield recovery. Aerial as well as other forms of resupply may be used, but each technique presents unique challenges during UW. Maintaining the security of the DZ (from both the enemy and civilians) is paramount. During OEF, for example, there were several instances of civilians rushing into DZs to procure items contained in the resupply bundles.

Chapter 8

CACHES AND MISSION SUPPORT SITES

8-28. Caches are hidden storage places for supplies and equipment. When properly planned and established, caches permit ARSOF and irregular forces considerable freedom to operate throughout the UWOA, independent of their base areas. Caches reduce the amount of supplies UW elements must carry, thus enhancing foot mobility. Caches are located to support projected operations.

8-29. An MSS is a temporary base used by personnel who are away from their base camp during an operation for periods in excess of two days. The MSS may provide food, shelter, medical support, ammunition, or demolitions. The use of an MSS eliminates unnecessary movement of supplies and allows the irregular force to move more rapidly to and from target sites.

HOSPITALS AND MEDICAL OPERATIONS

8-30. Medical operations in support of UW conserve the fighting strength of guerrilla forces and help secure the support of the local population for U.S. and guerrilla forces operating within the UWOA. Medical requirements within the UWOA differ from those posed by a conventional force in two key areas:
- Guerrilla forces typically suffer fewer battle casualties.
- Guerrilla forces typically have higher incidences of disease and malnutrition.

8-31. In UW, commanders must tailor the organization of medical elements to fit the particular situation. Depending upon the required skills, organizers may be able to bring personnel from other medical units into the UWOA. The basic medical organization may also expand by using guerrilla force members and recruiting professional medical personnel to establish and operate guerrilla hospitals.

8-32. Clandestine facilities are, at first, confined to emergency and expedient care with minimum preventive medicine. Once the area command develops sufficiently, the clandestine facilities can expand and become part of the unit's medical organization. Wounded guerrillas that fall into enemy hands may reveal critical intelligence that may compromise the mission. Patients with appropriate cover stories may infiltrate civilian or enemy military hospitals to receive care not otherwise available.

ADMINISTRATIVE ISSUES

8-33. Generally, not every group requires every routine administrative procedure. The prior development of the organization, its requirements, and the requirements of the theater and USG dictate the administrative procedures employed.

FUNDING

8-34. Section 1208, *Support of Military Operations to Combat Terrorism* (1 November 2004), of Public Law 108-375, FY05 National Defense Authorization Act, authorizes the SecDef up to $25 million per year to provide support to foreign forces, irregular forces, groups, or individuals engaged in supporting or facilitating ongoing military operations by U.S. SOF to combat terrorism. Security assistance or other uses not directly connected with ongoing or new SO cannot use Section 1208 funds. USSOCOM Policy Memorandum 05-10, *(C) Policy and Procedure for the Use of Section 1208 Funding Authority (U)*, details the request and authorization procedures for these funds.

8-35. The U.S. military uses intelligence contingency funds (ICF) to support USSOCOM-funded intelligence operations. Title 10 of the USC for the SecDef provides the funds for use as emergency and extraordinary expenses (E&EE). Army Regulation (AR) 381-141, *(C) Intelligence Contingency Funds (U)*, discusses the criteria for uses of ICF and intelligence property.

8-36. Confidential military purpose funds are available for E&EE in support of SO that are not provided for by other DOD procedures. Specific guidance for confidential funds is provided in USSOCOM Directive 37-4, *(S/NF) Confidential Military Purpose Funds (U)*. FM 3-05.220, Volume I, Chapter 14 (Special Funding and Support), defines specific procedures for request and use of funds

FORCE HEALTH PROTECTION

8-37. Before any UW deployment, ARSOF must acquire as much medical information as possible to ensure that the medical intelligence about the UWOA is current. This information will aid infiltrating detachments in developing a more thorough mission-planning profile.

MEDICAL AREA STUDY

8-38. SFODA medics prepare medical area studies of the UWOA as part of the overall detachment area study. Sources used to prepare this study include CA area studies (available through the CA database), OGA-provided information, and reports by UN agencies and NGOs operating in the area. Because this study is continuous, the SFODA medic updates applicable portions whenever he receives new medical intelligence.

8-39. Below is a general outline for a medical area study; the format is flexible enough to allow SFODA medics to tailor the report as required:
- *General.* Provide a brief summary of the nation's health status.
- *Environmental Health Factors.* Discuss the country's topography and climate, to include effects on health, medical evacuation, and logistics.
- *Demographics.* Include population, ethnic groups, life expectancy, and infant mortality.
- *Nutrition.* Discuss nutrition and facilities for refrigeration and food inspection programs.
- *Water Supply.* Discuss the method of supply, location, treatment, and health hazards of water as they apply to drinking, bathing, and swimming.
- *Fauna of Medical Importance.* Discuss disease vectors, hosts, reservoirs, and poisonous mammals, reptiles, and spiders.
- *Flora of Medical Importance.* Cover poisonous plants, plants with medical value, and edible plants used for survival.
- *Epidemiology.* Discuss prevalent diseases and their contributing factors. Focus on diseases of military importance, including communicable diseases and susceptibility to cold and heat injury. Discuss concerns of indigenous personnel, such as physical characteristics, unique attitudes, dress, religious taboos, and psychological attributes. Discuss preventative veterinary medicine programs that deal with prevalent animal diseases and diseases that animals can give to humans.
- *Public Health and Military Medical.* Focus on public health and military medical services.
- *Village Organization.* Cover such important village concerns as social, physical, and family organization; housing; diet; water and waste disposal; local medicinal practices; and rapport with neighboring tribes.
- *Domestic Animals.* Discuss the types and uses of domestic animals and any possible religious symbolism or taboos with these animals.

MEDICAL AREA ASSESSMENT

8-40. The initial medical area assessment begins immediately upon infiltration. The SFODA medic, using needed medical skills, establishes rapport with the local population and irregular forces. The medic seizes valuable opportunities to collect intelligence and information not readily available elsewhere. Such information might include captured medical order-of-battle intelligence from medical supplies, documents obtained through battlefield recovery, and intelligence garnered from indigenous sources. The SFODA medic uses the assessment to evaluate the actual extent of medical training for the irregular force, the availability of medical supplies and facilities, and the state of the sanitation and health within the UWOA.

8-41. The medical area assessment is an evolving process based upon observations and firsthand factual reports by the deployed SFODA medic. The assessment confirms, refutes, or clarifies previously researched information reported in the medical area study. The medical area assessment provides intelligence to other units, supplements and supports area studies, and forms the basis of the after action review. Results of (and information regarding) the medical area assessment should not be transmitted out of the UWOA unless significant differences exist between previous intelligence reports that impact current or planned operations.

MEDICAL ELEMENTS WITHIN THE UNCONVENTIONAL WARFARE OPERATIONS AREA

8-42. Historically, the lack of proper medical attention leads to serious illness and disability and results in reduced irregular unit combat and irregular organizational effectiveness. Health standards in many areas are well below those of the United States. Indigenous personnel may refuse treatment because of religious beliefs or superstitions. Also, certain natives may have an acquired immunity to diseases of the area.

8-43. Sometimes, a broad range of medical support may already be available in the UWOA. Although initial treatment may be limited to rudimentary medical procedures, some irregular forces may have developed highly organized and effective medical support units and installations. Their organizations typically parallel those of conventional forces, including the establishment of field hospitals in inaccessible areas.

Medical Requirements

8-44. Medical elements that support irregular forces must be mobile, responsive, and effective to prevent disease and restore the sick and wounded to duty. In many instances, there is no safe rear area where guerrilla forces can bring casualties for treatment. Wounded and sick personnel in such environments become tactical rather than logistical problems. Medical support must be a major tactical consideration when planning all operations. The civilian infrastructure of the irregular organization contributes to medical support by setting up and operating medical facilities. Medical personnel help during guerrilla combat operations by establishing casualty collection points, thereby permitting the remaining members of the guerrilla force to continue fighting. Casualties at these collection points are evacuated to a guerrilla base or a civilian care facility when possible.

8-45. In UW scenarios, the attitudes of the sick and wounded are extremely important. The emotional importance the individual soldier attributes to the medical service goes a long way toward care and treatment. When presented with difficult conditions, medical personnel do not lower standards of care. Experience has demonstrated that a soldier can undergo major surgery under extreme hardship conditions and still demonstrate remarkable recuperative power.

Medical Net

8-46. Medical personnel keep the medical net in the UWOA as simple as possible. The medical net entails just enough to provide security and fit the estimated future expansion of the UWOA. Medical personnel refine and modify the net after it is functioning and secure. When establishing a medical net, personnel must consider the following:

- The scale of activities already in existence and those planned.
- The potential increase in strength, activities, and operations.
- The physical factors, including topography, climate, transportation, and communications.
- The number, availability, and dependability of medically qualified (and semi-qualified) personnel in the UWOA.
- The attitude of the population, the government, and the irregular organization toward medical problems and the medical standards accepted in the area.
- The existing nonmedical operational facilities of the area command.

8-47. Medical personnel may use the existing intelligence and security nets to establish a separate medical net for the collection of medical intelligence. They may also use the existing logistics net to aid in the transport of medical supplies.

8-48. UW operations typically include some level of buildup in the irregular organization and guerrilla force, to include the force multiplication of irregular medical providers throughout the medical net. Depending on the situation and operational requirements, the SFODA medic—supported by the larger ARSOF organization—begins medical training of irregular forces at the earliest possible opportunity. FM 3-05.201 contains more detailed information on irregular medical force training.

Aid Station

8-49. Mission planning includes the positioning and operation of an aid station. Medical personnel provide emergency medical treatment at this location, and it is here that the evacuation of wounded personnel from a battle begins. Because the condition of the wounded may preclude movement to the unit base, medical personnel may need to hide the injured in secure locations while they notify the auxiliary. The auxiliary can then care for and hide the wounded or evacuate them to a treatment facility when the opportunity arises. As the UWOA develops and the situation increasingly favors the sponsor, evacuation of the more seriously injured or diseased personnel to friendly areas by clandestine air evacuation or other means may become possible.

Convalescent Facility

8-50. The area where medical personnel send patients to recuperate is the convalescent facility. Medical personnel discharge patients from a convalescent facility as quickly as possible. Convalescent facilities may be located in a safe house, where one or two convalescents may recuperate with their necessary cover stories; they may be located in any base camp in guerrilla-controlled areas or even outside of the UWOA.

Guerrilla Hospital

8-51. The guerrilla hospital is a medical treatment facility (MTF) or complex of smaller facilities that provides inpatient medical support to the guerrilla force. A guerrilla hospital is established during the classic organization and buildup phases of a resistance organization. The guerrilla hospital must be ready for operation at the start of any combat operations and must continue to provide medical support until directed otherwise. The hospital is generally located in the UWOA it supports; however, considerations of METT-TC may dictate otherwise. An indigenous medical officer—with advice and assistance of the U.S. SF group or battalion surgeon—will typically command the guerrilla hospital, although circumstances within the UWOA may require the group or battalion surgeon to serve as the commander.

8-52. The guerrilla hospital rarely (if ever) outwardly resembles a conventional hospital. The requirement for strict security, flexibility, and rapid mobility precludes visible comparison with conventional military or civilian MTFs. As the irregular forces consolidate their hold on the UWOA, all medical support functions also tend to consolidate. Safe areas allow the establishment of a centralized system of medical care. Sophisticated hospitals permit care that is more elaborate, because they provide a wider selection of trained personnel, specialized equipment, and the capability of more extensive and prolonged treatment. Guerrilla hospital considerations include the following:

- Location.
- Security.
- Communications.
- Medical supplies.
- Sections.

AVIATION SUPPORT

8-53. The SOAR is an integral part of ARSOF. Special operations aviation (SOA) units can operate as part of a SOTF or a JSOTF. They give the ground commander a means to infiltrate, resupply, and extract ARSOF. Since irregular forces supported in UW would rarely have aviation assets during the conduct of a UW campaign, SOAR support of ARSOF in UW resembles support to other SO in virtually all aspects. To properly employ the SOAR, commanders must understand the characteristics of SO in general and SOAR support of ARSOF UW in particular.

MISSION

8-54. The mission of the 160th SOAR in UW is to plan, conduct, and support ARSOF by clandestinely penetrating nonhostile, hostile, or denied airspace. The SOAR conducts air operations to support UW in any operational environment across the spectrum of conflict.

Chapter 8

MISSION-ESSENTIAL AND BATTLE TASKS PERTINENT TO UNCONVENTIONAL WARFARE

8-55. The mission-essential and battle tasks for SOAR pertinent to UW are to—
- Infiltrate, resupply, and exfiltrate U.S. ARSOF and other selected personnel.
- Insert and extract ARSOF land and maritime assault vehicles and vessels.
- Conduct DA or close air support (CAS) using organic attack helicopters to provide aerial firepower and terminal guidance for precision munitions, unilaterally or with other ARSOF.
- Provide forward air control for U.S. and multinational CAS and indirect fires in support of ARSOF UW.
- Conduct SR missions in support of ARSOF UW.
- Conduct electronic, photographic, and visual reconnaissance in support of ARSOF UW.
- Conduct limited electronic warfare (EW) in support of ARSOF UW.
- Recover personnel or sensitive materiel in support of ARSOF.
- Conduct assisted evasion and recovery when dedicated combat search and rescue (CSAR) assets are unavailable in support of ARSOF.
- Perform emergency air evacuation of ARSOF personnel during the conduct of UW.
- Conduct ARSOF water insertion and recovery operations in support of UW.
- Support and facilitate ground and aerial command, control, communications, computers, and intelligence operations for ARSOF UW.
- Provide the C2 element, when augmented with required USAF assets, specialties, and communications equipment, for SOA assets and attached conventional aviation assets supporting ARSOF UW.

EMPLOYMENT CONSIDERATIONS

8-56. The SOAR provides ARSOF the capability to penetrate hostile or denied territory and to accomplish UW missions. SOAR units have specialized aircraft with sophisticated state-of-the-art special mission equipment. SOAR aircrews undergo intense training in the tactical employment of the aircraft and the execution of SOA tasks. The SOAR supports the JFC's UW campaign plan throughout all phases, throughout the spectrum of conflict, and inside or outside of any designated UWOA. The SOAR should exploit the darkness, adverse weather conditions, and extended range and navigation systems to penetrate hostile territory from unexpected avenues of approach in the execution of tasks that support the UW campaign. Although organic SOAR assets can support most required tasks in UW, occasionally the need for flexibility and the limited range of rotary-wing assets will require support from sister Services. Moreover, the requirement for low visibility of many UW operations may require SOAR support from OGA-provided aviation assets.

8-57. SOAR missions and activities fall into two categories: direct and indirect. Direct contact with the adversary applies military resources to accomplish a task without relying on indigenous or surrogate forces not under direct U.S. control. Indirect contact with the adversary applies military resources to train, advise, or assist interagency activities, nations important to U.S. interests, or irregular surrogate forces pursuing objectives that further U.S. interests. These categories are not mutually exclusive. However, SOAR activities in UW will be predominantly in support of ARSOF interaction with irregular forces; direct contact with the adversary in UW will be the exception.

8-58. During UW, the SOAR supports the commander by conducting air movement of supported ARSOF teams, indigenous forces, and supplies. These air movements require the SOAR to conduct covert or clandestine penetration, precision navigation, and long-range infiltration and exfiltration. The SOAR can extract U.S., allied, or irregular personnel recovered by the unconventional assisted-recovery mechanism, a capability which is particularly relevant to UW. In addition, the SOAR can provide training and other support to irregular forces using nonstandard aviation platforms, equipment, and procedures.

Appendix A
The Diplomatic Instrument of National Power

INTERNATIONAL POLITICAL SYSTEM

A-1. Throughout history, mankind has existed in an environment of informational (cultural, philosophical, religious, mythical, and so on) and economic competition and a spectrum of conflict ranging from individual duels to societal wars of annihilation. This was an essentially anarchic environment, and force was the final judge between competition and conflict. Through natural development and for mutual protection, groups formed around kinship, ethnicity, and shared mythology and developed into historically identifiable bands, clans, tribes, and nations ("peoples") to compete and conflict more effectively. Starting in early modern Europe, many people recognized these groups as distinct sovereign states, increasingly aligned over time with a perceived distinct national identity.

INTERNATIONAL SYSTEM OF STATES

A-2. A state is a set of institutions that possess the authority to make the rules that govern the people in one or more societies, having internal sovereignty over a definite territory. The state includes institutions, such as the armed forces, civil service or state bureaucracy, courts, and police. By Max Weber's influential definition, a state has a "monopoly on the legitimate use of physical force within a given territory." By modern practice and the law of international relations, a state's sovereignty is not conditional upon the diplomatic recognition of the state's claim to independence by other states. However, the capacity of a state to enter into various international relations and treaties is conditional upon such recognition. Degrees of recognition and sovereignty may vary. However, any degree of recognition, even the majority recognition, is not binding on third-party states.

A-3. Within sovereign states, the ruling government uses all of the instruments of national ("state") power on its own people. The government is the political authority; it establishes and enforces the law, manages and develops the economy and allocates state finances, disseminates state-supporting information and gathers internal intelligence, and relies on the military as the final guarantor of internal state power.

A-4. Although the term often refers broadly to all institutions of government or rule—ancient and modern—the modern state system bears a number of characteristics that first consolidated in Western Europe, beginning in earnest in the 17th century. Since the late 19th century, all of the world's inhabitable land has been parceled up into states; earlier, quite large land areas had been either unclaimed or uninhabited or inhabited by nomadic peoples who were not organized as states.

A-5. Governments now used the same instruments of power that they had previously used internally against other states in interstate competition and conflict in an otherwise anarchic international environment. State governments could employ each of these instruments as a weapon in pursuit of their own interests. Despite the increased power of states, the international environment was still largely anarchic with each sovereign state interpreting international conduct by its own calculation. Using a mix of power instruments, groups of states formed ever-shifting blocks of alliance in the pursuit of advantage.

A-6. After the world wars of the 20th century, participating nations formed the UN. An increasing body of international law sought to reduce the anarchy in the international environment. Today's international environment is characterized by states—constrained by international law—using all of their instruments of national power for competition and conflict.

A-7. In the late 20th century, the globalization of the world economy, the mobility of people and capital, and the rise of many international institutions all combined to restrict the freedom of action of states. However, the state remains the basic political unit of the world and, therefore, the state is the most central concept in the study of politics. Currently, more than 200 states make up the international community, with the vast majority represented in the UN.

Appendix A

A-8. In casual usage, the terms "country," "nation," and "state" are often used synonymously, but in a more strict usage, they are distinguished as follows:
- Country is the geographical area.
- Nation designates a people; however, national and international both confusingly refer as well to matters pertaining to what are strictly states, as in national capital or international law.
- State refers to a set of governing institutions with sovereignty over a definite territory.

CURRENT GLOBAL GOVERNANCE SYSTEM

A-9. The UN is the primary formal organization coordinating activities between states on a global scale and the only intergovernmental organization with a truly universal membership (192 governments). In addition to the main organs and various humanitarian programs and commissions of the UN itself, there are about 20 functional organizations affiliated with the UN's Economic and Social Council (ECOSOC), such as the World Health Organization, the International Labor Organization (ILO), and International Telecommunications Union. Of particular interest politically are the WB, the IMF, and the World Trade Organization (WTO).

A-10. The WB and the IMF were formed together in Bretton Woods, New Hampshire in 1944 to foster global monetary cooperation and to fight poverty by financially assisting states in need. The WTO sets the rules of international trade. It has a semilegislative body (the General Council, reaching decisions by consensus) and a judicial body (the Dispute Settlement Body). Another influential international economic organization is the OECD, with a membership of 30 democratic members. A less formal but highly influential organization in global politics is the G8, an association of eight of the richest and most technologically advanced democracies in the world. The leaders of the G8 countries meet annually in person to coordinate their policies for confronting global issues, such as poverty, terrorism, infectious diseases, and climate change.

A-11. Militarily, the UN usually deploys only peacekeeping forces to build and maintain postconflict peace and stability. When a more aggressive international military action is undertaken, either ad hoc coalitions (for example, the MNF in Iraq) or regional military alliances (for example, NATO) are typically used.

A-12. International law encompasses international treaties, customs, and globally accepted legal principles. With the exceptions of cases brought before the International Criminal Court (ICC) and the International Court of Justice (ICJ), national courts interpret the laws. The ICJ (also known as the World Court) is the judiciary organ of the UN. It settles disputes voluntarily submitted to it by states (only) and gives advisory opinions on legal questions submitted to it by other organs of the UN, such as the General Assembly or Security Council. The ICC is a recent development in international law; it is the first permanent international criminal court. The ICC was established to ensure that the gravest international crimes do not go unpunished. One-hundred and thirty-nine national governments signed the ICC treaty. By October 2005, 100 of those nations had ratified the treaty into law.

A-13. In addition to the formal or semiformal international organizations and laws mentioned above, many other mechanisms regulate human activities across national borders. In particular, international trade in goods, services, and currencies (the "global market") has a tremendous impact on the lives of people in almost all parts of the world, creating deep interdependency among nations through globalization. Transnational (or multinational) corporations, some with resources exceeding those available to most governments, govern activities of people on a global scale. The rapid increase in the volume of transborder digital communications and mass-media distribution (for example, the Internet and satellite television [TV]) has allowed information, ideas, and opinions to rapidly spread across the world, creating a complex web of international coordination and influence, mostly outside the control of any formal organizations or laws.

INTERNATIONAL LAW

A-14. Codified or habitual relations and conduct between nations has developed over millennia of "natural law." The first formal attempts to develop modern international law stem from renaissance Europe and the

gradual development of the European national state. By the beginning of the 17th century, several generalizations could be made about the political situation:
- Self-governing, autonomous states existed; the Peace of Westphalia established states as sovereigns answering to no one within their own borders.
- Monarchs governed almost all states.
- Land, wealth, and trading rights were often the topics of wars between states.

A-15. The growth of nationalism in the 19th century pushed natural law farther from the legal realm. Commercial law became nationalized into private international law, distinct from public international law. The Congress of Vienna in 1815 marked formal recognition of the political and international legal system based on the conditions of Europe.

A-16. After World War I, many states decided to form an international League of Nations in the hope of preventing such conflicts. However, because of political wrangling in the U.S. Congress, the United States did not join the League of Nations, even though it was an initiative of U.S. President Wilson. When WWII broke out, the League of Nations foundered. Nevertheless, on 1 January 1942, U.S. President Roosevelt issued the "declaration by united nations" on behalf of 26 nations that had pledged to fight against the axis powers. Even before the end of the war, representatives of 50 nations met in San Francisco, California, to draw up the charter for an international body to replace the League of Nations. On 24 October 1945, the UN officially came into existence, setting a basis for much international law to follow.

A-17. In a global economy, law is global too. International law plays an increasingly important part in people's lives. The goods bought, the services consumed, and the work done by people are increasingly integrated with people far across the planet. International law can refer to three things:
- Public international law.
- Private international law or conflict of laws.
- Law of supranational organizations.

PUBLIC INTERNATIONAL LAW

A-18. Public international law concerns the structure and conduct of states and international organizations. The UN, founded under the UN charter and the Universal Declaration of Human Rights, is the most important international organization. Other international agreements, like the Geneva Conventions on the conduct of war and international bodies, such as the ILO, the WTO, or the IMF, also form a growing part of public international law. To a lesser degree, international law also affects multinational corporations and individuals, an impact increasingly evolving beyond domestic legal interpretation and enforcement. Public international law has increased in use and importance vastly over the 20th century, mainly because of the increase in global trade, armed conflict, environmental deterioration on a worldwide scale, human rights violations, rapid and vast increases in international transportation, and a boom in global communications. Public international law also is also known as the "law of nations." Public international law is not the same as "private international law," which is concerned with the resolution of conflicting laws.

Scope of Public International Law

A-19. Public international law establishes the framework and the criteria for identifying states as the principal actors in the international legal system. The existence of a state presupposes control and jurisdiction over territory. International law deals with the acquisition of territory, state immunity, and the legal responsibility of states in their conduct with each other. International law is similarly concerned with the treatment of individuals within state boundaries. Thus, there is a comprehensive regime dealing with group rights, treatment of aliens, rights of refugees, international crimes, nationality problems, and human rights in general. This regime further includes the important functions of the maintenance of international peace and security, arms control, the peaceable settlement of disputes, and the regulation of the use of force in international relations. Even when the law is not able to stop the outbreak of war, it has developed principles to govern the conduct of hostilities and the treatment of prisoners.

A-20. International law also governs issues relating to the global environment, the global commons, such as international waters, outer space, global communications, and world trade. Whereas municipal law is

Appendix A

hierarchical or vertical in its structure (meaning that a legislature enacts binding legislation), international law is horizontal in nature (meaning that all states are sovereign and theoretically equal). As a result of the notion of sovereignty, the value and authority of international law is dependent upon the voluntary participation of states in its formulation, observance, and enforcement. Although there may be exceptions, most states enter into legal commitments with other states out of enlightened self-interest rather than adherence to a body of law that is higher than their own.

A-21. Breaches of international law raise difficult questions for lawyers and statesmen. Since international law has no established compulsory judicial system for the settlement of disputes or a coercive penal system, managing breaches of international law is not as straightforward as managing breaches within a domestic legal system. However, there are ways that parties bring breaches to the attention of the international community, and there are ways to resolve conflict. For example, there are judicial or quasi-judicial tribunals in international law for certain areas, such as trade and human rights. The founders of the UN, for example, created the organization as a means for the world community to enforce international law upon members that violate its charter through the Security Council.

A-22. Traditionally, states and the Vatican were the sole subjects of international law. With the proliferation of international organizations over the last century, some organizations have been recognized as relevant parties as well. Recent interpretations of international human rights law, international humanitarian law, and international trade law have been inclusive of corporations, and even of certain individuals.

Sources of International Law

A-23. Public international law has three primary sources: international treaties, customary, and general principles of law. *International treaty law* includes obligations states expressly and voluntarily accept between themselves in treaties. *Customary international law* derives from the consistent practice of states accompanied by legal opinion that legal obligation requires the consistent practice. Those practicing international law traditionally look to judgments of international tribunals, as well as scholarly works, as persuasive sources for custom in addition to direct evidence of state behavior. Attempts to codify customary international law gained momentum after WWII with the formation of the International Law Commission (ILC), under the guidance of the UN. The binding interpretation of the underlying custom by agreement through treaty codifies customary law. For states not party to such treaties, the work of the ILC may still be accepted as custom applying to those states. *General principles of law* are those commonly recognized by the major legal systems of the world. Certain norms of international law achieve binding force to include all states with no permissible deviations. When there are disputes about the exact meaning and application of national laws, it is the responsibility of the courts to decide what the law means. In international law, there are no courts with the authority to do this. It is generally the responsibility of states to interpret the law for themselves. Unsurprisingly, this means that there is rarely agreement in cases of dispute.

A-24. Since international law exists in a legal environment without an overarching "sovereign," enforcement of international law is very different from enforcement in the domestic context. In many cases, enforcement takes on characteristics where the norm is self-enforcing. In other cases, defection from the norm can pose a real risk, particularly if the international environment is changing. When this happens and enough states (or enough powerful states) continually ignore a particular aspect of international law, the norm may actually change according to concepts of customary international law.

A-25. Apart from a state's natural inclination to uphold certain norms, the force of international law has always come from the pressure that states put upon one another to behave consistently and to honor their obligations. As with any system of law, many violations of international law obligations are overlooked. If addressed, it is usually done purely through diplomacy and the consequences of unwanted behavior upon an offending state's reputation. Though violations may be common in fact, states try to avoid the appearance of having disregarded international obligations. States may also unilaterally adopt sanctions against one another, such as the severance of economic or diplomatic ties or through reciprocal action. In some cases, domestic courts may render judgment against a foreign state (the realm of private international law) for an injury, though this is a complicated area of law where international law intersects with domestic law. States have the right to employ force in self-defense against an offending state that has used force to attack its territory or political independence. States may also use force in collective self-defense against another state.

A-26. The primary branches of public international law today include—
- International criminal law.
- Use-of-force law.
- International human rights law.
- International humanitarian law.
- Maritime law.
- Diplomatic law.
- Consular law.
- State responsibility law.
- International environmental law.
- International trade law.
- International space law.
- International aviation law.

PRIVATE INTERNATIONAL LAW

A-27. Private international law (or conflict of laws) is that branch of international law and interstate law that regulates all lawsuits involving a "foreign law" element, where a difference in result will occur depending on which laws are applied. First, it is concerned with determining whether the proposed forum has jurisdiction to adjudicate and is the appropriate venue for dealing with the dispute. Second, it is concerned with determining which of the competing state's laws the determining body will use to resolve the dispute. It also deals with the enforcement of foreign judgments. The object is the resolution of conflicts between competing law systems rather than resolution of the conflict itself.

SUPRANATIONAL LAW

A-28. The European Union (EU) is the only example of a supranational legal framework, where sovereign nations have pooled their authority through a system of courts and political institutions. It constitutes a new legal order in international law intended for the mutual social and economic benefit of the member states. EU law operates alongside the laws of the member states that have chosen by consent to limit some of their sovereign rights within certain limited fields.

INTERNATIONAL ORGANIZATIONS

A-29. An international organization, or more formally IGO, is an organization, such as the European Community or the WTO, with sovereign states or other IGOs as members. Such organizations function according to the principles of intergovernmentalism, which means that unanimity is required. NGOs are private organizations that can also be international in scope. Generally and correctly used, however, the term "international organization" is reserved for intergovernmental organizations only.

LEGAL NATURE

A-30. Legally speaking, a treaty must establish an international organization, which provides it with legal recognition. International organizations so established are subjects of international law, capable of entering into agreements among themselves or with states. Thus, international organizations in a legal sense are distinguished from mere groupings of states, such as the G8 and the G-77, neither of which have been founded by treaty, though in nonlegal contexts these are sometimes referred to as international organizations as well. International organizations must also be distinguished from treaties; although all international organizations are founded on a treaty, many treaties (for example, the North American Free Trade Agreement [NAFTA]) do not establish an international organization and rely purely on the member parties for their administration.

Appendix A

MEMBERSHIP AND FUNCTION

A-31. International organizations differ in function, membership, and membership criteria. Membership of some organizations (global organizations) is open to all the nations of the world. This category includes the UN and its specialized agencies and the WTO. Other organizations are only open to members from a particular region or continent of the world, like the EU, African Union, Association of Southeast Asian Nations (ASEAN), and so on. Finally, some organizations base their membership on other criteria, such as—

- Cultural or historical links (for example, the Commonwealth of Nations, la Francophonie, the Community of Portuguese Language Countries, and the Latin Union).
- Level of economic development or type of economy (for example, OECD and Organization of Petroleum-Exporting Countries [OPEC]).
- Religion (for example, Organization of the Islamic Conference).

Were it to come about, the ultimate international organization would be a federal world government.

Global and Regional Organizations

A-32. Examples of global organizations include the following:
- UN, its specialized agencies, and associated organizations.
- International Criminal Police Organization (INTERPOL).
- International Hydrographic Organization.
- WTO.
- Universal Postal Union.
- International Red Cross (IRC) and Red Crescent movement.

Figures A-1 through A-3, pages A-6 and A-7, show examples of regional organizations.

Financial International Organizations

A-33. Examples of financial international organizations include the following:
- Bank for International Settlements.
- IMF.
- The WB group.

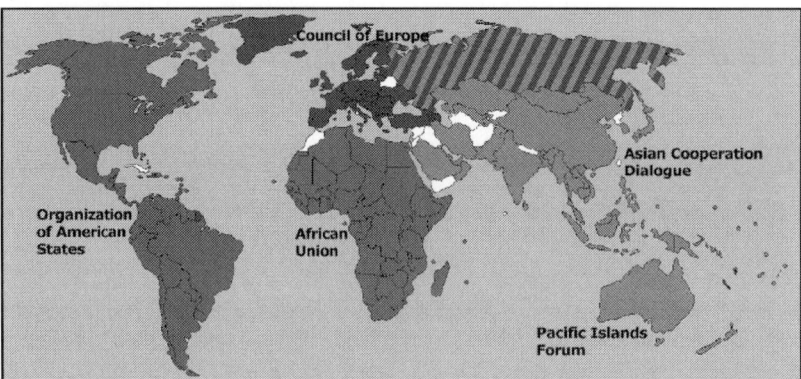

Figure A-1. Organizations grouping almost all countries in their respective continents

NOTE: Russia is a member of both the Council of Europe and the Asia Cooperation Dialogue, and Cuba is currently a suspended member of the Organization of American States.

The Diplomatic Instrument of National Power

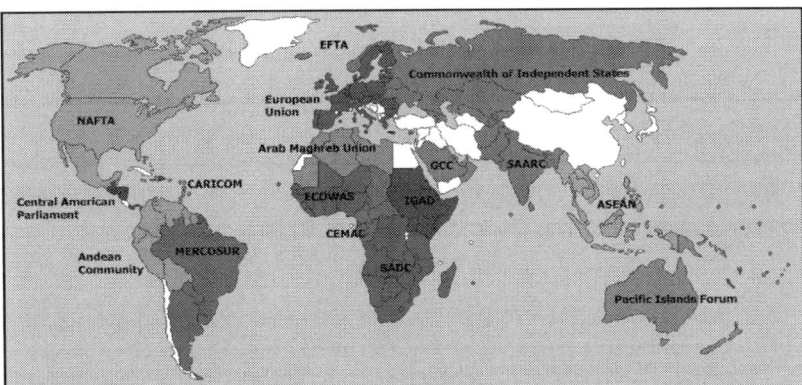

Figure A-2. Several smaller regional organizations with nonoverlapping memberships

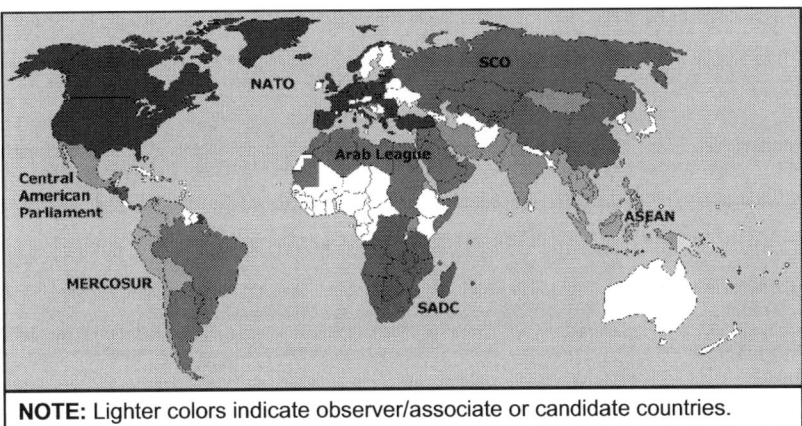

Figure A-3. Several nonoverlapping large alliances

Nongovernmental Organizations

A-34. The term "nongovernmental organization" is used in a variety of ways all over the world and, depending on the context in which it is used, can refer to many different types of organizations. In its broadest sense, an NGO is one that is not directly part of the structure of government. Depending on how an NGO is defined, they number in the 10,000s to several million worldwide.

History of Nongovernmental Organizations

A-35. Though voluntary associations of citizens have existed throughout history, NGOs along the lines seen today, especially on the international level, have developed in the past two centuries. One of the first such organizations, the IRC, was founded in 1863. The IRC and Red Crescent movement are the world's largest group of humanitarian NGOs. The phrase "nongovernmental organization" came into use with the establishment of the UN organization in 1945 with provisions in Article 71 of Chapter 10 of the UN charter for a consultative role for organizations that are neither governments nor member states. Resolution 288(x) of the UN ECOSOC on 27 February 1950 first gives the definition of international nongovernmental organization. The resolution defines an international nongovernmental organization as "any international organization that is not founded by an international treaty."

Appendix A

Types of Nongovernmental Organizations

A-36. NGOs are also known by alternative terms, such as independent sector, volunteer sector, civic society, grassroots organizations, transnational social movement organizations, private voluntary organizations, self-help organizations, and nonstate actors. NGOs are a dissimilar group. Some focus on small-scale relief or development, others do the same on much larger scales, and still others are primarily political organizations. The USAID refers to NGOs as "private voluntary organizations." However, many scholars have argued that this definition is highly problematic as many NGOs are in fact state and corporate funded and projects are managed with professional staffs.

A-37. There are also numerous classifications of NGOs. The typology the WB uses divides them into operational and advocacy:

- The primary purpose of an *operational* NGO is the design and implementation of development-related projects. One categorization that is frequently used is the division into relief-oriented or development-oriented organizations. They can also be classified according to whether they stress service delivery or participation, whether they are religious or secular, and whether they are more public or private. Operational NGOs can be community-based, national, or international.
- The primary purpose of an *advocacy* NGO is to defend or promote a specific cause. As opposed to operational project management, these organizations typically try to raise awareness, acceptance, and knowledge by lobbying, working with the press, and conducting activist events. An example of this type of NGO is Amnesty International, the largest human rights organization in the world. It forms a global community of human rights defenders with more than 1.8 million members, supporters, and subscribers in over 150 countries and territories.

Purposes and Methods

A-38. NGOs exist for a variety of purposes, usually to further the political or social goals of their members or funders. Examples include improving the state of the natural environment, encouraging the observance of human rights, improving the welfare of the disadvantaged, or representing a corporate agenda. However, there is a huge number of such organizations, and their goals cover a broad range of political and philosophical positions. These goals can also easily be applied to private schools and athletic organizations. NGOs also vary in their methods. Some primarily act as lobbyists, while others primarily conduct programs and activities.

Public Relations

A-39. NGOs need healthy relationships with the public to meet their goals. Foundations and charities use sophisticated public relations campaigns to raise funds and employ standard lobbying techniques with governments. Interest groups may be of political importance because of their ability to influence social and political outcomes. Some NGOs seek to mobilize public support.

Consulting

A-40. Many international NGOs have a consultative status with UN agencies relevant to their area of work. As an example, the Third World Network has a consultative status with the UN Conference on Trade and Development and the ECOSOC. In 1946, only 41 NGOs had consultative status with the ECOSOC. By 2003, this number had risen to 2,350.

Project Management

A-41. Management techniques are crucial to project success in NGOs. Generally, private NGOs private have a community or environmental focus. They address a variety of issues such as religion, emergency aid, and humanitarian affairs. They mobilize public support and voluntary contributions for aid. They often have strong links with community groups in developing countries and they often work in areas where government-to-government aid is not possible. States accept NGOs as a part of the international relations landscape. While they influence national and multilateral policy-making, their direct involvement in local action is increasing.

Funding

A-42. Large NGOs may have annual budgets in the millions of dollars. For instance, the budget of the American Association of Retired Persons was over $540 million dollars in 1999. Human Rights Watch spent and received $21.7 million U.S. dollars in 2003. Funding such large budgets demands significant fund-raising efforts on the part of most NGOs. Major sources of NGO funding include membership dues, the sale of goods and services, grants from international institutions or national governments, and private donations. Several EU grants provide funds accessible to NGOs.

A-43. Even though the term NGO implies independence of governments, some NGOs depend heavily on governments for their funding. The EU and the British government donated a quarter of the U.S. $162 million income in 1998 of the famine-relief organization OXFAM. The Christian relief and development organization World Vision collected $55 million (U.S.) worth of goods in 1998 from the American government. Médecins Sans Frontières (known in English as Doctors Without Borders) gets 46 percent of its income from government sources.

Legal Status, Criticism, and the Monitoring and Control of Nongovernmental Organizations

A-44. NGOs are not legal entities under international law. An exception is the International Committee of the Red Cross, which states consider a legal entity under international law because the organization's basis it the Geneva Convention. In general, states view NGOs as a beneficial and complementary source filling gaps in society not provided by the public or for-profit sectors. NGOs have also played a crucial role in upholding international law, especially UN treaties. However, critics argue that although NGOs have good intentions, they undermine outcomes.

A-45. Conservative critics have maintained that NGOs too often conflict with states activities, going so far as to subvert government actions, violate the law, and make common cause with criminals and terrorists. Progressive critics have suggested that imperialism and NGOs share a fine line. One of the first modern NGOs, for example, was the American Colonization Society that founded Liberia. Other famous examples include various Christian missionaries throughout the Americas, Asia, and Africa during colonial times.

A-46. Although most complaint literature is against multilateral or bilateral agencies, there are occasional criticisms of NGO operational strategies and inadvertent adverse impacts. For example, it is often argued that in poorer countries, northern-funded and managed NGOs tend to act as substitutes for popular movements in forums, like the World Social Forum, with negative consequences for the development of local civil society. In many developing countries with dysfunctional economies, entry into the aid industry is the most profitable professional career path for young college graduates. As NGOs provide services in the community for free or at subsidized rates (such as training), the private sector is unable to evolve and compete effectively at sustainable levels. If an NGO begins offering products or services for a fee (handicrafts, evaluations, digging wells, counseling, and so on), it eventually becomes a competitor with private-sector providers of these same services. However, with its donation-funding support or access to voluntary labor, the NGO has a significant competitive advantage.

A-47. Additional areas of concern include co-option (by political or other forces), mission-drift, changing core services based on an ever-changing funding landscape, transparency, accountability, moving beyond a charismatic founding leader, and donor-driven rather than self-defined strategies. New NGOs occasionally receive "do-gooder" complaints of engaging in action to help without understanding the full complexity and interplay of issues, which results in more harm than good.

UNITED STATES POLITICAL POWER IN THE INTERNATIONAL ENVIRONMENT

A-48. The international environment includes all modes of human interaction. This environment is not limited strictly to official political interaction between countries. Nevertheless, states generally consider international political power and foreign policy functions of sovereign nation-state governments. States primarily contend politically through government-to-government diplomacy and by leveraging the UN and international law against one another.

Appendix A

A-49. A state's foreign policy is a set of political goals that seeks to outline how that particular state will interact with other states of the world and, to a lesser extent, nonstate actors. Politicians generally design foreign policies to help guide and protect a state's national interests, national security, ideological goals, and economic prosperity. Successful foreign policy occurs as the result of peaceful cooperation with other states, wherever possible, through the exploitation of all instruments of national power. States may employ the military instrument of power up to the level of general war when differences between states are irreconcilable. The United States also uses the military instrument of power as the ultimate guarantor of U.S. foreign policy. Virtually every state in the world is now able to interact with one another in some diplomatic form. In many states, foreign policy ranks high on the list of factors that influence public opinion. The national and cultural values of all states and the foreign policy positions and activities that reflect those values have their disputants. Such is the nature of a large complex world with a troubled and imperfect history, finite resources, and differences of international perspective.

UNITED STATES FOREIGN POLICY

A-50. U.S. foreign relations are marked by a large economy, well-funded military, and notable political influence. According to estimates given in the Central Intelligence Agency (CIA) World Fact Book, the United States has the world's largest economy, the world's most well-funded military, and a large amount of political influence. The officially stated goals of U.S. foreign policy are—

- Protecting the safety and freedom of all American citizens, both within the United States and abroad.
- Protecting allied nations of the United States from attack or invasion and creating mutually beneficial international defense arrangements and partnerships to ensure this.
- Promoting peace, freedom (most notably of speech and enterprise), and democracy in all regions of the world.
- Furthering free trade, unencumbered by tariffs, interdictions, and other economic barriers, and furthering capitalism to foster economic growth, improve living conditions, and promote the sale and mobility of U.S. products to international consumers.
- Bringing developmental and humanitarian aid to foreign peoples in need.

DECISION MAKING

A-51. The President negotiates treaties with foreign states. The President is also Commander in Chief of the military. As the Commander in Chief, the President has broad authority over the armed forces once they deploy. The Secretary of State is the "foreign minister" of the United States and is the primary conductor of state-to-state diplomacy. The U.S. Congress has the power to declare war, but the President has the ability to commit military troops to an area for 60 days without congressional approval (though in all cases, Congress has granted approval afterward). The U.S. Senate also holds the exclusive right to approve treaties made by the President. Congress is likewise responsible for passing bills that determine the general character and policies of U.S. foreign policy. The Supreme Court traditionally has played a minimal role in foreign policy.

DIPLOMATIC RELATIONS

A-52. The United States has one of the largest diplomatic presences of any state. Almost every state in the world has both a U.S. Embassy and an embassy of its own in Washington, DC. Only a few nations do not have formal diplomatic relations with the United States. They are Bhutan, Cuba, Iran, North Korea, Somalia (no widely recognized government), Sudan, Republic of China (Taiwan), and Western Sahara (not recognized). In practical terms, however, this lack of formal relations does not impede the United States' communication with these states. In areas where no U.S. diplomatic post exists, the United Kingdom (UK), Canada, Switzerland, or another friendly third-party nation conducts American relations. In the case of the Republic of China, the American Institute in Taiwan conducts de facto relations. The United States also operates an Interests Section in Havana. Although this does not create a formal diplomatic relationship, it fulfills most other typical embassy functions. The United States maintains a normal trade relations list. There are several states excluded from the list, which means that their exports to the United States are subject to significantly higher tariffs.

ALLIES

A-53. The United States is a founding member of NATO, the world's largest military alliance. The 26-state alliance consists of Canada and much of Europe. Under the NATO Charter, the United States is compelled to defend any NATO state attacked by a foreign power. These mutual defense obligations are restricted to within the North American and European areas, and for this reason, the United States was not compelled to participate in the Falklands War between Argentina and the UK. The United States has also given major non-NATO ally status to fourteen states. Each such state has a unique relationship with the United States, involving various military and economic partnerships and alliances.

INSTRUMENTS OF UNITED STATES DIPLOMATIC POWER

A-54. The following paragraphs discuss the instruments of official U.S. diplomatic power as contained within the charter of the U.S. Department of State. However, many other USG departments, agencies, and other organizations play an adjunct or de facto diplomatic role under DOS leadership.

DEPARTMENT OF STATE

A-55. The DOS leads the United States in its relationships with foreign governments, international organizations, and the people of other countries. It aims to provide a free, prosperous, and secure world. The management of these relationships is called diplomacy. Diplomacy is vital to the United States because it is how the DOS formulates, implements, and represents to other nations the foreign policy goals of the President. Diplomacy is vital to U.S. interests. The DOS is a vital part of the USG because it—

- Represents the United States overseas and conveys U.S. policies to foreign governments and international organizations through American embassies and consulates in foreign countries and diplomatic missions.
- Negotiates and concludes agreements and treaties on issues ranging from trade to nuclear weapons.
- Coordinates and supports international activities of other U.S. agencies, hosts official visits, and performs other diplomatic missions.
- Leads interagency coordination and manages the allocation of resources for foreign relations.

A-56. There are more than 190 states in the world and the United States maintains diplomatic relations with some 180 of them, as well as with many international organizations. Advances in travel, trade, and technology have made the world more interconnected today than ever before, making interactions with other countries and their citizens more important for the United States. The DOS has four main foreign policy goals:

- Protect the United States and Americans.
- Advance democracy, human rights, and other global interests.
- Promote international understanding of American values and policies.
- Support U.S. diplomats, government officials, and all other personnel at home and abroad who make these goals a reality.

A-57. Diplomacy is one of the best ways to protect the United States and the American people. The United States uses diplomacy with other states of the world to successfully deal with a number of challenges that cross state boundaries and affect Americans in the United States, including—

- Terrorism.
- WMD.
- Human immunodeficiency virus/acquired immune deficiency syndrome and other infectious diseases.
- Illegal drug trafficking and crime.
- Humanitarian needs of migrants and refugees.
- Environmental degradation.

Appendix A

A-58. Americans at home and abroad face threats to their physical and economic well-being. The DOS protects the nation, its people, and its prosperity by helping to—
- Prevent terrorist attacks and strengthen international alliances to defeat global terrorism.
- Ensure America's homeland security by promoting policies and practices to keep travel, trade, and important infrastructure safe.
- Provide guidelines to manage the entry of visitors to the United States.
- Promote stability in all regions of the world.
- Prevent enemies from threatening the United States or its allies with WMD.
- Reduce the impact of international crime and illegal drugs on Americans.
- Protect and assist American citizens who travel, conduct business, and live abroad.

A-59. The following paragraphs discuss some of the many ways the DOS uses diplomacy to protect America.

Fighting Terrorism

A-60. After the attacks on 11 September 2001, the United States learned firsthand the serious threat it faces from terrorists and from states supporting them. The terrorists who performed these attacks had no respect for human life or state borders. Terrorists threaten not only Americans but also all people who believe in freedom and democracy. They are the enemy of all civilized states. They will be defeated only through the united action of states throughout the world. To provide leadership in the fight against terrorism, the DOS works with other U.S. agencies and foreign governments to—
- Identify terrorist organizations and states that support terrorists.
- Investigate the activities of terrorist organizations.
- Shut down terrorist financial networks.
- Bring terrorists to justice.

Department of State Support to Homeland Security

A-61. Security for Americans begins at home but extends beyond its borders. In pursuit of homeland security, the DOS conducts visa operations and leads U.S. diplomatic efforts to gain international cooperation on measures to deter threats to travel, communications, and other critical infrastructure networks—information systems, transportation, and energy—and to secure America's borders. The DOS also carefully reviews more than 7 million visa applications per year. The visa regulations help ensure that no visas are approved for foreign citizens who might harm the nation, thereby keeping America safe while continuing to welcome citizens from around the globe.

Regional Stability

A-62. The DOS uses diplomacy in all regions of the world to keep local conflicts from becoming wider wars that may harm U.S. interests. The DOS joins with other countries in international organizations to promote stability and economic prosperity.

Weapons of Mass Destruction

A-63. WMD—such as nuclear, chemical, or biological weapons—pose a serious danger to the United States and the world. The United States must be concerned about the possibility that terrorists may acquire these weapons for use against innocent people. The DOS works to ensure that more countries do not obtain these weapons and to verify that other countries are honoring international agreements restricting such weapons.

Democracy and Human Rights

A-64. Democracy and the protection of fundamental liberties were the basis for the creation of the United States more than 200 years ago. Since then, a central goal of U.S. foreign policy has been to promote respect for democracy and human rights throughout the world. The DOS—

- Promotes democracy as a way to achieve security, stability, and prosperity for the entire world.
- Helps establish and assist newly formed democracies.
- Identifies and denounces regimes that deny their citizens the right to choose their leaders in elections that are free and fair.

A-65. Human rights are a crucial foundation to create and maintain democracy. The DOS works to promote human rights in those countries where democracy is not firmly established. The DOS—

- Holds governments accountable to their promises to uphold universal human rights.
- Promotes greater respect for human rights, including freedom from torture, freedom of speech and other expression, freedom of religion, freedom of press, protection of the rights of women and children, and protection of minorities.
- Promotes the rule of law, such as fair judicial and voting procedures.
- Helps reform and strengthen the UN Commission on Human Rights.
- Coordinates support for human rights with America's allies.
- Releases an annual report on human rights practices.

Refugees, Migration, and Population Growth

A-66. The DOS helps millions of refugees and victims of conflict or natural disasters around the world. Each year, the United States also allows tens of thousands of refugees to live in the United States permanently. Population growth affects the environment and the ability of governments to provide services to the growing number of people who live in less space, use more fuel, and require more food. There is no country in the world untouched by America, and America is touched by every country in the world in some way. American principles of democracy, freedom, tolerance, and opportunity inspire people throughout the world. Recognition and understanding of these common values increases trust among states and peoples and betters the chances of resolving differences and reaching agreements. To achieve this understanding of other people and states, the DOS explains U.S. policies. While ensuring that its voice is heard in foreign affairs, good diplomacy dictates listening to the voices and concerns of other nations and peoples. The most effective way for others to hear the American message is to welcome their views, from which America has much to learn. The DOS provides information to foreign audiences, often in various foreign languages, through TV broadcasts, videos, print publications, and the Internet.

Department of State Personnel

A-67. Foreign Service and Civil Service personnel have the primary responsibility for executing U.S. foreign policy in the United States and at U.S. missions abroad. More than 11,000 employees make up the Foreign Service. These employees represent the United States in other countries. The Foreign Service can send its members to any embassy, consulate, or other diplomatic mission anywhere in the world, at any time, to serve the diplomatic needs of the United States. About 8,000 employees—mostly in Washington, DC—make up the Civil Service. These employees provide expertise, support, and continuity in accomplishing the mission of the department. Some Civil Service employees are the domestic counterparts to consular officers abroad, issuing passports and assisting U.S. citizens at home and abroad. U.S. missions abroad are supported by more than 31,000 locally engaged staff, formerly referred to as Foreign Service National employees, who are citizens of the country in which an embassy or other post is located. These employees provide continuity by remaining in their jobs, while the Foreign Service officers move in and out of the country.

COUNTRY TEAM ORGANIZATIONAL STRUCTURE (BAGHDAD, MARCH 2006)

A-68. The following recent description of a Country Team from the Congressional Research Service is especially useful because it shows the relationship between a JFC and his assets and the U.S. Ambassador

(Chief of Mission) enjoying a robust mission structure during wartime. Most U.S. embassies are not as big or complex during normal peacetime operations. Understanding this type of structure is useful to ARSOF UW commanders, staff, and their joint, interagency, and multinational partners.

A-69. "The U.S. Ambassador to Iraq…has full authority for the American presence in Iraq with two exceptions: 1—military and security matters, which are under the authority of the U.S. Commander of the Multinational Force-Iraq, and 2—staff working for international organizations. In areas where diplomacy, military, or security activities overlap, the ambassador and the U.S. Commander continue cooperating to provide co-equal authority regarding what is best for America and its interests in Iraq."

A-70. "The United States has a number of experts from the various agencies on the ground in Iraq working as teams to determine needs, such as security, skills, expenditures, contracting and logistics, communications/information technology, and real estate. In addition, the United States has consultants from the agencies working on an ongoing basis with the various Iraqi ministries, such as the Iraqi Health Ministry, Education Ministry, Foreign Ministry, and Ministry of Oil to help Iraq gain a strong foothold on democracy and administrative skills. "

Appendix B
The Informational Instrument of National Power

INTERNATIONAL INFORMATION ENVIRONMENT

B-1. The information environment is the total of individuals, organizations, and systems that collect, process, disseminate, or act on information. The actors include leaders, decision makers, individuals, and organizations. Resources include the materials and systems employed to collect, analyze, apply, or disseminate information. The information environment is where humans and automated systems observe, orient, decide, and act upon information, and is therefore the principal environment of decision making. Even though the information environment is considered distinct, it resides within each of the four domains of air, land, sea, and space.

B-2. The information environment is made up of three interrelated dimensions (Figure B-1, page B-2):

- *The physical dimension.* The physical dimension is made up of the C2 systems and supporting infrastructures that enable individuals and organizations to conduct operations across the four domains. It is also the dimension where physical platforms and the communications networks that connect them reside, which includes the means of transmission, infrastructure, technologies, groups, and populations. Comparatively, the elements of this dimension are the easiest to measure, and consequently, combat power has traditionally been measured primarily in this dimension.
- *The informational dimension.* The informational dimension is where information is collected, processed, stored, disseminated, displayed, and protected. It is the dimension where the C2 of modern military forces is communicated, and where commander's intent is conveyed. It consists of the content and flow of information. Consequently, it must be protected.
- *The cognitive dimension.* The cognitive dimension encompasses the mind of the decision maker and the TA. People think, perceive, visualize, and decide in this dimension. It is the most important of the three dimensions. A commander's orders, training, and other personal motivations affect this dimension. Battles and campaigns can be lost in the cognitive dimension. Factors such as leadership, morale, unit cohesion, emotion, state of mind, level of training, experience, situational awareness, as well as public opinion, perceptions, media, public information, and rumors influence this dimension.

B-3. Advancements in technology have enabled information to be collected, processed, stored, disseminated, displayed, and protected outside the cognitive process in quantities and at speeds that were previously incomprehensible. While technology makes great quantities of information available to audiences worldwide, perception-affecting factors provide the context that individuals use to translate data into information and knowledge.

B-4. There are criteria that define the quality of information relative to its purpose. The varying purposes of information require different applications of these criteria to qualify it as valuable. In addition, each decision relies on a different weighting of the information quality criteria to make the best decision. The finite amount of time and resources available to obtain information is a consideration. Whether decisions are made cognitively or preprogrammed in automated systems, the limited time and resources to improve the quality of available information leaves decision making subject to manipulation. In addition, there are real costs associated with obtaining quality information—that is, information well-suited to its purpose—such as those to acquire, process, store, transport, and distribute information. The overall impact of successful IO improves the quality of friendly information while degrading the quality of adversary information, thus providing friendly forces the ability to make faster, more accurate decisions (Figure B-2, page B-2).

Appendix B

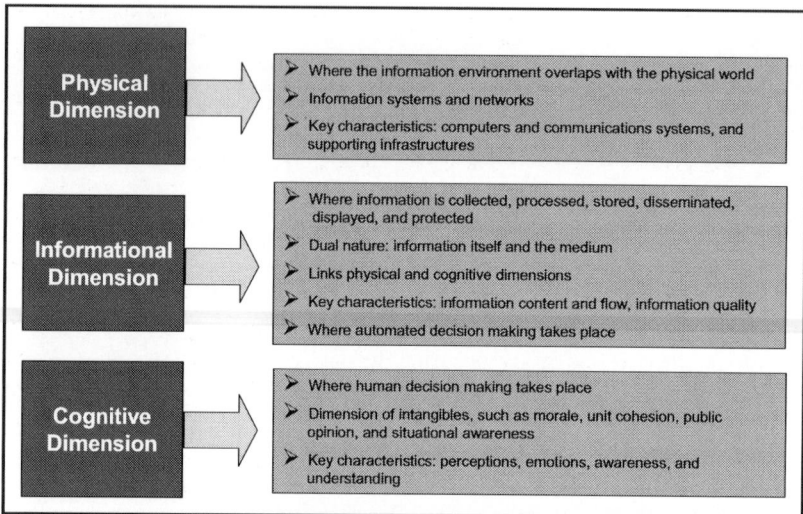

Figure B-1. The information environment

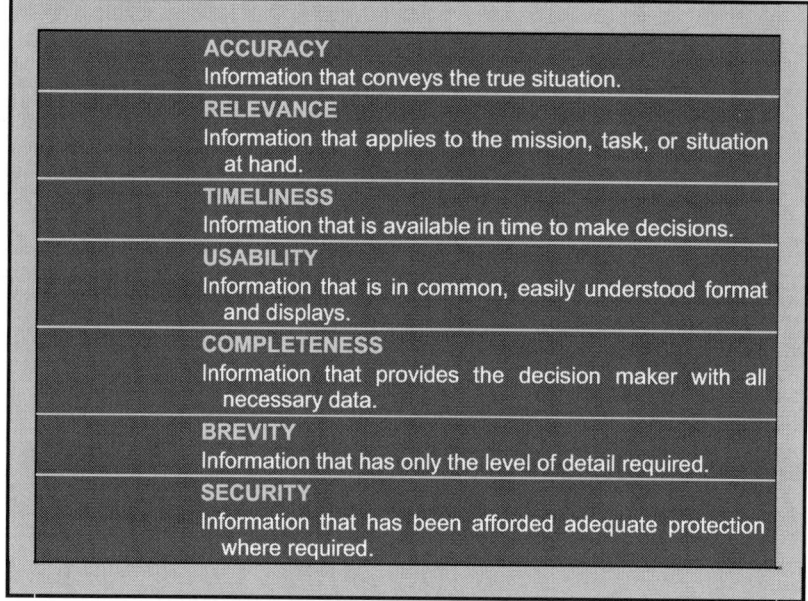

Figure B-2. Information quality criteria

B-5. Of the seven information quality criteria listed above, accuracy is distinct because it concerns truth. "Truth" is a combination of both scientifically verifiable fact and perception. ARSOF UW is an operation fundamentally focused on the human terrain, and Soldiers must understand the perceptions of the population to provide a militarily significant measure of truthfulness. This is a function of SC. JP 1-02 defines SC as "focused USG efforts to understand and engage key audiences to create, strengthen, or preserve conditions favorable for the advancement of USG interests, policies, and objectives through the use of coordinated programs, plans, themes, messages, and products synchronized with the actions of all instruments of national power." JP 3-13, *Information Operations*, states "history indicates that the speed and accuracy of information available to military commanders is the significant factor in determining the outcome on the battlefield." Appendix H discusses concepts fundamental to understanding the international human—and informational—environment in which Soldiers conduct UW.

INTERNATIONAL INFORMATION PROVIDERS

B-6. A medium of information is anything that conveys meaning to a person who perceives the conveyed information. It includes the symbolic meaning perceived in anything taken in by the one who perceives, to include stationary inanimate objects, nature, or man-made images. It also includes messages sent in human interaction—large or small—regardless of whether the message actually delivered was the one intended by the sender or whether the message received was understood as the sender intended. Very broadly, anything and anyone can be an information provider, intentionally or unintentionally.

B-7. This manual construes information as an instrument of power as the deliberate crafting, manipulation, and dissemination of information to convey an intended message or theme to a large TA. This manual narrowly focuses on media capable of and willing to influence audiences in the context of international relations and warfare. The media considered most broadly and profoundly influential is the so-called mass media. This is in contrast to nonmass, person-to-person, or point-to-point media, such as conversation, interpersonal gestures, telephony, postal mail, email, and some interactive media. Arguably, blogs and other first-person, Web-based communications are not mass media.

B-8. Media (the plural of medium) is a shortened version of the term "media of communication," referring to those organized means of dissemination of fact, opinion, entertainment, and other information, such as newspapers, magazines, banners, billboards, cinema films, radio, TV, the World Wide Web, books, compact discs (CDs), DVDs, videocassettes, computer games, and other forms of publishing.

MASS MEDIA

B-9. Mass media is a term used to denote that section of the media specifically conceived and designed to reach a very large audience, such as the population of a nation-state. The term "public media" has a similar meaning: it is the sum of the public mass distributors of news and entertainment across mediums such as newspapers, TV, radio broadcasting, and text publishers. The expansion of Internet media has complicated the concept of mass media because now individuals have a means of potential exposure on a scale comparable to what was previously restricted to a select group of mass media producers. Traditional mass media has a correspondingly lessened monopoly on information. These Internet media can include personal Web pages, podcasts, and blogs.

B-10. During the 20th century, technology that allowed the massive duplication of material drove the growth of mass media. Physical duplication technologies, such as printing, record pressing, and film duplication, allowed the duplication of books, newspapers, and movies at low prices to huge audiences. Radio and TV allowed the electronic duplication of information for the first time.

B-11. Mankind's ability to use informational power remained slow, small-scale, and expensive for millennia and then exploded exponentially in speed, scale, affordability, and accessibility throughout the 20th century. At the beginning of the 21st century, practically anyone with the freedom and means to do so can access, develop, and distribute information for any purpose. Mass media can be used for various purposes:

- Advocacy for business and social concerns, to include advertising, marketing, propaganda, public relations, and political communication.
- Journalism.
- Public service announcements.
- Personal enrichment and education.
- Entertainment.

B-12. Another description of mass media is central media, meaning that it emanates from a central point and provides an identical message to numerous recipients. Those who control centralized media are able to control the content and leverage public opinion, as well as inherently force certain intrinsic constraints on the kind of messages and information conveyed.

Appendix B

B-13. Hazards of centralized mass media include the following:
- A disproportion of power occurs. Disproportionate informational power accrues to those who control centralized mass media; arguably, it is inherently undemocratic.
- An inability to transmit tacit knowledge; the context of content presented must either be explicitly explained or is assumed to be understood by the receiver.
- An inclination to focus on the unusual and sensational to capture the receivers' attention, leading to a distortion and trivialization of reality.
- The deliberate promotion of emotions such as anxiety, fear, or greed can be used to sell a particular agenda.
- An inability to deal with complex issues because of time and economic constraints leads to simplification, further distorting and trivializing reality.

B-14. This view of central media can be contrasted with lateral media, such as email networks where messages are all slightly different and spread by a process of lateral diffusion. Democratic and independent use of media theoretically serves to educate the public or electorate about issues regarding government and society. Undemocratic use of media can lead to indoctrination, propaganda, and exploitation.

PUBLISHING

B-15. Publishing is the industry concerned with the production of literature or information—the activity of making information available for public view. In some cases, authors may be their own publishers. Traditionally, the term refers to the distribution of printed works, such as books and newspapers. With the advent of digital information systems and the Internet, the scope of publishing has expanded to include Web sites, blogs, and the like. As a business, publishing includes the development, marketing, production, and distribution of newspapers, magazines, books, literary works, music, and software.

B-16. The control of publishing and press freedom is relevant to the effectiveness of informational operations. The degree of press freedom is contentious and subjective. Critics contend that press freedom is constrained by concentration into conglomerates in the West and deliberately and severely censored by the state in undemocratic countries. One source for more information on freedom of the press internationally is "Reporters Without Borders," which provides assessments and a rank index of press freedom of 168 countries ranging from Finland ("most free" in 2006) to North Korea ("least free").

AUDIO RECORDING AND REPRODUCTION

B-17. Sound recording and reproduction is the electrical or mechanical re-creation or amplification of sound, often as music. Audio recording involves the use of audio equipment, such as microphones, recording devices, and loudspeakers. From early beginnings with the invention of the phonograph using purely mechanical techniques, the field has advanced with the invention of electrical recording, the mass production of the 78 record, the magnetic wire recorder followed by the tape recorder, and the vinyl LP record. The invention of the compact cassette in the 1960s, followed by Sony's Walkman, gave a major boost to the mass distribution of music recordings, and the invention of digital recording and the compact disc in 1983 brought massive improvements in ruggedness and quality. The most recent developments have been in digital audio players like the Apple IPOD.

BROADCASTING

B-18. Early radio engineers coined the term "broadcast" in the United States. Broadcasting is the distribution of audio or video signals (programs) to a number of recipients ("listeners" or "viewers"). This group may be the public in general, a relatively large audience within the public, or small, narrowly focused audiences. Thus, an Internet channel may distribute text or music worldwide, while a public address system in a workplace or school may broadcast very limited ad hoc sound bites to a small population within its range. The sequencing of content in a broadcast is called a schedule. TV and radio programs are distributed through radio broadcasting or cable and often through both simultaneously. By coding signals and having decoding equipment in homes, the latter also enables subscription-based channels and pay-per-view services.

B-19. A broadcasting organization may broadcast several programs at the same time through several channels (frequencies); British Broadcasting Corporation (BBC) One and Two, for example. On the other hand, two or more organizations may share a channel and each use it during a fixed part of the day. Digital radio and digital TV may also transmit multiplexed programming, with several channels compressed into one ensemble. When broadcasting via the Internet, the term "webcasting" is often used. In 2004, a new phenomenon occurred when a number of technologies combined to produce podcasting. Podcasting is an asynchronous broadcast/narrowcast medium. Broadcasting forms a very large segment of the mass media. Broadcasting to a very narrow range of audience is called narrowcasting.

B-20. Critics have accused the larger conglomerates of dominating media—especially news. Critics say that the larger conglomerates refuse to publicize or deem "newsworthy" information that would be harmful to their other interests and of contributing to the merging of entertainment and news at the expense of tough coverage of serious issues. Critics also accuse these larger conglomerates of being a leading force for the standardization of culture (globalization, or so-called "Americanization"). They are also a frequent target of criticism by partisan political groups that often perceive the news productions as biased toward their foes. Broadcasting companies and their supporters claim that they maintain a strict separation between the business end and the production end of news departments.

B-21. Some of the largest media conglomerates include AT&T (U.S.), Berlusconi Group (Italy), Bertelsmann AG (Germany), CanWest Global (Canada), Columbia Broadcasting System (CBS) Corporation (U.S.), General Electric (U.S.), Hearst Corporation (U.S.), Lagardère Media (France), Liberty Media (U.S.), News Corporation (Australia), NHST Mediagroup Norges Handels Og Sjøfartstidende (Norway), Organizações Globo (Brazil), Grupo Prisa (Spain), Sony (Japan), Time Warner (U.S.), the Times Group (India), Viacom (U.S.), Vivendi (France), and the Walt Disney Company (U.S.). Just seven of these conglomerates (Disney, CBS, Time Warner, News Corp, Bertelsmann AG, Viacom, and General Electric) together control more than 90 percent of the media market in western countries.

GEOGRAPHICAL USAGE OF TELEVISION

B-22. In addition to the explosion of informational technologies in the 20th century being relatively recent, the diffusion of such technologies has been uneven. Technological developments typically spread from the developed and democratic world outward with corresponding political effects on access to information and democratization. Authoritarian regimes severely curtail or influence some media in their countries.

Canadian Networks and Stations

B-23. In Canada, there are a number of national networks, including three main networks for English Canada. One, CBC Television, is owned by the Canadian Broadcasting Corporation, a government-funded Crown corporation. The other two, CTV and Global, are privately run. The private networks usually use most of their prime-time hours to rebroadcast U.S. shows, while the CBC airs more Canadian programming. Citytv, CH, and A-channel are private systems whose stations have a somewhat enhanced local focus. These stations do not reach all of Canada. In French Canada, particularly Quebec, the main networks are the CBC-owned Télévision de Radio-Canada and private networks TVA and TQS.

United States Networks and Stations

B-24. In the United States, the three traditional commercial TV networks (American Broadcasting Companies [ABC], CBS, and National Broadcasting Company [NBC]) provide prime-time programs for their affiliate stations to air from 8:00 p.m. to 11:00 p.m. Monday through Saturday and from 7:00 p.m. to 11:00 p.m. on Sunday. Most stations procure other programming, often syndicated, for off prime-time periods. Four newer broadcasting networks, FOX, the CW, ION, and My Network TV do not provide the same amount of network programming as do the traditional three networks. Over the past 30 years, cable and satellite TV have come to provide most homes with dozens or even hundreds of TV services.

Latin American Networks and Stations

B-25. More than 500 TV stations exist in Latin America. There are more than 60 million TVs in that same area. This represents a theoretical viewing audience of more than 200 million people. Because of the

Appendix B

financial and political troubles that occurred between the mid-1970s and the early 1990s, TV networks in some countries of this region had a more irregular development than did those of North American and European networks. In countries like Mexico or Brazil, one or two networks claim almost all the audience. In other countries, like Colombia, TV broadcasting had historically been state-dominated until the 1990s. In countries like Nicaragua or Peru, TV has had a troubled history.

European Networks and Stations

B-26. In much of Europe, TV broadcasting has historically been state-dominated rather than commercially organized, although commercial stations have grown in number recently. In the UK, the major national broadcaster is the BBC, which is funded by a television license granted by royal charter. Commercial TV is provided by Independent Television (ITV), Channels 4 and 5, as well as the satellite broadcaster British Sky Broadcasting. BBC1, BBC2, ITV, and Channels 4 and 5 are broadcast on analog terrestrial TV. An abundance of new broadcasters and channels have changed the market over the last few years, giving viewers a level of choice previously associated only with the United States.

B-27. Other leading European networks include SVT, Sweden; RAI, Italy; TF1, M6, and France Télévisions, France; ARD, Germany; ORF, Austria; ERT, Greece; YLE, MTV3, and Nelonen, Finland; RTE, Ireland; TVP, Poland; RTP, Portugal; TVR, Romania; TVE, Spain; RTV Slovenija, Slovenia; HRT, Croatia; and BNT, BTV, and Nova Televizia, Bulgaria. The largest commercial European broadcaster is the Luxembourg-based RTL Group. There are now also a few Europe-wide networks.

Asian Networks and Stations

B-28. In Asia, TV has traditionally been state-controlled, although the number of private stations is increasing, as is competition from satellite TV. Japan's NHK is a noncommercial network similar to the BBC funded by a TV license fee. NHK has more editorial independence over news and current affairs than broadcasters like India's state-run Doordarshan or China's China Central Television. From 2000 onward, India has encouraged development of new private stations. Star TV based in Hong Kong has expanded to other areas recently. The number of private broadcasters is increasing in some countries. For example, in 2004 Indonesia had 10 private national stations compared to only 1 in 1989.

Middle East Networks and Stations

B-29. Similarly in the Middle East, TV has been heavily state-controlled, with considerable censorship of both news coverage and entertainment—particularly that imported from the West. The increasing availability of satellite TV has eroded control over this medium, and the number of satellite channels in Arabic is second only to the number of satellite channels in English. The best known satellite channel in Arabic is the Qatar-based news service Al Jazeera.

African Networks and Stations

B-30. Despite being the most economically advanced country on the continent, South Africa did not introduce TV until 1976 because of opposition from the apartheid regime. Nigeria was one of the first countries in Africa to introduce TV in 1959. Zimbabwe followed (then Rhodesia) in 1961. Zanzibar was the first area in Africa to introduce color TV in 1973 (although mainland Tanzania did not introduce TV until 1994). The main satellite TV providers are the South African Multichoice Digital Satellite Television service and the predominantly French language Canal Horizons, which France's Canal Plus owns.

Australian and New Zealand Networks and Stations

B-31. Australian TV began in 1956, just in time for the Melbourne Olympics. Australia has three nationwide metropolitan commercial networks (Seven, Nine, and Ten), as well as the Australian Broadcasting Corporation, a government-owned, commercial-free network, and the Special Broadcasting Service, a commercial-supported, multilingual, government-owned station. The Australian Broadcasting Authority has also issued licenses to community groups to establish community TV stations in most capital cities on the ultrahigh frequency (UHF) Channel 31. In regional and rural areas, numerous commercial stations are affiliated with one of the three metropolitan networks and carry programming generally indistinguishable from those in the cities.

B-32. The New Zealand government owns two TV networks: Television One and TV2. Other, purely commercial networks include TV3 (owned by a Canadian media company), Prime Television (Australia), Sky Network Television, and a New Zealand government-funded Maori Television Service.

FILM

B-33. The making and showing of motion pictures became a source of profit almost at their invention. The film industry today spans the globe. There is also a large industry for educational and instructional films made in lieu of or in addition to lectures and texts. The major business centers of filmmaking are concentrated in India, the United States, China, and Nigeria. However, most developed nations have their own film industries.

B-34. Much like American popular music, American cinema has had a profound effect on cinema across the world since the early 20th century. During the 1930s and 1940s, big studios dominated American cinema. These studios virtually monopolized the production and distribution of film. The costs inherent in big-budget studio film production were also a hurdle to being able to produce, direct, or star in a traditional studio film. Production costs also led to conservative choices in content. Following technological advances and antitrust legislation, the big studios no longer enjoy such monopoly power. Hollywood, California, remains the primary nexus of the U.S. film industry, but today independent filmmaking often takes place outside of Hollywood and major studio systems.

B-35. With the advent of consumer camcorders in 1985 and the arrival of high-resolution digital video (DV) in the early 1990s, the technology barrier to movie production has been drastically lowered. Since the introduction of DV technology, filmmakers can conceivably shoot and edit a movie, create and edit the sound and music, and mix the final cut on a home computer. DVDs, professional-grade video connections, nonlinear editing systems, and other new technologies make moviemaking relatively inexpensive. However, while the democratization of production has occurred, financing, distribution, and marketing remain difficult to accomplish outside the traditional system. Most independent filmmakers rely on film festivals to get their films noticed and sold for distribution.

B-36. The Indian film industry is multilingual and the largest in the world in terms of number of annual movie releases and annual (domestic) ticket sales. Indian films have been gaining popularity in the rest of the world, especially in countries with large numbers of expatriate Indians. India's film industry is mostly concentrated in Bombay and is commonly referred to as "Bollywood." However, there are several smaller centers of Indian film industries in regional languages (Bollywood is largely in Hindi) centered in the states in which those languages are spoken.

B-37. Hong Kong, China, is a filmmaking hub for the Chinese-speaking world (including the worldwide Chinese diaspora) and East Asia in general. For decades, Hong Kong was the third-largest motion picture industry in the world (after India and Hollywood) and the second-largest exporter. Despite a return to Chinese sovereignty in July 1997, Hong Kong film retains much of its distinctive identity and continues to play a prominent part on the world cinematic stage. Unlike many film industries, Hong Kong enjoys little to no direct government support, through either subsidies or import quotas. It has always been a thoroughly commercial cinema, concentrating on crowd-pleasing genres, like comedy and action, and relying heavily on formulas, sequels, and remakes.

B-38. The cinema of Nigeria is a developing industry that has become increasingly productive in recent years. Although Nigeria has been producing films since the 1960s, the rise of digital cinema has resulted in a rapidly growing video film industry. The Nigerian video feature film industry is colloquially known as "Nollywood." Nigeria has a multibillion-dollar movie industry, churning out some 200 home videos every month to become the third largest in the world after the United States and India. In just over a decade, Nollywood has grown from nothing into an industry that employs thousands of people.

B-39. Nollywood has no studios in the Hollywood sense. Filmmakers shoot movies in locations all over Nigeria. Nigerian directors adopt new technologies as soon as they become affordable. Bulky videotape cameras gave way to their digital descendants. Filmmakers are now replacing those with high-definition cameras. Film industry personnel accomplish editing, music, and other postproduction work with common computer-based systems.

B-40. Currently, Nigerian films outsell Hollywood films in Nigeria and many other African countries. Some 300 producers churn out 1,000 and 2,000 new titles per year. The films go straight to DVDs and video compact discs. The industry delivers 30 new titles to Nigerian shops and market stalls every week, where an average film sells 50,000 copies. A hit may sell several hundred thousand. Discs sell for two dollars each, making them affordable for most Nigerians and providing astounding returns for the producers. Nigerian video movies are available in even the most remote areas of the continent, and Nollywood films are growing in popularity among the African communities in both Europe and North America. The content of the Nigerian film industry is primarily commercially oriented, but includes Christian- and Muslim-themed work as well.

INTERNET

B-41. The Internet is "a network of networks." Specifically, it is the worldwide, publicly accessible network of interconnected computer networks. This network transmits data by packet switching using the standard Internet protocol. It consists of millions of smaller domestic, academic, business, and governmental networks, which together carry various information and services, such as email, online chat, file transfer, and the interlinked Web pages and other documents of the World Wide Web. Contrary to common usage, the Internet and the World Wide Web are not synonymous: the Internet is a collection of interconnected computer networks, linked by copper wires, fiber-optic cables, wireless connections, and so on; the Web is a collection of interconnected documents linked by hyperlinks and uniform resource locators (URLs). The World Wide Web is accessible via the Internet.

B-42. Toward the end of the 20th century, the advent of the World Wide Web marked the first era in which any individual could have a means of exposure on a scale comparable to that of mass media. For the first time, anyone with a Web site can address a global audience, although serving to high levels of Web traffic is still relatively expensive. It is possible that the rise of peer-to-peer technologies will drive the cost of bandwidth down. Although a vast amount of information, imagery, and commentary (content) is available, it is often difficult to determine the authenticity and reliability of information contained in Web pages. In many cases, Web pages are self-published, and practically anyone can create a Web page. The invention of the Internet has also allowed breaking news stories to reach around the globe within minutes. This rapid growth of instantaneous, decentralized communication is likely to change mass media and its relationship to society.

B-43. An estimated 16 percent of the world population has access to the Internet with the highest concentration in North America (68.6 percent), Oceania/Australia (52.6 percent), and Europe (36.1 percent). In terms of broadband access, countries such as Iceland (26.7 percent), South Korea (25.4 percent), and the Netherlands (25.3 percent) lead the world. While Internet use is growing worldwide, some governments—such as those of Iran, the People's Republic of China, and Cuba—restrict what people in their countries can access on the Internet, especially political and religious content. The countries accomplish this restriction through content-control software that filters domains and content. This makes them difficult to access or obtain without elaborate circumvention. In Norway, Finland, and Sweden, major Internet service providers have voluntarily agreed to restrict access to sites listed by police. Although this list of forbidden URLs is only supposed to contain addresses of known child pornography sites, content of the list is secret. Many states have enacted laws making the possession or distribution of certain material illegal but do not use filtering software. Most governments and businesses, among others, use firewalls that restrict access to many sites to protect against cyberterrorism or cybercrime.

SOFTWARE PUBLISHING

B-44. Software can be considered a component of the modern international information environment because software—
- Can be made relatively easily and cheaply.
- Can carry any content.
- Can often be transmitted over the Internet.

- Can sometimes be endlessly multiplied through copying from computer to computer, which can avoid the net entirely.

Moreover, people can easily, discretely, and rapidly transport powerful software in tiny packages.

B-45. A software publisher is a publishing company in the software industry between the developer and the distributor. In some companies, two or all three of these roles may be combined (and indeed, may reside in a single person, especially in the case of shareware). Software publishers often license software from developers with specific limitations, such as a time limit or geographical region. The terms of licensing vary enormously and are typically secret. Developers may use publishers to reach larger or foreign markets or to avoid focusing on marketing. Conversely, publishers may use developers to create software to meet a market need that the publisher has identified. The United States is the largest and most profitable producer of software in the world by far, and the Microsoft Company dominates the industry. Other countries with large software industries include Japan, England, Canada, and Germany.

UNITED STATES DOMESTIC INFORMATION ENVIRONMENT

B-46. Individual liberty and freedom of speech protected by law and a tradition of competitive economic freedom in a diverse society provide the United States with an unusually broad array of information content. In the public commons, individuals exchange almost every perspective, counter perspective, and intervening gradation of meaning. As shown in the section above, the United States dominates or leads in many of the forms and technologies of international mass informational power. This section discusses current issues particular to informational power as it affects, or may affect, distribution of content to the U.S. domestic audience.

B-47. Little mass media regulation existed in the United States before the creation of the Federal Radio Commission in 1927. The Telecommunications Act of 1934 was a fundamental decision on how broadcast mass media would function from then on. At the time, radio technology was widespread among the public, and the electromagnetic spectrum was public property. The act reappropriated the spectrum to the government and claimed the right to assign spectrum ranges to private parties as long as they broadcast in the public interest. This act created the Federal Communications Commission (FCC) to replace the Federal Radio Commission.

B-48. Lobbyists from the largest radio broadcasters of the time, ABC and NBC, successfully petitioned to attach a cost to broadcast licenses. This enabled them to "price out" many amateur broadcasters. Such was the precedent for much of the following regulatory decisions, which have mostly focused on the percentage of a market deemed allowable to a single company.

B-49. The Telecommunications Act of 1996 set the modern tone of "deregulation," a relaxing of percentage restrictions that solidified the previous history of privatizing the utility and "commodifying" the spectrum. The legislation, touted as a step that would foster competition, actually resulted in the subsequent mergers of several large companies, a trend that continues. The FCC Forum of February 2003 approved new media ownership laws that removed many of the restrictions previously imposed to limit ownership of media within a local area. A few of the points included the following:

- Single-company ownership of media in a given market is now permitted up to 45 percent (formerly 35 percent, up from 25 percent in 1985) of that market.
- Restrictions on newspaper and TV station ownership in the same market were removed.
- All TV channels, magazines, newspapers, cable, and Internet services are now counted and weighted, based on people's average tendency to find news on that medium. At the same time, whether a channel actually contains "news" is no longer considered in counting the percentage of a medium owned by one owner. For example, it is now possible for two companies to own all of a city's two newspapers, three local TV stations, two national TV networks, and eight local radio stations (up to 45 percent of the media each), as long as there are other companies owning the "Shopping Channel" or the "Discovery Channel" and at least 10 percent of other non-news outlets.
- Previous requirements for periodic review of licenses have been changed. Licenses are no longer reviewed for public-interest considerations.

Appendix B

B-50. Depending on one's perspective (and political views) such media consolidation is capable of dominating the informational power to deliberately craft, manipulate, and disseminate information for conveyance of an intended message or theme to a domestic TA.

B-51. In opposition to this trend, some U.S. citizens promote a production and distribution model of "media democracy" that theoretically informs and empowers all members of society and enhances democratic values. The term also refers to a modern social movement evident in many other countries that attempts to make mainstream media more accountable to the publics they serve and to create democratic alternatives. Citizens base this concept and social movement on the assertion that increased corporate domination of mass media leads to a perceived shrinking of the marketplace of ideas. Its proponents advocate monitoring and reforming the mass media, strengthening public service broadcasting, and developing and participating in alternative media and citizen journalism.

B-52. Media democracy is a difficult term to define, because in addition to being a concept, it is also an advocacy movement. A number of academic and grassroots organizations, each with its own methods and goals, are advancing. Moreover, since suspicion of and hostility to corporate interests is a key tenet of the left end of the U.S. domestic political spectrum, much of the media democracy effort runs parallel with anticapitalist, even anti-American, agitation. Ironically, one of the central issues routinely assailed by the right end of the U.S. domestic political spectrum is a perceived monolithic and consolidated domestic media dominated by a "leftist agenda" in delivery of content.

B-53. Despite the difficulties in defining the term, the concept broadly encompasses the following notions:
- The health of the democratic political system depends on the efficient, accurate, and complete transmission of social, political, and cultural information in society.
- The media are the conduits of this information. As such, they should act in the public interest.
- The mass media have increasingly been unable and uninterested in fulfilling this role because of increased concentration of ownership and commercial pressures.
- The concept and practice of democracy are undermined if voters and citizens are unable to knowledgeably participate in public policy debates.

B-54. Without an informed and engaged citizenry, policy issues become defined by political and corporate elites. A related element of this concept asserts that corporate media interests lack a diversity of voices and viewpoints, particularly of traditionally marginalized sectors of the population. The following paragraphs discuss alternatives to traditional mass media.

PUBLIC BROADCASTING

B-55. Public broadcasting serves as one potential counterweight to commercial media. As such, it is a notable element of the so-called media democracy. The government and individual donations usually fund public TV and radio broadcasts. Therefore, they are not subject to the same commercial pressures as private broadcasters and, theoretically, provide a distinct source of more diverse, in-depth media content. However, public broadcasters are subject to funding instability, which jeopardizes their ability to operate consistently. Moreover, public broadcasting's editorial objectivity is susceptible to the editorial preferences of those who approve and provide grants, which jeopardizes its autonomy.

ALTERNATIVE AND CITIZEN MEDIA

B-56. As a response to the asserted shortcomings of the mainstream media, proponents of media democracy often advocate supporting and engaging in independent and alternative print and electronic media. Through citizen journalism and citizen media, individuals can produce and disseminate information and opinions that the mainstream media marginalizes. Practically anyone can now easily and cheaply publish audio, video, and written content to the Web. Home computing has empowered everyone to be a publisher of written documents. Every shade of opinion is now represented and there is a published viewpoint for every microconstituency. However, objectivity and credibility are endlessly disputed. In the absence of consensus over objectivity and credibility, such alternative media is unlikely to replace the mass persuasive power of the traditional, large-scale, information-providing institutions.

WIKIPEDIA AND WIKINEWS AS TOOLS OF MEDIA DEMOCRACY

B-57. A similar claim for media democracy is asserted for the online dictionary "Wikipedia." Anyone—regardless of educational background, experience, or in-depth knowledge—can edit, expand, or remove content. Individuals do not have to get the approval of an editorial board to post content. Although there are administrators on Wikipedia, they have roughly the same powers as ordinary users. Wikipedia also lacks corporate control: it operates as a not-for-profit entity and accepts no advertising or corporate investment, which can influence or theoretically silence particular ideas. Typically, small individual donations pay its operating costs. Creators of a related site called "Wikinews" intend to provide an alternative news source using the same open collaborative philosophy.

B-58. As with other forms of alternative media, such as weblogs, the appeal of Wikipedia is that anyone can access and contribute to the site. This site provides a wide range of information in a free format and can be a handy quick reference similar to a traditional encyclopedia. However, its accessibility diminishes its authority. Although individuals can dispute inserted content, the shaping of much content has no objective peer review. This allows individuals to easily craft content to convey a slanted editorial position.

ROLE OF UNITED STATES DOMESTIC MEDIA

B-59. U.S. domestic media includes stationary visuals, such as billboards and other advertisements, and print documents, such as newspapers, periodicals, and books. Publishers typically craft these products for and disseminate them to specific, narrowly defined TAs to address specific, narrowly defined interests (predominantly commercial advertising and entertainment). In keeping with this manual's focus on mass media, however, this section will outline U.S. broadcast media—specifically, news media, which is theoretically a transmission of objective truth imparting serious information about society and matters of state.

B-60. Regular but rudimentary broadcast programming occurred in the United States and several European countries before WWII. Regular network broadcasting began in the United States in 1946, and TV became common in American homes by the middle of the 1950s. In the last half of the 20th century, TV news in the United States evolved from a simple 10-to-15-minute format in the evenings to a variety of programs and channels. Today, viewers can receive local, regional, and national news programming in many different ways, any time of the day.

ORIGIN AND DEVELOPMENT OF TELEVISION NEWS

B-61. The reach, appeal, and centrality of TV news is taken so much for granted in the early 21st century that it is difficult to remember how recently it developed and how limited it was, and how few media stars have represented its visual front. NBC and CBS only initiated regular network news broadcasts in 1948. The third major network broadcast news (ABC) did not join NBC and CBS until 1965. For decades, these three national broadcasters of TV news were the public's only choice. Moreover, in the 1960s and 1970s national news was only available at set times of the evening (after the conclusion of a standard workday), requiring the news-viewing public to arrange their personal schedules around the limited availability of broadcast national news.

B-62. Moreover, many news anchor personalities remained in their positions so long that they took on a familiar and authoritative iconic status. For example, Walter Cronkite (CBS news anchor 1963 to 1981) was alternately known as "Uncle Walter," or "the most trusted man in America." Critics have claimed that Cronkite's opinion after the Vietnamese Tet Offensive that "the war was now lost" significantly influenced American public opinion against continued involvement in the war. Since the 1940s, fewer than two dozen personalities have been the influential public face of such mainstream broadcast news by the three traditional networks.

TODAY'S TELEVISION NEWS

B-63. TV news has come a long way since its beginning. Today, electronic news gathering has enabled reporters to capture video and audio more easily and edit the footage faster than in the days of film.

Appendix B

Journalists also employ microwave and satellite feeds and even videophone to transmit live video and audio signals from remote locations.

B-64. Programmable video recorders, such as videocassette recorders and the digital video recorder free viewers from dependence on artificial schedules. Consumers can now watch programs on their own schedule once they are broadcast and recorded. TV service providers also offer video on demand, a set of programs that viewers can watch at any time. Mobile phone networks and the Internet are capable of carrying video streams. In addition, Internet TV (either live or as downloadable programs) and video-sharing Web sites have become more popular.

PROGRAMMING

B-65. Aside from TV news production, news providers must market and deliver the "product" to whatever markets are willing to use it. TV is a commercial business. Selling the product and generating revenues from advertising drive programming decisions more than any other factor. Despite the inherent substantive importance of "news information," news broadcasts are a small segment of the total TV menu. News broadcasts must compete with other first-run and syndicated TV entertainment, the Internet, traditional newspapers, and so on, which has affected the availability and format—and some would argue quality—of TV news. TV news programming in the United States is separated into three different categories: local news, network news, and cable news.

Local News

B-66. Many local broadcast TV stations have in-house news departments that produce their own newscasts. Newscasters gear content toward viewers in specific, designated market areas in which the stations operate. The content of such stories have a strong local focus and are relevant to local lives.

Network News

B-67. The three traditional networks all operate news divisions named ABC News, CBS News, and NBC News respectively. Their schedules are broadly similar. They each air half-hour early weekday morning programs, and, following intervening local news, they each run a longer morning news show with a significant entertainment approach. All three also have morning weekend news programs. On Sunday mornings, the three networks and FOX News Channel air political interview programs. In the evenings, the networks' flagship news programs air seven nights a week. During prime time, all three traditional networks air newsmagazine programs with a more in-depth and thematic focus on select topics. On late weeknights, the networks air similar half-hour newsmagazine programs.

Cable News

B-68. The advent of cable TV in the United States led to the eventual birth of cable news. The first 24-hour cable news operation, Cable News Network (CNN), was launched in 1980 and gained a significant reputation with its 1991 coverage of the Gulf War. The success of CNN inspired many other 24-hour cable news stations. Today, CNN, CNN Headline News, FOX News Channel, MSNBC, and CNBC compete for viewers in the national cable news arena. Regional cable news operations, such as New England Cable News, NY1 for New York City, Northwest Cable News, and Texas Cable News, have also gained prominence among regional viewers. The programming styles vary among these cable channels, but during prime time, their key personalities strongly drive the channels. Typically, such programming is in a TV show format based on a particular host rather than continuous broadcasts of breaking news.

CURRENT DEVELOPMENTS

B-69. As the Internet has become more prevalent in American lives, TV news operations have had to adapt and embrace new technologies. Today, most TV news operations publish the text and video of the stories aired during their newscasts on dedicated Web sites. Such information posting is contributing to a convergence between TV and Internet media formats accessible 24 hours a day to computer-savvy viewers.

B-70. Technological advancement is also changing the way news is gathered and edited. Reporters do not use film anymore. TV journalists are now capturing and reporting images and sound on video, DV, and even high-definition. Even editing and archiving systems are evolving as more stations convert to nonlinear editing systems and store file footage on computer servers rather than tapes.

B-71. With digital cable comes on-demand news programming. News operations have begun to feel the burden to generate news content on a 24-hour news cycle, while keeping material "fresh" on their regularly scheduled newscasts. Such around-the-clock coverage means that rather than having a certain deadline for scheduled newscasts to meet, reporters have to file stories as fast as they can. Producers, on the other hand, have to find more innovative ways to package news stories as fresh to the viewers. Such immediate, worldwide coverage of news events has speeded the pace of cause-and-effect and reaction times in international statecraft.

FORMATS

B-72. Over the years, TV news in the United States has evolved into a variety of formats. Local news and network news, once similar in having slow paces and low story counts, are now quite different in style:

- *Traditional.* In the early days of TV, the public viewed local newscasts as a public service. The style was straightforward. Stations and networks divided newscasts into three blocks: news, sports, and weather. They further divided the news block into national, international, and local stories. These newscasts usually had a white male anchor, with white males announcing sports and weather as well. This format is no longer prevalent.
- *Eyewitness news.* This style developed in the late 1960s. Networks and stations hired reporters to leave the newsroom and become "eyewitnesses" of news stories, recording them on film. Later, they asked reporters to join the anchors in the studio to talk about the stories. Most TV news operations are working under some variation of the eyewitness format.
- *Action news.* TV executives devised this style to compete against the eyewitness news format. The action news format features short stories, high story counts in newscasts, and a strong focus on spot news. The "action" refers to the fast pacing of the newscast.
- *Franchise news.* This style is a variation of eyewitness news. Some stations decide to brand their news with slogans such as "News You Can Use" or "8 On Your Side." The newscasts at these stations tend to focus more on franchises—stories that cover a topic important to local viewers. The most successful franchises are health and consumer news, but other examples include parenting, pets, environment, and crime fighting. Almost every news operation uses some franchises, and a few stations build their news identities around these topical stories entirely.
- *Interview news shows.* Many cable news channels run these shows, which incorporate lots of talk and often heated debates between anchors and guests. Interview news programs typically promote discernable editorial positions on the topics covered.
- *Tabloid news.* This style blurs the line between news and entertainment with sensational writing and energetic reporters. Tabloid news programs generally confine stories to popular culture items.

ALLEGED SOCIAL DANGERS

B-73. Paralleling TV's entrenched informational primacy in current U.S. family life and society, a vocal chorus of legislators, scientists, parents, and political commentators raise objections to an uncritical acceptance of the medium. Continuous disputes over the effect TV viewing may have on children, whether it influences individuals to misbehave and leads to erosion of social mores or health, and how aired content is controlled to further particular (political) agendas are now common complaints. Judgments on such issues are beyond the scope of this manual. However, given the assumed fundamental mission of U.S. domestic news to deliver truth—and the example of Cronkite declaring the Vietnam War "unwinnable after Tet" (referenced above), and the effect that declaration may have had on public opinion—it is reasonable to assume that news programs do exert influence on domestic support for U.S. foreign policy.

B-74. The extent of such media influence and the forces and agendas behind it are subjects of continuous debate. A neutral understanding of the term "mainstream media" (MSM) suggests outlets that are in harmony with the prevailing direction of influence in the culture at large. In the United States, usage of this term often depends on the connotations the speaker wants to invoke. The term "corporate media" is often used by left-wing media critics to imply that MSM is made up of large multinational corporations, which primarily promote corporate, capitalist interests. By contrast, right-wing media critics' use of the term MSM often connotes a majority of mass media sources dominated by politically left-leaning elites that are furthering a leftist political agenda.

INSTRUMENTS OF UNITED STATES INFORMATIONAL POWER

B-75. U.S. engagement in the world and the DOS's engagement of the American public are indispensable to the conduct of foreign policy. Where conflict between states is absent or low, the United States attempts to influence other states' populations through PD.

B-76. The Under Secretary for Public Diplomacy and Public Affairs has oversight of the PD functions of cultural and educational exchange, as well as international information programs, and the PA function of providing information to the U.S. audience. The long-term and comprehensive strategy of the bureau is based on three strategic objectives:
- Offer people throughout the world a positive vision of hope and opportunity that is rooted in America's belief in freedom, justice, opportunity, and respect for all.
- Isolate and marginalize violent Muslim extremists; confront their ideology of tyranny and hate. Undermine their efforts to portray the West as in conflict with Islam by empowering mainstream voices and demonstrating respect for Muslim cultures and contributions.
- Foster a sense of common interests and common values between Americans and people of different countries, cultures, and faiths throughout the world.

PUBLIC DIPLOMACY AND TRADITIONAL DIPLOMACY

B-77. In traditional diplomacy, U.S. Embassy officials conduct official USG business with the officials of the host government. The emphasis is on state-to-state relations through their respective government apparatus. In PD, U.S. Embassy officials primarily engage a wide range of nongovernment audiences. The U.S. Country Team sometimes conducts these activities directly but often acts a facilitator of private American and individual engagements with various sectors of the HN society.

B-78. The Undersecretary for Public Diplomacy and Public Affairs oversees the following offices and bureaus:
- The Office of Policy, Planning, and Resources for Public Diplomacy and Public Affairs.
- The Bureau of Public Affairs.
- The Bureau of Educational and Cultural Affairs (ECA).
- The Bureau of International Information Programs (IIP).

Office of Policy, Planning, and Resources for Public Diplomacy and Public Affairs

B-79. This office provides long-term strategic planning and performance measurement capability for PD and PA programs. It enables the Undersecretary to better advise on the allocation of PD and PA resources, to focus those resources on the most urgent national security objectives, and to provide realistic measurement of PD's and PA's effectiveness. The office also coordinates the department's PD presence in the interagency, in close consultation with relevant bureaus.

Bureau of Public Affairs

B-80. The Bureau of Public Affairs carries out the Secretary of State's mandate to help Americans understand the importance of foreign affairs, and to feed their concerns and comments back to policy makers. It accomplishes this in a variety of ways, which include—
- Planning—both strategic and tactical—for the advancement of the administration's priority foreign policy goals.
- Conducting press briefings for domestic and foreign press corps.

- Pursuing media outreach, enabling Americans everywhere to hear directly from key department officials through local, regional, and national media interviews.
- Managing the State Department's Web site at state.gov and developing Web pages with up-to-date information about U.S. foreign policy.
- Answering questions from the public about current foreign policy issues by phone, email, or letter.
- Arranging town meetings and scheduling speakers to visit communities to discuss U.S. foreign policy and why it is important to all Americans.
- Producing and coordinating audiovisual products and services in the United States and abroad for the public, the press, the Secretary of State, and department bureaus and offices.
- Preparing historical studies on U.S. diplomacy and foreign affairs matters.

Bureau of Educational and Cultural Affairs

B-81. The ECA fosters mutual understanding between the people of the United States and other countries. It works in close cooperation with State Department posts through cultural and professional exchanges and presenting U.S. history, society, art, and culture in all of its diversity to overseas audiences.

Bureau of International Information Programs

B-82. The IIP is the principal international strategic communications entity for the foreign affairs community. The IIP informs, engages, and influences international audiences about U.S. policy and society to advance American interests. The IIP develops and implements PD strategies that measurably influence international audiences through quality programs and cutting-edge technologies. The IIP provides localized context for U.S. policies and messages, reaching millions worldwide in English, Arabic, Chinese, French, Persian, Russian, and Spanish.

B-83. The IIP's mission statement is to "inform, engage, and influence international audiences about U.S. policy and society to advance America's interests." The IIP delivers America's message to the world through a number of key products and services. The IIP created this outreach strictly for international audiences, such as international media, government officials, opinion leaders, and the public in more than 140 countries around the world. The IIP—

- Delivers America's message to the world, counteracting negative preconceptions, maintaining an open dialogue, and building bridges of understanding to help build a network of communication, promote American voices, and forge lasting relationships in international communities.
- Delivers clear and meaningful U.S. policy information and articles about U.S. society in the languages that attract the largest number of viewers—English, Arabic, Chinese, French, Persian, Russian, and Spanish.
- Produces news articles and electronic and print publications that provide context to U.S. policies, as well as products on U.S. values, culture, and daily life, that serve as a window on positive American values.
- Engages audiences through lectures, workshops, and seminars to promote understanding of U.S. policies.
- Provides current and authoritative information on U.S. policy issues, legislation, business and trade issues, and U.S. political and social processes to local decision makers and opinion leaders.

INTERNATIONAL BROADCASTING BUREAU

B-84. The USG created the IBB as a federal agency in 1994 to produce political radio and TV broadcasts that intended for audiences in foreign countries. The IBB replaces the defunct Bureau of Broadcasting agency that superseded the Voice of America. The legislation that originally placed the IBB within the United States Information Agency (USIA) also created a Broadcasting Board of Governors (BBG) with oversight authority over all nonmilitary USG international broadcasting. When the government disbanded USIA in 1999, it established the IBB and BBG as independent federal government entities. The IBB and

BBG do not fall under the oversight of the Undersecretary for Public Diplomacy and Public Affairs. The IBB includes—

- The Voice of America (VOA).
- Radio Martí and TV Martí (broadcasting exclusively to Cuba).
- An office of engineering and technical services.

B-85. The BBG funds other international broadcasting services as private corporations that are not part of the IBB. These include Radio Sawa (Arab world), Radio Farda (Persian Farsi to Iran), Radio Free Europe/Radio Liberty, and Radio Free Asia. The IBB provides the technical support of transmission sites in three U.S. states and operates shortwave and mediumwave relay stations in Europe, Africa, and Asia.

B-86. The BBG is made up of nine bipartisan members with expertise in the fields of journalism, broadcasting, and public and international affairs. The President appoints eight members and the U.S. Senate confirms them. The ninth, an ex-officio member, is the Secretary of State. The BBG oversees all USG and government-sponsored, nonmilitary international broadcasting. The BBG board also evaluates the mission and operation of U.S. international broadcasters to ensure statutory compliance, to assess quality and effectiveness, to determine the addition and deletion of language services, and to submit annual reports to the President and Congress.

INFORMATION OPERATIONS

B-87. When some percentage of another state is hostile to U.S. interests to the point that it becomes a defense concern, the United States may engage in IO (PSYOP, EW, physical strike, and so on) against that adversarial percentage.

MILITARY OPERATIONS AND THE INFORMATION ENVIRONMENT

B-88. Information is a strategic resource vital to national security. Dominance of the information environment is a reality that extends to the armed forces of the United States at all levels. Military operations, in particular, are dependent upon many simultaneous and integrated activities that, in turn, depend upon information and information systems, which the United States must protect.

B-89. In modern military operations, commanders face a variety of information challenges. Technical challenges include establishing and maintaining connectivity, particularly in austere and distributed locations. Operational challenges include the complexities of modern combat against adversaries with growing information capabilities. For example, regardless of size, adversaries, including terrorist groups, can counter U.S. efforts through propaganda campaigns or develop, purchase, or download from the Internet tools and techniques enabling them to attack U.S. information and information systems, which may result in tangible impacts on U.S. diplomatic, economic, or military efforts. The global information environment and its associated technologies are potentially available to everyone, and as a result, U.S. military commanders face another challenge. Adversaries now have the capability to pass information, coordinate, exchange ideas, and synchronize their actions instantaneously.

B-90. The commander visualizes, plans, and directs operations—IO are a part of those operations. The commander's intent should specify a visualization of the desired effects of IO and other operations for the staff to develop IO objectives. The commander must not only be able to visualize the desired effects of IO but also to understand the adversary's capabilities to limit the impact of U.S. operations while the adversary strives to acquire information superiority from the United States. These effects can vary based on the objectives of the mission, ranging from disrupting an enemy commander in combat to assuring friendly nations through combined or multinational military training or exercises during peacetime. The nature of the conflict determines the role of the military and the desired end state or effect. If conducting a humanitarian assistance mission, then generating goodwill for the services rendered and departing with a favorable impression of U.S. activities becomes a primary objective. The commander's intent must include the concept of how these effects will help achieve force objectives.

B-91. Military forces operate in an information environment of constantly changing content and tempo. This evolution adds another layer of complexity to the challenge of planning and executing military operations at a specific time and in a specific location. A continuum of long-, medium-, and short-term factors, each of which must be considered together when planning and executing military operations, shapes the information environment. Commanders and IO cell chiefs must be prepared to adapt or modify IO plans to meet their desired IO effects. Long-term factors that may shape the information environment include the various ways by which humans—

- Organize (nation-states, tribes, families).
- Govern.
- Interact as groups (culture, sociology, religion).
- Experience regional influence (stability, alliances, economic relationships).
- Advance technologically.

Medium-term factors may include—

- The rise and fall of leaders.
- The competition between groups over resources or goals.
- The incorporation of specific technologies into information infrastructure.
- The employment of resources by organizations to take advantage of IT and infrastructure.

Short-term factors may include—

- The weather.
- The availability of finite resources to support or employ specific information technology (IT).
- The ability to extend or maintain sensors and portable information infrastructure to the specific location of distant military operations.

B-92. The pervasiveness of the information environment in human activity combined with the speed and processing power of modern IT enhance and complicate military efforts to organize, train, equip, plan, and operate. Today, technology has opened the way to an ever-increasing span of control.

B-93. U.S. forces perform their missions in an increasingly complex information environment. To succeed, it is necessary for U.S. forces to gain and maintain information superiority. DOD policy describes information superiority as the operational advantage gained by the ability to collect, process, and disseminate an uninterrupted flow of information while exploiting or denying an adversary's ability to do the same. The forces possessing better information and using that information to more effectively gain understanding have a major advantage over their adversaries. A commander who gains this advantage can use it to accomplish missions by affecting perceptions, attitudes, decisions, and actions. However, information superiority is not static; during operations, all sides continually attempt to secure their own advantages and deny useful information to adversaries. The operational advantages of information superiority can take several forms, ranging from the ability to create a common operational picture to the ability to delay an adversary's decision to commit reinforcements.

B-94. Recognizing information superiority can be difficult to attain over certain adversaries, but its advantages are significant. When it exists, the information available to commanders allows them to accurately visualize the situation, anticipate events, and make appropriate, timely decisions more effectively than adversary decision makers.

B-95. In essence, information superiority enhances commanders' freedom of action and allows them to execute decisions and maintain the initiative while remaining inside the adversary's decision cycle. However, commanders recognize that without continuous IO designed to achieve and maintain information superiority, adversaries may counter those advantages and possibly attain information superiority themselves. Commanders can achieve information superiority by maintaining accurate situational understanding while controlling or affecting the adversaries' or TAs' perceptions. The more a commander can shape this disparity, the greater the friendly advantage.

B-96. Potential information adversaries come in many shapes. However, they traditionally are hostile countries who wish to gain information on U.S. military capabilities and intentions, malicious hackers who wish to steal from or harm the USG, terrorists, and economic competitors, just to name a few. Potential adversarial information attack techniques are numerous. Some, particularly electronic means, can be prevented by the consistent application of encryption, firewalls, and other network security techniques. Others are considerably more difficult to counter. Possible threat information techniques include but are not

Appendix B

limited to deception, electronic attack (EA), computer network attack (CNA), propaganda and PSYOP, and signals intelligence (SIGINT) operations.

B-97. With the free flow of information present in all theaters, such as TV, phone, and Internet, conflicting messages can quickly emerge to defeat the intended effects. As a result, continuous synchronization and coordination between IO, PA, PD, and U.S. allies is imperative. It also helps to ensure that information themes employed during operations involving neutral or friendly populations remain consistent.

B-98. IO may involve complex legal and policy issues and require careful review. Beyond strict compliance with legalities, U.S. military activities in the information environment, as in the physical domains, are conducted as a matter of policy and societal values on a basis of respect for fundamental human rights. U.S. forces, whether operating physically from bases or locations overseas or from within the boundaries of the United States or elsewhere, are required by law and policy to act in accordance with (IAW) U.S. law and the law of armed conflict.

PRINCIPLES OF INFORMATION OPERATIONS

B-99. Success in military operations depends on collecting and integrating essential information while denying it to the adversary and other TAs. IO encompass planning, coordinating, and synchronizing the employment of current capabilities to deliberately affect or defend the information environment to achieve the commander's objectives. IO are integrated into joint operations as follows:

- Core capabilities (EW, computer network operations [CNO], PSYOP, MILDEC, and OPSEC) are integrated into the planning and execution of operations in the information environment.
- Supporting IO capabilities (IA, physical security, physical attack, CI, and combat camera [COMCAM]) have military purposes other than IO, but they either operate in or affect the information environment.
- Related IO capabilities (PA, CMO, and DSPD) may be constrained by U.S. policy or legal considerations. Although these capabilities have common interfaces with IO, their purposes and rules make them separate and distinct. As a result, it is essential that commanders and their staffs coordinate their efforts when exercising their functions within the information environment.

B-100. IO are primarily concerned with affecting decisions and decision-making processes, while defending friendly decision-making processes. Primary mechanisms used to affect the information environment include influence, disruption, corruption, or usurpation. Table B-1, page B-19, describes how joint operations integrate IO.

B-101. The ability of IO to affect and defend decision making is based on five fundamental assumptions. Although each of these assumptions is an important enabling factor for IO, they will not all necessarily be true for every operation. For any specific operation where one or more of these assumptions are not met, the risk assessment provided to the commander would be adjusted accordingly. The five fundamental assumptions are as follows:

- It is generally accepted that the quality of information that is considered valuable to human and automated decision makers is universal. However, the relative importance of each quality criterion of information may vary based on the influences of geography, language, culture, religion, organization, experience, or personality.
- It is known that decisions are made based on the information available at the time.
- It is possible, with finite resources, to understand the relevant aspects of the information environment to include the processes decision makers use to make decisions.
- It is possible to affect the information environment in which specific decision makers act through psychological, electronic, or physical means.
- It is possible to measure the effectiveness of IO actions in relation to an operational objective.

B-102. Since human activity takes place in the information environment, it is potentially subject to IO. However, IO should only target mission-related critical psychological, electronic, and physical points in the information environment.

B-103. IO capabilities can produce effects and achieve objectives at all levels of war and across the range of military operations. The nature of the modern information environment complicates the identification of

The Informational Instrument of National Power

the boundaries between these levels. Therefore, at all levels, information activities (including IO) must be consistent with broader national security policy and strategic objectives. Sometimes only a small TA is an adversary within an otherwise nonadversarial state. At the other end of the spectrum of conflict, when conflict between states is elevated to potential or actual employment of armed forces, the entire population of an adversarial state may be the TA of IO.

Table B-1. Information operations integration into joint operations

Core, Supporting, Related Information Activities	Activities	Audience/ Target	Objective	Information Quality	Primary Planning/Integration Process	Who Does It?
Electronic Warfare	Electronic Attack	Physical, Informational	Destroy, Disrupt, Delay	Usability	Joint Operation Planning and Execution System (JOPES)/Targeting Process	Individuals, Governments, Militaries
	Electronic Protection	Physical	Protect the Use of Electromagnetic Spectrum	Security	JOPES/Defense Planning	Individuals, Businesses, Governments, Militaries
	Electronic Warfare Support	Physical	Identify and Locate Threats	Usability	Joint Intelligence Preparation of the Operational Environment (JIPOE)/SIGINT Collection	Militaries
Computer Network Operations	Computer Network Attack	Physical, Informational	Destroy, Disrupt, Delay	Security	JIPOE/JOPES/Targeting Process	Individuals, Governments, Militaries
	Computer Network Defense	Physical, Informational	Protect Computer Networks	Security	JOPES/J-6 Vulnerability Analysis	Individuals, Businesses, Governments, Militaries
	Computer Network Exploitation	Informational	Gain Information From and About Computers and Computer Networks	Security	JIPOE/Targeting Process	Individuals, Governments, Militaries
PSYOP	PSYOP	Cognitive	Influence	Relevance	JOPES/Joint Operation Planning	Businesses, Governments, Militaries
Military Deception	Military Deception	Cognitive	Mislead	Accuracy	JOPES/Joint Operation Planning	Militaries
OPSEC	OPSEC	Cognitive	Deny	Security	JOPES/Joint Operation Planning	Businesses, Governments, Militaries
Supporting Capabilities	CI	Cognitive	Mislead	Accuracy	JIPOE/HUMINT Collection	Governments, Militaries
	Combat Camera	Physical	Inform/ Document	Usability, Accuracy	JOPES/Joint Operation Planning	Governments, Militaries
Related Capabilities	CMO	Cognitive	Influence	Accuracy	JOPES/Joint Operation Planning	Governments, Militaries
	Public Affairs	Cognitive	Inform	Accuracy	JOPES/Joint Operation Planning	Businesses, Governments, Militaries
	Public Diplomacy	Cognitive	Inform	Accuracy	Interagency Coordination	Governments

B-104. IO are conducted across the range of military operations. IO can make significant contributions before major operations begin. Because of these factors, the IO environment should be prepared and assessed through a variety of engagement and intelligence activities. In addition to affecting the environment before the onset of military operations, IO are essential to postcombat operations. Therefore, integration, planning, employment, and assessment of core, supporting, and related IO are vital to ensuring a rapid transition to a peaceful environment.

Appendix B

B-105. The ultimate strategic objective of IO is to deter a potential or actual adversary or other TA from taking actions that threaten U.S. national interests. In addition, IO actions executed through civilian-controlled portions of the global information environment must account for U.S. policy and legal issues, as well as potentially disruptive infrastructure issues, through civil-military coordination at all levels. IO actions that may cause unintended reactions from U.S. or foreign populaces also require civil-military coordination.

B-106. IO may target human decision making or automated decision support systems with specific actions. Technology allows for increasingly precise targeting of automated decision making and affords more sophisticated ways to protect it. However, targeting automated decision making is only effective if the adversary is relying on it.

B-107. The focus of IO is on the decision maker and the information environment to affect decision making and thinking processes, knowledge, and understanding of the situation. IO can affect data, information, and knowledge in three basic ways:

- By taking specific psychological, electronic, or physical actions that add, modify, or remove information from the environment of various individuals or groups of decision makers.
- By taking actions to affect the infrastructure that collects, communicates, processes, and stores information in support of targeted decision makers.
- By influencing the way people receive, process, interpret, and use data, information, and knowledge.

B-108. Commanders use IO capabilities in both offensive and defensive operations simultaneously to accomplish the mission, increase their force effectiveness, and protect their organizations and systems. Fully integrating IO capabilities requires planners to treat IO as a single function. Commanders can use IO capabilities to accomplish the following:

- *Destroy.* Destruction is damaging a system or entity so badly that it cannot perform any function without being replaced or entirely rebuilt.
- *Disrupt.* Disruption is breaking or interrupting the flow of information.
- *Degrade.* Degradation is reducing the effectiveness or efficiency of adversary C2 or communications systems and information collection efforts or means. IO can also degrade the morale of a unit, the target's value, or the quality of adversary decisions and actions.
- *Deny.* Denial is preventing the adversary from accessing and using critical information, systems, and services.
- *Deceive.* Deception is causing a person to believe what is not true. MILDEC seeks to mislead adversary decision makers by manipulating their perception of reality.
- *Exploit.* Exploitation is gaining access to adversary C2 systems to collect information or to plant false or misleading information.
- *Influence.* Influence is causing others to behave in a manner favorable to U.S. forces.
- *Protect.* Protection is taking action to guard against espionage or capture of sensitive equipment and information.
- *Detect.* Detection is discovering or discerning the existence, presence, or fact of an intrusion into information systems.
- *Restore.* Restoration is bringing information and information systems back to their original state.
- *Respond.* Response is reacting quickly to an adversary's or others' IO attack or intrusion.

B-109. SC constitutes focused USG efforts to understand and engage key audiences to create, strengthen, or preserve conditions favorable for the advancement of USG interests, policies, and objectives through coordinated programs, plans, themes, messages, and products synchronized with the actions of all elements of national power. DOD efforts must be part of a governmentwide approach to develop and implement a more robust SC capability. The DOD must also support and participate in USG SC activities to understand, inform, and influence relevant foreign audiences, including the DOD's transition to and from hostilities, security, military forward presence, and stability operations. PA, DSPD, and IO capabilities primarily accomplish DOD transition and coordination.

B-110. DOD PA, DSPD, and IO are distinct functions that can support SC. The synchronization of these functions is essential for SC to be effective. CCDRs should ensure IO, PA, and DSPD planning is consistent with overall USG SC objectives. CCDRs also must ensure that the Office of the Secretary of Defense (OSD) approves the planning. CCDRs should integrate an information strategy into planning for peacetime and contingency situations. CCDRs plan, execute, and assess PA, DSPD, and IO activities to implement theater security cooperation plans, to support U.S. Embassies' information programs, and to support other agencies' PD and PA programs that directly support DOD missions.

B-111. IO enables the accuracy and timeliness of information required by U.S. military commanders by defending U.S. systems from exploitation by adversaries. IO are used to deny adversaries access to their C2 information and other supporting automated infrastructures. Adversaries are increasingly exploring and testing IO actions as an asymmetric threat that can be used to thwart U.S. military objectives that are heavily reliant on information systems. This threat requires the U.S. military to employ defensive technologies and utilize leading-edge tactics and procedures to protect U.S. forces and systems from attacks.

CORE, SUPPORTING, AND RELATED INFORMATION OPERATIONS CAPABILITIES

B-112. Of the five core IO capabilities, PSYOP, OPSEC, and MILDEC have played a major part in military operations for many centuries. In this modern age, they have been joined first by EW and most recently by CNO. Together these five capabilities, used in conjunction with supporting and related capabilities, provide the JFC with the principal means of influencing an adversary and other TAs by enabling the joint forces freedom of operation in the information environment.

Psychological Operations

B-113. PSYOP are planned operations to convey selected information and indicators to foreign audiences to influence their emotions, motives, objective reasoning, and ultimately, the behavior of their governments, organizations, groups, and individuals. The purpose of PSYOP is to induce or reinforce foreign attitudes and behaviors favorable to the originator's objectives. PSYOP are a vital part of the broad range of U.S. activities to influence foreign audiences and are the only DOD operations authorized to influence foreign TAs directly through radio, print, and other media. PSYOP personnel advise the supported commander on methods to capitalize on the psychological impacts of every aspect of force employment and on how to develop a strategy for developing and planning the dissemination of specific PSYOP programs to achieve the overall campaign objectives.

B-114. During a crisis, a Psychological Operations assessment team (POAT) deploys at the request of the supported commander. A POAT is a small, tailored team of PSYOP planners, product distribution and dissemination specialists, and logistics specialists. The POAT assesses the situation, develops PSYOP objectives, and recommends the appropriate level of support to accomplish the mission. A POAT can augment a unified command or JTF staff and provide PSYOP planning support. The senior PSYOP officer in the operational area, normally the joint psychological operations task force commander, may also serve as the de facto joint force PSYOP officer. Working through the various component operations staffs, the joint force PSYOP officer ensures continuity of psychological objectives and identifies themes to stress and avoid.

B-115. PSYOP have a central role in the achievement of UW objectives in support of the JFC. In today's information environment, even PSYOP conducted at the tactical level can have strategic effects. Therefore, PSYOP have an approval process that Soldiers must understand. The necessity for timely decisions is fundamental to effective PSYOP and IO. Anticipating PSYOP involvement in the early stages of an operation is particularly important given the time it takes to develop, design, produce, distribute, disseminate, and evaluate PSYOP products and actions. Interagency-coordinated and OSD-approved PSYOP programs oversee the conduct of all PSYOP. The PSYOP program approval process at the national level requires time for sufficient coordination and resolution of issues; hence, JFCs should begin PSYOP planning as early as possible to ensure the execution of PSYOP in support of operations. A JFC must have an approved PSYOP program, execution authority, and delegation of product approval authority before PSYOP execution can begin. JFCs should request PSYOP planners immediately during the initial crisis stages to ensure the JFC has plenty of time to obtain the proper authority to execute PSYOP. PSYOP assets

Appendix B

may be of particular value to the JFC in precombat and postcombat operations when other means of influence are restrained or not authorized.

Military Deception

B-116. MILDEC are deliberately misleading actions executed for adversary decision makers as to friendly military capabilities, intentions, and operations, thereby causing the adversary to take specific actions (or inactions) that contribute to the accomplishment of the friendly forces' mission. MILDEC and OPSEC are complementary activities—MILDEC seeks to encourage incorrect analysis, causing the adversary to arrive at specific false deductions, while OPSEC seeks to deny real information to an adversary and prevent correct deduction of friendly plans. To be effective, a MILDEC operation must be susceptible to adversary collection systems and "seen" as credible to the enemy commander and staff. A plausible approach to MILDEC planning is to employ a friendly COA that friendly forces can execute and that adversary intelligence can verify. However, MILDEC planners must not fall into the trap of ascribing to the adversary particular attitudes, values, and reactions that "mirror image" likely friendly action in the same situation; for example, assuming that the adversary will respond or act in a particular manner based on how U.S. forces would respond.

B-117. Core, supporting, and related IO capabilities always represent competing priorities for the resources required for deception and the resources required for the real operation. For this reason, the deception plan should be developed concurrently with the real plan, starting with the commander's and staff's initial estimate, to ensure proper resourcing of both. To encourage incorrect analysis by the adversary, it is usually more efficient and effective to provide a false purpose for real activity than to create false activity. OPSEC of the deception plan is at least as important as OPSEC of the real plan, since compromise of the deception may expose the real plan. This requirement for close-hold planning while ensuring detailed coordination is the greatest challenge to MILDEC planners. On joint staffs, MILDEC planning and oversight responsibility is normally organized as a staff deception element in the operations directorate of a joint staff (J-3).

B-118. MILDEC is fundamental to successful UW. It exploits the adversary's information systems, processes, and capabilities. Successful MILDEC rely on an understanding of how the adversary commander and his staff think and plan and how both use information management to support their efforts. Effective MILDEC requires a high degree of coordination with all elements of friendly forces' activities in the information environment, as well as with physical activities. Each of the core, supporting, and related capabilities has a part to play in the development of successful MILDEC and in maintaining its credibility over time. While PA should not be involved in the provision of false information, it must be aware of the intent and purpose of MILDEC in order not to inadvertently compromise it.

Operations Security

B-119. OPSEC is a process of identifying critical information and subsequently analyzing friendly actions and other activities to—

- Identify what friendly information is necessary for the adversary to have sufficiently accurate knowledge of friendly forces and intentions.
- Deny adversary decision makers critical information about friendly forces and intentions.
- Cause adversary decision makers to misjudge the relevance of known critical friendly information because other information about friendly forces and intentions remains secure.

B-120. On joint staffs, the J-3 is normally responsible for OPSEC. A designated OPSEC program manager supervises other members of the command-assigned OPSEC team and oversees the coordination, development, and implementation of OPSEC as an integrated part of IO in the operational area.

B-121. OPSEC denies the adversary the information needed to correctly assess friendly capabilities and intentions. In particular, OPSEC complements MILDEC by denying an adversary information required to both assess a real plan and to disprove a deception plan. For those IO capabilities that exploit new opportunities and vulnerabilities, such as EW and CNO, OPSEC is essential to ensure uncompromised friendly capabilities.

B-122. The process of identifying essential elements of friendly information and taking measures to mask them from disclosure to adversaries is only one part of a defense-in-depth approach to securing friendly information. To be effective, other types of security must complement OPSEC. Examples of other types of security include physical security, IA programs, computer network defense (CND), and personnel programs that screen personnel and limit authorized access.

Electronic Warfare

B-123. EW plays a limited role in UW. EW refers to any military action involving the use of electromagnetic (EM) and directed energy to control the EM spectrum or to attack the adversary. EW includes three major subdivisions: EA, electronic protection (EP), and electronic warfare support (ES). EA involves the use of EM energy, directed energy, or antiradiation weapons to attack personnel, facilities, or equipment with the intent of degrading, neutralizing, or destroying adversary combat capability. EP ensures the friendly use of the EM spectrum. ES consists of actions tasked by or under direct control of an operational commander to search for, intercept, identify, and locate or localize sources of intentional and unintentional radiated EM energy for the purpose of immediate threat recognition, targeting, planning, and conduct of future operations. ES provides information required for decisions involving EW operations and other tactical actions, such as threat avoidance, targeting, and homing. Forces can use ES data to produce SIGINT, provide targeting for electronic or other forms of attack, and produce measurement and signature intelligence (MASINT). SIGINT and MASINT can also provide battle damage assessment (BDA) and feedback on the effectiveness of the overall operational plan.

B-124. EW contributes to the success of IO by using offensive and defensive tactics and techniques in a variety of combinations to shape, disrupt, and exploit adversarial use of the EM spectrum while protecting friendly freedom of action in that spectrum. Expanding reliance on the EM spectrum for informational purposes increases both the potential and the challenges of EW in IO. The increasing prevalence of wireless telephone and computer usage extends both the utility and threat of EW, offering opportunities to exploit an adversary's electronic vulnerabilities and a requirement to identify and protect such U.S. assets from similar exploitation.

Computer Network Operations

B-125. CNO are one of the latest capabilities developed in support of military operations. CNO stem from the increasing use of networked computers and supporting infrastructure systems by military and civilian organizations. Forces use CNO, along with EW, to attack, deceive, degrade, disrupt, deny, exploit, and defend electronic information and infrastructure. For the purpose of military operations, CNO are divided into CNA, CND, and related computer network exploitation (CNE) enabling operations. CNA consists of actions taken through the use of computer networks to disrupt, deny, degrade, or destroy information resident in computers and computer networks, or the computers and networks themselves. CND involves actions taken through the use of computer networks to protect, monitor, analyze, detect, and respond to unauthorized activity within DOD information systems and computer networks. CND actions not only protect DOD systems from an external adversary but also from exploitation from within, and are now a necessary function in all military operations. CNE is enabling operations and intelligence collection capabilities conducted through the use of computer networks to gather data from target or adversary automated information systems or networks. Because of the continued expansion of wireless networking and the integration of computers and radio frequency communications, there will be operations and capabilities that blur the line between CNO and EW, and that may require case-by-case determination when EW and CNO are assigned separate release authorities.

B-126. The increasing reliance of unsophisticated militaries and terrorist groups on computers and computer networks to pass information to C2 forces reinforces the importance of CNO in UW plans and activities. As the capability of computers and the range of their employment broaden, new vulnerabilities and opportunities will continue to develop. CNO offer both opportunities to attack and exploit an adversary's computer system weaknesses and a requirement to identify and protect U.S. systems from similar attack or exploitation.

B-127. Capabilities supporting IO include IA, physical security, physical attack, CI, and COMCAM. These are either directly or indirectly involved in the information environment and contribute to effective

Appendix B

IO. They should be integrated and coordinated with the core capabilities, but also serve other wider purposes.

Information Assurance

B-128. The U.S. military defines IA as measures that protect and defend information and information systems by ensuring their availability, integrity, authentication, confidentiality, and nonrepudiation. IA includes providing for restoration of information systems by incorporating protection, detection, and reaction capabilities. IA is necessary to gain and maintain information superiority. IA requires a defense-in-depth approach that integrates the capabilities of people, operations, and technology to establish multilayer and multidimensional protection to ensure survivability and mission accomplishment. IA assumes others can gain access to information and information systems from inside and outside DOD-controlled networks. In joint organizations, IA is a responsibility of the J-6.

B-129. UW depends on IA to protect information and information systems, thereby assuring continuous capability. IA and IO have an operational relationship in which IO are concerned with the coordination of military activities in the information environment, while IA protects the electronic and automated portions of the information environment. IA and all aspects of CNO are interrelated and rely upon each other to be effective. IO relies on IA to protect infrastructure to ensure its availability to position information for influence purposes and for the delivery of information to the adversary. Conversely, IA relies on IO to provide operational protection with coordinated OPSEC, EP, CND, and CI against adversary IO or intelligence efforts directed against friendly electronic information or information systems.

Physical Security

B-130. Physical security is that part of security concerned with physical measures designed to safeguard personnel and to prevent unauthorized access to equipment, installations, material, and documents against espionage, sabotage, damage, and theft. The physical security process includes determining vulnerabilities to known threats; applying appropriate deterrent, control, and denial safeguarding techniques and measures; and responding to changing conditions.

B-131. Just as IA protects friendly electronic information and information systems, physical security protects physical facilities containing information and information systems worldwide. Physical security often contributes to OPSEC, particularly in the case of MILDEC, when compromise of the MILDEC activity could compromise the real plan. UW plans may require significant physical security resources and the J-3 must understand this requirement as early as possible in the planning process.

Physical Attack

B-132. Physical attack disrupts, damages, or destroys adversary targets through destructive power. Forces can also use physical attack to create or alter adversary perceptions or drive an adversary to use certain exploitable information systems. Physical attack can be employed in support of UW as a means of attacking C2 nodes to affect enemy ability to exercise C2 and to influence TAs. Commanders can employ IO capabilities, for example PSYOP, in support of physical attack to maximize the effect of the attack on the morale of an adversary. The integration and synchronization of fires with IO through the targeting process is fundamental to creating the necessary synergy between IO and more traditional maneuver and strike operations. To achieve this integration, commanders must be able to define the effects they seek to achieve and staffs will incorporate these capabilities into the commander's plan. Specifically, because of the fast-paced conduct of air operations, it is crucial that the planning and execution of both IO and air operations be conducted concurrently to produce the most effective targeting plan.

Counterintelligence

B-133. CI consists of information gathered and activities conducted to protect against espionage, other intelligence activities, sabotage, or assassinations conducted by or on behalf of foreign governments or elements thereof, foreign organizations, foreign persons, or international terrorist activities. The CI programs in joint staffs are a responsibility of the CI and human intelligence staff element of the intelligence directorate. CI procedures are a critical part of guarding friendly information and information systems. A robust security program that integrates IA, physical security, CI, and OPSEC with risk management procedures offers the best chance to protect friendly information and information systems from adversary actions. CNO provide some of the tools needed to conduct CI operations. For the IO planner, CI analysis offers a view of the adversary's information-gathering methodology. From this, CI can develop the initial intelligence target opportunities that provide access to the adversary for MILDEC information, PSYOP products, and CNA/CNE actions.

Combat Camera

B-134. The COMCAM mission is to provide the OSD, the CJCS, the military departments, the COCOMs, and the JTF with an imagery capability in support of operational and planning requirements across the range of military operations. The COMCAM is responsible for rapid development and dissemination of products that support strategic and operational IO objectives. The COMCAM program belongs to the defense visual information directorate, which falls under the assistant secretary of defense for public affairs. The JFC and subordinate commanders can delegate operational control of COMCAM forces to any echelon of command. The IO staff at the JFC, component, and subordinate unit levels may coordinate the COMCAM. The commander with operational control can assign COMCAM teams to SOF or other specific units.

B-135. COMCAM supports all of the capabilities of IO that use images of U.S. or friendly force operations, whether to influence an adversary or other TAs or support U.S. forces or allies. COMCAM provides images for PSYOP, MILDEC, PA, and CMO use. However, COMCAM can also be used for BDA/MOE analysis. COMCAM can also provide records of IO actions for subsequent rebuttal proceedings. However, the command must control COMCAM imagery to ensure that OPSEC is maintained and valuable information is not released to the adversary. The quality and format, including digital video/still photography and night and thermal imagery, means that COMCAM products can be provided to professional news organizations by PA when they are unable to provide their own imagery.

B-136. There are three military functions—PA, CMO, and DSPD—specified as related capabilities for IO. These capabilities make significant contributions to IO and must always be coordinated and integrated with the core and supporting IO capabilities. However, IO must not compromise the primary purpose and rules under which PA, CMO, and DSPD operate. Avoiding compromise requires additional care and consideration in the planning and conduct of UW. For this reason, the PA and CMO staffs particularly must work in close coordination with the IO planning staff.

Public Affairs

B-137. PA are those public information, command information, and community relations activities directed toward both external and internal audiences with interest in the DOD. PA is essential for joint forces information superiority, and credible PA operations are necessary to support the commander's mission and maintain essential public liaisons. PA's principal focus is to inform domestic and international audiences of joint operations to support COCOM public information needs.

B-138. PA and IO must be coordinated and synchronized to ensure that personnel communicate consistent themes and messages to maintain credibility. As with other core, supporting, and related IO capabilities related IO capabilities, PA has a role in all aspects of DOD's missions and functions. Communication of operational matters to internal and external audiences is just one part of PA's function. In performing duties as one of the primary spokesmen, the PA officer's interaction with the IO staff enables PA activities to be integrated, coordinated, and deconflicted with IO. While intents differ, PA and IO ultimately support the dissemination of information, themes, and messages adapted to their audiences. PA contributes to the achievement of military objectives, for instance, by countering adversary misinformation and disinformation through the publication of accurate information. PA also assists OPSEC by ensuring that the media are aware of the implications of premature release of information. The embedding of media in combat units offers new opportunities, as well as risks, for the media and the military; the PA staff has a key role in establishing rules for embedding media personnel. Many adversaries rely on limiting their population's knowledge to remain in power; PA and IO provide ways to get the joint forces' messages to these populations.

Civil-Military Operations

B-139. CMO are the activities of a commander that establish, maintain, influence, or exploit relations between military forces, governmental and nongovernmental civilian organizations and authorities, and the civilian populace. CMO are conducted across the spectrum of conflict to address root causes of instability, assist in reconstruction after conflict or disaster, or support U.S. national security objectives. CMO can occur in friendly, neutral, or hostile operational areas to facilitate military operations and achieve U.S. objectives. CMO may include performance by military forces of activities and functions that are normally the responsibility of local, regional, or national government. These activities may occur before, during, or subsequent to other military actions. CMO may be performed by designated CA, by other military forces, or by a combination of CA and other forces. Certain types of organizations are particularly suited to this mission and form the nucleus of CMO. These units are typically CA and PSYOP units. Others units, such as other SOF, engineers, health service support, transportation, military police, and security forces, may act as enablers. Personnel skilled in the language and culture of the population are essential to CMO.

B-140. CMO can be particularly effective in peacetime and precombat and postcombat operations when other capabilities and actions may be constrained. Early consideration of the civil-military environment in which operations will take place is important. As with PA, the CMO staff also has an important role to play in the development of broader UW plans and objectives. As the accessibility of information to the widest public audiences increases and as forces increasingly conduct military operations in open environments, the importance of CMO to the achievement of UW objectives will increase. At the same time the direct involvement of CMO with core, supporting, and related IO capabilities (for instance, PSYOP, CNO, and CI) will also increase. CMO, by their nature, usually affect public perceptions in their immediate locale. Distribution of information about CMO efforts and results through PA and PSYOP can affect the perceptions of a broader audience and favorably influence key groups or individuals.

Defense Support to Public Diplomacy

B-141. DSPD consists of activities and measures taken by DOD components, not solely in the area of IO, to support and facilitate public diplomacy efforts of the USG. The DOD contributes to PD, which includes those overt international information activities of the USG designed to promote U.S. foreign policy objectives by seeking to understand, inform, and influence foreign audiences and opinion makers and by broadening the dialogue between American citizens and institutions and their counterparts abroad. When approved, commanders may employ PSYOP assets in support of DSPD as part of security cooperation initiatives or in support of U.S. Embassy PD programs. Much of the operational-level IO activity conducted in any theater will be directly linked to PD objectives. DSPD requires coordination with both the interagency and among DOD components.

Appendix C
The Intelligence Instrument of National Power

INSTRUMENTS OF UNITED STATES INTELLIGENCE POWER

Our job is to effectively integrate foreign, military, and domestic intelligence in defense of the homeland and of United States interests abroad.

John Negroponte,
Director of National Intelligence

MISSION AND AUTHORITIES OF THE DIRECTOR OF NATIONAL INTELLIGENCE

C-1. The Director of National Intelligence (DNI) serves as the head of the IC, overseeing and directing the implementation of the National Intelligence Program (NIP) and acting as the principal advisor to the President, the NSC, and the Homeland Security Council for intelligence matters. Working together with the Principal Deputy Director of National Intelligence (PDDNI) and with the assistance of mission managers and four deputy directors, the goal of the Office of the Director of National Intelligence (ODNI) is to protect and defend American lives and interests through effective intelligence. With this goal in mind, Congress provided the DNI with a number of authorities and duties, as outlined in the Intelligence Reform and Terrorism Prevention Act (IRTPA) of 2004. These charge the DNI to—

- Ensure that the President, the heads of departments and agencies of the executive branch, the CJCS, senior military commanders, and the Congress receive timely and objective national intelligence.
- Establish objectives and priorities for collection, analysis, production, and dissemination of national intelligence.
- Ensure maximum availability of and access to intelligence information within the IC.
- Oversee coordination of relationships with the intelligence or security services of foreign governments and international organizations.
- Support national security needs by ensuring that the analysis of intelligence is the most accurate derivation available.
- Develop personnel policies and programs to enhance the capacity for joint operations and to facilitate staffing of community management functions.

OFFICE OF THE DIRECTOR OF NATIONAL INTELLIGENCE LEADERSHIP

C-2. The ODNI includes four directorates that focus on management, collection, requirements, and analysis. The deputy directors in each of these areas, along with the PDDNI, work closely with each other to lead community-wide efforts to budget for, collect, analyze, and support intelligence needs on a national level.

C-3. The mission of the Deputy Director of National Intelligence (DDNI) for Management is administrative management of the IC, strategic planning and coordination, and the development and execution of the NIP budget.

C-4. The Office of the DDNI for Collection coordinates collection throughout the IC and ensures that the National Intelligence Strategy priorities are appropriately reflected in future planning and systems acquisition decisions. The Office of the DDNI for Collection looks across the entire collection business enterprise to develop corporate understanding of needs, requirements, and capabilities to ensure that personnel view current and future collection systems holistically. The DDNI for Collection brings together key IC stakeholders to get senior-level insight into issues. Four assistant deputies support the DDNI for Collection. They are the Assistant DDNI for Collection Strategies, the Assistant DDNI for HUMINT, the Assistant DDNI for Open Source, and the Assistant DDNI for Technical Means.

Appendix C

C-5. Requirements drive intelligence, and the Office of the DDNI for Requirements ensures decision makers receive timely and actionable information that allows them to fulfill their respective national security missions by articulating, advocating, and coordinating requirements within the IC. The DDNI for Requirements interfaces with intelligence customers at the national, state, and local levels and acts as an advocate for them. The DDNI for Requirements provides organizations not traditionally associated with national intelligence with a link to information, products, and avenues for sharing; anticipates customer requirements; and evaluates and reports on how the IC's effectiveness and timeliness in meeting the needs of senior decision makers.

C-6. The Office of the DDNI for Analysis manages and establishes common policies and standards to ensure the highest quality, timeliness, and utility of synthesized analytic resources. The DDNI for Analysis works to increase expertise and to improve analytic tradecraft at individual, agency, and community levels through specialization, training, collaboration, and cross-fertilization. Some of the most important functions of the DDNI for Analysis include establishing analytic priorities; ensuring timely and effective analysis and dissemination of analysis; tasking of analytic products; and encouraging sound analytic methods, all-source analysis, competitive analysis, and resource recommendations regarding the need to balance collection and analytic capabilities. The DDNI for Analysis can only accomplish these key functions in close coordination with the DDNIs for Collection and Requirements. Finally, the DDNI for Analysis manages the production of the President's Daily Brief and serves concurrently as the Chairman of the National Intelligence Council (NIC).

C-7. The NIC is a key component of the ODNI structure. The NIC serves as a unique bridge between the intelligence and policy communities, a source of deep substantive expertise on intelligence matters, and as a facilitator of IC collaboration. Added to the ODNI structure by the IRTPA, the NIC supports the DNI in his role as head of the IC and serves as the center for midterm and long-term strategic thinking. The NIC's core missions are to produce National Intelligence Estimates (NIEs), the IC's most authoritative written assessments on national security issues, and a broad range of other products; to reach out to nongovernmental experts in academia and the private sector to broaden the IC's perspective; and to articulate substantive intelligence priorities and procedures to guide intelligence collection and analysis.

MISSION MANAGERS

C-8. The DNI also has six mission managers who serve as the principal IC officials overseeing all aspects of intelligence related to their targets. These significant areas of focus are—
- Iran.
- North Korea.
- Cuba and Venezuela.
- Counterterrorism—led by the Director of the National Counterterrorism Center (NCTC).
- Counterproliferation—led by the Director of the National Counterproliferation Center.
- Counterintelligence—led by the Director of the National Counterintelligence Executive.

C-9. In each area, mission managers are responsible for understanding the requirements of intelligence consumers; providing consistent overall guidance on collection priorities, integration, and gaps; assessing analytic quality and capabilities and gaps; sharing of intelligence information on the target; and recommending funding, investment, and research and development resource allocations.

C-10. Of note is the NCTC—a multiagency organization dedicated to eliminating the terrorist threat to U.S. interests at home and abroad. The NCTC is the primary organization in the USG for integrating and analyzing all intelligence pertaining to terrorism and CT and for conducting operational planning by integrating all instruments of national power. Finally, the Program Manager for the Information-Sharing Environment oversees the policies, procedures, and technologies linking the resources (people, systems, databases, and information) of federal, state, local, and tribal entities and the private sector to facilitate terrorism information sharing, access, and collaboration among users to combat terrorism more effectively.

Central Intelligence Agency

C-11. The CIA is responsible to the President through the DNI and accountable to the American people through the Intelligence Oversight Committees of the Congress. The Director of Central Intelligence Agency (DCIA) also serves as the National HUMINT Manager. The core mission of the CIA is to support the President, the NSC, and all officials who make and execute U.S. national security policy by—

- Providing accurate, comprehensive, and timely foreign intelligence and analysis on national security topics.
- Conducting CI activities, special activities, and other functions related to foreign intelligence and national security as directed by the President.

C-12. To accomplish the mission, the CIA works closely with the rest of the IC and OGAs to ensure that intelligence consumers—whether administration policy makers, diplomats, or military commanders—receive the best intelligence possible. The CIA is organized into four mission components called directorates, which together carry out the intelligence process—the cycle of collecting, analyzing, and disseminating intelligence.

C-13. The National Clandestine Service (NCS) is the clandestine arm of the CIA. Its core mission is to support U.S. security and foreign policy interests by conducting clandestine activities to collect information that is not obtainable through other means. Analysts review the information that the NCS collects for reliability before disseminating it to policy makers. Although the primary focus of the NCS is the collection and dissemination of foreign intelligence, it also conducts CI activities abroad and special activities as authorized by the President. The Director of the National Clandestine Service (DNCS) serves as the national authority for the integration, coordination, deconfliction, and evaluation of clandestine HUMINT operations across the IC, under the authorities delegated to the DCIA as the National HUMINT Manager. The NCS develops common standards for all aspects of clandestine HUMINT operations, including human-enabled technical operations, across the IC. The DNCS also oversees the CIA's clandestine operations.

C-14. The Directorate of Intelligence (DI) supports the President, administration policy makers, the Congress, Pentagon planners and warfighters, law enforcement agencies, and negotiators with timely, comprehensive all-source intelligence analysis about a wide range of national security issues. The DI integrates, analyzes, and evaluates information collected through clandestine and other means, including open sources, to generate value-added insights. The substantive scope of the DI is worldwide and covers functional as well as regional issues; its products range from quick-reaction, informal oral briefings to complex, long-term research studies. The DI works closely with the NCS and other collectors to enhance the quality and timeliness of intelligence support to consumers. This partnership provides a single focal point within the CIA for the consumer and strengthens CIA's analytical efforts in support of policy makers' needs.

C-15. The Directorate of Science and Technology (DS&T) works closely with the NCS and DI to access, collect, and exploit critical intelligence by applying innovative scientific, engineering, and technical solutions. DS&T officers engage in programs to assure clandestine access to intelligence targets worldwide, to obtain intelligence through technical means, to provide technical support to clandestine operations, and to discover new technologies that will enhance intelligence collection. The DS&T maintains extensive contacts with the scientific and technical communities nationwide and can rapidly assemble experts in many fields to bring the technological prowess of the United States to bear on fast-breaking intelligence and national security issues.

C-16. The Directorate of Support (DS) provides integrated, mission-critical support to the NCS, DI, DS&T, and the IC. The DS has a significant number of personnel with professional certifications, including doctors, lawyers, accountants, engineers, law enforcement officers, and architects. Its workforce supports the CIA's mission worldwide, providing around-the-clock support that is international in focus and clandestine in nature. The DS embeds about half of its workforce within various mission partners, with the largest concentration these workers serving in the NCS and elsewhere in the IC. The DS maintains a broad range of capabilities to support CIA's unique mission.

Appendix C

Defense Intelligence Agency

C-17. The DIA is a major producer and manager of foreign military intelligence for the DOD and is a principal member of the IC. The DIA's mission is to provide timely, objective, all-source military intelligence to policy makers, the U.S. armed forces, U.S. acquisition community, and U.S. force planners to counter a variety of threats and challenges across the range of military operations. The Director of the DIA is a three-star military officer who serves as the principal advisor on substantive military intelligence matters to the SecDef and the CJCS. In addition, he is the Program Manager for the General Defense Intelligence Program (GDIP), which funds a variety of military intelligence programs at and above the corps level, and is the Chairman of the Military Intelligence Board, which examines key intelligence issues and provides defense intelligence inputs to the NIE.

C-18. DIA's Defense Intelligence Operations Coordination Center (DIOCC) integrates all defense intelligence resources on transnational threats to U.S. national security and enhances defense intelligence collaboration. The DIOCC collaborates with DOD and national intelligence resources to manage risk and resource requirements. It integrates and synchronizes all-source military and national-level intelligence capabilities in support of warfighters.

C-19. The Joint Functional Component Command for Intelligence, Surveillance, and Reconnaissance (JFCC-ISR) works closely with the DIOCC to manage risk and intelligence resources. The DIA director is the commander of this U.S. strategic command organization. The JFCC-ISR monitors COCOM ISR information needs, serves as the IC's entry point into the DOD ISR system, and works to maximize efficient use of ISR assets and identify gaps in ISR coverage.

C-20. Through the Joint Staff J-2, DIA operates the National Military Joint Intelligence Center (NMJIC), which is collocated with the National Military Command Center. The NMJIC provides real-time indicators and warnings of breaking situations and serves as the national focal point for crisis intelligence support to military operations. During a crisis or contingency, the DIA establishes intelligence task forces, working groups, or cells in the NMJIC to monitor unfolding events.

C-21. The DIA centrally manages defense intelligence analysis and production using a distributed analytical process known as the Defense Intelligence Analysis Program (DIAP). This program integrates general military intelligence and scientific and technical intelligence production conducted at DIA, COCOMs, and Service intelligence centers. The DIAP allows the DIA to focus all-source defense intelligence analysis efforts on compelling issues for defense customers while limiting duplication of effort. The DIA employs extensive analytic expertise in a number of areas, including—

- Foreign military forces, intentions, and capabilities.
- Foreign military leadership analysis.
- Proliferation of WMD.
- Defense-related political and economic developments.
- Advanced military technologies and material production.
- Information warfare.
- Missile and space developments.
- Defense-related medical and health issues.

C-22. To support all-source analytical efforts, the DIA directs and manages DOD intelligence collection requirements for the various intelligence collection disciplines, such as HUMINT, MASINT, imagery intelligence (IMINT), and SIGINT. The Defense Human Intelligence Management Office (DHMO) ensures a strong defense HUMINT program by centrally managing all DOD HUMINT methodology, techniques, and procedures while decentralizing execution. DHMO accomplishes this task by linking the various components of the Defense HUMINT community through common communication architecture, common standards, and common training, thereby eliminating gaps between all levels of operation.

C-23. DIA's Directorate for Human Intelligence (DH) conducts HUMINT operations worldwide to obtain critical intelligence often not available from technical collection means. DH operations provide in-depth and actionable intelligence to policy makers and military forces in the field. DH manages the Defense Attaché System. This system currently has military attachés assigned to more than 135 U.S. Embassies. These attachés are an integral part of the U.S. diplomatic presence abroad. Attachés develop working relationships with foreign military forces. They represent the SecDef and other senior DOD officials to their overseas military counterparts.

C-24. The DIA manages various national and DOD activities related to MASINT, which is technically derived information that measures, detects, tracks, and identifies unique characteristics of fixed and dynamic targets. To further MASINT usefulness, the DIA spearheads significant advances in complex collection technology, such as unattended sensors for chemical and biological programs. MASINT technologies allow the DOD to confidently monitor arms control agreements, to make "smart" weapons even smarter, and to support FP and missile defense efforts.

C-25. DIA's Joint Intelligence Task Force for Combating Terrorism consolidates and produces all-source terrorism-related intelligence and leads and manages the DOD CT intelligence effort to warn U.S. forces and to support offensive CT operations. It collects, analyzes, and shares intelligence with military commanders, government officials, and other intelligence agencies. The DIA also serves as executive agent for the U.S. IC's Prisoner of War/Missing in Action Analytic Cell. This unit provides actionable, national-level intelligence support to locate missing, isolated, evading, or captured U.S. military or USG personnel.

C-26. DIA's Armed Forces Medical Intelligence Center provides medical profiles of foreign countries and assesses real and potential health hazards to support U.S. armed forces operations worldwide to include humanitarian operations.

C-27. To support the growing demand for intelligence agility and global collaboration, DIA provides state-of-the-practice data and information management capabilities and operates one of the world's most robust communications systems, the Joint Worldwide Intelligence Communications System (JWICS)—essentially a very secure Internet. JWICS is a secure, high-bandwidth system providing full motion video teleconferencing and data exchange that serves the entire IC. The DIA is also responsible for the intelligence IT management of the COCOMs, which creates greater efficiency and promotes sharing of information. Intelligence IT management also allows the development of a single DOD data standard for information metadata tagging and ensures that every DOD system tracks, tags, and stores data the same way. This consolidation of resource management ensures integrated and interoperable intelligence information architecture.

Department of Energy Office of Intelligence and Counterintelligence

C-28. The Department of Energy's (DOE's) Office of Intelligence and Counterintelligence (IN) core mission is to—
- Defend the DOE complex from foreign penetration.
- Gauge the worldwide threat of nuclear terrorism.
- Counter the spread of nuclear technologies, materials, and expertise.
- Enrich IC access to information in DOE core areas, particularly with respect to energy.
- Evaluate emerging foreign technology threats to U.S. economic and military interests.

C-29. The DOE's intelligence program continues to evolve in close concert with changing policy needs and the strengths of the DOE's unique scientific and technological base, from the world energy crisis of the 1970s to the emergence of nuclear terrorism as an urgent national security priority in the new millennium. The IN supports senior policy officials at the DOE, the White House, and elsewhere among national security agencies by identifying and evaluating policy opportunities and challenges in areas of unique IN expertise and providing ongoing support to policy in the development and implementation phases. The IN serves as a bridge between the intelligence, special operations, and law enforcement communities on the one hand and the DOE's technology development base on the other, providing near-term technology applications and operational support.

Department of Homeland Security Office of Intelligence and Analysis

C-30. Intelligence in the DHS consists of the Office of Intelligence and Analysis (I&A) and intelligence offices located within the DHS's operational components. DHS intelligence analysts track terrorists and their networks and assess threats to U.S. critical infrastructures from bioterrorism, nuclear terrorism, pandemic diseases, U.S. border (air, land, and sea) weaknesses, and radical elements within U.S. society.

C-31. The chief intelligence officer established the Homeland Security Intelligence Council, which includes intelligence principals from DHS's operating components, to integrate DHS intelligence. The DHS I&A works with Customs and Border Protection, the Immigration and Naturalization Service, and Immigration and Customs Enforcement to ensure the full capabilities of the national IC are used to increase intelligence collection along U.S. borders. The DHS I&A embeds intelligence officers in state and local fusion centers nationwide, and its Homeland Infrastructure and Threat Reduction Assessment Center shares terrorist threat capacities and U.S. vulnerability awareness with the private sector.

Department of State Bureau of Intelligence and Research

C-32. The Bureau of Intelligence and Research (INR) provides the Secretary of State with timely, objective analysis of global developments, as well as real-time insights from all-source intelligence. It serves as the focal point within the DOS for all policy issues and activities involving the IC. The INR's expert, independent foreign affairs analysts draw on all-source intelligence, diplomatic reporting, INR's public opinion polling, and interaction with U.S. and foreign scholars. Their strong regional and functional backgrounds allow them to respond rapidly to changing policy priorities and to provide early warning and in-depth analysis of events and trends that affect U.S. foreign policy and national security interests. INR analysts—a combination of Foreign Service officers with extensive in-country experience and Civil Service specialists with in-depth expertise—cover all countries and regional or transnational issues.

C-33. INR products cover the globe on foreign relations issues such as political and military developments, terrorism, narcotics, and trade. The INR contributes to the IC's NIEs, the Presidential Daily Brief, and other analyses. The INR disseminates many of its products on the IC's Intelink system. In support of the statutory authority of the Secretary of State and Chiefs of Mission for the conduct of foreign policy and oversight of USG activities overseas, the INR coordinates on behalf of the DOS on issues concerning intelligence, CI, and special operations.

C-34. The INR develops DOS intelligence policy and works to harmonize all agencies' intelligence activities abroad with U.S. policy. The INR analyzes geographical and international boundary issues. Its Humanitarian Information Unit serves as a nucleus for unclassified information related to complex emergencies and provides a coordinating mechanism for data sharing among the USG, the UN, NGOs, and foreign governments.

Department of the Treasury Office of Intelligence and Analysis

C-35. The Office of Intelligence and Analysis (OIA) is responsible for the receipt, analysis, collation, and dissemination of foreign intelligence and foreign CI information related to the operation and responsibilities of the Treasury. The OIA is within the Treasury's Office of Terrorism and Financial Intelligence. The OIA is a member of the IC. Some of OIA's strategic goals are to—

- Support the formulation of policy and execution of Treasury authorities by providing expert analysis and intelligence production on financial and other support networks for terrorist groups, proliferators, and other key national security threats.
- Provide timely, accurate, and focused intelligence support to the Treasury on the full range of economic, political, and security issues.

C-36. The OIA's strategic priorities are—

- *Terrorist financing.* Terrorist threats have become far more decentralized in nature. Many terrorist groups, especially those affiliated with al-Qaeda, now pose a serious threat to U.S. national security. The OIA continues to develop its analytic expertise and expand its analytic coverage on the financial and other support networks of the various terrorist groups and networks intent on attacking the United States and its allies.
- *Insurgent financing.* The OIA continues to improve its understanding of insurgency financing, primarily through the Baghdad-based Iraq Threat Finance Cell, which the Treasury leads together with the DOD. Insurgent financing intelligence is critical to support and strengthen

U.S., Iraqi, and coalition efforts to disrupt and eliminate financial and other material support to the insurgency.
- *Rogue regimes and proliferation financing.* The OIA combats other national security threats, including rogue regimes involved in WMD proliferation, such as Iran, Syria, and North Korea.

Drug Enforcement Administration Office of National Security Intelligence

C-37. The Drug Enforcement Administration Office of National Security Intelligence (DEA/NN) is a part of the DEA Intelligence Division. This office works with other IC members on issues of national security interest in an integrated fashion. The DEA/NN assigns personnel to analysis, liaison, and central tasking management functions.

C-38. The DEA/NN establishes and manages centralized tasking of requests for and analysis of national security information obtained during the DEA's drug enforcement mission. The office also centrally manages requests from the IC for information either stored in the DEA under the authority the DEA derives from Title 21 USC or obtained for the IC through existing assets operating pursuant to DEA's law enforcement missions.

C-39. The DEA/NN's membership in the IC optimizes the overall USG counternarcotics interdiction and security effort and furthers creative collaboration between the many organizations involved in countering the threats from narcotics trafficking, human smuggling and trafficking, immigration crimes, and global terrorism. Some of the most serious threats to national security exist at the core of these transnational threats. The DEA's membership in the IC permits greater exploitation of its intelligence capabilities. The DEA has the largest U.S. law enforcement presence abroad with 86 offices in 63 countries, and it has over 33 years of operational experience in the foreign arena.

Federal Bureau of Investigation National Security Branch

C-40. The traditional responsibilities of the FBI are to uphold and enforce federal criminal laws of the United States and to provide leadership and criminal justice services to federal, state, municipal, tribal, and international agencies and partners. Since 9/11, the FBI's overriding priority has been protecting the United States by preventing future attacks. In this national security role, the FBI's top three priorities are—
- Protecting the United States from terrorist attack.
- Protecting the United States against foreign intelligence operations and espionage.
- Protecting the United States against cyber-based attacks and high-technology crimes.

C-41. The National Security Branch (NSB) integrates the FBI's primary national security programs under a single FBI official who is under the leadership of the DNI. The NSB consists of the CT Division, the CI Division, and the Directorate of Intelligence.

C-42. The CT Division develops and executes an integrated investigative and intelligence strategy to use criminal law enforcement and nonprosecutorial sanctions to identify, disrupt, and neutralize individuals and groups with the capacity to organize, plan, and carry out terrorist acts against the United States at home and against U.S. interests abroad.

C-43. As the lead CI agency in the United States, the FBI is responsible for identifying and neutralizing ongoing national security threats. The CI Division provides centralized management and oversight for all foreign CI investigations. It ensures that offensive operations and investigations are fully coordinated within the IC and focused on those countries, foreign powers, or entities that pose the most significant threat to the United States.

C-44. The FBI uses intelligence to investigate and solve cases. The mission of the Directorate of Intelligence is to optimally position the FBI to meet current and emerging national security and criminal threats by—
- Aiming core investigative work proactively against threats to U.S. interests.
- Building and sustaining enterprise-wide intelligence policies and capabilities.

Appendix C

- Providing useful, appropriate, and timely information and analysis to the national security, homeland security, and law enforcement communities.

National Geospatial-Intelligence Agency

C-45. The National Geospatial-Intelligence Agency (NGA) provides timely, relevant, and accurate geospatial intelligence in support of national security objectives. Geospatial intelligence is the exploitation and analysis of imagery and geospatial information to describe, assess, and visually depict physical features and geographically referenced activities on the Earth. The NGA tailors information collected and processed for customer-specific solutions. By giving customers ready access to geospatial intelligence, the NGA provides support to civilian and military leaders and contributes to the state of readiness of U.S. military forces. The NGA also contributes to humanitarian efforts, such as tracking floods and fires.

C-46. The NGA is a member of the IC and is a DOD Combat Support Agency. It is the functional manager for the National System for Geospatial Intelligence (NSG). The NSG integrates technology, policies, capabilities, and doctrine necessary to conduct geospatial intelligence in a multi-intelligence environment. The NGA's strategy supports operational readiness through geospatial foundation data. These may include controlled imagery, digital elevation data, and selected feature information, which the NSG can augment and fuse with other spatially referenced information, such as intelligence, weather, and logistics data. The result is an integrated, digital view of the mission space.

National Reconnaissance Office

C-47. The National Reconnaissance Office (NRO) is the "nation's eyes and ears in space." The NRO develops and operates unique and innovative overhead reconnaissance systems. The NRO's conduct of intelligence-related activities is essential for U.S. national security. The Director of National Reconnaissance is responsible to the DNI. This person also serves as the Assistant to the Secretary of the Air Force (for Intelligence Space Technology). The NRO's workforce is assigned primarily from the USAF, the CIA, and the USN. However, the other uniformed Services and other DOD and IC elements are also represented.

National Security Agency/Central Security Agency

C-48. The NSA is the United States' cryptologic organization that coordinates, directs, and performs highly specialized activities to produce foreign intelligence and protect U.S. information systems. The NSA is a high-technology organization at the forefront of communications and information technology. The NSA is also one of the most important centers of foreign language analysis and research within the USG. The NSA is part of the DOD and is a member of the IC. The NSA supports military customers, national policy makers, and the CT and CI communities, as well as key international allies. The NSA's two strategic missions are SIGINT and IA.

C-49. SIGINT is the exploitation of foreign signals for national foreign intelligence and CI purposes. IA is the protection of U.S. IC and allied information through technical solutions and defensive IO. Therefore, the NSA is responsible for the inherent activity of cryptology and for all U.S. communications security.

C-50. The NSA faces an increasingly dynamic set of customer demands, including terrorism, narcotics trafficking, organized crime, CI, and various other asymmetric threats. American military forces are more likely to be involved in coalition warfare, regional conflicts, peacekeeping operations, and nontraditional operations than in the past. Moreover, the rapid growth of global information technology makes NSA's missions of SIGINT and IA more significant than ever in gaining information superiority for U.S. warfighters and policy makers.

United States Air Force

C-51. USAF intelligence harnesses the integration of manned and unmanned aeronautical vehicles and space-based systems to provide persistent situational awareness and executable decision-quality information to national decision makers and the joint warfighter. Through its ISR assets, USAF intelligence plays the dominant role in the conduct and analysis of aerial reconnaissance and surveillance operations.

The USAF carries out these missions in an increasingly dynamic environment amid rapid proliferation of information technologies and against adversaries that have no geopolitical boundaries.

C-52. The USAF continues to operate the U-2. The USAF has added unmanned aircraft systems (UASs), like the Global Hawk and Predator, as intelligence platforms. In addition, the USAF is vital to the development and use of intelligence gathered from space platforms. USAF ISR is fully engaged in worldwide operations in the WOT. USAF ISR assets, including the U-2, RC-135, Global Hawk, Predator, Senior Scout, Theater Airborne Reconnaissance System, Scathe View, and USAF Distributed Common Ground System, are providing continuous support to U.S. Central Command and other COCOMs as they execute their WOT operations.

C-53. USAF intelligence also provides the United States with technical collection against foreign ballistic missile development, using a global network of airborne, shipborne, and ground-based collectors. Further, through the National Air and Space Intelligence Center, the USAF is the executive agent for the technical analysis of adversary aircraft, long-range ballistic missiles, and space-based technologies. Increased investment in MASINT and UAS capabilities will enhance future USAF ISR capabilities.

C-54. Each unified command's air component, down to the wing and squadron levels, contain embedded USAF ISR resources. USAF ISR personnel work at every level of command and across the entire IC, continuously preparing for and conducting operations from full-scale conflict to peacekeeping, counterdrug, CT, and humanitarian and disaster relief.

United States Coast Guard

C-55. The USCG is a military, multimission, maritime service within the DHS. The mission of the USCG is maritime security with core roles in protecting the public and environment and guarding U.S. economic and security interests. It performs those missions in any maritime region where those interests may be at risk, including international waters, as well as U.S. coasts, ports, and inland waterways. Because the USCG employs unique expertise and capabilities in the maritime environment where other USG agencies typically are not present, there exists the opportunity to collect intelligence that supports not only USCG missions but also other national security objectives.

C-56. The mission of the USCG's Intelligence and Criminal Investigations Program is to direct, coordinate, and oversee intelligence and investigative operations and activities that support all USCG objectives by providing actionable (timely, accurate, and relevant) intelligence to strategic decision makers, as well as operational and tactical commanders.

United States Navy

C-57. Naval intelligence is a global intelligence enterprise. The Director of Naval Intelligence serves as the lead intelligence advisor to the Secretary of the Navy (SECNAV) and Chief of Naval Operations in his role as USN staff intelligence officer. The director also serves as the Senior Official of the Intelligence Community for the Navy.

C-58. The naval intelligence primary production organization is the Office of Naval Intelligence (ONI), located at the National Maritime Intelligence Center (NMIC). The ONI is the lead DOD production center for maritime intelligence. The ONI supports a variety of missions including U.S. military acquisition and development, CT, counterproliferation, counternarcotics, customs enforcement and, through partnerships and information-sharing agreements with the USCG and U.S. Northern Command, homeland security and homeland defense.

C-59. The ONI is the largest naval intelligence organization. It has the largest concentration of naval intelligence civilians. However, most naval intelligence personnel are active duty military personnel who are serving in joint intelligence centers, cryptologic elements, and afloat units and are supporting strike warfare, special warfare, collections, HUMINT and operational intelligence. A cadre of USN reservists who provide intelligence production support while training for mobilization in time of crisis augment these active duty personnel. The USN's cryptologic professionals form the maritime component of the Unified Cryptologic System and integrate fully with the Navy's warfighting organizations from major combatants to Fleet Command staffs, as well as at Navy/National Cryptologic field locations worldwide. Afloat and

Appendix C

forward detachments that deploy from Naval Network Warfare Command, Fleet Information Operations Centers, and Navy elements at each of the NSA/Central Security Service USG Regional Operations Centers provide additional cryptologic direct support. The breadth of naval intelligence experience and technical expertise applied to the analysis of foreign naval weapons, systems, and activities, combined with the operational expertise of its assigned operators and warfare specialists, provide U.S. decision makers and joint and operational commanders worldwide with fully integrated maritime intelligence support on demand.

United States Marine Corps

C-60. The USMC intelligence mission is to provide commanders at every level with seamless, tailored, timely, and mission-essential intelligence and to ensure integration of this intelligence into the operational planning process. Intelligence encompasses the policy, planning, direction, collection, processing, dissemination, and use of information to meet USMC service and operational missions in maritime, expeditionary, land, and air warfare.

C-61. The USMC orients its intelligence activities toward tactical support because of the USMC's primarily tactical employment posture. Accordingly, two-thirds of all Marines in the intelligence field serve in the Fleet Marine Force, with the majority assigned to the staffs and units of tactical commands.

C-62. The USMC's Director of Intelligence is the commandant's principal intelligence staff officer and the functional manager for intelligence, CI, and cryptologic matters. The Service allocates resources and manpower to develop and maintain specific expertise in the areas of human and technical reconnaissance and surveillance, general military and naval intelligence duties, HUMINT, CI, IMINT, SIGINT, and Tactical Exploitation of National Capabilities. USMC resources allocated to the Master Intelligence Program provide for tactical capabilities necessary to support the operational forces with the U.S. Fleet or as otherwise assigned to the COCOMs.

C-63. The USMC participates in three component programs of the NIP: the Consolidated Cryptologic Program (CCP), the Foreign Counterintelligence Program (FCIP), and the GDIP. The CCP funds most USMC participation in NSA activities worldwide. The FCIP provides Marines to the Naval Criminal Investigative Service for CI activities. The GDIP provides funds for USMC's participation in the Defense HUMINT Service, COCOM staff, Joint Intelligence Center and Joint Analysis Center, and Service and DIA-distributed production functions of the Marine Corps Intelligence Activity (MCIA). The MCIA is collocated with the USN's NMIC and at facilities in Quantico, Virginia. The MCIA is the USMC's intelligence production center for threat assessments, estimates, and intelligence for Service planning and decision making tailored to the needs of the NMS and the complexities and rigors of expeditionary service.

United States Army

C-64. The United States is adapting to face a changed model of warfare. The Army Intelligence Campaign Plan drives military intelligence (MI) transformation efforts to increase full-spectrum operational capacity at the brigade combat team (BCT) level and provides fused, all-source actionable intelligence along tactically useful timelines to Soldiers and commanders at all levels. There are four key components:

- Increasing MI capacity and skills balance.
- Enabling distributed access to an all-source, "flat" integrated network.
- Revitalizing Army HUMINT.
- Increasing intelligence readiness.

C-65. The complex nature of contemporary warfare makes it essential that each BCT and subordinate battalion intelligence section (S-2) are capable of fusing all sources of information to detect, identify, track, and target enemy activities in near-real time. Modular BCT S-2 sections have more than doubled in size; each BCT now has an organic MI company with HUMINT, UAS, SIGINT, and analysis capabilities. MI collection battalions with additional HUMINT and SIGINT capabilities form the core of new, multifunctional battlefield surveillance brigades (BFSBs). Joint interrogation and debriefing center battalions provide interrogation capacity at the theater and JTF levels. The net result is a better-balanced, modular MI force capable of operating effectively in complex environments against both irregular and conventional enemies.

C-66. Close-access HUMINT collection (military source operations, interrogation, and CI) provides critical capabilities needed for successful full-spectrum operations. HUMINT is a fundamental ingredient in effective CT and COIN operations. MI is significantly expanding its HUMINT capacity—every BCT MI company now includes a HUMINT platoon. Two robust HUMINT companies are incorporated into every BFSB MI battalion and experienced S-2X HUMINT management sections are embedded at BCT and division levels. Expansion of HUMINT training is also underway with the formation of a Joint HUMINT Center of Excellence at the USA Intelligence Center, Fort Huachuca, Arizona.

C-67. Concurrent efforts are underway to increase the Soldier's ability to understand their environment and recognize and report useful information:

- "Every Soldier is a Sensor" training is designed to increase tactically relevant reporting about the environment, baseline norms, and changes.
- Cultural awareness training complements "Every Soldier is a Sensor" training by helping Soldiers understand the complex, interwoven dynamics of foreign societies, religions, and regions.
- Language training complements cultural awareness training and increases the Soldier's ability to interact with regional counterparts and citizens.

This page intentionally left blank.

Appendix D
The Economic Instrument of National Power

INTERNATIONAL ECONOMIC SYSTEM

D-1. International trade is the exchange of goods and services across international boundaries or territories. In most countries, it represents a significant share of the gross domestic product (GDP). While international trade has been present throughout much of history, its economic, social, and political importance has been on the rise in recent centuries. Industrialization, advanced transportation, globalization, multinational corporations, and outsourcing all have a major impact on what is politically and militarily possible. Increasing international trade—an economic and financial function—is the primary meaning of globalization.

REGULATION OF INTERNATIONAL TRADE

D-2. Traditionally, bilateral treaties between states regulated trades. For centuries, most states maintained high tariffs and many other restrictions on international trade through a belief in mercantilist trade theory. In the 19th century, especially in Britain, a belief in free trade became paramount. Since that time, this view has dominated the thinking among western nations. In the years since WWII, multilateral treaties and organizations, such as the General Agreement on Tariffs and Trade and the WTO, have attempted to create a globally regulated trade structure enforced through diplomatic pressure and international law.

D-3. Usually, the most economically powerful nations support free trade, although they often engage in selective protectionism of some domestic industries that are politically important (the protective tariffs applied to agriculture and textiles by the United States, Europe, and Japan, for example). The Netherlands and Great Britain were both strong advocates of free trade when they were economically dominant. Today, the United States, the UK, Australia, and Japan are free trade's greatest proponents. However, many other countries, such as India, China, and Russia, are increasingly advocating free trade as their economic power increases. As tariff levels fall, there is also an increasing willingness to negotiate nontariff measures, including foreign direct investment, alternative procurement, and trade facilitation.

D-4. At the global level, the WTO regulates international trade. Several other regional arrangements, such as Mercosur in South America; NAFTA between the United States, Canada, and Mexico; and the EU between 27 independent states, regulate international trade as well. The 2005 Buenos Aires talks on the planned establishment of the Free Trade Area of the Americas failed, largely because of opposition from the populations of Latin American nations. Similar agreements, such as the Multilateral Agreement on Investment, have also failed in recent years.

D-5. Some nations support the regulation of international trade because of risks inherent in the free trade ideal. Free trade makes economic sense because the elimination of artificial costs and barriers lowers the cost of goods and services. However, comparative advantage would automatically flow to those producers with natural advantages (such as favorable climates for agriculture or natural resources) or artificial advantages based on preexisting conditions (such as cheap—or even "slave"—labor or a well-developed industrial base). While free trade theory may be economically sound, it can be disruptive to markets, industries, and entire societies. Throughout history, unresolved trade disputes, perceptions of interstate exploitation, seizure of assets, or denial of access to markets or resources have caused wars. Given the political consequences inherent in such international trade, it is unsurprising that states attempt to use state power to seek advantage for their economic enterprises through various economic weapons. Some of the economic weapons employed by nations throughout history include—
- Market penetration.
- Protectionism or trade sanctions.
- Trade wars.

Appendix D

D-6. Market penetration is the "offensive" (deliberate) attempt to enter another nation's economy to secure a market for one's goods and services. Because this penetration competes with indigenous suppliers, it may be unwelcome for economic, political, cultural, or other reasons. As businesses compete for market dominance, some market penetration may involve the use of aggressive techniques to subdue and even eliminate market competitors. Typical tools of market penetration used throughout history include—

- *Military and political conquest.* An invader can impose controls on supply and market access. This extreme action can be a pretext for broad-based general war.
- *Market creation.* This comprises fostering a demand for goods and services that traditionally is unprecedented. Developing a widespread demand for opium in China or a taste for Asian tea in Britain by British companies are examples.
- *Monopoly.* If an external power can control the only supply of a good or service that is in demand, it can not only dominate the indigenous market but also demand higher prices.
- *Subsidized industry and dumping.* If a government provides subsidies to its industry such that the industry does not compete for inputs similar to its international competitors, that industry will have an artificial advantage in producing goods and services. Competitors can then sell those goods and services at a lower price than indigenous products. Left unchallenged, such "dumping" can force the indigenous suppliers to go out of business, leading in theory to a supply monopoly and market domination by the foreign provider.

D-7. Protectionism is the economic policy of restraining trade between nations through methods such as high tariffs on imported goods, restrictive quotas, a variety of restrictive government regulations designed to discourage imports, and antidumping laws in an attempt to protect domestic industries in a particular nation from foreign takeover or competition. This policy contrasts with theoretical free trade. Free trade institutes no artificial barriers to entry. Protectionism is mostly understood as policies that protect businesses and stable labor forces by restricting or regulating trade between foreign nations. Protectionist "weapons" of the economic instrument of power include—

- *Intervention.* Any use of state power to bolster an economic entity. Such "artificial" actions are outside of the normal economic laws of supply and demand in a free market. Economic interventions have political dimensions that may or may not be obvious to all. All of the following specific weapons are examples of intervention.
- *Subsidies.* These are targeted government allocations of money to protect existing businesses from risk associated with change, such as the costs of labor, materials, and so on.
- *Protective tariffs.* Tariffs are a form of tax designed to increase the price of a foreign competitor's goods by artificially increasing the cost of imports on par or higher-than-domestic prices.
- *Quotas.* By restricting the amount of imports, quotas prevent the introduction of competitive goods and services. Sometimes, states impose quotas to prevent the dumping of cheaper foreign goods that would overwhelm the market and drive indigenous suppliers out of business.
- *Tax cuts.* Tax cuts can function as a "reverse or shadow subsidy." If the indigenous government makes targeted tax relief that alleviates the normal burdens of social and business costs, these cuts can provide an artificial advantage to the indigenous business relative to foreign competitors.
- *Trade restrictions.* Trade restrictions include all means to frustrate the free import and competition of foreign goods. Typical restrictions include bureaucratic requirements (red tape) for licensing, quality controls, safety inspections, quarantine, cultural-sensitivity protestations, and so on.

D-8. Protectionism has frequently been associated with economic theories such as mercantilism, the belief that it is beneficial to maintain a positive trade balance and import substitution. Protectionist actions may be standard policy or may be a reaction to the aggressive, sometimes unfair actions of foreign competitors. Such defensive, retaliatory actions are trade sanctions. They tend to arise in the context of an unresolved trade or policy dispute, such as a disagreement about the fairness of a policy affecting international trade (imports or exports). For example, in 2002 the United States placed import tariffs on steel to protect the U.S. steel industry from more efficient foreign producers, such as China and Russia. The WTO ruled that these tariffs were illegal. The EU threatened retaliatory tariffs (sanctions) on a range of U.S. goods, forcing the USG to remove the steel tariffs in early 2004.

D-9. Trade sanctions are only one specific type of economic power. Trade sanctions are regarded as political interventions in an otherwise free flow of economic goods and services. Recently, the United States and multilateral partners threatened sanctions against Iran and North Korea in response to those regimes' threat to develop nuclear arsenals. This is not primarily a trade sanction because the normal volume of trade between these nations and the United States is already limited. States can manipulate other economic variables, such as grants of aid, credit, currency value manipulation, and access to financing, to put direct or indirect pressure on other governments to modify political behavior.

D-10. Being frequently retaliatory in nature, trade and economic sanctions can ratchet out of control and lead to trade wars. A trade war refers to two or more nations increasing or creating tariffs or other trade barriers in retaliation for other trade barriers. It is the opposite of free trade. Economists believe trade wars are nonproductive. They also believe that trade wars decrease the economic welfare and total social surplus of all nations involved. Politically, however, the threat of a trade war is helpful in winning concessions. This is another example of the complex relationship between more than one instrument of power—the diplomatic (political) and the economic. The WTO is the world governing body for trade disputes.

D-11. Economic and financial flows are a natural characteristic of the international environment and a fundamental activity of human society. When economic relations between two countries exist, most activity is conducted by economic sectors of society in general. The degree of state government direction or intervention in the economy will vary with the nature of each ruling regime. When state governments take action in international trade or economic disputes, they attempt to solve the dispute through bilateral diplomacy, multilateral diplomacy, and recourse to international trade and legal bodies to seek honoring of agreements and international law enforcement. Failing a diplomatic solution or successful international arbitration, state governments can also intervene domestically by restricting or blocking natural economic and financial flows.

CORPORATIONS

D-12. Just as the state remains the central structural concept of international political relations, the company or corporation is the central structural concept of international economics. A corporation is a legal entity collectively owned by a number of natural persons or other legal entities. However, a corporation can exist completely separate from those entities. This separation gives the corporation unique powers that other legal entities lack. The laws of place of incorporation determine the extent and scope of a corporation's status and capacity.

D-13. Investors and entrepreneurs often form joint stock companies and incorporate them to facilitate a business; as this form of business is now extremely prevalent, the term "corporation" is often used to refer specifically to such business corporations. Corporations may also be formed for local government (municipal corporation); political, religious, and charitable purposes (not-for-profit corporation); or government programs (government-owned corporation).

Legal Status

D-14. The law typically views a corporation as a fictional person, a legal person, or a moral person (as opposed to a natural person). Under such a doctrine, a corporation enjoys many of the rights and obligations of individual persons, such as the ability to own property, sign binding contracts, pay taxes, exercise certain constitutional rights, and otherwise participate in society. On the other hand, corporations often have rights not granted to individuals, such as treaty rights.

D-15. The most salient features of incorporation include—
- *Limited liability*. Unlike in a partnership or sole proprietorship, members of a corporation have "limited" liability for the corporation's debts and obligations. Limited liability allows anonymous trading in the shares of the corporation, greatly increases its ability to raise more funds for enterprises, and reduces investor risk. This, in turn, greatly increases both the number of willing investors and the amount they are likely to invest, thus adding liquidity and volume to the stock market.

- *Perpetual lifetime.* The assets and structure of the corporation exist beyond the lifetime of any of its members or agents. Perpetual lifetime allows for stability and accumulation of capital, which becomes available for investment in projects of a larger size and over a longer term than if the corporate assets remained subject to dissolution and distribution. The perpetual lifetime feature is an indication of the unbounded potential duration of the corporation's existence, as well as its accumulation of wealth and thus power. In theory, a corporation can have its charter revoked at any time, putting an end to its existence as a legal entity. However, in practice, dissolution only occurs for corporations that request it or fail to meet annual filing requirements.
- *Ownership and control.* Humans and other legal entities composed of humans (such as trusts and other corporations) can have the right to vote or share in the profit of corporations. In the case of for-profit corporations, these voters hold shares of stock as proof of ownership of the corporation. This is why they are called shareholders or stockholders. When no stockholders exist, a corporation may exist as a nonstock corporation. In this situation, the corporation has members who have the right to vote on the corporation's operation instead of stockholders. If the nonstock corporation is not operated for profit, it is called a not-for-profit corporation. In either category, the corporation includes a collection of individuals with a distinct legal status and with special privileges not provided to ordinary unincorporated businesses, voluntary associations, or groups of individuals.

D-16. Typically, a board of directors governs a corporation on the behalf of the members. The corporate members elect the directors, and the board has a fiduciary duty to look after the interests of the corporation. The board chooses the corporate officers, such as the chief executive officer, president, treasurer, and other titled officers, to manage the affairs of the corporation.

D-17. Creditors, such as banks, can also control (in part) corporations. In return for lending money to the corporation, creditors can demand a controlling interest similar to that of a shareholder, including one or more seats on the board of directors. Creditors do not "own" the corporation as shareholders do but can outweigh the shareholders in practice, especially if the corporation is experiencing financial difficulties and cannot survive without credit.

D-18. Members of a corporation have a "residual interest." Should the corporation end its existence, the members are the last to receive its assets, following creditors and others with interests in the corporation. This can make investment in a corporation risky; however, the corporation's limited liability, which ensures that the members will only be liable for the amount they contributed, outweighs the risk. This only applies in the case of for-profit corporations; nonprofits are not allowed to have residual benefits available to the members.

Formation

D-19. Historically, special charter of governments created corporations. Today, corporations are usually registered with the state, province, or federal government and are regulated by the laws enacted by that government. As part of this registration, corporations are often required to designate the principal address and registered agent of the corporation.

D-20. Generally, a corporation files articles of incorporation with the government, laying out the general nature of the corporation, the amount of stock it is to issue, and the names and addresses of directors. Once the government approves the articles, the corporation's directors meet to create bylaws that govern the internal functions of the corporation, such as meeting procedures and officer positions.

D-21. The law of the jurisdiction in which a corporation operates will regulate most of its internal activities, as well as its finances. If a corporation operates outside its home state, it is often required to register with other governments as a foreign corporation and is usually subject to laws of its host state pertaining to employment, crimes, contracts, and civil actions. The nature of the corporation continues to evolve through existing corporations pushing new ideas and structures, courts responding, and governments regulating in response to new situations.

Development of Modern Commercial Corporations

D-22. Early commercial corporations were formed under frameworks set up by governments of states to undertake tasks that appeared too risky or too expensive for individuals or governments. Many European nations chartered corporations to lead colonial ventures, such as the Dutch East India Company, and these corporations came to play a large part in the history of corporate colonialism.

D-23. The 20th century saw a proliferation of corporation-enabling law across the globe, which drove national economic booms, international development, and globalization. Starting in the 1980s, many countries with large, state-owned corporations moved toward privatization—the selling of publicly owned services and enterprises to private, normally corporate, ownership. Deregulation—reducing the public-interest regulation of corporate activity—often accompanied privatization IAW policies based on minimal government interference economic theory. Another major postwar shift was toward development of conglomerates, in which large corporations purchased smaller corporations to expand their industrial base. Japanese firms developed a horizontal conglomeration model, the *keiretsu*, which other countries later duplicated. While corporate efficiency (and profitability) skyrocketed, small shareholder control diminished and directors of corporations assumed greater control over business, contributing in part to the hostile takeover movement of the 1980s and the accounting scandals that brought down Enron and WorldCom following the turn of the century.

D-24. More recent corporate developments include downsizing; contracting-out, or outsourcing; offshoring; and narrowing activities to core business as information technology, global trade regimes, and cheap fossil fuels enable corporations to reduce and externalize labor costs, transportation costs, and transaction costs and thereby maximize profits.

Types of Corporations

D-25. Most corporations register with the local jurisdiction as either a stock corporation or a nonstock corporation. Stock corporations represent ownership of the corporation by shares of stock. A stock corporation is generally a for-profit corporation. A nonstock corporation does not have owners. However, it may have members who have voting rights in the corporation. Some jurisdictions (for example, Washington, DC) separate corporations into for-profit and nonprofit instead of stock and nonstock.

D-26. The institution most often referenced by the word "corporation" is a public or publicly traded corporation, the shares of which are traded on a public market (for example, the New York Stock Exchange or NASDAQ) specifically designed for the buying and selling of shares of stock of corporations by and to the general public. Most of the largest businesses in the world are publicly traded corporations. However, the majority of corporations are closely held, privately held, or close corporations, meaning that no ready market exists for the trading of ownership interests. A small group of businesspeople or companies own and manage many such corporations, although the size these corporations can be as vast as the largest public corporations.

D-27. The affairs of publicly traded and closely held corporations are similar in many respects. The main difference in most countries is that publicly traded corporations have the burden of complying with additional securities laws and stricter corporate governance standards. Though the laws governing organizations may differ, the courts often interpret provisions of the law that apply to profit-making enterprises in a similar manner when applying principles to nonprofit organizations—as the underlying structures of these two types of entities often resemble each other.

Multinational Corporations

D-28. Following on the success of the corporate model at a national level, many corporations have become MNCs or transnational corporations (TNCs), growing beyond national boundaries to attain sometimes remarkable positions of power and influence in the process of globalizing.

D-29. The typical TNC or MNC may fit into a web of overlapping ownerships and directorships, with multiple branches and lines in different regions, and many such subgroupings comprising corporations in their own right. Growth by expansion may favor national or regional branches; growth by acquisition or merger can result in an excess of groupings spanning the globe, with structures and names that do not

Appendix D

always make the structures of ownership and interaction clear. In the spread of corporations across multiple continents, the importance of corporate culture has grown as a unifying factor and a counterweight to local-national sensibilities and cultural awareness.

D-30. MNCs can powerfully influence international relations, given their large economic influence in politicians' representative districts, as well as their extensive financial resources available for public relations and political lobbying. MNCs play an important role in globalization. Given their international reach and mobility, prospective countries and sometimes regions within countries must compete with each other to have MNCs locate their facilities (and subsequent tax revenue, employment, and economic activity) within their borders. To compete, countries and regional political districts offer incentives to MNCs, such as tax breaks, pledges of governmental assistance or improved infrastructure, or lax environmental and labor standards.

D-31. MNCs try to affect government policy through lobbying and donating to politicians that management feels will be supportive of corporate goals on topics ranging from tariff structures through labor laws to environmental regulations. However, there is no unified multinational perspective on any of these issues because MNCs have different competitive goals between and within industries.

D-32. By contrast, there are many more actions taken by governments to affect corporate behavior. From nationalization (forcing a company to sell local assets to the government or to other local nationals) to a host of changes in laws and regulations to which business must respond, it is more realistic to think of business-government relations as a constant push-and-pull between adversaries that periodically make peace and move together in a single direction.

INSTRUMENTS OF UNITED STATES ECONOMIC POWER

D-33. The following paragraphs discuss the instruments of U.S. economic power. Most of these instruments are units of the DOC. The United States Agency for International Development, however, is an independent agency under the general guidance of the State Department.

DEPARTMENT OF COMMERCE

D-34. The mission of the department is to foster, promote, and develop the foreign and domestic commerce of the United States. Because of legislative and administrative additions, this mission evolved to encompass the responsibility to foster, serve, and promote the nation's economic development and technological advancement. Some of the ways the department fulfills this mission is by—

- Participating with OGAs in the creation of national policy through the President's cabinet and its subdivisions.
- Promoting and assisting international trade.
- Strengthening the international economic position of the United States.
- Ensuring effective use and growth of the nation's scientific and technical resources.
- Acquiring, analyzing, and disseminating information regarding the nation and the economy to achieve increased social and economic benefit.
- Assisting states, communities, and individuals with economic progress.

D-35. The USG divided the department into several primary operating units, among which the International Trade Administration (ITA) is the primary instrument of official U.S. economic power abroad. The ITA includes the following subunits: Trade Promotion and the United States and Foreign Commercial Service (TP/US&FCS), the Import Administration, Market Access and Compliance, and Manufacturing and Services (M&S).

International Trade Administration

D-36. The ITA plans, determines, and coordinates policy; directs the programs; and oversees all activities of ITA. The ITA coordinates all issues concerning import administration, trade law enforcement, agreements compliance, international trade and commercial policy, trade promotion, and trade competitiveness. In the absence of the Secretary of Commerce, the Under Secretary for ITA represents the DOC on the Trade Policy Committee as an ex officio member of the board of the Export-Import Bank of the United States and as chair of the Trade Promotion Coordinating Committee (TPCC). The Under Secretary also serves, as assigned, on all other secretarial-level boards, committees, or panels focusing on international trade. The Under Secretary has primary responsibility for developing and implementing the President's National Export Strategy in conjunction with the TPCC.

United States and Foreign Commercial Service

D-37. The United States and Foreign Commercial Service (US&FCS) is a subunit that directs the ITA's export promotion programs and develops and implements a unified goal-setting and evaluation process to increase trade assistance to small and medium-sized businesses. The US&FCS integrates its activities with the rest of the ITA. It directs a program of international trade events, market research, and export-related trade-information products and services. It also directs programs that help U.S. firms to compete successfully for major projects and procurements worldwide through strategic, comprehensive, and focused advocacy support.

Trade Promotion and the United States and Foreign Commercial Service (International Operations)

D-38. The TP/US&FCS (International Operations) subunit administers a system of overseas posts located in commercial centers throughout the world that, IAW the annual country commercial guide, support and carry out trade promotion activities. It develops marketing and commercial intelligence, facilitates U.S. investments, and assists in the monitoring and compliance with U.S. rights and opportunities created by trade agreements. It also supports ITA import administration activities and provides representation to host governments on behalf of U.S. business firms. The senior commercial officer in a country has overall responsibility for all ITA activities and personnel in that country.

Trade Promotion and the United States and Foreign Commercial Service TP/US&FCS (Domestic Operations)

D-39. The TP/US&FCS (Domestic Operations) subunit administers a system of U.S. export assistance centers located in commercial centers throughout the United States that offer export-ready U.S. firms overseas marketing counseling, technical export information, and marketing opportunities and strategies guidance. It disseminates information on trade developments and trade policy issues to the business community. The subunit provides a comprehensive platform of export assistance services throughout the United States to assist U.S. firms in entering or expanding their presence in overseas markets, including counseling, trade events, and outreach. It establishes program partnerships with state and federal agencies and other public and private sector entities to create an efficient export-assistance network for U.S. companies.

Market Access and Compliance

D-40. This subunit advises on the analysis, formulation, and implementation of U.S. international economic policies of a bilateral, multilateral, or regional nature and ensures that trade objectives align with U.S. foreign policy. It improves market access by U.S. companies to overseas markets and strengthens the international trade and investment position of the United States.

Import Administration

D-41. This subunit ensures the proper administration of antidumping and countervailing duty (AD/CVD) laws. These duties include the timely conduct of investigations and administrative reviews, the administration of AD/CVD findings and orders, the issuance of instructions directing the U.S. Customs and Border Protection to collect duties under those findings and orders, and the administration of AD/CVD suspension agreements and other related bilateral and multilateral trade agreements. It assists the Office of the Chief Counsel for Import Administration in its responsibilities for the defense of litigation challenging actions taken by the department under the AD/CVD laws and other laws and conducts negotiations with foreign manufacturers or governments to suspend AD/CVD investigations.

D-42. In conjunction with the Bureau of Industry and Security, the Import Administration subunit recommends remedial action to the President upon a finding by the Bureau of Industry and Security that imports threaten national security. It administers trade agreements with foreign governments in product areas and ensures the continued full access to trade remedy laws by U.S. industry. Import Administration implements WTO and key bilateral agreements by strengthening enforcement efforts to combat illegal transshipment and participating in negotiations or consultations on matters of transshipment, classification, and investigation. It also administers classification and categorization seminars for foreign governments, issues visa agreements and visa waivers, and identifies barriers to trade.

Manufacturing and Services

D-43. This subunit serves as the primary liaison with U.S. industry and trade associations to help address the U.S. industry's concerns and to support U.S. industry's competitiveness. It advises on domestic and international trade and investment policies affecting the competitiveness of U.S. industry and carries on a program of research and analysis on manufacturing and services. Based on this analysis and interaction with U.S. industry, it develops strategies, policies, and programs to strengthen the competitive position of U.S. industries in the domestic and world markets.

D-44. M&S administers the market development cooperator program and congressionally mandated grants. It manages the industry trade advisory program (jointly with the U.S. Trade Representative) and other advisory committees. M&S provides staff support for the President's export council and coordinates the department's participation on the interagency Committee on Foreign Investment in the United States.

UNITED STATES AGENCY FOR INTERNATIONAL DEVELOPMENT

D-45. The USAID is an independent agency that receives general direction and overall foreign policy guidance of the Secretary of State. The USAID administers U.S. economic and humanitarian assistance programs designed to promote sustainable development in countries worldwide. Overseas missions that work in close coordination with U.S. Embassies administer USAID assistance programs. The USAID works to advance U.S. foreign policy objectives of shaping a freer, more secure, and more prosperous world by focusing its programs in five interrelated areas. These include—
- Improving health and population conditions.
- Protecting the environment.
- Promoting economic growth and agricultural development.
- Building human capacity through education and training.
- Supporting democracy.

D-46. In addition to providing humanitarian assistance, USAID promotes democratic values and international cooperation and helps establish economic conditions that expand markets for U.S. goods and services in developing countries. The agency funds technical assistance and commodity assistance, trains thousands of foreign students each year at U.S. colleges, and supports development research. USAID also enlists the collaboration of the United States for-profit private sector, nongovernmental and private organizations, and universities in its programs. Money spent on foreign assistance programs in the United States is usually in the form of purchases of food, equipment, and services sent overseas. Nearly 80 percent of USAID contracts and grants go to U.S. firms for such purchases.

Appendix E
The Financial Instrument of National Power

THE INTERNATIONAL FINANCIAL ENVIRONMENT

E-1. In addition to its economic functions and capacities, money has acquired other secondary social and psychological powers that may be exercised either by the expenditure of money or by its mere possession. These include the power to enhance popularity, status, and prestige; the capacity to enhance the sense of self-worth; and the power to attain or influence political power.

E-2. A number of commodity money systems were among the earliest forms of money to emerge. Examples include iron bars; cowry shells; salt; ingots of copper, silver, and gold; rum; and cash crops, such as tobacco, rice, indigo, or maize. In recent experience struggling against al-Qaeda and global terrorist networks, it was discovered that the "hawala system" of clandestine terrorist financing was organized around a trade in honey. Under a commodity money system, the objects used as money have intrinsic value; that is, they have value beyond their use as money. For example, gold coins retain value because of gold's useful physical properties besides its value because of monetary usage, whereas paper notes are only worth as much as the monetary value assigned to them. Groups usually adopt commodity money to simplify transactions in a barter economy, and so it functions first as a medium of exchange.

E-3. Some forms of commodity money are too bulky and difficult to transport, leading to the invention of more practical symbolic substitutes. Goldsmiths' receipts became an accepted substitute for gold in 17th century England. The goldsmiths were the precursors of banks, and the receipts they issued were the precursors of the banknote. Through most of the 19th century, commercial banks in Europe and North America issued their own banknotes based on the same principle of partial backing. From there it was only one further step to create true fiat money, currency with negligible inherent value and no backing of a commodity. A central authority (government) creates new money by issuing paper currency or creating new bank deposits. The central authority mandating the money's acceptance as legal tender under penalty of law and demanding this money in payment of taxes or tribute most frequently enhances fiat money's widespread acceptance. By the early 1970s, almost all countries had abandoned the gold standard and converted their national currencies to pure fiat money.

SOCIAL EVOLUTION OF MONEY

E-4. Money is an invention of the human mind. The creation of money is possible because human beings have the capacity to accord value to symbols. Money is a symbol that represents the value of goods and services. The acceptance of any object as money—be it wampum, a gold coin, a paper currency note, or a digital bank account balance—involves the consent of both the individual user and the community. Thus, all money has a psychological and social as well as an economic dimension.

Characteristics

E-5. Money is generally considered to have the following three characteristics and associated features:
- *It is a medium of exchange.* A medium of exchange is an intermediary used in trade to avoid the inconveniences of a pure barter system. It should have liquidity and be easily tradable, easily transportable, and durable.
- *It is a unit of account.* A unit of account is a standard numerical unit of measurement of the market value of goods, services, and other transactions. A unit of account is a prerequisite for the formulation of commercial agreements that involve debt. It should be divisible into small units without destroying its value; fungible (one unit or piece must be exactly equivalent to another); and it must be a specific weight, measure, or size to be verifiably countable.

Appendix E

- *It is a store of value.* To act as a store of value, commodity, form of money, or financial capital, it must be able to be reliably saved, stored, and retrieved—and be predictably useful when retrieved. Therefore, it should be durable, of stable value, and difficult to counterfeit (and the genuine must be easily recognizable). Money also is typically that which has the least declining marginal utility (meaning that as more units accumulate, each unit is worth about the same as the prior units and not substantially less).

E-6. Moreover, libertarians and most laissez-faire economists would argue that an additional characteristic is that money is anonymous. This view requires that money is not subject to government tracking or does not require any equipment, tools, or electricity to use and is useable for purchases in a black market.

Modern Forms

E-7. People commonly use banknotes (also known as paper money) and coins (the most liquid forms of tangible money) for small person-to-person transactions. Today, people commonly use gold as a store of value but not often as a medium of exchange or a unit of account (although central banks do use gold as a unit of account). Less tangible forms of money exist that nevertheless serve the same functions as money. Checks, debit cards, and wire transfers are an easy means to transfer larger amounts of money between bank accounts. Electronic money is an entirely nonphysical currency that people use and trade over the Internet.

Credit

E-8. People often loosely refer to credit as money. People use money to buy goods and services, whereas people use credit to buy goods and services on the promise to pay with money in the future. This distinction between money and credit causes much confusion in discussions of monetary theory. In lay terms, people frequently use the terms credit and money interchangeably. For example, bank deposits are generally included in summations of the national broad money supply. However, any detailed study of monetary theory recognizes the proper distinction between money and credit.

Creation of Money

E-9. Although people easily identify and distinguish types of money, the actual nature of money and the manner in which it is created is less easily understood. The fact that commodities, such as gold, silver, furs, or tobacco leaves, have value does not make any of them money. Commodities only become money when people widely accept them as a symbol representing a certain value of goods and services and in exchange for other goods and services of commensurate perceived value. Trust in the commodity's authenticity and universal acceptance and confidence in the availability of goods and services for redemption are essential criteria.

E-10. Later, banks became the principle source of new money. Banks take in deposits and issue loans to borrowers either by paying out some of the currency receipted on deposit or simply by creating a new deposit in the borrower's account without receiving currency to back it up. By this means, banks create many times more money than the amount they receive or hold on deposit. In turn, central banks further multiply the amount of currency and demand deposits by printing additional currency and using it to purchase government bonds or by lending it to commercial banks by creating fresh deposits at the central bank for the bank just as the bank does for its own borrowers.

Economic Value of Money

E-11. The value of money depends on what it can purchase, not what it is made of. Fiat money has value because people can use it to purchase goods and services, even though it has no intrinsic value or utility other than as a medium of exchange. The intrinsic value of gold and silver remains unaltered by the quantity available. However, their value as a medium of exchange is directly dependent on the availability of goods and services for sale. When explorers discovered huge quantities of gold and even larger amounts of silver in the New World and brought the gold and silver back to Europe for conversion into coin, the purchasing power of those coins fell by 60 to 80 percent. Prices of commodities rose because the supply of goods for sale did not keep pace with the increased supply of money. In addition, the relative value of silver to gold shifted dramatically downward. The governments that issue today's national currencies back them, not gold or silver. The governments are backed by the productive capacity of the societies they represent.

Problems With Paper as Money

E-12. Because of the ease of production, paper money may lose value through inflation, and in today's electronic era, vast quantities of money can be created with a few key strokes. Perhaps the biggest criticism of paper money is that its stability is generally subject to the whim of government regulation rather than the disciplines of market phenomena.

Money and Economy

E-13. Money is one of the most central topics studied in economics, and the value of money is the central concept in finance. Monetarism is an economic theory that predominantly deals with the supply and demand for money. Monetary policy aims to manage money supply, inflation, and interest to affect output and employment. Inflation is the decrease in the value of a specific currency over time. Dramatic increases in the money supply can cause such a decrease of value. The interest rate (the cost of borrowing money) is an important tool used to control inflation and economic growth in monetary economics. Governments often make central banks responsible for monitoring and controlling the money supply, interest rates, and banking.

E-14. A monetary crisis can have very significant economic effects, particularly if it leads to monetary failure and the adoption of a much less efficient barter economy. This happened in Russia, for example, after the fall of the Soviet Union. There have been many historical arguments regarding the combination of money's functions, some arguing that they need more separation and that a single unit is insufficient to deal with them all. Financial capital is a more general and inclusive term for all liquid instruments, whether or not they are a uniformly recognized tender.

Money Supply

E-15. The money supply is the amount of money available within a specific economy available for purchasing goods or services. The money supply in the United States exists in four escalating categories: M0, M1, M2, and M3. The categories grow in size with M3 representing all forms of money (including credit) and M0 representing only base money (coins, bills, and central bank deposits). M0 is also money that can satisfy private banks' reserve requirements. In the United States, the Federal Reserve is responsible for controlling the money supply, while in the Euro area, the respective institution is the European Central Bank. Other central banks with significant impact on global finances are the Bank of Japan, People's Bank of China, and the Bank of England.

Social and Psychological Value of Money

E-16. Money is so universally valued that people consider its value self-evident. Money today is valued for the products and services for which it can be exchanged, the security it provides against unexpected needs, the economic power it generates, the political influence it exerts, the social status it offers to those who possess it, and the self-confidence and sense of accomplishment it fosters in those who earn it.

Linkages Between Money and Other Social Institutions

E-17. The evolution of money illustrates how each new social institution creates linkages with other existing social institutions as it develops and how those linkages gradually expand into complex networks of relationships until they become inseparable elements of a single social web. The evolution of money began as a medium of exchange and measure of value. Money thus served as a stimulant for the exchange of goods and services. As a medium for storage of value, it gave rise to banking. By creating and lending money, banks became catalysts for the further development of trade and industry. In the form of taxation, money supported the development of government. These linkages are direct expressions of the primary powers of money to facilitate transactions.

Appendix E

E-18. In addition, money exercises secondary influences on the society. Politically, the right to collect taxes helped monarchies centralize power and influence into national governments. At a later stage, the ever-increasing need of that government for more funds made it increasingly dependent and subject to those sections of society that possessed or controlled large sums of money. The English Parliament eventually wrested power from the king by first acquiring the sole right to raise taxes, paving the way for democracy. Later, the wealthy merchant class acquired increasing influence over the political establishment. Socially, money has helped breakdown the rigid class structure that allocated privileges according to one's birth. In a money economy, access to goods and services is based on the capacity to pay rather than one's social origins. Thus, it helps eliminate social discrimination based on caste and class.

Private Currencies

E-19. In many countries, laws have severely restricted the issue of private paper currencies. In the so-called free banking era (1837 to 1866), some 8,000 private banks in the United States issued private money. In Scotland and Northern Ireland, the government licensed private sector banks to print their own paper money. Today, privately issued electronic money is in circulation. Historic forms of money, such as gold (as in the case of digital gold currency), back some of these private currencies. Transactions in these currencies represent an annual turnover value in billions of U.S. dollars.

E-20. Any material can back privately issued money. The material used to back money changes with the times—and sometimes to avoid legal scrutiny. This makes things, such as energy, transport capacity, food, honey, illegal drugs, and so on, more useful for backing money. It is important for Soldiers to understand that money is, above all, an agreement to use something as a medium of exchange. It is up to a community (or to the entity that holds the power within a community—state government, MNC, nonstate actor) to decide whether money should be backed by a certain material or should be totally virtual.

Future of Money

E-21. In recent years, the European Monetary Union introduced the Euro to many European nations. Now, almost all use one currency (the UK and Sweden are notable exceptions). West Africa is proposing the 2009 introduction of the Eco, a new currency for 5 or 6 nations. Some speculate that a North American currency, such as the Amero, might come next. Some are proposing an Asian currency unit as well. In the Middle East, many nations use the dinar. An Islamic gold dinar is also proposed. In Mexico, there is a movement to return to using silver as money. One difficulty with currency blocks unifying paper currencies is that it may eliminate the ability to exchange trillions of dollars on currency markets. If this kind of trading were to move into the gold and silver markets, the prices for gold and silver could soar. Today, people can trade gold and paper money electronically via online systems.

Practice and Organizations of International Finance

E-22. International finance is the branch of economics that studies the dynamics of exchange rates and foreign investment, as well as their affects on international trade. International financial organizations study and influence the effects of these phenomena.

Exchange Rates

E-23. The exchange rate (also known as the foreign exchange rate) between two currencies specifies how much one currency is worth in terms of the other. For example, an exchange rate of 120 Japanese yen (JPY) to the United States dollar (USD) means that 120 JPY is worth the same as 1 USD. The foreign exchange market is one of the largest markets in the world. Experts estimate that approximately 2 trillion USD worth of currency changes hands on the market every day. The spot exchange rate refers to the current exchange rate. The forward exchange rate is an exchange rate that members of the financial arena quote and trade today for delivery and payment at specified later date.

E-24. In the international arena, currency exchange rates matter to a state's economy for inverse reasons. A relatively strong or appreciating currency provides the home country with more purchasing power abroad. Moreover, foreigners will want to hold strong currencies in their financial holdings (U.S. debt, for example). In this case, such foreign-held debt can be used by the USG to finance major expenditures (like the WOT or massive infrastructure projects). However, domestic goods for export will be more expensive for foreigners to purchase, which reduces export sales and affects the balance of international trade. Conversely, a relatively weak or depreciating home currency reduces purchasing power abroad but increases the affordability to foreigners of domestic goods for export, thus increasing sales. In addition, depreciating currencies will become increasingly unattractive to foreign currency investors, decreasing the amount of debt they are willing to hold. In the case of the USG, such foreign unwillingness to hold U.S. debt constrains the ability to finance massive expenditures.

Free or Pegged

E-25. If a currency is free-floating, its exchange rate varies against that of other currencies and market forces determine supply and demand. Exchange rates for such currencies are likely to change almost constantly as quoted on financial markets, mainly banks, around the world. By contrast, a movable or adjustable peg system is a system of artificially fixed exchange rates determined by one or more state governments. For example, between 1994 and 2005, the Chinese yuan (CNY) was pegged to the USD at 8.2768 CNY to 1 USD. Many countries have pegged their currencies to the USD at various times, as Japan and Western Europe did from World War II until the 1970s. Fixed exchange rates can have benefits for both the U.S. and foreign states. For example, export-driven economies, such as Japan, can benefit by stability and predictability, resulting in cheap imports for the United States and increased export growth for Japanese industry. Pegged exchange rates facilitated postwar reconstruction of U.S. allies during the Cold War, and the United States and its allies therefore benefited politically, militarily, and economically relative to the Communist threat. However, artificial manipulation of currency exchange represents an artificial manipulation of free trade, which can threaten the survival of domestic industry.

Nominal and Real Exchange Rates

E-26. International finance also distinguishes between nominal and real exchange rates. The nominal exchange rate is the rate at which an organization can trade the currency of one country for the currency of another. The real exchange rate is an economic theory that attempts to reflect the complexity of currencies' and price levels' real value. In practical usage, there are many foreign currencies and price level values to take into consideration. For example, if the price of a product increases 10 percent in the UK and the Japanese currency simultaneously appreciates 10 percent against the UK currency, the price of the product remains constant for someone in Japan. The people in the UK, however, would still have to deal with the 10 percent increase in domestic prices.

E-27. Government-enacted tariffs or legal restrictions can affect the actual rate of exchange for protectionist economic or other political reasons. For example, if the Thai baht is more valuable than the Bangladeshi rupiah but Bangladesh makes direct trading in Baht illegal, the transaction costs of converting each currency into dollars or yen first makes the real exchange rate more costly.

E-28. Finally, considerations of nominal and real currency values must account for purchasing power parity. If a state's currency is relatively weaker than another state's currency but the cost of living in the former state is also lower, the nominal exchange rate does not necessarily reflect real value. For example, the CNY may be weaker than the USD if used to buy rice in Tokyo, but less yuan is needed to buy that same amount of rice within China.

Fluctuations in Exchange Rates

E-29. A market-based exchange rate will change whenever the values of either of the two component currencies change. A currency will tend to become more valuable whenever demand for it is greater than the available supply. It will become less valuable whenever demand is less than available supply. This does not mean people no longer want money; it just means they prefer holding their wealth in some other form, possibly another currency. Increased demand for a currency is due to either an increased transaction demand for money or an increased speculative demand for money.

E-30. The transaction demand for money is highly correlated to the country's level of business activity, GDP, and employment levels. The greater the unemployment, the less the public as a whole will spend on goods and services. Central banks routinely adjust the available money supply to accommodate changes in

Appendix E

the demand for money because of business transactions. The speculative demand for money is much harder for a central bank to accommodate but they try to do this by adjusting interest rates.

E-31. In choosing what type of asset to hold, people are also concerned that the asset will retain its value in the future. Most people will not be interested in a currency if they think it will devalue. A currency will tend to lose value, relative to other currencies, if the country's level of inflation is relatively higher, if the country's level of output is expected to decline, or if a country is troubled by political uncertainty. For example, when Russian President Putin dismissed his government on 24 February 2004, the price of the ruble dropped.

Foreign Exchange Markets

E-32. Because the world's main international banks provide a market around-the-clock, the foreign exchange markets are highly liquid. The biggest foreign exchange trading center is London, followed by New York and Tokyo.

Foreign Investment

E-33. Foreign direct investment (FDI) is a long-term investment by a foreign direct investor in an enterprise residing in an economy not his own. The FDI relationship consists of a parent enterprise and a foreign affiliate that together form a TNC. To qualify as an FDI, the investment must afford the parent enterprise control over its foreign affiliate. The UN defines control in this case as owning 10 percent or more of the ordinary shares or voting power of an incorporated firm or its equivalent for an unincorporated firm. There are several recognized types of FDI:
- *Greenfield investments are direct investment in new facilities or the expansion of existing facilities.* Greenfield investments are the primary target of an HN's promotional efforts because they create new production capacity and jobs, transfer technology and know-how, and lead to linkages to the global marketplace. However, Greenfield investments often accomplish this by crowding out local industry. MNCs are able to produce goods more cheaply because of advanced technology and efficient processes. In addition, they compete for local resources (labor, intermediate goods, and so on). Another downside of Greenfield investments is that profits from production feed back into the MNC's home economy instead of the local economy. This is in contrast to local industries whose profits flow back into the domestic economy to promote growth.
- *Mergers and acquisitions transfer existing assets from local firms to foreign firms.* These are the most common types of FDIs. Cross-border mergers occur when the assets and operation of firms from different countries combine to establish a new legal entity. Cross-border acquisitions occur when the control of assets and operations transfer from a local to a foreign company, with the local company becoming an affiliate of the foreign company.

E-34. Unlike Greenfield investments, acquisitions provide no long-term benefits to the local economy. In such deals, the acquiring entity typically pays owners of the local firm in stock, meaning that the money from the sale never reaches the local economy. Nevertheless, mergers and acquisitions are a significant form of FDI and until the late 1990s accounted for nearly 90 percent of the FDI flow into the United States.

E-35. FDI can be characterized by structure:
- Horizontal FDI represents investments in the same industry abroad as a firm operates in at home.
- Vertical FDI takes two forms:
  - When an industry abroad provides inputs for a firm's domestic production process, it is a backward vertical FDI.
  - When an industry abroad sells the outputs of a firm's domestic production, it is a forward vertical FDI.

E-36. The motives of the investing firm can also characterize FDI:
- Resource-seeking investments attempt to acquire more efficient production factors than those in the firm's home economy. In some cases, these resources may not exist in the home economy

The Financial Instrument of National Power

(for example, cheap labor or scarce natural resources). This typifies FDI into developing countries.
- Market-seeking investments attempt to either penetrate new markets or maintain existing ones.
- Efficiency-seeking investments attempt to exploit the benefits of economies of scale and scope and also those of common ownership.

INTERNATIONAL FINANCIAL ORGANIZATIONS

E-37. The following paragraphs discuss various international financial organizations. These paragraphs will cover the World Bank, the International Monetary Fund, the Organization for Economic Coordination and Development, the Bank for International Settlements, and additional types of international banks and financial institutions.

World Bank

E-38. The WB is a group of five international organizations responsible for providing finance and advice to countries for the purposes of economic development and poverty elimination. The bank came into formal existence in 1945 following international ratification of the Bretton Woods agreements. It approved its first loan on 9 May 1947 ($250 million to France for postwar reconstruction), which in real terms is the largest loan ever issued by the bank. Its five agencies are the—
- International Bank for Reconstruction and Development (IBRD).
- International Finance Corporation (IFC).
- International Development Association (IDA).
- Multilateral Investment Guarantee Agency (MIGA).
- International Centre for Settlement of Investment Disputes.

E-39. The WB focuses its activities in developing countries on fields, such as human development (for example, education or health), agriculture and rural development (for example, irrigation or rural services), environmental protection (for example, pollution reduction or establishing and enforcing regulations), infrastructure (for example, roads, urban regeneration, or electricity), and governance (for example, anticorruption or legal institutions development).

E-40. The IBRD and IDA provide loans at preferential rates to member countries, as well as grants to the poorest countries. The granting agency often links loans or grants for specific projects to wider policy changes in the sector or the economy. For example, the entity granting the loan may link a loan to improve coastal environmental management to the development of new environmental institutions at national and local levels and to the implementation of new regulations to limit pollution. The activities of the IFC and MIGA include investment in the private sector and providing insurance respectively.

E-41. The WB is an international organization owned by member governments. The headquarters of the WB is in Washington, DC. Although it makes profits, the WB uses profits to support continued efforts in poverty reduction. The WB technically is part of the UN system, but its governance structure is different. Each institution in the WB group is owned by its member governments, which subscribe to its basic share capital with votes proportional to shareholding. Membership gives certain voting rights that are the same for all countries but there are also additional votes that depend on financial contributions to the organization.

E-42. As a result, developed countries primarily control the WB. Most of the WB's clients are developing countries. Some critics argue that a different governance structure would take greater account of developing countries' needs. As of 2006, the United States held 16.4 percent of total votes; Japan, 7.9 percent; Germany, 4.5 percent; and the UK and France each held 4.3 percent. As major decisions require an 85 percent super majority, the United States can block any major changes.

International Monetary Fund

E-43. The IMF is an international organization that oversees the global financial system by observing exchange rates and balance of payments, as well as offering financial and technical assistance when

Appendix E

requested. The IMF's headquarters is in Washington, DC. However, the IMF describes itself as an organization of 185 countries working to foster global monetary cooperation, secure financial stability, facilitate international trade, promote high employment and sustainable economic growth, and reduce poverty.

E-44. The primary mission of the IMF is to provide financial assistance to countries that experience serious financial difficulties. Member states with balance-of-payment problems may request loans or organizational management of their national economies. In return, the countries are usually required to launch certain reforms. Critics have often derisively dubbed the reforms as the "Washington consensus." The IMF generally requires these reforms because countries with fixed exchange rate policies can engage in fiscal, monetary, and political practices that may lead to the crisis. For example, states with severe budget deficits, rampant inflation, strict price controls, or significantly overvalued or undervalued currencies run the risk of facing balance-of-payment crises in the future. Thus, the IMF's structural adjustment programs ostensibly attempt to ensure that the IMF is actually helping to prevent financial crises rather than merely funding financial recklessness.

Organization for Economic Cooperation and Development

E-45. The OECD is an international organization of developed countries that accept the principles of representative democracy and a free market economy. It originated in 1948 to help administer the Marshall Plan for the reconstruction of Europe after WWII. Later, however, the OECD extended its membership to non-European states.

E-46. The OECD Secretariat in Paris provides a setting for governments to compare policy experiences, seek answers to common problems, and identify good practice and coordinate domestic and international policies. It is a forum where peer pressure can act as a powerful incentive to improve policy and implement "soft law"—nonbinding instruments that can occasionally lead to binding treaties. The Secretariat collects data, monitors trends and analyses, and forecasts economic developments. It also researches social changes or evolving patterns in trade, environment, agriculture, technology, taxation, and other areas. The OECD is also a premium statistical agency, because it publishes highly comparable statistics on a wide number of subjects.

E-47. Over the past decade, the OECD has tackled a range of economic, social, and environmental issues while deepening its engagement with businesses, trade unions, and other representatives of civil society. Activities have included negotiating taxation and transfer pricing, coordinating international action on corruption and bribery, and reporting on the effects of Internet spam problems in developing countries. Twenty-four nonmembers currently participate as regular observers or full participants in OECD committees, and the OECD conducts policy dialogues and capacity building activities with nonmembers (country programs, regional approaches, and global forums) to share best policy practices.

Bank for International Settlements

E-48. The BIS is an international organization of central banks that exists to foster cooperation among central banks and other agencies in pursuit of monetary and financial stability. It carries out its work through subcommittees, the secretariats it hosts, and through its annual general meeting of all members. The BIS also provides banking services, but only to central banks or to other international financial organizations. The headquarters of the BIS is in Basel, Switzerland.

E-49. As an organization of central banks, the BIS seeks to increase predictability and transparency in monetary policy among its 55 member central banks. While monetary policy is determined by each sovereign state, policy is subject to central and private banking scrutiny and potentially to speculation that affects foreign exchange rates and the fate of export economies. Failures to keep monetary policy in line with reality and to make timely monetary reforms—preferably as a simultaneous policy among all 55 member banks and the IMF—have historically led to financial losses in the billions of dollars as banks try to maintain a policy using open market methods that have proven to be unrealistic.

E-50. Central banks do not unilaterally "set" exchange rates; they set goals and intervene using their massive financial resources and regulatory powers to achieve monetary targets that they set. One reason to coordinate policy closely at the BIS and elsewhere is to ensure that this does not become too expensive and that opportunities for private arbitrage exploiting shifts in policy or difference in policy are rare and quickly removed. The BIS therefore has two specific goals: to regulate capital adequacy and to make reserve requirements transparent.

Additional Bank and Financial Institution Types

E-51. A multilateral development bank (MDB) is an institution created by a group of states that provides financing and professional advice for development. MDBs have large memberships including both developed donor countries and developing borrower countries. MDBs finance projects in the form of long-term loans at market rates, very long-term loans (also known as credits) below market rates, and through grants. The five main MDBs are the WB, African Development Bank, Asian Development Bank, European Bank for Reconstruction and Development, and the Inter-American Development Bank Group.

E-52. There are also several "subregional" MDBs. These banks typically only include borrowing nations as members and do not include developed donor nations. The banks borrow from and lend to its developing members. Examples include the Caribbean Development Bank and the West African Development Bank.

E-53. There are also several multilateral financial institutions. These institutions are similar to MDBs but they are sometimes separated because their memberships are more limited and their financing often focuses on financing certain types of projects. Examples include the European Investment Bank, the Islamic Development Bank, and the OPEC Fund for International Development.

INSTRUMENTS OF UNITED STATES FINANCIAL POWER

E-54. The Department of the Treasury is the primary federal agency responsible for the economic and financial prosperity and security of the United States. As such, the Department of the Treasure is responsible for a wide range of activities, including advising the President on economic and financial issues, promoting the President's growth agenda, and enhancing corporate governance in financial institutions. In the international arena, the Treasury works with other federal agencies, the governments of other nations, and the international financial institutions to encourage economic growth, raise standards of living, and predict and prevent, to the extent possible, economic and financial crises.

E-55. The basic functions of the Treasury include—
- Managing federal finances.
- Collecting taxes, duties, and monies paid to and because of the United States.
- Paying all bills of the United States.
- Producing all postage stamps, currency, and coinage.
- Managing government accounts and the U.S. public debt.
- Supervising national banks and thrift institutions.
- Enforcing federal finance and tax laws.
- Advising the President and Congress on domestic and international financial, monetary, economic, trade, and tax policy.
- Investigating and prosecuting tax evaders, counterfeiters, forgers, smugglers, illicit spirits distillers, and gun law violators.

E-56. Various offices and bureaus exist within the Treasury that support USG power abroad and, in some cases, function as U.S. financial "weapons." The Treasury includes 10 offices, among which is International Affairs. The mission of International Affairs is to protect and support economic prosperity at home by encouraging financial stability and sound economic policies abroad. International Affairs performs constant surveillance and in-depth analysis of global economic and financial developments and then engages with financial market participants, foreign governments, international financial institutions, and in multilateral meetings to develop and promote good policies. It advises and assists in the formulation and execution of U.S. international economic and financial policy, as well as international financial, economic, monetary, trade, investment, bilateral aid, environment, debt, development, and energy programs, including U.S. participation in international financial institutions.

Appendix E

E-57. Another Treasury office is Terrorism and Financial Intelligence (TFI). TFI marshals the department's intelligence and enforcement functions with the twin aims of safeguarding the financial system against illicit use and combating rogue nations, terrorist facilitators, money launderers, drug kingpins, and other national security threats. TFI develops and implements USG strategies to combat terrorist financing domestically and internationally, develops and implements the national money-laundering strategy, as well as other policies and programs to fight financial crimes.

E-58. TFI gathers and analyzes information from the intelligence, law enforcement, and financial communities concerning how terrorists and other criminals earn, move, and store money. Based on this analysis, TFI takes appropriate policy, regulatory, or enforcement action to—

- Freeze the assets of terrorists, drug kingpins, and their support networks.
- Cut off corrupt foreign jurisdictions and financial institutions from the U.S. financial system.
- Develop and enforce regulations to address U.S. vulnerabilities to terrorist financing and money laundering.
- Promote the international adoption and implementation of counterterrorist financing and anti-money-laundering standards.
- Trace and repatriate assets looted by corrupt foreign officials in such countries as Iraq, Liberia, and Haiti.
- Promote a meaningful exchange of information with the private financial sector to detect and address threats to the financial system.

E-59. TFI's subordinate offices include an Office of Terrorist Finance and Financial Crime, an Office of Intelligence and Analysis (OIA), and an OFAC. TFI is also affiliated with the Treasury bureau FinCEN.

E-60. OIA is responsible for the receipt, analysis, collation, and dissemination of foreign intelligence and foreign CI information related to the operation and responsibilities of the Treasury. OIA is a member of the U.S. IC. Its mission is to support the formulation of policy and execution of treasury authorities by providing—

- Expert analysis and intelligence production on financial and other support networks for terrorist groups, proliferators, and other key national security threats.
- Timely, accurate, and focused intelligence support on the full range of economic, political, and security issues.

E-61. OFAC administers and enforces economic and trade sanctions based on U.S. foreign policy and national security goals against targeted foreign countries, terrorists, international narcotics traffickers, and those engaged in activities related to the proliferation of WMD. OFAC acts under Presidential wartime and national emergency powers, as well as authority granted by specific legislation, to impose controls on transactions and to freeze foreign assets under U.S. jurisdiction. UN and other international mandates are the basis for many of the sanctions, which are multilateral in scope and involve close cooperation with allied governments.

E-62. The Treasury has a long history of dealing with sanctions dating back to before the War of 1812 when it administered sanctions imposed against Great Britain for the harassment of American sailors. During the Civil War, Congress approved a law that prohibited transactions with the Confederacy, called for the forfeiture of goods involved in such transactions, and provided a licensing regime under rules and regulations administered by the Treasury.

E-63. OFAC is the successor to the Office of Foreign Funds Control (FFC), which was established in WWII following the German invasion of Norway in 1940. The Secretary of the Treasury administered the FFC program throughout the war. The FFC's initial purpose was to prevent Nazi use of the occupied countries' holdings of foreign exchange and securities and to prevent forced repatriation of funds belonging to nationals of those countries. The United States later extended these controls to protect assets of other invaded countries. After the United States formally entered WWII, the FFC played a leading role in economic warfare against the Axis powers by blocking enemy assets and prohibiting foreign trade and financial transactions. The Treasury formally created OFAC in 1950, following the entry of China into the Korean War. OFAC blocked all Chinese and North Korean assets subject to U.S. jurisdiction.

E-64. The Treasury also includes 11 bureaus, among which is the FinCEN. The FinCEN supports law enforcement investigative efforts and fosters interagency and global cooperation against domestic and international financial crimes. It also provides U.S. policy makers with strategic analyses of domestic and worldwide trends and patterns.

E-65. Since 1995, the United States has pursued an aggressive policy of promoting a worldwide network of financial intelligence units (FIUs) in its overall strategy of fighting money laundering and terrorist financing. The FinCEN is the FIU of the United States. As such, the FinCEN is a member of the Egmont Group of FIU. The Egmont group is an international network of 100 countries that have implemented national centers to collect information on suspicious or unusual financial activity from the financial industry, to analyze the data, and to make it available to appropriate national authorities and other financial intelligence units for use in combating terrorist funding and other financial crimes.

E-66. Information exchange is at the heart of the Egmont group. There are limitations, however. All information exchanged by an FIU is subject to strict controls and safeguards to ensure that its use is in an authorized manner consistent with national provisions on privacy and data protection. No entity can use the information in an administrative, investigative, prosecutorial, or judicial purpose without the prior consent of the FIU that disclosed the information.

E-67. The FinCEN also provides strategic analysis support to international law enforcement through identification of trends, patterns, and issues associated with money laundering and other financial crimes. Strategic analysis information, especially suspicious activity reports filed by the nation's financial industries, forms the heart of FinCEN's strategic analysis knowledge base. FinCEN's strategic analysis products are intended to assist partners in the improvement of money-laundering prevention and detection programs while providing support for the enforcement of anti-money-laundering laws and regulations.

E-68. The objectives of strategic analysis at the FinCEN include—
- Disseminating information on money-laundering trends and methods to law enforcement, regulatory agencies, and the banking industry.
- Assessing industry, geographic, and other systemic money-laundering vulnerabilities.
- Undertaking research and analysis to identify newly emerging or inadequately understood money-laundering methodologies.
- Providing support to federal, state, local, and international law enforcement efforts in connection with illicit funds movement methodologies associated with complex financial or money-laundering investigations.
- Providing feedback to the U.S. financial community on the use and utility of suspicious activity reports and other Bank Secrecy Act data.

This page intentionally left blank.

Appendix F
The Law Enforcement Instrument of National Power

INTERNATIONAL CRIMINAL POLICE ORGANIZATION

F-1. The INTERPOL is the world's largest international police organization, with 186 member countries. Created in 1923, it facilitates cross-border police cooperation and supports and assists all organizations, authorities, and services whose mission is to prevent or combat international crime. The INTERPOL aims to facilitate international police cooperation even where diplomatic relations do not exist between particular countries. Action is taken within the limits of existing laws in different countries and in the spirit of the Universal Declaration of Human Rights. INTERPOL's constitution prohibits "any intervention or activities of a political, military, religious, or racial character." The INTERPOL has three core functions, which provide—

- Secure global police communications.
- Data services and databases for police.
- Operational police support services.

SECURE GLOBAL POLICE COMMUNICATIONS SERVICES

F-2. The ability of police to exchange crucial data quickly and securely is a cornerstone of effective international law enforcement. This is why INTERPOL developed the I-24/7 global police communications system. The system connects the INTERPOL General Secretariat in Lyon, France, with the National Central Bureaus (NCBs) in member countries and regional offices, creating a global network for the exchange of police information and providing law enforcement authorities in member countries with instant access to the organization's databases and other services.

F-3. Member countries can also choose to grant consultative access to authorized law enforcement entities outside of NCBs, such as border control units or customs officials. INTERPOL continues to develop new services and training programs to ensure that users are able to make full use of the I-24/7 system. As of the end of 2006, 183 countries and 25 additional sites, including INTERPOL Sub-Regional Bureaus, were connected. For countries unable to connect because of technical or financial limitations, a sophisticated, cost-efficient satellite system is in place to enable all member countries to be active participants of the international law enforcement community.

OPERATIONAL DATA SERVICES AND DATABASES FOR POLICE

F-4. To fight international crime, police need access to information that can assist investigations or prevent crime. INTERPOL manages several databases, accessible to the INTERPOL bureaus in all member countries through its I-24/7 communications system, which contain critical information on criminals and criminality. These include—

- MIND/FIND.
- Suspected terrorists.
- Nominal data on criminals (names, photos).
- Fingerprints.
- Deoxyribonucleic acid (DNA) profiles.
- Lost or stolen travel documents.
- Child sexual abuse images.
- Stolen works of art.
- Stolen motor vehicles.

Appendix F

OPERATIONAL POLICE SUPPORT SERVICES

F-5. INTERPOL seeks to enhance the role of NCBs and regional offices and to increase the General Secretariat's responsiveness to their needs. This includes the development of emergency support and operational activities centered on the organization's priority crime areas: fugitives, public safety and terrorism, drugs and organized crime, trafficking in human beings, and financial and high-tech crime. The Command and Coordination Centre (CCC) operates around the clock in all of INTERPOL's four official languages (English, French, Spanish, and Arabic) and serves as the first point of contact for any member country faced with a crisis. The CCC staff monitors news channels and INTERPOL messages exchanged between member countries to ensure the full resources of the organization are ready and available whenever and wherever needed. If a terrorist attack or natural disaster occurs, the CCC and the Crisis Support Group mobilize to offer and coordinate the organization's response. INTERPOL treats all messages and requests for information and assistance from the affected member countries with the highest priority.

F-6. Terrorism poses a grave threat to individuals' lives and national security around the world. INTERPOL has therefore made available various training and resources to support member countries in their efforts to protect their citizens from terrorism, including bioterrorism, firearms and explosives, attacks against civil aviation, maritime piracy, and WMD.

F-7. INTERPOL collects, stores, analyzes, and exchanges information about suspected individuals and groups and their activities. The organization also coordinates the circulation of alerts and warnings on terrorists, dangerous criminals, and weapons threats to police in member countries. A chief initiative in this area is the Fusion Task Force, which INTERPOL created in the aftermath of the 11 September attacks in the United States.

F-8. INTERPOL has long cooperated with the UN in law enforcement matters and has observer status in the General Assembly. This cooperation includes—

- Responding to the needs of the international community in fighting crime.
- Assisting states in their efforts to combat organized crime.
- Cooperating in the implementation of the mandates of international judicial bodies.
- Carrying out joint investigations and other police-related matters in the context of peacekeeping.
- Establishing joint databases related to penal law.

INSTRUMENTS OF UNITED STATES LAW ENFORCEMENT

F-9. The following paragraphs discuss the instruments of U.S. law enforcement. Most of these instruments reside within the Department of Justice, although there are significant agencies in the Departments of Homeland Security and State as well.

DEPARTMENT OF JUSTICE

F-10. The mission of the Department of Justice (DOJ) is to enforce the law and defend the interests of the United States according to the law, to ensure public safety against threats foreign and domestic, to provide federal leadership in preventing and controlling crime, to seek just punishment for those guilty of unlawful behavior, and to ensure fair and impartial administration of justice for all Americans. The attorney general represents the United States in legal matters and advises the President and heads of the executive departments of the government when so requested. The DOJ is the world's largest law office and the central agency for enforcement of federal laws.

F-11. Among its other offices, the DOJ includes a National Security Division that combines the CT and counterespionage sections of the Criminal Division with the Foreign Intelligence Surveillance Act experts from the Office of Intelligence Policy and Review (OIPR). This organization enables a vigorous effort to combat terrorism and other threats to national security. The National Security Division improves coordination against terrorism between the DOJ, CIA, DOD, and other IC agencies.

F-12. The DOJ also has several subordinate elements that function as part of the U.S. law enforcement instrument of national power abroad, including the United States National Central Bureau (USNCB) of INTERPOL, the FBI, and the DEA.

United States National Central Bureau of INTERPOL

F-13. The USNCB operates in conjunction with the DHS and within the guidelines prescribed by the DOJ. The mission of the USNCB is to facilitate international law enforcement cooperation as the U.S. representative with INTERPOL on behalf of the attorney general. The major functions of the USNCB are to—

- Transmit information of a criminal justice, humanitarian, or other law enforcement-related nature between NCBs of INTERPOL member countries and law enforcement agencies of the United States.
- Respond to requests by law enforcement agencies and legitimate organizations, institutions, and individuals when in agreement with the INTERPOL constitution.
- Coordinate and integrate information for investigations of an international nature and identify those involving patterns and trends of criminal activities.

Federal Bureau of Investigation

F-14. The FBI has an international presence to protect Americans. The globalization of crime—whether terrorism; international trafficking of drugs, contraband, and people; or cybercrime—requires the United States to integrate law enforcement efforts with willing international partners. This integration includes having FBI agents work directly with law enforcement counterparts abroad, where possible, to solve and prevent crimes and terrorism. The FBI's international presence currently consists of more than 50 small legal attaché offices in U.S. Embassies and consulates around the world. Their goals include stopping foreign crime as far from American shores as possible and helping solve international crimes that do occur as quickly as possible. The activities of agents and support staff include coordinating international investigations with their colleagues, covering international leads for domestic U.S. investigations, and linking U.S. and international resources in critical criminal and terrorist areas that better ensure the safety of the American public at home and abroad.

F-15. The FBI solicits information on suspected criminal and terrorist activity, including possible terrorist threats to the United States. The FBI's CI section is responsible for exposing, preventing, and investigating intelligence activities on U.S. soil. The FBI is the lead law enforcement agency for investigating cyber-based attacks by foreign adversaries and terrorists. The FBI works with the DOJ's National Security Division, which consolidates the resources of the Criminal Division's CT and counterespionage sections and the OIPR. The Criminal Division supervises the investigation and prosecution of cases affecting national security, exercises the exclusive responsibility for authorizing the prosecution of criminal cases relating to espionage and sabotage, and plays a key role in coordinating U.S. efforts to combat and disrupt terrorist activity against U.S. interests around the world.

Drug Enforcement Administration

F-16. Another arm of the U.S. law enforcement instrument abroad is the foreign cooperative investigations and corollary activities of the DEA. Cooperation with foreign law enforcement agencies is essential to the DEA mission because the trafficking syndicates responsible for the drug trade inside the United States do not operate solely within U.S. borders. Since its creation in 1973, the number of DEA agents stationed in foreign countries has grown as drug syndicates possess greater financial and technological resources that enable them to operate on a global scale. International cooperation has increasingly become more crucial to effective drug law enforcement. By 2002, the DEA was operating in 58 foreign countries.

F-17. In 1976, the Mansfield Amendment required the USG to adopt formal rules concerning DEA agents' duties and activities while working abroad. Among the amendment's many restrictions, DEA agents were prohibited from active involvement in arrests of suspects in host countries. They were also prohibited from participating in unilateral enforcement actions without the approval of officials from the host government.

Appendix F

Operating strictly within these guidelines, DEA agents participate in five different law enforcement functions while working abroad:
- *Bilateral investigations*. DEA special agents assist their foreign counterparts by developing sources of information and interviewing witnesses. Agents work undercover and assist in surveillance efforts on cases that involve drug traffic affecting the United States.
- *Foreign liaison*. The DEA actively participates in several international forums to promote international law enforcement cooperation.
- *Institution building*. The DEA helps host countries fight the criminals by working with the people who have the integrity and the courage to pass strong antidrug laws and build strong law enforcement institutions.
- *Intelligence gathering*. The DEA, respected for its drug intelligence-gathering abilities, supports its foreign counterparts' investigations by providing information, such as who controls the drug trade; how drugs are distributed; how the profits are being laundered; and how the entire worldwide drug system operates at the source level, transportation level, and wholesale and retail levels.
- *International training*. The DEA conducts training for host-country police agencies at the DEA training facilities in Quantico, Virginia, and on-site in host countries.

UNITED STATES SECRET SERVICE, DEPARTMENT OF HOMELAND SECURITY

F-18. Statue and executive order mandate that the U.S. Secret Service carry out two significant missions: protection and criminal investigations. The Secret Service protects the President and Vice President, their families, heads of state, and other designated individuals; investigates threats against these protectees; protects the White House, Vice President's residence, foreign missions, and other buildings within Washington, DC; and plans and implements security designs for designated national special security events. The Secret Service also investigates violations of laws relating to counterfeiting of obligations and securities of the United States, and financial crimes that include, but are not limited to, access device fraud, financial institution fraud, identity theft, computer fraud; and computer-based attacks on the nation's financial, banking, and telecommunications infrastructure.

UNITED STATES COAST GUARD, DEPARTMENT OF HOMELAND SECURITY

F-19. The USCG's roles and missions support national policies and objectives along the United States' coast and waterways. It also plays a role at select times and locations in foreign waters. In an environment shaped by globally interlinked economies, revolutions in maritime transportation and information systems, emerging threats to the marine environment, and changing national security concerns, the USG has an abiding interest in continuing the USCG's active presence and exertion of influence in the nation's inland waters, coastal regions, and on the high seas.

F-20. The fundamental roles of the USCG are to save lives and property at sea; provide a safe, efficient marine transportation system; protect the marine environment; enforce laws and treaties in the maritime region; and defend U.S. national security interests and maritime borders in America's inland waterways, ports and harbors, and along the approximately 95,000 miles of U.S. coastlines. The USCG also defends U.S. interests in U.S. territorial seas, the more than 3.4 million square miles of U.S. exclusive economic zones, in international waters, and in other maritime regions of importance to the United States. The USCG has unique characteristics as a maritime agency with regulatory authority, law enforcement authority, and military capability.

BUREAU OF INTERNATIONAL NARCOTICS AND LAW ENFORCEMENT AFFAIRS, DEPARTMENT OF STATE

F-21. The Bureau of International Narcotics and Law Enforcement Affairs (INL) advises the President, Secretary of State, other bureaus in the DOS, and other USG departments and agencies on the development of policies and programs to combat international narcotics and crime. The INL is under the direction of the

Under Secretary for Political Affairs. INL programs support two of the department's strategic goals: to reduce the entry of illegal drugs into the United States and to minimize the impact of international crime on the United States and its citizens. Counternarcotics and anticrime programs also complement the WOT both directly and indirectly by promoting modernization of and supporting operations by foreign criminal justice systems and law enforcement agencies charged with the CT mission.

This page intentionally left blank.

Appendix G
The Military Instrument of National Power

ORGANIZATION

G-1. Under the U.S. Constitution, the U.S. President is the Commander-in-Chief of the armed forces. To coordinate military action with diplomatic action, the President has an advisory NSC headed by a National Security Advisor. Under the President is the SecDef, a cabinet secretary responsible for the DOD. The Joint Chiefs of Staff (JCS) is made up of the Service chiefs and is led by the CJCS and the Vice Chairman of the JCS. The JCS advises both the President and SecDef. The Goldwater-Nichols Act streamlined the military chain of command, which now runs from the President through the SecDef directly to unified CCDRs, bypassing the JCS, who were assigned to an advisory role. Each Service is responsible for organizing, training, and equipping military units for the commanders of the various unified commands.

G-2. There are 10 unified COCOMs—6 geographic and 4 functional. These commands and their responsibilities are as follows:

- U.S. Northern Command, Peterson Air Force Base, Colorado (responsible for North American homeland defense and coordinating homeland security with civilian forces).
- U.S. Central Command, MacDill Air Force Base, Florida (responsible for Egypt through the Persian Gulf region and into Central Asia).
- U.S. European Command (also Supreme Allied Commander Europe and Supreme Headquarters Allied Powers Europe), Belgium and Stuttgart, Germany (responsible for Europe and Israel).
- U.S. Pacific Command, Camp H. M. Smith, Oahu, Hawaii (responsible for the Asia-Pacific region including Hawaii).
- U.S. Southern Command, Miami, FL (responsible for South and Central America and the surrounding waters).
- U.S. Africa Command, Stuttgart, Germany presently but relocation to the African continent is planned (responsible for Africa excluding Egypt).
- USSOCOM, MacDill Air Force Base, FL (responsible for providing special operations for the Army, Navy, Air Force, and Marine Corps).
- U.S. Joint Forces Command (also Supreme Allied Commander Transformation and Naval Support Activity Headquarters) Norfolk, Virginia (responsible for supporting other commands as a joint force provider).
- U.S. Strategic Command, Offutt Air Force Base, Nebraska (responsible for the strategic deterrent force and coordinating the use of space assets).
- U.S. Transportation Command, Scott Air Force Base, Illinois (responsible for global mobility of all military assets for all regional commands).

G-3. The armed forces fulfill unique and crucial roles, defending the United States against all adversaries and serving the nation as a bulwark and guarantor of its security and independence. When called to action, they support and defend national interests worldwide. They fulfill their roles, missions, and functions within the American system of civil-military relations. The interests of the United States and the nature of the challenges it faces demand that the armed forces operate as a fully integrated joint team across the range of military operations. U.S. forces may conduct these operations with the military forces of allies and coalition partners, U.S. and foreign government agencies, state and local government agencies, IGOs, and NGOs. The best way to meet today's challenges is through the unified action of the armed forces eliciting the maximum contribution from each Service and their unique but complementary capabilities and through the synergy that results from their synchronized and integrated action.

Appendix G

JOINT FORCE

G-4. The term "unified action" is a broad generic term that describes the wide scope of actions directed by national civilian and military authorities and the commanders of unified commands, subordinate unified commands, or JTFs. It includes the synchronization and integration of joint or multinational military operations with the activities of local, state, and federal government agencies; IGOs; and NGOs. "Unity of effort" is the result of successful unified action. National unified action is governed by the constitution, federal law, international law, and the national interest. Responsibilities for strategic coordination established by the Constitution and federal law and practice are as follows:

- The President of the United States, advised by the NSC, is responsible to the American people for national strategic unified action.
- The SecDef is responsible to the President for creating, supporting, and employing military capabilities. The SecDef provides authoritative direction and control over the Military Departments through the Service secretaries. The SecDef retains control of and authority over those logistics and logistics support forces not specifically assigned to the COCOMs and administers this authority through the Military Departments, the Service secretaries, and applicable chains of command. The Military Departments organize, train, and equip forces for combat and provide for the administration and support of those forces assigned or attached to the CCDRs.
- The CJCS is the principal military advisor to the President, the NSC, and the SecDef. The CJCS functions under the authority of the President and the direction and control of the President and SecDef. The CJCS transmits communications between the President, SecDef, and CCDRs and oversees activities of CCDRs as directed by the SecDef.
- CCDRS exercise COCOM over assigned forces. They are responsible to the President and SecDef for the performance of assigned missions and the preparedness of their commands to perform assigned missions.
- In a foreign country, the U.S. Ambassador is responsible to the President for directing, coordinating, and supervising all USG elements in the HN, except those under the command of a CCDR. GCCs are responsible for coordinating with U.S. Ambassadors in their geographic AORs as necessary across the range of military operations and for negotiating memoranda of agreement with the Chiefs of Mission in designated countries in support of military operations. Force protection is an example of a military operation or requirement where a memorandum of agreement would enhance coordination and integration.

G-5. Unified action within joint commands synchronizes and integrates joint, single-service, and multinational operations with the operations of other USG agencies, NGOs, and IGOs (for example, the UN) to achieve unity of effort in the operational area. Unified action within the military instrument of national power supports the national strategic unified action through close coordination with the other instruments of national power. Success depends on unified actions. The CJCS and all CCDRs are in pivotal positions to ensure that unified actions are planned and conducted IAW the guidance and direction received from the President and SecDef ICW other authorities (for example, alliance or coalition leadership).

G-6. Unified action of the U.S. armed forces starts with unified direction. For U.S. military operations, unified direction is normally accomplished by establishing a joint force, assigning a mission to the designated JFC, establishing command relationships, assigning or attaching appropriate Service and special operations forces to the joint force, and empowering the JFC with sufficient authority over the forces to accomplish the assigned mission.

OBJECTIVES

G-7. In the abstract sense, an objective is the clearly defined, decisive, and attainable goal toward which every military operation should be directed—the military objective. Objectives provide the focus for military action; they are essential for unity of effort. In the concrete sense, an objective may be a physical object of the action taken (for example, a definite terrain feature, the seizure or holding of which is essential to the commander's plan or the destruction of an adversarial force without regard to terrain features). This is more accurately termed the "physical objective." Soldiers must not confuse physical objectives with military objectives, although occasionally they may overlap. Usually, physical objectives contribute to the attainment of military objectives. Military objectives must contribute to the achievement of national objectives (for example, defend the territorial integrity of an ally, ensure the freedom of maritime commerce, and so on.).

ROLES, MISSIONS, AND FUNCTIONS

G-8. The terms "roles, missions, and functions" are often used interchangeably, but the distinctions between them are important:

- *Role*: A role is a position or function. This is the broad term for which the services and USSOCOM were established in law.
- *Mission*: The mission is the task, together with the purpose, that clearly indicates the action to be taken and the reason therefore. In common usage, and especially when applied to lower military units, a mission is a duty assigned to an individual or unit. The mission is a task.
- *Functions*: Functions are the appropriate or assigned duties, responsibilities, missions, or tasks of an individual, office, or organization. As defined in the National Security Act of 1947, as amended, the term "function" includes functions, powers, and duties.

CHAIN OF COMMAND

G-9. The President and SecDef exercise authority and control of the armed forces through two distinct branches of the chain of command. One branch runs from the President through the SecDef to the commanders of unified commands for missions and forces assigned to their commands. The other branch (used for purposes other than operational direction of forces assigned to the COCOMs) runs from the President through the SecDef to the secretaries of the Military Departments. The Military Departments, organized separately, operate under the authority, direction, and control of the SecDef. The secretaries of the Military Departments exercise authority through their respective Service chiefs over their forces not assigned to the CCDRs. The Service chiefs, except as otherwise prescribed by law, perform their duties under the authority, direction, and control of the secretaries. The Service chiefs are directly responsible to their secretaries.

G-10. CCDRs exercise COCOM of assigned forces. They are directly responsible to the President and SecDef for the performance of assigned missions and the preparedness of their commands. CCDRs prescribe the chain of command within their COCOMs and designate the appropriate command authority that subordinate commanders can exercise.

G-11. The Military Departments operate under the authority, direction, and control of the SecDef. This branch of the chain of command is responsible for all military forces within the respective Service not assigned to commanders of COCOMs. For those forces not assigned to COCOMs, the Service secretary has authorities and responsibilities equal to COCOM (command authority) and administers these through the appropriate chain of command. This branch is separate and distinct from the branch of the chain of command that exists within a COCOM.

COMBATANT COMMANDS

G-12. The President, through the SecDef and with the advice and assistance of the CJCS, establishes combatant (unified or specified) commands for the performance of military missions and prescribes the force structure of such commands. The CJCS assists the President and SecDef in performing their command functions. The CJCS transmits to the CCDRs the orders given by the President or SecDef and, as directed by the SecDef, oversees the activities of those commands. Orders issued by the President or SecDef are normally conveyed by the CJCS under the authority and direction of the SecDef. CCDRs normally submit reports through the CJCS. The CJCS will then forward them to the SecDef and will act as the spokesman for the CCDRs.

G-13. Commanders in the chain of command exercise COCOM, OPCON, TACON, or a support command relationship, as prescribed by law or a superior commander, over the military capability made available to them. Unless otherwise directed by the President or SecDef, COCOM is reserved for the commanders of the COCOMs over forces assigned to that command. For those forces not assigned to COCOMs the Service secretary has authorities and responsibilities equal to COCOM (command authority) and administers these through the appropriate chain of command. During contingency planning, the majority of forces are apportioned to support the missions of more than one CCDR. This requires CCDRs that do not exercise COCOM over an apportioned force to continuously coordinate with the CCDR that exercises COCOM to fully prepare for mission success.

MILITARY DEPARTMENTS, SERVICES, AND FORCES

G-14. The authority vested in the secretaries of the Military Departments in the performance of their role to organize, man, train, equip, and provide forces runs from the President through the SecDef to the secretaries. Then, to the degree established by the secretaries or specified in law, this authority runs through the Service chiefs to the Service component commanders assigned to the CCDRs and to the commanders of forces not assigned to the CCDRs. This administrative control (ADCON) provides for the preparation of military forces and their administration and support, unless the SecDef specifically assigns those responsibilities to another DOD component.

G-15. The secretaries of the Military Departments are responsible for the administration and support of the Service forces assigned or attached to CCDRs. They fulfill their responsibilities by exercising ADCON of Service forces through the Service chiefs (as determined by the secretaries) to the commanders of the Service component commands assigned to CCDRs.

G-16. Each of the secretaries of the Military Departments, coordinating as appropriate with the other department secretaries and with the CCDRs, has the responsibility for organizing, manning, training, equipping, and providing forces to fulfill specific roles and for administering and supporting these forces. This responsibility, however, is subject to the CCDR's authority to organize assigned forces and ensure their preparedness as necessary to accomplish a specific mission.

G-17. Commanders of forces are responsible to their respective Service chiefs for the administration, training, and readiness of their units. Commanders of forces assigned to the COCOMs are under the authority, direction, and control of (and are responsible to) their CCDR to carry out assigned operational missions, joint training and exercises, and logistics.

G-18. The USG manages the USCG differently. Although it is a military Service and a branch of the U.S. armed forces at all times, federal law establishes it separately as a service in the DHS, except when transferred to the DN during time of war or when the President so directs. Authorities vested in the USCG under Title 10 as an armed Service and Title 14 as a federal maritime safety and law enforcement agency remain in effect at all times, including when USCG forces are operating within the DOD/DN chain of command. USCG commanders and forces may be assigned to JFCs in performance of any activity for which they are uniquely qualified. USCG units routinely serve alongside USN counterparts operating within a naval task organization in support of a maritime component commander.

G-19. In addition to the Services above, a number of defense agencies provide a spectrum of logistics or sustainment to joint forces. The USG designates these agencies as combat support agencies (CSAs). Included among CSAs are the DIA, NGA, Defense Information Systems Agency, Defense Logistics Agency, Defense Contract Management Agency, and Defense Threat Reduction Agency. These CSAs provide CCDRs with specialized support. Executive authority over these CSAs resides with the SecDef.

RELATIONSHIP BETWEEN COMBATANT COMMANDS AND MILITARY DEPARTMENTS, SERVICES, AND FORCES

G-20. The military Services and USSOCOM share the division of responsibility for developing military capabilities for the COCOMs. All components of the DOD coordinate on matters of common or overlapping responsibility. The joint staff, Service, and USSOCOM HQ play a critical role in ensuring that CCDRs' concerns and comments are included or advocated during the coordination.

G-21. Unified action demands maximum interoperability. The forces, units, and systems of all Services must operate together effectively. This effectiveness is achieved in part through interoperability, which includes the development and use of joint doctrine (to include joint TTP), joint operation plans, joint and interoperable doctrine, and policy governing unified direction of armed forces communications and information systems. Other key elements of this effectiveness are the conduct of joint training and exercise, and a materiel development and fielding process that provides materiel that is fully compatible with and complementary to systems of all Services.

G-22. A key to successful interoperability is to ensure that planning processes are joint from their inception. Those responsible for systems and programs intended for joint use establish working groups that fully represent the Services and functions affected. Planners consider interoperability in all joint program reviews. CCDRs ensure maximum interoperability and identify interoperability issues to the CJCS, who has overall responsibility for the joint interoperability program.

G-23. The synchronized employment of land, air, maritime, space, and special operations forces provides JFCs with a wide range of strategic, operational, and tactical options. All Service components contribute their distinct capabilities to the joint campaign, each dominating a domain. However, their operational and tactical interdependence is critical to overall joint force effectiveness. Joint interdependence is the purposeful reliance by one Service's forces on another Service's capabilities to maximize complementary and reinforcing effects of both.

JOINT SPECIAL OPERATIONS

G-24. USSOCOM is the unified COCOM charged with overseeing the various SO commands of each U.S. military branch. The command is part of the DOD. When SOF of different branches participate in the same operation, USSOCOM acts as the joint command center of all the forces for the operation. The Joint Special Operations Command is the USSOCOM branch working on CT.

AIR AND SPACE POWER

G-25. The USAF is the aerospace branch of the armed forces. The USAF is currently the largest and the most technologically advanced air force in the world, with about 6,057 manned aircraft in service (4,273 USAF, 1,313 Air National Guard, and 400 Air Force Reserve), approximately 160 unmanned combat air vehicles, 2,161 air-launched cruise missiles, and 1,900 intercontinental ballistic missiles. The stated mission of the USAF today is to "deliver sovereign options for the defense of the United States of America and its global interests—to fly and fight in air, space, and cyberspace."

G-26. The USAF does not operate all U.S. military combat aircraft. The USA operates its own helicopters, mostly for support of ground combatants. The USN is responsible for the aircraft operating on its aircraft carriers and naval air stations, and the USMC operates its own combat and transport aircraft. The USCG also maintains transport and search-and-rescue aircraft, which may be used in either a combat or law enforcement role. All branches of the U.S. military operate helicopters.

ORGANIZATION

G-27. The (civilian) Department of the Air Force manages and the Secretary of the Air Force (SECAF) leads the USAF and the uniformed air staff. The office of the SECAF handles acquisition and auditing, comptroller issues (including financial management), inspector general matters, legislative affairs, and public affairs. USAF subordinate commands and echelons are the major commands (MAJCOMs), field operating agencies, and direct reporting units (DRUs).

MAJOR COMMANDS

G-28. The USAF is organized on a functional basis in the United States and a geographical basis overseas. A MAJCOM represents a major USAF subdivision having a specific portion of the USAF mission. Each MAJCOM is directly subordinate to HQ USAF. MAJCOMs are interrelated and complementary, providing offensive, defensive, and support elements. An operational command consists (in whole or in part) of strategic, tactical, space, or defense forces, or of flying forces that directly support such forces. A support command may provide supplies, weapon systems, support systems, operational support equipment, combat material, maintenance, surface transportation, education and training, or special services and other supported organizations.

Appendix G

NUMBERED AIR FORCES

G-29. The numbered air forces (NAFs) are a level of command directly under a MAJCOM. NAFs are tactical echelons that provide operational leadership and supervision. They are not management HQ. They do not have complete functional staffs. Many NAFs are responsible for MAJCOM operations in a specific geographic region or theater of operations. A NAF is assigned subordinate units, such as wings, groups, and squadrons.

Wings

G-30. The wing is a level of command below the NAF. It is responsible for maintaining the installation and may have several squadrons in more than one dependent group. A wing may be an operational wing, an air base wing, or a specialized mission wing. A colonel or brigadier general usually commands a wing.

Operational Wing

G-31. An operational wing is one that has an operations group and related operational mission activity assigned to it. When an operational wing performs the primary mission of the base, it usually maintains and operates the base. In addition, an operational wing is capable of self-support in functional areas like maintenance, supply, and munitions, as needed. When an operational wing is a tenant organization, the host command provides it with base and logistics support.

Air Base Wing

G-32. Some bases that do not have operational wings or are too large or diverse for one wing will have an air base wing (ABW). The ABW performs a support function rather than an operational mission. It maintains and operates a base. An ABW often provides functional support to a MAJCOM HQ. Several groups with different functional responsibilities make up wings. Several squadrons, each of which has one major responsibility of flying one type of aircraft, make up groups. Two or more flights make up a squadron.

Independent Groups

G-33. The last level of independent operation is the group level. When an organization is not part of the primary mission of the base, it will be made an independent group. Independent groups may report to a wing, or they may be completely independent. They may also be organized as an expeditionary unit, independent but too small to warrant a wing designation. The organization of the independent group is usually similar to the operations group. Independent groups have a few squadrons or flights from the support side added to make the organization more self-sufficient. However, this does not make the independent group large enough to become a wing.

OPERATIONAL ORGANIZATION

G-34. The above organizational structure is responsible for the peacetime organization, equipping and training of aerospace units for operational missions. When required to support operational missions, the SecDef directs a change in operational control (chop) of these units from their peacetime alignment to a CCDR.

AEROSPACE EXPEDITIONARY TASK FORCE

G-35. Chopped units are referred to as "forces". The top-level structure of these forces is the Air and Space Expeditionary Task Force (AETF). The AETF is the USAF presentation of forces to a CCDR for the employment of air power. A standing warfighting headquarters (WFHQ) supports each CCDR to provide planning and execution of aerospace forces in support of CCDR requirements. Each WFHQ consists of a Commander, Air Force Forces (COMAFFOR), and Air Force forces staff, and an air operations center (AOC). The WFHQ may deploy air component coordinate elements to liaise with and support JFCs in the CCDR's AOR as needed.

G-36. The COMAFFOR is the senior USAF officer responsible for the employment of air power in support of JFC objectives. The COMAFFOR has a special staff and an A-staff to ensure assigned or attached forces are properly organized, equipped, and trained to support the operational mission. The AOC is the COMAFFOR's C2 center. This center is responsible for planning and executing air power missions in support of JFC objectives.

AIR EXPEDITIONARY WINGS, GROUPS, AND SQUADRONS

G-37. The AETF generates air power to support CCDR objectives from air expeditionary wings or air expeditionary groups. These units are responsible for receiving combat forces from USAF MAJCOMs, preparing these forces for operational missions, launching and recovering these forces, and eventually returning forces to the MAJCOMs. Theater air control systems control employment of forces during these missions.

UNITED STATES AIR FORCE SPECIAL WARFARE

G-38. Air Force Special Operations Command (AFSOC) provides AFSOF for worldwide deployment and assignment to regional unified commands. AFSOF are highly trained, rapidly deployable airmen who are equipped with specialized aircraft. These forces conduct global SO missions that include precision application of firepower, infiltration, aviation FID, exfiltration, resupply, and refueling of SOF operational elements. AFSOC's unique capabilities include airborne radio and TV broadcast for PSYOP, as well as combat aviation advisors to provide other governments with military expertise for their internal development. AFSOC's special tactics squadrons combine combat controllers, SO weathermen, and pararescuemen to form versatile SOF teams.

G-39. AFSOC core tasks are grouped into nine mission areas: air-to-surface interface, agile combat support, combat aviation advisory operations, IO, ISR, personnel recovery/recovery operations, precision fires, PSYOP dissemination, and specialized air mobility.

G-40. AFSOC's active duty and reserve component flying units operate fixed-wing, rotary-wing, unmanned, and tilt-rotor aircraft, including the CV-22, AC-130H/U, C-130, EC-130, MC-130E/H/W, MH-53J/M, UH-1N/H, CN-235-100, AN-26, U-28A, Casa 212, MQ-1 Predator/MQ-1A/B Predator, and MI-17. AFSOC currently oversees the following active units:

- 1st SOW, Hurlburt Field, FL.
- 352d Special Operations Group, RAF Mildenhall, England.
- 353d Special Operations Group, Kadena Air Base, Japan.
- 720th Special Tactics Group, Hurlburt Field, FL.
- USAF Special Operations School, Hurlburt Field, FL.
- 18th Flight Test Squadron, Hurlburt Field, FL.

AFSOC oversees the following Reserve and National Guard units:

- 919th SOW, Duke Field, FL.
- 193d SOW, Harrisburg, Pennsylvania.
- 123d Special Tactics Squadron, Standiford Field, Kentucky.
- 209th Civil Engineer Squadron, Gulfport, Mississippi.
- 280th Combat Communication Squadron, Dothan, Alabama.
- 107th Weather Flight, Selfridge Air National Guard Base, Michigan.
- 146th Weather Flight, Pittsburgh, Pennsylvania.
- 181st Weather Flight, Dallas, Texas.

SEA POWER

G-41. The USN is the branch of the U.S. armed forces primarily responsible for conducting naval operations. Its stated mission is to maintain, train, and equip combat-ready naval forces capable of winning wars, deterring aggression, and maintaining freedom of the seas. The USN currently operates 276 ships in active service and more than 4,000 aircraft. The USN's ability to project force onto the littoral regions of

Appendix G

the world, engage in forward areas during peacetime, and rapidly respond to regional crises makes it an active player in American foreign and defense policy. Despite decreases in ships and personnel following the Cold War, the USN has continued to spend more on technology development than any other navy. The USN is the world's largest navy with a tonnage greater than that of the next 17 largest navies combined.

ORGANIZATION

G-42. The USN falls under the administration of the DN and under the civilian leadership of the SECNAV. The most senior naval officer is the Chief of Naval Operations, a four-star admiral who reports to the SECNAV and is a member of the JCS. The SECNAV and Chief of Naval Operations are responsible for organizing, recruiting, training, and equipping the USN so that it is ready for operation under the command of the unified CCDRs.

OPERATING FORCES

G-43. There are nine components to USN operating forces: Atlantic Fleet, Pacific Fleet, Naval Forces Central Command (NAVCENT), Naval Forces Europe (NAVEUR), Naval Network Warfare Command, Navy Reserve, Naval Special Warfare Command, Operational Test and Evaluation Forces, and the Military Sealift Command. USN fleets take on the role of force provider. USN fleets do not carry out military operations independently. They train and maintain naval units that will subsequently be provided to the naval forces component of each unified COCOM.

G-44. The USN has five active numbered fleets, each led by a vice admiral. These five fleets are grouped under Fleet Forces Command (the former Atlantic Fleet), Pacific Fleet, NAVEUR—all led by four-star full admirals—and NAVCENT, whose commander is also commander of the Fifth Fleet.

Fleet Forces Command

G-45. Fleet Forces Command is made up of the following:
- Submarine Force U.S. Atlantic Fleet, Surface Forces Atlantic, and Naval Air Forces Atlantic.
- Second Fleet, which operates in the Atlantic Ocean from the North to South Pole, from the eastern United States to Western Europe and Africa, and along both the eastern and western shores of Central and South America. Second Fleet is the sole numbered operational fleet within Fleet Forces Command, providing forces to Joint Forces Command. Second Fleet is based in Norfolk, Virginia, and its flagship is USS Wasp (LHD-1).

Pacific Fleet

G-46. The Pacific Fleet is made up of the following:
- Submarine Forces Pacific, Surface Force Pacific, and Naval Air Forces Pacific.
- Third Fleet, whose jurisdiction is the northern, southern, and eastern Pacific Ocean along with the west coast of the United States. Normally, units assigned to Third Fleet undergo training cruises before deployment with either the Fifth Fleet or Seventh Fleet. These units are not intended for immediate use in battle. Only in the event of general war does Third Fleet participate in active combat operations. Forming part of the Pacific Fleet, Third Fleet is a part of the USPACOM and is based in San Diego, California. The USS Coronado (AGF-11) is its flagship.
- Seventh Fleet, which is the largest forward-deployed U.S. fleet, operates in the western Pacific and the Indian Ocean, stretching to the Persian Gulf and including much of the east coast of Africa. It forms the fully combat-ready part of the Pacific Fleet and provides naval units to the USPACOM. At any given time, Seventh Fleet consists of 40 to 50 ships operating from bases in South Korea, Japan, and Guam. Seventh Fleet's headquarters is in Yokosuka, Kanagawa, Japan. Its flagship is the USS Blue Ridge (LCC-19).

Naval Forces Europe

G-47. Sixth Fleet is deployed in the Mediterranean Sea and Black Sea, under the administrative direction of NAVEUR and the operational command of the European Command. Sixth Fleet also provides the HQ and core of Naval Striking and Support Forces NATO, a multinational force supporting NATO objectives in the Mediterranean. Sixth Fleet is based in Gaeta, Italy, and its flagship is USS Mount Whitney (LCC-20).

Naval Forces Central Command

G-48. NAVCENT includes a number of task forces that are not part of the Fifth Fleet. These include combined Task Force 150, carrying out maritime surveillance activities in the Gulf of Oman and around the Horn of Africa, and Task Force 152, covering the southern Persian Gulf with the same role. Both task forces report to Commander NAVCENT in his role as Combined Maritime Forces Component Commander.

G-49. Fifth Fleet's AOR is the Middle East, including the Persian Gulf, Red Sea, Gulf of Oman, and parts of the Indian Ocean. Consisting of approximately 25 ships, including a carrier strike group and an expeditionary strike group, Fifth Fleet is effectively fused with NAVCENT, which is the naval component of the larger USCENTCOM. Fifth Fleet's headquarters is in Manama, Bahrain.

SHORE ESTABLISHMENTS

G-50. Shore establishment commands exist to support the mission of the afloat fleets through facilities on land. Focusing on logistics and combat readiness, they are essential for the full, smooth, and continuous operation of operating forces. The varieties of commands reflect the complexity of the modern USN and range from naval intelligence to personnel training to maintaining repair facilities. Two of the major logistics and repair commands are Naval Sea Systems Command and Naval Air Systems Command. Other commands, such as the ONI, the U.S. Naval Observatory, and the Navy War College are focused on intelligence and strategy. Training commands include the Naval Strike and Air Warfare Center and the U.S. Naval Academy.

G-51. The Navy maintains several "naval forces commands" that operate naval shore facilities and serve as liaison units to local ground forces of the USAF and USA. Such commands are answerable to a fleet commander as the shore protector component of the afloat command. During times of war, all naval forces commands augment to become task forces of a primary fleet. Some of the larger naval forces commands in the Pacific Ocean include Commander, Naval Forces Korea; Commander, Naval Forces Marianas; and Commander, Naval Forces Japan.

MILITARY SEALIFT COMMAND

G-52. The Military Sealift Command (MSC) serves not only the USN but also the entire DOD as the ocean carrier of materiel during peacetime and war. It transports equipment, fuel, ammunition, and other goods essential to the smooth function of U.S. armed forces worldwide. The MSC can move up to 95 percent of all supplies needed to sustain the U.S. military. It operates approximately 120 ships with 100 more in reserve. The MSC is unique in that its ships are manned not by active duty Navy personnel but by civil service or contract merchant mariners.

G-53. Four programs make up MSC: Sealift, Naval Fleet Auxiliary Force (NFAF), Special Mission, and Pre-positioning. The Sealift program provides the bulk of the MSC's supply-carrying operation and operates tankers for fuel transport and dry-cargo ships that transport equipment, vehicles, helicopters, ammunition, and supplies. The NFAF directly replenishes ships that are underway at sea, enabling them to deploy for long periods without having to come to port. NFAF also runs the USN's two hospital ships, which provide emergency health care to both military personnel and civilians. The Special Mission Program operates vessels for unique military and federal government tasks. These vessels perform such duties as oceanographic and hydrographic surveys, submarine support, and missile flight data collection and tracking. The Pre-positioning Program sustains the U.S. military's forward presence strategy by deploying supply ships in key areas of the ocean before actually needed. In the event of a contingency,

Appendix G

these ships would be available to support military operations on short notice and before full-scale supply lines are established.

NAVAL SPECIAL WARFARE

G-54. The U.S. Naval Special Warfare Command is in charge of USN SOF. The command currently oversees the following:
- Naval Special Warfare Group (NSWG) One (sea-air-land teams [SEALs], Naval Air Base, Coronado, California [CA]).
- NSWG Two (SEALs, Naval Amphibious Base, Little Creek, Virginia).
- NSWG Three (SEAL delivery vehicle teams, Naval Air Base, Coronado, CA).
- NSWG Four (Special boat teams, Naval Amphibious Base, Little Creek, Virginia).
- Naval Special Warfare Development Group (Dam Neck, Virginia).

UNITED STATES MARINE CORPS

G-55. Historically, the USN has enjoyed a unique relationship with the USMC, partly because they both specialize in seaborne operations. The USMC is a branch of the U.S. military responsible for providing power projection from the sea, using the mobility of the USN to rapidly deliver combined-arms task forces to global crises.

G-56. The USMC serves as an amphibious force-in-readiness. It has three primary AORs:
- The seizure or defense of advanced naval bases and other land operations to support naval campaigns.
- The development of tactics, techniques, and equipment used by amphibious landing forces.
- The duties other than the above that the President may direct.

G-57. The third clause is a codification of the expeditionary duties of the USMC. The Corps has most often performed actions of a non-naval nature, including its famous actions in the War of 1812, at Tripoli, Chapultepec (during the Mexican American War), and numerous counterinsurgency and occupational duties in Central America and East Asia, World War I, and the Korean War. While these actions are not accurately described as support of naval campaigns or amphibious warfare, their common thread is that they are of an expeditionary nature, using the mobility of the USN to provide timely intervention in foreign affairs on behalf of American interests.

G-58. At the top level of civilian organization, the USMC is part of the DN and reports to the SECNAV. However, the USMC is a distinct Service branch and not a subset of the USN. The highest-ranking Marine officer, the Commandant of the Marine Corps, does not report to a naval officer. The Commandant is responsible for organizing, recruiting, training, and equipping the USMC so that it is ready for operation under the command of the unified CCDRs. There are four principal subdivisions in the USMC: HQ Marine Corps, the operating forces, the supporting establishment, and the Marine Forces Reserve.

G-59. The operating forces are further subdivided into three categories: Marine Corps forces assigned to unified commands; Marine Corps security forces guarding high-risk naval installations; and Marine Corps security guard detachments at American embassies, legations, and consulates at over 110 DOS posts overseas. The USMC assigns its forces to each of the regional unified commands at the discretion of the SecDef and with the approval of the President. Since 1991, the USMC's component HQ are at each of the regional unified COCOMs. Marine Corps forces are further divided into Marine Forces Command (MARFORCOM) and Marine Forces Pacific (MARFORPAC), each headed by a lieutenant general. MARFORCOM has operational control of the II Marine Expeditionary Force (MEF); MARFORPAC has operational control of the I MEF and the III MEF. The supporting establishment includes Marine Corps Combat Development Command, Marine Corps recruit depots, Marine Corps Logistics Command, Marine bases and air stations, and the Recruiting Command.

Capabilities

G-60. Although the USMC does not employ any unique combat arms, it has, as a force, the unique ability to rapidly deploy a combined-arms task force to almost anywhere in the world within days. The basic structure for all deployed units is the Marine Air-Ground Task Force (MAGTF), a flexible structure of varying size that integrates a ground combat element, an air combat element, and a logistics combat element under a common command element. A MAGTF can operate independently or as part of a larger coalition. It is a temporary organization formed for a specific mission and dissolved after completion of that mission. The MAGTF structure reflects a strong tradition in the Corps toward self-sufficiency and a commitment to combined arms—both essential assets of an expeditionary force often called upon to act independently in discrete, time-sensitive situations.

G-61. A MAGTF varies in size. The smallest element is a MEU, based around a reinforced infantry battalion and a composite squadron. The largest element is a MEF, which ties together a division, an air wing, and a logistics group under a MEF HQ Group. There are usually three MEUs assigned to each of the USN Atlantic and Pacific fleets, with a seventh MEU based on Okinawa. While one MEU is on deployment, one MEU is training to deploy and one is standing down, resting its Marines and refitting. Each MEU is capable of performing SO. The three MEFs are—

- I MEF located at Camp Pendleton, California.
- II MEF located at Camp Lejeune, North Carolina (NC).
- III MEF located at Camp Courtney, Okinawa, Japan (relocating to Guam in 2008).

Relationship With Other Services

G-62. The USMC and USN are partner Services with a closer relationship than exists with other branches of the U.S. military. Marine air squadrons operate alongside Navy air squadrons from USN aircraft carriers, though they frequently have distinct missions and rarely fly sorties together, except to directly support Marine ground troops. Conversely, the USMC is responsible for conducting land operations to support naval campaigns, including the seizure of naval and air bases. Both Services operate a network security team in conjunction. As amphibious assault specialists, Marines often deploy on and attack from Navy vessels. While being transported on a Navy ship, Marines must obey the orders of its captain.

G-63. The Corps' combat capabilities in land warfare overlap those of the USA. Originally organized as the Continental Marines in 1775 to serve as naval infantry, the USMC's mission has evolved with changing military doctrine and American foreign policy.

G-64. Although the USA now maintains light infantry units capable of rapid worldwide deployment, they do not match the combined-arms integration of a MAGTF. In addition, the USA does not have the logistical train that the USN provides. For this reason, the USMC is often assigned to noncombat missions, such as the evacuation of Americans from unstable countries and humanitarian relief of natural disasters. In larger conflicts, Marines act as a stopgap—to get into and hold an area until larger units mobilize. The USMC performed this role in World War I, the Korean War, and Operation DESERT STORM, where Marines were the first significant combat units deployed from the United States. Those Marines held the line until the country could mobilize for war.

G-65. While the creation of joint commands under the Goldwater-Nichols Act has improved inter-Service coordination between the U.S. military Services, the Corps' ability to permanently maintain integrated multielement task forces under a single command provides a smoother implementation of combined-arms warfare principles.

G-66. The USMC is the smallest of the U.S. Armed Forces in the DOD (the USCG, about one-fifth the size of the USMC, is under the DHS). The Corps is nonetheless larger than the entire armed forces of many significant military powers; for example, it is larger than the active troop level of the Israeli Defense Forces.

Marine Special Warfare

G-67. In addition to the "special operations-capable" MEUs noted above, in 2006 the USMC agreed to supply a 2,600-strong unit, the Marine Forces Special Operations Command (MARSOC), which answers directly to USSOCOM. MARSOC trains, organizes, equips—and when directed by the Commander,

Appendix G

USSOCOM—deploys task-organized, scalable, and responsive USMC SOF worldwide in support of CCDRs and other agencies. Component units of MARSOC include the following:
- Marine Special Operations Advisor Group, Camp Lejeune, North Carolina.
- 1st Marine Special Operations Battalion (1st MSOB), Camp Pendleton, California.
- 2nd MSOB, Camp Lejeune, North Carolina.
- Marine Special Operations Support Group.
- Marine Special Operations School (including a Special Missions Training Branch on each coast).

UNITED STATES COAST GUARD

G-68. The USCG is a branch of the U.S. armed forces involved in maritime law enforcement, mariner assistance, search and rescue, and national defense. As the smallest of the five U.S. armed Services, its stated mission is to protect the public, the environment, and the economic and security interests of the United States in any maritime region in which those interests may be at risk, including international waters and America's coasts, ports, and inland waterways.

G-69. The USCG is a component of the DHS, unlike the other branches of the military, which are components of the DOD. Because the Posse Comitatus Act prohibits the USN from enforcing U.S. laws, the USCG fulfills this role in naval operations.

G-70. The USCG has a broad and important role in homeland security; law enforcement; search and rescue; marine environmental pollution response; and the maintenance of river, intracoastal, and offshore aids to navigation. The USCG has participated in every U.S. conflict from landing troops on D-Day and on the Pacific islands in WWII through conducting extensive patrols and shore bombardment during the Vietnam War to OIF. Maritime interception operations, coastal security patrols, and law enforcement detachments are the major roles in Iraq. The USCG provides law enforcement detachments to USN vessels to perform arrests and other law enforcement duties during Navy boarding and interdiction missions. At other times, coast guard port security units are sent overseas to guard the security of ports and other assets. The USCG also jointly staffs the USN's naval coastal warfare groups and squadrons (previously known as harbor defense commands), which oversee defense efforts in foreign littoral combat and inshore areas.

G-71. The USCG carries out five basic missions:
- Maritime safety.
- Maritime mobility.
- Maritime security.
- National defense.
- Protection of natural resources.

The USCG has no designated SO element.

LAND POWER

G-72. The USA is the largest branch of the U.S. armed forces and has primary responsibility for land-based military operations. The USA is managed by the Department of the Army, which is led by the Secretary of the Army. The highest-ranking military officer in the department is the Chief of Staff of the Army, who is a member of the JCS.

STRUCTURE

G-73. Three components make up the USA: the Active Army and two reserve components, the ARNG and the USAR. Both reserve components are primarily made up of part-time Soldiers who train once a month and conduct two to three weeks of annual training each year. Title 10 of the U.S. Code provides the organization of both the Active Army and the USAR, while Title 32 of the U.S. Code provides the organization of the ARNG. The USA organizes, trains, and equips the ARNG as one of its components. However, when it is not in federal service, it is under the command of individual states' governors. However, a presidential order can federalize the ARNG against the governor's wishes.

G-74. Since the Militia Act of 1903, all ARNG Soldiers have held dual status: as National Guardsmen under the authority of the governor of their state and as a reserve of the USA under the authority of the President. Since the adoption of the total force policy in the aftermath of the Vietnam War, reserve component Soldiers have taken a more active role in U.S. military operations. USAR and ARNG units took part in the Persian Gulf War, peacekeeping in Kosovo, and the 2003 invasion of Iraq. Various state defense forces also exist, sometimes known as state militias, which are sponsored by individual state governments and serve as an auxiliary to the ARNG. Except in times of extreme national emergency, such as a mainland invasion of the United States, state militias operate independently of the USA. These militias are seen as state government agencies rather than a component of the military.

G-75. Although the present-day USA exists as an all-volunteer force, augmented by USAR and ARNG forces, measures exist for emergency expansion in the event of a catastrophic occurrence, such as a large-scale attack against the United States or the outbreak of a major global war. The current "call-up" order of the USA is as follows:
- The Active Army volunteer force.
- The total mobilization of the USAR.
- The full-scale activation of ARNG forces.
- The recall of all retired personnel fit for military duty.
- The reestablishment of the draft and creation of a conscript force within the Active Army.
- The recall of previously discharged officers and enlisted personnel who were separated under honorable conditions.
- The activation of the state defense forces/state militias.
- The full-scale mobilization of the unorganized U.S. militia.

G-76. The final stage of USA mobilization, known as "activation of the unorganized militia," would effectively place all able-bodied males in the service of the USA. The last time an approximation of this occurred was during the American Civil War when the Confederate States of America activated the "home guard" in 1865, drafting all males, regardless of age or health, into the Confederate Army.

ADAPTING THE MAJOR ARMY COMMAND STRUCTURE

G-77. The Army Campaign Plan adapts major Army commands and specified HQ to reflect the most effective C2 structure for supporting the modular force. This decision defines three HQ—Army command, ASCC, and DRU. The definitions align responsibilities of these HQ to the Department of the Army and Secretary of the Army and assign theater support relationships and responsibilities. This decision establishes—
- Three Army commands:
  - Forces Command.
  - Training and Doctrine Command.
  - Army Materiel Command.
- Nine ASCCs:
  - United States Army, Central Command (Third Army).
  - United States Army, Northern Command (Fifth Army).
  - United States Army, Southern Command (Sixth Army).
  - United States Army, European Command (Seventh Army).
  - United States Army, Pacific Command.
  - Eighth United States Army.
  - USASOC.
  - Surface Deployment and Distribution Command.
  - Space and Missile Defense Command.
- 11 Army DRUs:
  - Network Command.
  - Medical Command.

Appendix G

- Intelligence and Security Command.
- Criminal Investigation Division Command.
- United States Army Corps of Engineers.
- Military District of Washington.
- Army Test and Evaluation Command.
- United States Military Academy.
- United States Army Reserve Command.
- Acquisition Support Center.
- Installation Management Agency.

G-78. The Army Campaign Plan accomplishes three objectives: it recognizes the global role and multidiscipline functions of the three Army commands, establishes the theater Army as an ASCC reporting directly to the Department while serving as the Army's single point of contact for a unified combatant or functional component command, and acknowledges DRUs as the functional proponent at the Department of the Army level.

G-79. As part of the same transformation plan, the USA is currently undergoing a transition from being a division-based force to a brigade-based force. The central part of this plan is that each brigade will be modular; that is, all brigades of the same type will be the same. This allows any division to command any brigade. There will be three major types of ground combat brigades:

- Heavy brigades will have approximately 3,700 troops. They will be equivalent to a mechanized infantry brigade.
- Infantry brigades will have approximately 3,300 troops. They will be equivalent to a light infantry or airborne brigade.
- Stryker brigades will have approximately 3,900 troops. They will be based around the Stryker family of vehicles.

G-80. In addition, the Army Campaign Plan will establish logistics and sustainment modular brigades, aviation brigades in heavy and light varieties, fires (artillery) brigades, and several varieties of sustainment brigades that will function in a standard support role.

ARMY SPECIAL WARFARE

G-81. Of these commands, the USA's major command in charge of USA SOF, which has the primary responsibility for conducting UW, is the USASOC. USASOC currently oversees the following:

- USASFC(A). SF units are tasked with seven specific missions: UW, FID, SR, DA, CT, counterproliferation, and IO. Other duties include coalition warfare and support, CSAR, security assistance, peacekeeping, humanitarian assistance, humanitarian demining and counterdrug operations. USASFC(A) oversees the following SF units:
    - 1st SFG(A): 1st Battalion stationed in Okinawa, the 2d and 3d Battalions and 1st SFG(A) HQ at Fort Lewis, Washington. 1st SFG(A) is responsible for the Pacific.
    - 3d SFG(A): HQ at Fort Bragg, North Carolina. 3d SFG(A) is responsible for all of Africa except for the Middle East and the Horn of Africa (HOA).
    - 5th SFG(A): HQ at Fort Campbell, Kentucky. 5th SFG(A) is responsible for the Middle East, Persian Gulf, Central Asia, and the HOA.
    - 7th SFG(A): HQ at Fort Bragg, North Carolina. 7th SFG(A) is responsible for Latin and Central America, as well as the Caribbean (along with 20th SFG[A]).
    - 10th SFG(A): 1st Battalion stationed near Stuttgart, Germany and the 2d and 3d Battalions and 10th SFG(A) HQ at Fort Carson, Colorado. 10th SFG(A) is responsible for Europe (primarily Central, Eastern, and the Balkans), Turkey, Israel, and Lebanon.
    - 19th SFG(A): An ARNG SF unit. 19th SFG(A) is responsible for Southwest Asia (shared with 5th SFG[A]), as well as the Pacific (shared with 1st SFG[A]).
    - 20th SFG(A): An ARNG SF unit. 20th SFG(A) has an AOR covering 32 countries, including Latin America south of Mexico; the waters, territories, and nations in the

Caribbean Sea; the Gulf of Mexico; and the southwestern Atlantic Ocean. The total area covers 15.6 square miles. This area is shared with 7th SFG(A).
- 75th Ranger Regiment (Rangers, light infantry).
- 160th SOAR (Night Stalkers, helicopters).
- 4th POG(A).
- 95th CA BDE(A).

NOTE: The 95th CA BDE(A) and the 4th POG(A) represent Active Army CA and PSYOP and remain under USASOC. USASOC retains proponency for all CA and PSYOP doctrine and training.

- SB(SO)(A).
- 112th SO Signal Battalion (A).
- Five SO theater support elements.
- USAJFKSWCS.

This page intentionally left blank.

Appendix H
The Role of History and Culture

INTRODUCTION

H-1. In this manual, history does not mean the profession of history—the study of the past—so much as the concept of worldview. History is related and is perceived as a narrative story. It is this narrative that allows for the widest range of interpretation from many perspectives. Historians as scholars strive to achieve an "objective" view of cause-and-effect in the past based on conclusive or reasonable evidence by academic criteria. Nonhistorians interpret their individual and cultural history by their own criteria; that is, the "historical narrative" by which each individual interprets the world as a matter of perception. Individual perceptions are a matter of subjective individual and cultural interpretation. They are not necessarily valid. Nevertheless, such interpretations remain powerful.

H-2. It is beyond the scope of this manual to judge the relative merits of "objective" and "subjective" truth. It is pertinent, however, to identify the many ways in which people perceive individuals organized in various groups and how they prescribe to a given set of beliefs over time. Familiarization with how such historical and cultural issues are defined, analyzed, and disputed provides useful insights into the context within which the informational instrument of power is effective and the manner in which forces conduct UW. As a primer for considering many of the facets of the human terrain, this appendix will survey the concepts of culture, society, civilization, state, nation, race, ethnic group, tribe, clan, band, tradition, mythology, folklore, and religion. The importance of these concepts will vary by UWOA and specific target audience, which warrants further study of how each of these applies to various situations.

CULTURE

H-3. Anthropologists use the term culture to refer to the universal human capacity to symbolically classify, codify, and communicate their experiences. As a scientific concept, it refers to patterns of human activity and the symbolic structures that give such activity significance. In the most general sense, the term culture denotes the whole product of an individual, group, or society. It includes technology, art, science, and the moral systems and characteristic behaviors and habits of the population under examination. Individuals dispute the idea of culture, which reflects different theoretical bases for understanding or criteria for evaluating human activity.

H-4. Some classify culture as the way of life for an entire society. As such, it includes codes of manners; dress; language; religion; rituals; norms of behavior, such as law and morality; and systems of belief. Edward Burnett Taylor, writing from the perspective of social anthropology in the UK in 1871, described culture in the following way: "Culture, or civilization, taken in its wide ethnographic sense, is that complex whole which includes knowledge, belief, art, morals, law, custom, and any other capabilities and habits acquired by man as a member of society." In 2002, the United Nations Educational, Scientific, and Cultural Organization described culture as follows: "Culture should be regarded as the set of distinctive spiritual, material, intellectual, and emotional features of society or a social group, and that it encompasses, in addition to art and literature, lifestyles, ways of living together, value systems, traditions, and beliefs."

KEY COMPONENTS OF CULTURE

H-5. A common way of understanding culture is that it consists of four elements that are passed on from generation to generation. The four elements are—
- *Values*. Values include ideas about what is important in life. They guide the rest of the culture.
- *Norms*. Norms are expectations of how people will behave in various situations.

- *Institutions*. Institutions are the structures of a society that transmit values and norms.
- *Artifacts*. Artifacts are things or aspects of material culture that derive from a culture's values and norms.

CULTURE AS CIVILIZATION

H-6. The culture that developed in Europe during the 18th and early 19th centuries reflected inequalities within European societies and between European powers and their colonies. According to this perspective, people can classify some countries as more civilized than others and some people as more cultured than others.

H-7. From the 19th century onward, Marxists and other social critics have recognized this contrast between high and low culture but claimed that the refinement and sophistication of high culture were corrupting and unnatural developments that obscure and distort people's essential nature. For example, in this view, folk music (as produced by working-class people) honestly expresses a natural way of life, and classical music seems a superficial and decadent representation of a particular social class. This view often romanticizes indigenous peoples as "noble savages" living "authentic," unblemished lives, "uncomplicated" and "uncorrupted" by the highly stratified capitalist systems of the West. This view rejects the opposition of culture to nature. Those that subscribe to this view assert that nonelites are as cultured as elites (and nonwesterners just as civilized as westerners, simply regarding them as just cultured—or civilized—in a different way). This perspective underlies an egalitarian, multicultural worldview in reaction to more ethnocentric and nationalistic worldviews emphasized in the 19th and 20th centuries.

CULTURE AS SHARED SYMBOLS

H-8. Culture holds symbols to be both the practices of social actors and the context that gives such practices meaning. Symbols provide the limits of cultured thought.

CULTURE AS A STABILIZING MECHANISM FOR SURVIVAL

H-9. The view of culture as a "stabilizing mechanism" considers the possibility that culture itself is a product of stabilization tendencies. For example, individuals identify with those cultural artifacts, symbols, and practices that foster feelings of survival, security, and (eventually) self-actualization. Allegiance to a culture for these reasons tends to perpetuate it.

CULTURE AS UNBOUNDED ACTIVITY

H-10. Some scholars (particularly sociologists and Marxists) focus on the study of "artifacts" to understand culture. The patterns involving value and transfer of consumption goods (such as fashion, art, and literature) have been a common means of analyzing cultural patterns. With modern reactions to the 18th- and 19th-century distinction between "high" and "low" culture, such scholars tend to emphasize mass-produced and mass-marketed consumption goods of "popular" culture.

H-11. However, other contemporary scholars (particularly anthropologists) reject the identification of culture with consumption goods and de-emphasize the defining role of any artifacts. This view rejects the notion of culture as "bounded" by a set class of defining attributes. Such scholars consequently reject the notion of mainstream "culture" or "subculture" altogether. Instead, they see culture as a complex web of shifting patterns at any given time that link people in different locales into social formations of different scales. According to this view, any group can construct its own cultural identity.

CULTURAL CHANGE

H-12. Each culture, however defined, is predisposed to either embrace or resist change based on its particular cultural traits. Two kinds of influence cause change or resistance to it: forces at work within or

between cultures and changes in the natural environment. Some of the terms associated with cultural change include the following:
- *Diffusion.* The form of something moves directly from one culture to another. For example, a culture adopts fashion or music styles unchanged from another culture.
- *Stimulus diffusion.* Exposure of one culture to another that leads to new and different activity or products. For example, exposure to American blues music in the early 20th century led to newly developed styles of rock and roll in mid-20th-century Britain.
- *Acculturation.* In this context, it refers to replacement of the traits of one culture with those of another. For example, certain indigenous peoples across the globe adopted the culture of the entering power during the process of colonization.
- *Assimilation.* This term reflects a more complete level of acculturation wherein those assimilated effectively become a part of the mainstream culture. For example, the descendents of 19th-century European immigrants to America have largely assimilated into "American" culture.

H-13. Cultural change or resistance to change can be difficult to measure—especially the diffusion, acceptance, and rejection of ideas. In the context of 21st-century globalization and with a view of culture as "unbounded," culture can be a complex and subjective matter of definition, interpretation, and self-identification.

CULTURES WITHIN A SOCIETY

H-14. The idea of culture is inexact. Large societies often have subcultures, or groups of people with distinct sets of behavior and beliefs. Subculture may be distinctive because of many factors: age, race, ethnicity, class, gender, behavior patterns, and so on.

CULTURES BY REGION

H-15. In practical terms, world region can identify current broad cultural influences. Throughout history, contact with others through conquest, colonization, trade, migration, mass media, and religion has influenced all predominant regional cultures. Examples of this influence follow:
- *Africa.* European colonialism and Arabic and Islamic culture.
- *America.* Colonialism, immigration and Christianity.
- *Asia.* Chinese language and culture, Buddhism, Taoism, Hinduism, and Islam.
- *Oceania.* Aboriginal culture, the indigenous Maori people, and Christianity.
- *Europe.* Ancient Greece and Rome; Christianity; European culture and languages, such as English, Spanish, and French.
- *Middle East and North Africa.* Persian culture and Arabic language.

SOCIETY

H-16. Closely related to the term culture is the notion of society. A society is a grouping of individuals characterized by common interest and, sometimes, a distinctive culture and institutions. In a society, members can be from a different ethnic group. A society may refer to a particular people, such as the Nuer, to a nation-state, such as Switzerland, or to a broader cultural group, such as western society.

CHARACTERISTICS OF SOCIETY

H-17. The three components common to all definitions of society are—
- Social networks.
- Criteria for membership.
- Characteristic patterns of organization.

Social Networks

H-18. Social networks are relationships between people. Examples of social networks are relatives, friends, and colleagues.

Criteria for Membership

H-19. The most common entrance to membership of any given society is to be born into it, where the individual generally accepts and reflects its norms. In this sense, society and culture are sometimes indistinguishable. Continued self-identification with and support of the original society is the most common method of sustaining membership.

H-20. Society is not necessarily synonymous with state or nation. Sometimes, peoples of many nations united by common political and cultural traditions, shared beliefs or values, or common goals form a society (such as Judeo-Christian, eastern, and western). When used in this context, the term is a means of contrasting two or more large "societies" whose members represent alternative conflicting and competing worldviews. Other examples include some small academic, learned, and scholarly associations that describe themselves as societies or as used in some countries to denote a partnership between commercial investors.

Characteristic Patterns of Organization

H-21. Experts classify societies in various ways. For example:
- Hunters and gatherers.
- Simple agricultural.
- Advanced agricultural.
- Industrial.

H-22. Societies may also organize according to their political structure or by the status of individuals, complexity, and the role of the state:
- Hunter-gatherer bands.
- Tribal societies.
- Kingdoms and early modern European nation-states.
- Civilizations with complex social hierarchies.

CONCEPT OF SOCIETY

H-23. Some societies disappear, while others have progressed toward ever more complex forms. Some dispute the concept of society. Some sociologists and anthropologists question whether society as an entity exists. Some Marxist theorists argue that society is nothing more than an effect of the ruling ideology of a certain class system. They contend that people should not use society as a sociological notion. Marx held that society was merely the sum total of social relations among members of a community. Many Muslims identify more readily with "Islamic society" than they do with any particular state or nation. Regardless of ideology, the way people define society explains much about them.

CIVILIZATION

H-24. The term "civilization" has a variety of meanings related to human society. Most often, civilization refers to complex societies—those that have an intensive practice of agriculture, have a significant division of labor, and have population densities sufficient to form cities. People may use civilization more broadly to refer to the sum or current extent of human accomplishment and diffusion (human civilization or global civilization).

H-25. The term "civilization" in common speech has both a normative and a descriptive dimension. In the past, to be "civilized" was linked to the act of being "civil"—a term for politeness and propriety. To be "uncivilized" in this usage means to be rude, barbaric, or savage. In this sense, civilization implies sophistication and refinement. The problem with this concept is that some people who lived outside of a given, recognized civilization could nonetheless be quite civilized in their behavior. Many world cultures throughout history have used the normative definition of "civilization" to justify imperialism.

H-26. In reaction to this disparaging meaning of civilization, academia has broadened the term so that "civilization" can often refer to any distinct society, whether complex and city dwelling or simple and tribal (for example "Australian aboriginal civilization"). People often perceive this sense of the term as less exclusionary and ethnocentric, because it does not make distinctions between civilized or barbaric. However, this less-ethnocentric approach to the term weakens its descriptive power. Such a usage is both less useful and meaningful than the first. In this sense, civilization becomes nearly synonymous with culture.

H-27. In contrast, civilization can also legitimately describe the culture of a complex society, not just simple societies or society itself. Every society has a specific set of ideas, customs, items, and arts that make it unique. However, civilizations have even more intricate cultures, including literature, professional art, architecture, organized religion, and complex customs. It is a matter of degree. The description of a "culture" as a "civilization," therefore, is another contentious and vaguely defined concept.

CHARACTERISTICS OF CIVILIZATION

H-28. Civilizations are complex systems or networks of cities that emerge from preurban cultures and are defined by the economic, political, military, diplomatic, and cultural interactions between them. Therefore, as a descriptive and literal term, a civilization is a complex society, as distinguished from a simpler society. Historically, civilizations have shared some or all of the following traits:

- Agricultural techniques.
- Division of labor.
- Permanent settlements.
- Social organization.
- Institutional food control.
- Complex social institutions.
- Complex economic exchange.
- Material possessions.
- Advanced technology.
- Advanced arts.
- Long existence.

H-29. By these characteristics, some societies, like Greece, are clearly civilizations, whereas others, like the Bushmen or the early nomadic Native Americans, clearly are not. However, the distinction is not always clear and is often in dispute.

CIVILIZATION AS HUMAN-SOCIETY-AS-A-WHOLE

H-30. Some argue that the entire world is already integrated into a single world system, by a process known as "globalization." Different civilizations and societies all over the globe are economically, politically, and even culturally interdependent in many ways. There is debate over when this integration began and what sort of integration—cultural, technological, economic, political, or military/diplomatic—is the key indicator in determining the extent of a civilization.

H-31. In this broader sense, "civilization" can refer to human society as a whole—the "global civilization." What globalization means and how to characterize are also in dispute. Critics of "globalization" reject such a coupling of the terms, saying that what is called "globalization" is in fact a form of "global corporatization" and that other forms of "globalization" are possible (such as Communist world government or a worldwide Islamic caliphate). Others argue that globalization and ongoing future integration inherently erode the distinct sovereignty of states. Still others believe that states will continue to be politically meaningful despite the technological and economic integration of continued globalization. Despite ideology, people widely accept that the "world civilization" is increasingly integrating.

STATE

H-32. As noted above, a state is a set of institutions that possess the authority to make the rules that govern the people in one or more societies with internal sovereignty over a definite territory. It is casually and most commonly confused with "country," which refers to a geographic area and "nation," which designates a people.

NATION

H-33. A nation is a group of humans that people assume share a common identity and a common language, religion, ideology, culture, or history. People often assume that individuals in groups have a common origin, in the sense of ancestry, parentage, or descent.

H-34. The national identity refers both to the distinguishing features of the group and to the individual's sense of belonging to it. People use a very wide range of criteria with very different applications to determine national identity. Small differences in pronunciation may be enough to categorize someone as a member of another nation. However, two people may be separated by difference in personalities, belief systems, geographical locations, time, and even spoken language yet regard themselves (and others may regard them as well) as members of the same nation. Members of a nation are considered to share certain traits, values, and norms of behavior; certain duties toward other members; and certain responsibilities for the actions of the members of the same nation.

H-35. Nations extend across generations and include the dead as full members. More vaguely, people include future generations as members. People frame past events in this context; for example, referring to "our soldiers" in conflicts that took place hundreds of years ago.

H-36. People often use the term "nation" as a synonym for ethnic group. However, although ethnicity is now one of the most important aspects of cultural or social identity for the members of most nations, people with the same ethnic origin may live in different nation-states, and people may treat them as members of separate nations for that reason. People often dispute national identity, down to the level of the individual.

H-37. Almost all nations are associated with a specific territory, the national homeland. Some live in historical communities outside of their original national homeland. A state that explicitly identifies as the homeland of a particular nation is a nation-state, and most modern states fall into this category, although there may be violent disputes about their legitimacy. When nations dispute territory, the nations may base their claims on which nation lived there first. Especially in areas of European colonial settlement (1500-1950), the term "first nations" is used by some groups that share an aboriginal culture and seek official recognition or autonomy.

AMBIGUITY IN USAGE

H-38. In the strict sense, terms such as "nation," "ethnos," and "people" (for example, the "Danish people") name a group of human beings. The concepts of nation and nationality have much in common with ethnic group and ethnicity but have a more political connotation, since they imply the possibility of a nation-state. Country names a geographical territory, whereas state expresses a legitimized administrative and decision-making institution. Confusingly, some use the terms "national" and "international" as technical terms applying to states. International law, for instance, applies to relations between states and occasionally between states on the one side and individuals or legal persons on the other. Likewise, the UN represents states, while nations are not admitted to the body (unless a respective nation-state exists, which can become a member).

H-39. Usage also varies from country to country. For example, the UK is an internationally recognized sovereign state, which is also a country whose inhabitants have British nationality. It is, however, traditionally divided into four home nations—England, Scotland, Wales, and Ireland. Three of these are not sovereign states. Ireland, however, is now divided into the sovereign Republic of Ireland and Northern Ireland, which remains part of the UK.

H-40. Usage of the term "nation" not only is ambiguous but also is the subject of political disputes, which may be extremely violent. When the term "nation" has any implications of claims to independence from an existing state, its use is controversial. Finally, the term "nation" is widely used by extension or metaphor to describe any group promoting some common interest or common identity, such as "Red Sox nation," "rhythm nation," or "religious nation."

NATIONALISM

H-41. In Europe, especially since the late 18th century, the idea of nation assumed a fundamental political significance with the rise of the ideology and philosophy of nationalism. Nationalists saw a nation not simply as a descriptive term for a group of people but as an entity entitled to sovereignty, if necessary, by the absorption or destruction of nonnational states.

H-42. There is no consensus among the theorists of nationalism on whether nations were a significant political factor before that time. Some historians see England and Portugal as early examples of nation-states, with a developed sense of national identity. Others see the nation-state as a 19th century creation, either as the result of the political campaigns of nationalists or as a top-down and indoctrinated creation by preexisting states. Some Marxists and world civilization-oriented theorists are hostile to the idea of "centuries-old nations" that nationalists claimed to represent, arguing that nations are often imagined communities constructed through a variety of techniques using state power. The generally accepted but eroding idea that populations divide Europe into nations has existed since at least the 19th century.

H-43. In the course of the 20th century, partly through decolonization, a world of nation-states came into existence, at least nominally. That does not mean that there is any agreement on the number of nations, on whether they correspond with a nation-state, or on whether any particular existing state is necessarily legitimate. Very few nation-state's territory and borders are 100 percent undisputed. Political actors make claims on behalf of stateless nations, such as the Kurds, Assyrians, Palestinians, or Roma people (gypsies). Secessionist movements may oppose the very existence of the nation-state, as in Belgium. Some nationalist movements request greater autonomy within the framework of the broader state (for example, the Basque in Spain, Quebecois in Canada, or Native Americans in the western hemisphere). Claimed national territory may be partitioned or divided, as in the Republic of Ireland and Northern Ireland. There are also examples of national identity without a corresponding state or claim to a state. Although it is common to attribute political and territorial aspirations to a nation itself, political movements speaking on behalf of that nation make these aspirations.

H-44. People sometimes use the term "state-nation" for nations in which the common identity derives from shared citizenship of a state. This term implies that the state formed first followed by a sense of national identity or that it developed in tandem. Examples of state-nations are Italy and France. However, both countries also have a strong ethnic and cultural identity. If the people defined the nation only by citizenship, then the people would accept naturalized citizens as equal members of the nation and that is not always the case. Citizenship may itself be conditional on a citizenship test, which usually includes language and cultural knowledge tests.

DEFINING A NATION

H-45. Nations are defined by a limited number of characteristics that apply to both the individual members and the nation. The first requirement for the definition is that the characteristics should be shared—a group of people with nothing in common cannot be a nation. Because they are shared, the national population also has some degree of uniformity and homogeneity. Finally, at least some of the characteristics must be exclusive—to distinguish the nation from neighboring nations. All of the characteristics can be disputed and opposition to secessionist nationalism often includes the denial that a separate nation exists.

COMMON DESCENT

H-46. Almost all nationalist movements make some claim to shared origins and descent, and it is a component of the national identity in most nations. The fact that members of the nation share ancestry unites them and sets them apart from other nations that do not share that ancestry. The question is: descent from whom? Often, the answer is simply from previous generations of the same nation. More specifically—

- The nation may be defined as the descendants of the past inhabitants of the national homeland.
- The nation may be defined as the descendants of past speakers of the national language or past groups that shared the national culture.

H-47. Usually, people assume these factors coincide. Iceland provides an example. People assume the well-defined Icelandic nation consists of the descendants of the island of Iceland in, for example, 1850. Those people also spoke the Icelandic language. They were known as Icelanders at that time. They had a recognized culture of their own. However, the present population of Iceland cannot coincide exactly with their descendants; that would mean that no Icelander since 1850 ever had children by a non-Icelander. Most European nations experienced border changes and migration over the last few centuries and members intermarried with other national groups. Statistically, their current national population cannot coincide exactly with the descendants of the nation in 1850 or 1500, even if it was then known by the same name. The shared ancestry is more of a national myth than a genetic reality—but still sufficient for a national identity.

COMMON LANGUAGE

H-48. People often view a shared language as a defining feature of a nation. In some cases, the language is exclusive to the nation. This language may be central to the national identity. The Basque language is a unique language isolate and prominent in the self-definition of the Basque people and in Basque nationalism, although not all Basques speak it. In other cases, other nations also speak the national language (shared among the nation, but not exclusive to the nation). Some peoples, such as the Swiss, identify themselves as multilingual. Conversely, Papua New Guinea promotes a "Papuan" national identity, despite having around 800 distinct languages. People do not define any nation solely by language—that would effectively create an open membership for anyone who learned the language.

COMMON CULTURE

H-49. People define most nations partly by a shared culture. Unlike a language, a national culture is usually unique to the nation, although it may include many elements shared with other nations. In addition, people assume that previous generations shared the national culture and that they share a cultural heritage from these generations, as if it were an inheritance. As with the common ancestry, this identification of past culture with present culture may be largely symbolic. The archaeological site of Stonehenge is owned and managed by English heritage, although no "English" people or state existed when it was constructed 4,000 to 5,000 years ago. Other nations have similarly appropriated ancient archaeological sites, literature, art, and even entire civilizations as a national heritage.

COMMON RELIGION

H-50. People sometimes use religion to define a nation, although some nationalist movements de-emphasize it as a divisive factor. Again, it is the sharing of the religion that makes it national. It may not be exclusive. Several nations define themselves partly as Catholic although the religion itself is Universalist. Irish nationalism traditionally sees Catholicism as an Irish national characteristic, in opposition to the largely Protestant British colonial power (although the Irish Republic usually recognizes the Protestant minority in Ireland as Irish). Some religions are largely specific to one ethnic group, notably Judaism. Nevertheless, the Zionist movement generally avoided a religious definition of the "Jewish people," preferring an ethnic and cultural definition. Since Judaism is a religion, people can become a Jew by religious conversion, which in turn can facilitate their obtaining Israeli citizenship. Jews in Israel who convert to other religions do not lose Israeli citizenship, although their national identity might then be questioned by others.

VOLUNTARY DEFINITIONS

H-51. Some ideas of a nation emphasize not shared characteristics, but rather on the shared choice for membership. In practice, this always applies to a group of people who are also a nation by other definitions. The most famous "voluntarist" definition is that of Ernest Renan. In a lecture in 1882, he rhetorically asked "What is a nation?" and answered that it is a "daily plebiscite." Renan meant that the members of the nation by their daily participation in the life of the nation show their consent to its existence and to their own continued membership. Renan saw the nation as a group "having done great things together and wishing to do more."

STALIN'S DEFINITION

H-52. Many definitions of a nation combine several of these factors. One influential example of these combined definitions is that of Joseph Stalin given in 1913: "A nation is a historically constituted, stable community of people, formed on the basis of a common language, territory, economic life, and psychological makeup manifested in a common culture."

RACE

H-53. The term "race" serves to distinguish between populations or groups of people based on different sets of characteristics that can be determined either through scientific conventions or, more commonly, through social conventions. Visual traits are the most widely used human racial categories (especially skin color, facial features, and hair texture), genes, and self-identification. Conceptions of race and specific racial groupings vary by culture and over time. They are often controversial for scientific reasons and because of their impact on social identity and identity politics. Many contemporary biological and social scientists regard the concept of race primarily as a social construct, while some maintain it has a genetic basis.

ETHNIC GROUP

H-54. An ethnic group or ethnicity is a population of humans whose members identify with each other, usually on a presumed common genealogy or ancestry. Recognition by others as a separate ethnic group and a specific name for the group also contribute to defining it. Certain common cultural, behavioral, linguistic, and ritualistic or religious traits also usually unite ethnic groups. In this sense, an ethnic group is also a cultural community.

H-55. Because of closely related definitions, an ethnic group can overlap or even coincide with a nation, especially when terms of common origin primarily define national identity. Members of nations also identify with each other. They often presume a common ancestry. In addition, others recognize them as a distinct group with a specific name. Nations also have a common identity: always cultural, usually linguistic, and sometimes religious. An ethnic group that is also a nation can be the named head of a nation-state; however, ethnic groups as such are not a state and possess no territorial sovereignty. Members of an ethnic group generally claim a strong cultural continuity over time.

H-56. While ethnicity and race are related concepts, the concept of ethnicity is rooted in the idea of social groups and is marked especially by shared nationality, tribal affiliation, genealogy, religious faith, language, or cultural and traditional origins, whereas race is traditionally rooted in the idea of a biological classification.

TRIBE

H-57. A tribe, viewed historically or developmentally, consists of a social group existing before the development of or outside of states, although some modern theorists hold that contemporary tribes can only be understood in terms of their relationship to states. People often use the term loosely to refer to any nonwestern or indigenous society. Many anthropologists use the term to refer to societies organized largely based on kinship, especially descent groups. In the common modern understanding, the word tribe is a social division within a traditional society consisting of a group of interlinked families or communities sharing a common culture and dialect. In the contemporary western mind, the modern tribe is typically associated with a seat of traditional authority (tribal leader) with whom the representatives of external (for example, state or occupying) powers interact.

H-58. Considerable debate takes place over how best to characterize tribes. Some of this debate stems from perceived differences between prestate tribes and contemporary tribes. Some of this debate reflects controversy over cultural evolution and colonialism. In the popular imagination, tribes reflect a way of life that predates and is more natural than that in modern states. Tribes also grant primary social ties, contain clear boundaries, demonstrate uniform culture, manifest a narrow outlook, and establish stability. Thus, many believed that tribes organize links between families (including clans and lineages) and provide them with a social and ideological basis for solidarity that is in some way more limited than that of an "ethnic group" or of a "nation."

H-59. Anthropological and ethnohistorical research challenges all of these notions. In his 1972 study, *The Notion of the Tribe*, Morton Fried provided numerous examples of tribes in which members spoke different languages and practiced different rituals or shared languages and rituals with members of other tribes. Similarly, he provided examples of tribes in which people followed different political leaders or followed the same leaders as members of other tribes. He concluded that generally fluid boundaries and dissimilarity characterized tribes, in general. He determined that tribes have open outlooks and are dynamic.

CLAN

H-60. A clan is a group of people united by kinship and descent, which is defined by perceived descent from a common ancestor. Even if actual lineage patterns are unknown, clan members nonetheless recognize a founding member or original ancestor. As kinship-based bonds can be merely symbolical, some clans share a "stipulated" common ancestor, which is a symbol of the clan's unity. Sometimes this ancestor is not human. Generally, kinship differs from biological relation, as it also involves adoption, marriage, and fictional genealogical ties. Clans can be most easily described as subgroups of tribes and usually constitute groups of 7,000 to 10,000 people.

H-61. Some clans are patrilineal, meaning its members are related through the male line. Others are matrilineal; its members are related through the female line. Still other clans are bilateral, consisting of all the descendants of the original ancestor through both the male and female lines. Whether a clan is patrilineal, matrilineal, or bilateral depends on the kinship rules and norms of their society.

H-62. In different cultures and situations, a clan may mean the same thing as other kin-based groups, such as tribes and bands. Often, the distinguishing factor is that a clan is a smaller part of a larger society, such as a tribe, chiefdom, or a state. Examples include Irish, Scottish, Chinese, and Japanese clans, which exist as kin groups within their respective nations. However, tribes and bands can also be components of larger societies. Arab tribes are small groups within Arab society, and Ojibwa bands are smaller parts of the Ojibwa tribe.

H-63. Apart from these different traditions of kinship, further confusion arises from common use of the term. In post-Soviet countries, for example, it is quite common for the term to refer to informal networks within the economic and political sphere. This usage reflects the assumption that their members act toward each other in a particularly close and mutually supportive way approximating the solidarity among kinsmen.

H-64. People sometimes better refer to clans as a "house" or "line." In some cases, a house or line consists of a collection of families bearing the same coat of arms, as opposed to actually claiming a common descent. Most clans are exogamous, meaning that its members cannot marry one another. Some clans have an official leader, such as a chieftain, matriarch, or patriarch.

BANDS

H-65. A band society is the simplest form of human society. A band generally consists of a small kin group no larger than an extended family or clan. Bands have very informal leadership. There are no written laws in bands. In addition, the coercion normally present in more complex societies does not exist in bands. Younger members of the band look to older members for guidance and advice. Band members usually transmit customs orally. Formal social institutions are few or nonexistent. Generally, family tradition, individual experience, or shamanic counsel is the basis of the band's religion. All known band societies hunt and gather to obtain their food.

H-66. Fried defined bands as "small, mobile, and fluid social formations with weak leadership that do not generate surpluses, pay no taxes, and support no standing army." Bands are distinguished from tribes in that tribes are generally larger and consist of many families. Social roles exist in tribes, such as a chief or elders. Tribes are also more permanent than bands. A band can cease to exist if only a small group walks out. Many tribes are in fact subdivided into bands. In the United States, some tribes are made up of official bands that live in specific locations. With the spread of the modern nation-state to all corners of the globe, there are very few true band societies left. Some historic examples include the Inuit of northern North America, the Shoshone of the great basin, the bushmen of southern Africa, and some groups of indigenous Australians.

TRADITION

H-67. A tradition is a story or a custom that a person memorizes and passes down from generation to generation. Traditions are usually thought of as—
- A meme, which is a unit of cultural information passed down orally.
- A set of customs or practices.
- A broad religious movement made up of religious denominations or church bodies that have a common history, customs, culture, and body of teachings.

H-68. On a more basic theoretical level, traditions are information brought into the present from the past in a particular societal context. This is even more fundamental than particular acts or practices even if repeated over a long sequence of time. For such acts or practices, once performed, disappear unless they are transformed into some manner of communicable information.

H-69. Although people usually presume that traditions are ancient, unalterable, and deeply important, this is not necessarily true. People or groups sometimes deliberately invent some "traditions" for one reason or another, often to highlight or enhance the importance of a certain institution. People also change traditions to suit the needs of the day, and the changes quickly become accepted as a part of the ancient tradition. Some examples include "the invention of tradition" in Africa and other colonial holdings by the occupying forces. Requiring legitimacy, the colonial power would sometimes invent a tradition that they could use to legitimize their own position. For example, a force might recognize a certain succession to chiefdom by a colonial power as traditional to favor their favorite candidate for the job. Often the force based these inventions on some form of tradition. However, these were grossly exaggerated, distorted, or biased toward a particular interpretation.

MYTHOLOGY

H-70. A mythology is a narrative, oral tradition, or a popular belief or assumption based on the heroes of a culture. Mythology sometimes involves supernatural events or characters to explain the nature of the universe and humanity. The term myth is often used interchangeably with legend or allegory.

CHARACTERISTICS

H-71. Myths are narratives about divine or heroic beings arranged in a coherent system. Myths often explain the universal and local beginnings, natural phenomena, inexplicable cultural conventions or rituals, and anything else for which no simple explanation exists.

H-72. Individual myths may be classified in various categories:
- Ritual myths.
- Origin myths.
- Creation myths.
- Cult myths.
- Prestige myths.
- Eschatological myths.

Appendix H

- Social myths.
- Trickster myths.

FORMATION OF MYTHS

H-73. Myths authorize the cultural institutions of a tribe, a city, or a nation by connecting them with universal truths. All cultures have developed their own myths, consisting of narratives of their history, their religions, and their heroes.

FOLKLORE

H-74. Folklore is the body of expressive culture, including tales, music, dance, legends, oral history, proverbs, jokes, popular beliefs, customs, and material culture common to a particular population, comprising the traditions of that culture. The definition most widely accepted by current scholars of the field is "artistic communication in small groups." The term, and the associated field of study, now includes nonverbal art forms and customary practices.

H-75. Contemporary narratives common in the western world include the urban legend. There are many forms of folklore that are so common, however, that most people do not realize they are folklore, such as riddles, children's rhymes, ghost stories, rumors, gossip, ethnic stereotypes, holiday custom, and life-cycle rituals.

RELIGION

H-76. A religion is a set of beliefs and practices held by a community that involves adherence to codified beliefs and rituals and the study of ancestral or cultural traditions and mythology, as well as personal faith and mystic experience.

H-77. The *Encyclopedia of Religion* describes religion in the following way: "In summary, it may be said that almost every known culture involves the religious in the sense of a 'depth dimension' in cultural experiences at all levels—a push, whether ill-defined or conscious, toward some sort of ultimacy and transcendence that will provide norms and power for the rest of life. When more or less distinct patterns of behavior are built around this depth dimension in a culture, this structure constitutes religion in its historically recognizable form. Religion is the organization of life around the depth dimensions of experience—varied in form, completeness, and clarity IAW the environing culture."

RELIGION AS A SOCIAL CONSTRUCTION

H-78. Those who assert that religion—however defined—is an overall positive are as numerous as the number of religious adherents. Inherently, each individual's religious adherence entangles with the ways he identifies with all of the other characteristics of human organization. Therefore, most individual's religious adherence interweaves with tradition and ideas of culture, society, mythology, and so on. Conversely, all philosophies and orthodoxies—including religious philosophies and orthodoxies—have their disputants. In the 21st century western world, most Marxists and some scientists are the most strident critics of "religion."

RELIGIONS AS PROGRESSIVELY TRUE

H-79. Within these models, religions reflect an essential truth that is revealed as society develops. Models that view religion as progressively true include the following:

- *The Baha'i model of prophetic revelation.* This model holds that god has sent a series of prophets to earth, each brining teachings appropriate for his culture and context but originating from the same god and, therefore, teaching the same essential message. While religious truth is seen as being relative because of its varied cultural and developmental expression, this model accepts that the underlying essential truth being expressed is absolutely true, if incompletely and progressively presented.
- *The study of history model.* This model holds that prophets are given to extraordinary spiritual insight during periods of social decay and act as surveyors of the course of secular civilization

who report breaks in the road and breakdowns in the traffic and plot a new spiritual course that will avoid those pitfalls.
- *The great awakening model.* This model states that religion proceeds along a Hegelian dialectic of thesis, antithesis, synthesis, in cycles of approximately 80 years as a result of the interaction between four archetypal generations, by which old religious beliefs (the thesis) face new challenges for which they are unprepared (the antithesis) and adapt to create new and more sophisticated beliefs (the synthesis).

RELIGIONS AS ABSOLUTELY TRUE

H-80. Some models see religion as absolutely and unchangingly true. Models that view a particular religion as absolutely true include the Jewish, Christian, and Islamic models. Exclusivist models hold that one particular set of religious doctrines is the one true religion and all others are false to the extent that they conflict with the true one. In this model, all other religions are seen as either distortions of the original truth or original fabrications resulting from either ignorance or imagination or a more devious influence, such as false prophets.

RELIGIOUS BELIEF

H-81. Religious belief usually relates to the existence, nature, and worship of a deity or deities and divine involvement in the universe and human life. It may also relate to values and practices transmitted by a spiritual leader. Religious beliefs are found in virtually every society throughout human history. All religions generally seek to provide answers to metaphysical and cosmological questions about the nature of being, of the universe, humanity, and the divine.

H-82. Many early scientists held strong religious beliefs and many theories exist as to why religions sometimes seem to conflict with scientific knowledge. In the case of Christianity, a relevant factor may be that it was among Christians that science in the modern sense was developed. Unlike other religious groups, as early as the 17th century the Christian churches had to deal directly with this new way to investigate nature and seek truth. The practice of literally interpreting the Bible partially explains the perceived conflict between science and Christianity. This way to read the sacred texts became especially prevalent after the rise of the Protestant Reformation, with its emphasis on the Bible as the only authoritative source concerning ultimate reality. In contrast, this view is often shunned by both religious leaders who prefer a metaphorical interpretation and many scientists who regard it as an impossibility. The proper relationship of religion to science remains an unsettled matter of widely varied opinion.

H-83. Some Christians disagree with scientists on astronomy, the theory of evolution, and the nature of creation and origin of life. Others find no contradiction in a metaphorical interpretation of their faith with scientific inquiry. Islam sees all endeavor as god's will, so scientific endeavor is theoretically unobjectionable. However, particular Muslim observance and tolerance for scientific consensus varies widely in Muslim societies ranging from theocratic Iran through democratic Malaysia to Muslim minorities in the United States. Other faiths such as Baha'ism and Hinduism maintain there is no disharmony between true science and true religion, because they are aspects of the same "truth."

This page intentionally left blank.

Appendix I
A Historical Survey of Unconventional Warfare

INTRODUCTION

I-1. The United States has considerable experience in conducting UW. The best known U.S. UW campaigns include OSS activities in Europe and the Pacific (1942–45), Philippines (1941–44), Guatemala (1950), Cuba (1960–61), North Vietnam (1964–72), South Vietnam (1967–72), Iraq (1991–96), OEF (2001–02), and OIF (2002–03). Below is a brief but expanded representative sampling of such operations.

UNITED STATES-PHILIPPINE RESISTANCE TO JAPANESE OCCUPATION (1942–1945)

I-2. U.S. support to and in some cases leadership of irregular resistance to Japanese forces in the Philippine archipelago was an unqualified success. It stands as a premier example of what military planners today call operational preparation of the environment. The Philippine resistance movement, made up of a number of groups spread throughout the archipelago but most numerous on the main island of Luzon, collected and transmitted intelligence on adversary order of battle, conducted hit-and-run raids against Japanese forces, and provided de facto government services in a number of villages. The resistance movement benefited from environmental factors that contributed to the overall success of the campaign. These factors included the size of the archipelago (almost 115,000 square meters) spread out over 7,100 islands and the imposing jungle and mountain terrain on the largest islands. Both factors, as well as the requirement to maintain lines of communications and supply between garrisons, severely stretched the occupying Japanese forces. Although the Japanese initially offered positive or neutral incentives not to resist, such as amnesty to military stragglers and those under arms, increasing negative measures (including collective reprisals against villagers for attacks; imprisonment, torture, or execution of suspected guerrillas; and seizing crops and livestock) turned the population against them.

UNITED NATIONS PARTISAN OPERATIONS IN KOREA (1951–1953)

I-3. Success and failure in waging UW can be difficult to judge. In the case of UW conducted during the Korean War, the evidence seems contradictory. Although UN partisan forces contributed to allied interdiction efforts in the operational rear areas of North Korea, the movement nevertheless failed to achieve more widespread strategic success. Most if not all of the preconditions for UW success existed on the Korean peninsula, but a number of factors inhibited the success of UN partisan forces. First, the responsibility for UN partisan operations shifted between different command instruments, none of which had developed a comprehensive plan or phasing for UW in the theater. Second, the command used UN partisan forces primarily for seaborne raids not unlike British commando raids in WWII—not for organization of an indigenous organization. The purpose of these raids was to interdict main supply routes, inflict casualties, and boost the morale of anticommunist instruments in North Korea. The command applied little effort to establishing sanctuaries and base areas on the peninsula itself or cultivating the population to support an insurgency. From 1952 onward, the North Koreans placed greater emphasis on rear area counterpartisan operations that limited the mobility and access of UN partisan forces to the North Korean population. Finally, and most significantly, U.S. advisors to UN partisan forces neither spoke Korean nor understood the culture. This lack of preparation seriously influenced the ability of UN partisan forces to undertake UW actions more complicated than episodic raids-in-force.

UNITED STATES UNCONVENTIONAL WARFARE IN NORTH VIETNAM (1964–1972)

I-4. With few possible exceptions, U.S. UW efforts in North Vietnam were among the least successful of any it has attempted. According to Conboy and Andrade, U.S. UW efforts failed because of a "lack of imagination in planning, faulty execution of missions, and poor operational security." Although originally planned and controlled by the CIA in 1960, responsibility for U.S. UW activities was shifted to the DOD in 1964. Most of the activities subsequently conducted in Northern Vietnam bore a striking similarity to missions conducted by the OSS during WWII. These missions included parachuting lone Vietnamese agents or teams of agents deep into North Vietnam to gather and report intelligence or conduct attacks. Maritime missions included short-term seaborne raids, agent insertion, and deception/psychological warfare operations. Such UW was designed to distract North Vietnamese attention, as well as resources, to combating saboteurs operating in their homeland. The results of these UW efforts were dismal. The fact that such operations continued despite persistent evidence of their failure is a testament to the lack of imagination mentioned above, as well as the bravery of most of the Vietnamese volunteers. The inability of U.S. planners to set meaningful strategic and operational objectives for UW and the haphazard and uncoordinated use of UW troops simply because the option existed—without any hope of generating support among the local populous—ultimately doomed such efforts.

UNITED STATES UNCONVENTIONAL WARFARE IN SOUTH VIETNAM (1967–1972)

I-5. The successful U.S.-led UW efforts in South Vietnam had their genesis in the Mike Force and Mobile Guerrilla Force concepts, which were initially corps-level reserve forces designed to react quickly to contingencies such as Viet Cong attacks on SF or Civilian Irregular Defense Group camps. Instead of responding to the adversary and ceding the local initiative to them the newly developed Mobile Guerrilla Force would operate autonomously for extended periods of time to take the fight to areas of South Vietnam controlled by the Viet Cong. A crucial difference between the Mobile Guerrilla Forces and their predecessors was operational control. An SF corps-level commander directly controlled the force, instead of a conventional corps commander in each of the four corps of South Vietnam. The United States designed the Mobile Guerrilla Forces for extended operations, including long-range reconnaissance patrolling and ambushing, to fight the Viet Cong using their own tactics against them. Comprised of any combination of Vietnamese, Montagnard (tribal hill peoples), and ethnic Cambodians, these forces were led by U.S. and/or South Vietnamese SF personnel. Operating largely in sparsely populated areas, the Mobile Guerrilla Forces combined cultural awareness; local knowledge and support; U.S. supply, mobility, and firepower; and guerrilla tactics offensively and successfully against the Viet Cong.

UNITED STATES UNCONVENTIONAL WARFARE IN THE SOVIET-AFGHAN WAR (1981–1989)

I-6. Not all offensive UW efforts involve the United States working with indigenous forces directly, as was the case with U.S. support to Afghan Mujahideen forces during the Soviet-Afghan War. Initially, the United States funneled financial support for the Afghan fighters from other government agencies through the intelligence service of Pakistan. The Pakistani Inter-Service Intelligence maintained direct links with a number of Mujahideen leaders and dispensed the funds to favored groups so that they could buy arms and other supplies. In addition, some of these Afghan groups maintained training bases and safe areas within Pakistan. Although financial support was important to sustaining the Mujahideen, one of the key turning points in the war occurred when the United States and the British introduced shoulder-fired surface-to-air missiles, such as Stinger and Blowpipe, into the conflict. The Mujahideen were effective at ambushing the largely road-bound motorized and mechanized Soviet forces. Soviet airpower, especially in the form of helicopter transports and gunships, inflicted serious losses on Mujahideen forces. The introduction of man-portable surface-to-air missiles severely constrained the Soviet use of their airpower. Continued numbers of casualties on the ground, as well as mounting domestic opposition to the war, convinced Soviet leaders to withdraw from Afghanistan. The United States was able to achieve its goals by waging UW through third-party actors without directly confronting the Soviet Union.

UNITED STATES UNCONVENTIONAL WARFARE IN AFGHANISTAN (2001–2002)

I-7. Experience in Afghanistan from 2001 to 2002 demonstrates that waging UW need not be prolonged, costly undertakings. Waging UW can quickly and efficiently achieve policy goals if the conditions for success are right. In this specific case, a standing indigenous force was already in existence. The forces of the Northern Alliance, although somewhat demoralized from previous losses, were armed and many were combat veterans, including some who had fought against the Soviets. The introduction of American military and paramilitary advisors and resources was critical in defeating and scattering Taliban and al-Qaeda forces in less than four months. Conventional force options would have taken too long to implement and, according to at least one account, CIA Director George Tenet suggested more unconventional uses of force including UW. Supported by Army and Air Force SOA assets, USA SF teams conducted two primary missions in the subsequent UW campaign. The first was political in nature and involved close liaison with Northern Alliance faction commanders to prevent jealousy and rivalries from adversely affecting the campaign. A key to the success of the SF teams was their cultural sensitivity and willingness to engage the Afghan and Uzbek leaders on their terms, creating considerable trust between U.S. and Northern Alliance forces. The second mission was military in nature and involved combat advice and leadership, C2, and precise fires against Taliban strong points and key force concentrations. The flexibility and adaptability of joint SO teams, connected to awe-inspiring levels of firepower, greatly boosted Northern Alliance confidence and, in one particular case, led to the first horse-mounted charge against armored forces in over sixty years. Although the character of the campaign changed, from overthrowing the Taliban regime to stabilizing the country and chasing the Taliban and al-Qaeda remnants, the success of the U.S. UW campaign is undeniable. It also underscores the necessity of achieving a close working relationship with indigenous forces based on trust and mutual competence.

UNITED STATES UNCONVENTIONAL WARFARE IN IRAQ (2003)

I-8. Experience in the early stages of OIF in 2003 demonstrates that waging UW continues to have utility in the present global environment and in the context of ongoing major combat operations. Elements of the 10th SFG(A) were infiltrated by SOF aircraft from the 353d SOW across denied airspace after Turkey refused U.S. passage over its border in the opening stages of the conflict. Once the 10th SFG(A) Soldiers successfully infiltrated Kurdistan in northern Iraq and linked up with Kurdish *peshmerga* units, the anticipated second operational front was achieved using initially unanticipated methods. The SF Soldiers' presence acted as a force multiplier by providing evidence of the political support desired by the Kurds. Thus emboldened, Kurdish forces with SF support tied down Hussein's entire northern army. In addition, the SF Soldiers provided and reinforced the legitimacy of U.S. support to Kurdish aspirations and provided additional legitimacy to Kurdish forces' participation in the larger coalition effort. Moreover, seeing that the second front established despite its objections, Turkey eventually relented and allowed subsequent border crossings to reinforce the effort. This example illustrates that the ability to conduct UW not only can support the larger conventional operation but also can use national strategy to achieve second- and third-order effects that are significant, practical, and timely.

This page intentionally left blank.

Appendix J
An Outline History of the Unconventional Warfare Definition

CURRENT DEFINITION

J-1. It is common for definitions to evolve, and ARSOF have recently refined the definition below to highlight the essentials of UW and eliminate everything that is nonessential. Words matter. In this era of definitional and conceptual change, ARSOF must be unified with a clear and concise understanding of the UW core task. The UW definition is *operations conducted by, with, or through irregular forces in support of a resistance movement, an insurgency, or conventional military operations.*

PREVIOUS DEFINITIONS FOR UNCONVENTIONAL WARFARE

J-2. The initial doctrinal concept for the United States to conduct UW lies with the creation of the OSS. Doctrine generally defined UW in terms of guerrilla and covert operations in enemy-held or influenced territory. In August 1950, the *Dictionary of United States Army Terms* defined "partisan warfare" as an "Activity carried on against an enemy by people who are devoted adherents to a cause, but who are not members of organized and recognized military forces. It includes guerrilla action, passive resistance by underground groups, espionage, sabotage, and propaganda." (Special Regulation 350-5-1.)

J-3. In 1951, the Army consolidated its UW assets under the Office of Psychological Warfare. It was then that the Army published the first two manuals for the conduct of SO. They were FM 31-21, *Organization and Conduct of Guerrilla Warfare*, and FM 31-20, *Operations Against Guerrilla Forces*.

J-4. FM 31-21 (October 1951) defined "guerrilla warfare" as "Operations carried out by small independent forces, generally in the rear of the enemy, with the objective of harassing, delaying, and disrupting military operations of the enemy. The term is sometimes limited to the military operations and tactics of small forces whose objective is to inflict casualties and damage upon the enemy rather than to seize or defend terrain. The extensive use of surprise and an emphasis on the avoidance of casualties characterize these operations. The term includes organized and directed passive resistance, espionage, assassination, sabotage and propaganda, and, in some cases, ordinary combat. Guerrilla warfare is ordinarily carried on by irregular or partisan forces; however, regular forces that have been cut off behind enemy lines or have infiltrated into the enemy rear areas may use guerrilla tactics."

J-5. FM 31-21 (October 1951) also noted, "Guerrilla warfare...is capable of gaining political and economic decisions."

J-6. In March 1955, FM 31-21, *Guerrilla Warfare*, stated, "The broad aims of guerrilla strategy are to lessen the enemy's combat effectiveness; delay and disrupt operations of the enemy forces; and weaken the morale and will to resist of a hostile military force."

J-7. In August 1955, FM 31-20, *Special Forces Group* (which superseded FM 31-20, February 1951), stated, "UW consists of the interrelated fields of guerrilla warfare, escape and evasion, and subversion against hostile states."

J-8. In May 1958, FM 31-21, *Guerrilla Warfare and Special Forces Operations* (which superseded FM 31-21, March 1955, and FM 31-20, August 1955), stated, "Guerrilla warfare comprises that part of UW which is conducted by relatively small groups employing offensive tactics to reduce enemy combat effectiveness, industrial capacity, and morale. Guerrilla operations are normally conducted in enemy-controlled territory by units organized on a military basis. It must be emphasized that UW is an activity which, in addition to guerrilla warfare, includes evasion and escape and subversion against hostile states."

Appendix J

J-9. In May 1961, FM 31-15, *Operations Against Irregular Forces*, stated, "The term irregular, used in combinations such as irregular forces, irregular activities, and counter-irregular operations, is used in the broad sense to refer to all types of nonconventional forces and operations. It includes guerrilla, partisan, insurgent, subversive, resistance, terrorist, revolutionary, and similar personnel, organizations, and methods. Irregular activities include acts of military, political, psychological, and economic nature, conducted predominately by inhabitants of a nation for the purpose of eliminating or weakening the authority of the local government or occupying power, and using primarily irregular and informal groupings and measures."

J-10. In September 1961, FM 31-21, *Guerrilla Warfare and Special Forces Operations* (which superseded FM 31-21, May 1958) stated, "UW consists of the interrelated fields of guerrilla warfare, evasion and escape, and subversion against hostile states (resistance). UW operations are conducted in enemy-controlled territory by predominately indigenous personnel, usually supported and directed in varying degrees by an external source."

J-11. In June 1965, FM 31-21, *Special Forces Operations* (which superseded FM 31-21, September 1961) stated, "UW includes the three interrelated fields of guerrilla warfare, evasion and escape, and subversion. UW operations are conducted within enemy or enemy-controlled territory by predominately indigenous personnel, usually directed and supported in varying degrees by an external force."

J-12. The broadest classic conceptions of UW doctrine did not apply to COIN situations. However, select UW tactics and techniques—such as establishing intelligence nets and methods to gain support of the population and combat techniques, such as raids and ambushes—had obvious application to COIN—a growing concern during the Vietnam conflict.

J-13. In December 1965, FM 31-20, *Special Forces Operational Techniques* (which superseded FM 31-20, October 1961) omitted a direct definition of UW from the manual. However, by the early 1960s, definitions began to take more of an "insurgent" nature, whereby UW expanded to include "forces [that] may have political aspirations inimical to our own." The February 1969 issue of FM 31-21, *Special Forces Operations* (which superseded FM 31-21, June 1965), changed this idea. FM 31-21, February 1969, included the following definitions and amplifications:

- "UW includes the three related fields of guerrilla warfare, evasion and escape, and subversion, conducted within hostile areas by predominately indigenous personnel, usually supported and directed in varying degrees by an external source. UW consists of military, political, psychological, or economic actions of covert, clandestine, or overt nature within areas under the actual or potential control or influence of a force or state whose interests and objectives are inimical to those of the United States. These actions are conducted unilaterally by U.S. resources or in conjunction with indigenous assets, and avoid formal military confrontation."

- "The UW Concept. UW is conducted to exploit military, political, economic, or psychological vulnerabilities of an enemy. It is implemented by providing support and direction to indigenous resistance forces where appropriate, or by unilateral operations of U.S. UW forces. Its conduct involves the application of guerrilla warfare and selected aspects of subversion, political warfare, economic warfare, and psychological operations in support of national objectives."

- "UW Operations. UW operations may be covert, clandestine, or overt in nature. Covert operations are conducted in such a manner as to conceal the identity of the sponsor, while clandestine operations place emphasis on concealment of the operation rather than the identity of the sponsor. Overt operations do not try to conceal either the operation or the identity of the sponsor. In an established theater of operations in which significant ground operations by conventional U.S. military force will be undertaken, UW is conducted primarily to complement, support, or extend conventional operations. Within geographical areas under enemy control or influence, to which conventional U.S. forces will not be deployed, UW may be conducted as an economy-of-force measure, and to reduce or dissipate the enemy potential."

J-14. In February 1971, FM 31-20, *Special Forces Operational Techniques* (which superseded FM 31-20, December 1965) continued to omit a direct definition of UW from the manual.

J-15. In December 1974, FM 31-21, *Special Forces Operations*, stated, "UW is defined as a broad spectrum of military and paramilitary operations conducted in enemy, enemy-held, enemy-controlled, or politically sensitive territory. UW includes, but is not limited to, the interrelated fields of guerrilla warfare, evasion and escape, subversion, sabotage, direct action missions, and other operations of a low-visibility, covert, or clandestine nature. These interrelated aspects of UW may be prosecuted singly or collectively by predominantly indigenous personnel, usually supported and directed in varying degrees by (an) external source(s) during all conditions of war or peace."

J-16. Also in December 1974, FM 31-21A, *Special Forces Operations*, expanded on the above definition by stating that "UW operations may be conducted against the external sponsor of an insurgent (movement in a host country), or against insurgent (movement in a host country), or against insurgent activities in a third country, which either willingly or unwillingly accepts the use of its territory by the insurgents for bases, movement, or actuary. Their purpose is to support or complement IDAD in the host country."

J-17. In April 1990, FM 31-20, *Doctrine for Special Forces Operations*, defined UW as "A broad spectrum of military and paramilitary operations, normally of long duration, predominantly conducted by indigenous or surrogate forces who are organized, trained, equipped, supported, and directed in varying degrees by an external source. It includes guerrilla warfare and other direct offensive, low-visibility, covert, or clandestine operations, as well as the indirect activities of subversion, sabotage, intelligence collection, and evasion and escape."

J-18. In April 1998, JP 3-05, *Doctrine for Joint Special Operations*, essentially copied the above definition: UW is "a broad spectrum of military and paramilitary operations, normally of long duration, predominantly conducted by indigenous or surrogate forces who are organized, trained, equipped, supported, and directed in varying degrees by an external source. It includes guerrilla warfare and other direct offensive low-visibility, covert, or clandestine operations, as well as the indirect activities of subversion, sabotage, intelligence activities, and evasion and escape."

J-19. In December 1998, FM 31-20 (Initial Draft), *Doctrine for Special Forces Operations*, added to the two definitions above stating—

- "UW is a broad spectrum of military and paramilitary operations, predominantly conducted by indigenous or surrogate forces organized, trained, equipped, supported, and directed in varying degrees by an external source. It includes guerrilla warfare and the indirect activities of subversion, sabotage, intelligence activities, and unconventional assisted recovery (UAR). UW is the military and paramilitary aspect of an insurgency or other armed resistance movement. UW is thus a protracted political-military activity."
- "Contemporary UW is significant for several reasons. Historically, SF has focused on UW as an adjunct to a major theater of war. The new strategic environment, however, requires SF to focus on UW during military operations other than war, especially as it relates to UAR. Moreover, global urbanization dictates a shift in SF emphasis from rural guerrilla warfare to all aspects of clandestine UW."

NONDOCTRINAL TERMS

J-20. Other currently influential but nondoctrinal terms further complicate the goal of maintaining an up-to-date, authoritative, and clearly articulated ARSOF UW doctrine. Incorrect usage of doctrinal terms sows confusion and aggravates mission accomplishment. Incorrect usage of unapproved terms does so exponentially. Individuals throughout the government, academia, and the press so widely and often incorrectly use these terms that they demand a brief summary.

J-21. One such imprecise term often confused for UW is "asymmetric warfare." Despite the frequent usage of the term, JP 1-02 has no approved definition for it. "Symmetric warfare" assumes the legacy concept of two roughly equal nation-states who fight each other directly, using standing, uniformed armies, navies, and air forces. WWII countries and combats are a classic example. Asymmetric warfare is generally understood to be a conflict in which the strengths and sizes of the opponents do not mirror each other. The side with the conventional disadvantage is probably incapable of winning through direct, conventional warfare. It must seek victory through other methods that exploit weaknesses in the superior conventional power's capacity to prevail. Examples include the Maoist Peoples' War against the Imperial Japanese Army, the Vietnamese dau trahn strategy in the First and Second Indochina Wars, and al-Qaeda's tactics in

Appendix J

the WOT. In these cases, political organization, proselytizing, and PSYOP were fundamental to their effectiveness.

J-22. Although symmetric warfare is the loose conceptual equivalent of conventional warfare, it is not an approved doctrinal definition. The discussion of "asymmetry," however, is obviously useful to the characterization of IW, UW, and COIN. IW does include the concept of seeking asymmetric advantages. IW also uses terms such as "asymmetric applications" of TTP and drawing attention to "asymmetric activities." ARSOF—and its joint, interagency, and multinational partners—must therefore understand and use the unapproved term "asymmetric warfare" with care. It is not synonymous with UW.

J-23. A second term often used in discussions of UW, IW, and COIN is so-called fourth-generation warfare, or 4GW. 4GW proponents maintain that the world is in a new era, or generation, of warfare. The first generation was characterized by massed manpower, the second by firepower, and the third by maneuver. 4GW proponents claim that the new generation is characterized by the use of all instruments of power—not just the military—to defeat the will of enemy decision makers. 4GW has its detractors. 4GW borrows heavily from concepts previously developed by Mao, the Vietnamese, and others. It is not accepted DOD doctrine or terminology and is not a synonym for UW.

J-24. A third term that is sometimes mistakenly confused with UW is "unrestricted warfare." This term refers to the title of a monograph written by two army colonels from the Peoples' Republic of China. They advocate "a multitude of means, both military and particularly nonmilitary, to strike at the United States during times of conflict." Hacking into Web sites, targeting financial institutions, conducting terrorism, using the media, and conducting urban warfare are among the methods proposed. The first rule of unrestricted warfare is that there are no rules. Strong countries would not use the same approach against weak countries because "strong countries make the rules, while rising ones break them and exploit loopholes."

J-25. The similarity of these ideas to those in the previous terms is unmistakable. Whether or not the authors break any new ground or establish a new theory is debatable. Their monograph has generated interest in the West primarily for what it may signify in Peoples' Republic of China strategic thinking—such ideas could not be published without some official sanction in the often inscrutable Chinese government. ARSOF Soldiers—and their joint, interagency, and multinational partners—should be aware of unrestricted warfare, but they must understand that the term is not synonymous with the aforementioned terms, is not approved doctrine, and has a very specific international context and usage.

Glossary

SECTION I – ACRONYMS AND ABBREVIATIONS

4GW	fourth-generation warfare
A	airborne
ABC	American Broadcasting Companies
ABW	air base wing
ADCON	administrative control
AD/CVD	antidumping and countervailing duty
AETF	Air and Space Expeditionary Task Force
AFSOC	Air Force Special Operations Command
AO	area of operations
AOB	advanced operational base
AOC	air operations center
AOR	area of responsibility
AR	Army regulation
ARNG	Army National Guard
ARSOF	Army special operations forces
ASCC	Army Service component command
ASCOPE	areas, structures, capabilities, organizations, people, and events
ASEAN	Association of Southeast Asian Nations
BBC	British Broadcasting Corporation
BBG	Broadcasting Board of Governors
BCT	brigade combat team
BDA	battle damage assessment
BDE	brigade
BFSB	battlefield surveillance brigade
BIS	Bank for International Settlements
C2	command and control
CA	Civil Affairs; California
CAO	Civil Affairs operations
CAPT	Civil Affairs planning team
CAS	close air support
CAT	Civil Affairs team
CBS	Columbia Broadcasting System
CBT	combat
CCC	Command and Coordination Centre
CCDR	combatant commander
CCP	Consolidated Cryptologic Program
CD	compact disc
CDR	commander

Glossary

CERP	commander's emergency response program
CI	counterintelligence
CIA	Central Intelligence Agency
CJCS	Chairman of the Joint Chiefs of Staff
CMO	civil-military operations
CMOC	civil-military operations center
CNA	computer network attack
CND	computer network defense
CNE	computer network exploitation
CNN	Cable News Network
CNO	computer network operations
CNY	Chinese yuan
COA	course of action
COCOM	combatant command
COIN	counterinsurgency
COMAFFOR	Commander, Air Force Forces
COMCAM	combat camera
CSA	combat support agency
CSAR	combat search and rescue
CT	counterterrorism
DA	direct action
DC	dislocated civilian
DCIA	Director of Central Intelligence Agency
DDNI	Deputy Director of National Intelligence
DEA	Drug Enforcement Administration
DEA/NN	Drug Enforcement Administration Office of National Security Intelligence
DH	Directorate for Human Intelligence
DHMO	Defense Human Intelligence Management Office
DHS	Department of Homeland Security
DI	Directorate of Intelligence
DIA	Defense Intelligence Agency
DIAP	Defense Intelligence Analysis Program
DIME	diplomatic, informational, military, and economic
DIMEFIL	diplomatic, informational, military, economic, financial, intelligence, and law enforcement
DIOCC	Defense Intelligence Operations Coordination Center
DN	Department of the Navy
DNA	deoxyribonucleic acid
DNCS	Director of the National Clandestine Service
DNI	Director of National Intelligence
DOC	Department of Commerce
DOD	Department of Defense

DOE	Department of Energy
DOJ	Department of Justice
DOS	Department of State
DRU	direct reporting unit
DS	Directorate of Support
DSPD	defense support to public diplomacy
DS&T	Directorate of Science and Technology
DV	digital video
DVD	digital video disc
DZ	drop zone
E&EE	emergency and extraordinary expenses
EA	electronic attack
ECOSO	Economic and Social Council
EM	electromagnetic
EP	electronic protection
ES	electronic warfare support
ESC	Expeditionary Sustainment Command
EU	European Union
EW	electronic warfare
FBI	Federal Bureau of Investigation
FCC	Federal Communications Commission
FCIP	Foreign Counterintelligence Program
FDI	foreign direct investment
FFC	Foreign Funds Control
FHA	foreign humanitarian assistance
FID	foreign internal defense
FinCEN	Financial Crimes Enforcement Network
FIU	financial intelligence unit
FL	Florida
FM	field manual
FP	force protection
G-9	Deputy/Assistant Chief of Staff for Civil-Military Operations
GCC	geographic combatant commander
GDIP	General Defense Intelligence Program
GDP	gross domestic product
GIG	Global Information Grid
GW	guerrilla warfare
HF	high frequency
HN	host nation
HOA	Horn of Africa
HQ	headquarters

Glossary

HUMINT	human intelligence
I&A	Office of Intelligence and Analysis
IA	information assurance
IAW	in accordance with
IBB	International Broadcasting Bureau
IBRD	International Bank for Reconstruction and Development
IC	intelligence community
ICC	International Criminal Court
ICF	intelligence contingency funds
ICJ	International Court of Justice
ICW	in coordination with
ID	identify
IDA	International Development Association
IDAD	internal defense and development
IFC	International Finance Corporation
IGO	intergovernmental organization
IIP	Bureau of International Information Programs
ILC	International Law Commission
ILO	International Labor Organization
IMF	International Monetary Fund
IMINT	imagery intelligence
IN	Office of Intelligence and Counterintelligence
INR	Bureau of Intelligence and Research
INTERPOL	International Criminal Police Organization
IPB	intelligence preparation of the battlefield
IPI	indigenous populations and institutions
IPOE	intelligence preparation of the operational environment
IO	information operations
IR	information requirement
IRC	International Red Cross
IRTPA	Intelligence Reform and Terrorism Prevention Act
ISO	in support of
ISR	intelligence, surveillance, and reconnaissance
IT	information technology
ITA	International Trade Administration
ITV	Independent Television
IW	irregular warfare
J-2	intelligence directorate of a joint staff
J-3	operations directorate of a joint staff
J-6	communications system directorate of a joint staff
JCS	Joint Chiefs of Staff

JFC	joint force commander
JFCC-ISR	Joint Functional Component Command for Intelligence, Surveillance, and Reconnaissance
JIIM	joint, interagency, intergovernmental, and multinational
JOA	joint operations area
JOC	joint operating concept
JP	joint publication
JPY	Japanese yen
JSOTF	joint special operations task force
JTF	joint task force
JWICS	Joint Worldwide Intelligence Communications System
LNO	liaison officer
M&S	Manufacturing and Services
MAGTF	Marine Air-Ground Task Force
MAJCOM	major command
MARFORCOM	Marine Forces Command
MARFORPAC	Marine Forces Pacific
MARSOC	Marine Forces Special Operations Command
MASINT	measurement and signature intelligence
MCIA	Marine Corps Intelligence Activity
MCO	major combat operations
MDB	multilateral development bank
MEF	Marine Expeditionary Force
METT-TC	mission, enemy, terrain and weather, troops and support available–time available and civil considerations
MEU	Marine Expeditionary Unit
MI	military intelligence
MIGA	Multilateral Investment Guarantee Agency
MILDEC	military deception
MNC	multinational corporation
MNF	multinational force
MOE	measure of effectiveness
MOS	military occupational specialty
MSC	Military Sealift Command
MSM	mainstream media
MSOB	Marine special operations battalion
MSS	mission support site
MTF	medical treatment facility
NA	nation assistance
NAF	numbered air force
NAFTA	North American Free Trade Agreement
NATO	North Atlantic Treaty Organization

Glossary

NAVCENT	Naval Forces Central Command	
NAVEUR	Naval Forces Europe	
NBC	National Broadcasting Company	
NC	North Carolina	
NCB	National Central Bureau	
NCO	noncommissioned officer	
NCS	National Clandestine Service	
NCTC	National Counterterrorism Center	
NDS	national defense strategy	
NFAF	Naval Fleet Auxiliary Force	
NGA	National Geospatial-Intelligence Agency	
NGO	nongovernmental organization	
NIC	National Intelligence Council	
NIE	National Intelligence Estimate	
NIP	National Intelligence Program	
NMIC	National Maritime Intelligence Center	
NMJIC	National Military Joint Intelligence Center	
NMS	national military strategy	
NRO	National Reconnaissance Office	
NSA	National Security Agency	
NSB	National Security Branch	
NSC	National Security Council	
NSG	National System for Geospatial Intelligence	
NSS	national security strategy	
NSWG	Naval Special Warfare Group	
ODNI	Office of the Director of National Intelligence	
OECD	Organization for Economic Cooperation and Development	
OEF	Operation ENDURING FREEDOM	
OFAC	Office of Foreign Assets Control	
OGA	other government agency	
OHDACA	Overseas Humanitarian Disaster and Civic Aid	
OIA	Office of Intelligence and Analysis	
OIF	Operation IRAQI FREEDOM	
OIPR	Office of Intelligence Policy and Review	
o/o	on order	
OPCON	operational control	
OPEC	Organization of Petroleum-Exporting Countries	
OPLAN	operation plan	
OPSEC	operations security	
OSD	Office of the Secretary of Defense	
OSS	Office of Strategic Services	

PA	public affairs
PD	public diplomacy
PDDNI	Principal Deputy Director of National Intelligence
PDS	product distribution system
PE	preparation of the environment
PIR	priority intelligence requirement
PN	partner nation
PO	Psychological Operations objective
POAT	Psychological Operations assessment team
POG	Psychological Operations group
POL/MIL	political/military
PRC	populace and resources control
PRS	populace and resources shaping
PSYACT	Psychological Operations action
PSYOP	Psychological Operations
ROE	rules of engagement
S-2	intelligence staff officer
S-2X	counterintelligence/human intelligence operations staff officer
S-9	civil-military operations staff officer
SATCOM	satellite communications
SB(SO)(A)	Sustainment Brigade (Special Operations) (Airborne)
SC	strategic communication
S/CRS	State Department's Office of the Coordinator for Reconstruction and Stabilization
SEAL	sea-air-land team
SECAF	Secretary of the Air Force
SecDef	Secretary of Defense
SECNAV	Secretary of the Navy
SF	Special Forces
SFG(A)	Special Forces group (airborne)
SFODA	Special Forces operational detachment A
SFODB	Special Forces operational detachment B
SIGINT	signals intelligence
SO	special operations
SOA	special operations aviation
SOAR	Special Operations Aviation Regiment
SOF	special operations forces
SOP	standing operating procedure
SOT-A	special operations team A
SOTF	special operations task force
SOW	special operations wing
SR	special reconnaissance

Glossary

SSTR	stability, security, transition, and reconstruction
TA	target audience
TAA	target audience analysis
TACON	tactical control
TFI	Terrorism and Financial Intelligence
TNC	transnational corporation
TPCC	Trade Promotion Coordinating Committee
TP/US&FCS	Trade Promotion and the United States and Foreign Commercial Service
TSC	Theater Sustainment Command
TSOC	theater special operations command
TTP	tactics, techniques, and procedures
TV	television
UAR	unconventional assisted recovery
UAS	unmanned aircraft system
UHF	ultrahigh frequency
UK	United Kingdom
UN	United Nations
URL	uniform resource locator
U.S.	United States
US&FCS	United States and Foreign Commercial Service
USA	United States Army
USAF	United States Air Force
USAID	United States Agency for International Development
USAJFKSWCS	United States Army John F. Kennedy Special Warfare Center and School
USAR	United States Army Reserve
USASFC(A)	United States Army Special Forces Command (Airborne)
USASOC	United States Army Special Operations Command
USC	United States Code
USCENTCOM	United States Central Command
USCG	United States Coast Guard
USD	United States dollar
USG	United States Government
USIA	United States Information Agency
USMC	United States Marine Corps
USN	United States Navy
USNCB	United States National Central Bureau
USPACOM	United States Pacific Command
USSOCOM	United States Special Operations Command
UW	unconventional warfare
UWOA	unconventional warfare operational area
VA	Virginia

WB	World Bank
WFHQ	warfighting headquarters
WMD	weapons of mass destruction
WOT	War on Terrorism
WTO	World Trade Organization
WWII	World War II

SECTION II – TERMS

area assessment

The commander's prescribed collection of specific information that commences upon employment and is a continuous operation. It confirms, corrects, refutes, or adds to previous intelligence acquired from area studies and other sources before employment. (JP 1-02) In unconventional warfare, the collection of specific information prescribed by the commander to commence immediately after infiltration. It is a continuous operation, and it confirms, corrects, refutes, or adds to intelligence required from area studies or other sources before infiltration. (FM 3-05.130)

area command

A command which is composed of those organized elements of one or more of the Armed Services, designated to operate in a specific geographical area, which are placed under a single commander. (JP 1-02) In unconventional warfare, the organizational structure established within an unconventional warfare operational area to command and control irregular forces. It consists of the area commander, his staff, representatives of the irregular organization, and ARSOF elements after infiltration. (FM 3-05.130)

area study

The prescribed collection of specific information pertaining to a given unconventional warfare operational area developed from sources available before infiltration. (FM 3-05.130)

asset (intelligence)

Any resource—person, group, relationship, instrument, installation, or supply—at the disposition of an intelligence organization for use in an operational or support role. Often used with a qualifying term, such as agent asset or propaganda asset. (JP 1-02)

asymmetric threat

A weapon, tactic, or strategy intended to capitalize on differences in organization, equipment, doctrine, capabilities, values and/or norms between adversaries that is dangerous or could have serious consequences. (Proposed DA G-3, Mar 07)

asymmetry

An exploitable difference in organization, equipment, doctrine, capabilities, values, and norms between adversaries. (Proposed DA G-3, Mar 07)

auxiliary

The support element of the irregular organization whose organization and operations are clandestine in nature and whose members do not openly indicate their sympathy or involvement with the irregular movement. (FM 3-05.130)

cadre

A nucleus of trained personnel around which a larger organization can be built and trained. In unconventional warfare such cadres often share and spread the political goals of the irregular organization. (FM 3-05.130)

clandestine operation

An operation sponsored or conducted by governmental departments or agencies in such a way as to assure secrecy or concealment. A clandestine operation differs from a covert operation in that emphasis is placed on concealment of the operation rather than on concealment of the identity of the

Glossary

sponsor. In special operations, an activity may be both covert and clandestine and may focus equally on operational considerations and intelligence-related activities. See also **covert operation; overt operation.** (JP 1-02)

conventional warfare

A form of warfare between states that employs direct military confrontation to defeat an adversary's armed forces, destroy an adversary's war-making capacity, or seize or retain territory in order to force a change in an adversary's government or policies. The focus of conventional military operations is normally an adversary's armed forces with the objective of influencing the adversary's government. It generally assumes that the indigenous populations within the operational area are nonbelligerents and will accept whatever political outcome the belligerent governments impose, arbitrate, or negotiate. A fundamental military objective in conventional military operations is to minimize civilian interference in those operations. (This term and its definition are applicable only in the context of this manual and cannot be referenced outside this manual.)

covert operation

An operation that is so planned and executed as to conceal the identity of or permit plausible denial by the sponsor. A covert operation differs from a clandestine operation in that emphasis is placed on concealment of the identity of the sponsor rather than on concealment of the operation. See also **clandestine operation; overt operation.** (JP 1-02)

government in exile

An institutional body with a legitimate claim to represent a state government which has been overthrown or displaced by occupation, revolution, or coup. Such bodies usually contain core members of a previously recognized legitimate government and are most often exiled outside of the state's sovereign boundaries. (FM 3-05.130)

guerrilla

A combat participant in guerrilla warfare. See also unconventional warfare. (JP 1-02) An irregular, usually indigenous actor that conducts paramilitary operations in enemy-held, hostile, or denied territory. (FM 3-05.130)

guerrilla base

A temporary site where guerrilla installations, headquarters, and some guerrilla units are located. A guerrilla base is considered to be transitory and must be capable of rapid displacement by personnel within the base. (FM 3-05.130)

guerrilla force

A group of irregular, predominantly indigenous personnel organized along military lines to conduct military and paramilitary operations in enemy-held, hostile, or denied territory. (JP 1-02)

guerrilla warfare

Military and paramilitary operations conducted in enemy-held or hostile territory by irregular, predominantly indigenous forces. Also called **GW**. See also **unconventional warfare.** (JP 1-02)

insurgency

An organized movement aimed at the overthrow of a constituted government through use of subversion and armed conflict. (JP 1-02)

insurgent

Member of a political party who rebels against established leadership. (JP 1-02) Member of an organized movement who rebels against established leadership. (FM 3-05.130)

irregular forces

Armed individuals or groups who are not members of the regular armed forces, police, or other internal security forces. (JP 1-02)

irregular organization

In the context of unconventional warfare, the total members, structures, and capabilities of a group of nonstate actors organized to achieve a political goal. (FM 3-05.130)

Glossary

irregular warfare

A violent struggle among state and nonstate actors for legitimacy and influence over the relevant populations. Irregular warfare favors indirect and asymmetric approaches, though it may employ the full range of military and other capacities, in order to erode an adversary's power, influence, and will. Also called **IW.** (JP 1-02)

mass base

The population indigenous to an unconventional warfare operational area from which irregular forces are drawn, or from whom support for an unconventional warfare campaign can be wittingly or unwittingly drawn. (FM 3-05.130)

nonstate actor

A group or organization that is not within the formal structure of any state, not limited by any state boundary, and operates beyond the control of any state and without loyalty to any state. Examples include international organizations, nongovernmental organizations, private volunteer organizations, political parties, labor unions, commercial trade associations, criminal enterprises, and armed groups such as insurgent and terrorist organizations, informal armed militias, and private military companies. (Proposed IW JOC V 1.0)

overt operation

An operation conducted openly, without concealment. See also **clandestine operation; covert operation.** (JP 1-02)

paramilitary forces

Forces or groups distinct from the regular armed forces of any country, but resembling them in organization, equipment, training, or mission. (JP 1-02)

paramilitary operation

An operation undertaken by a paramilitary force. (FM 3-05.130)

partisan warfare

Not to be used. See **guerrilla warfare.** (JP 1-02)

pilot team

A preplanned, ad hoc, typically interagency element composed of individuals possessing specialized skills who infiltrate a specified area to evaluate and report on the potential to conduct unconventional warfare and the compatibility of U.S. and local interests and objectives. (FM 3-05.130)

political warfare

Aggressive use of political means to achieve national objectives. (JP 1-02) In the context of unconventional warfare, all efforts to persuade other actors to act in concert with U.S. national objectives. (FM 3-05.130)

resistance

Truncated version of resistance movement. (FM 3-05.130)

resistance force

That portion of the population within a specified area which is engaged in the resistance movement as guerrillas, auxiliaries, or members of the underground. (FM 3-05.130)

resistance movement

An organized effort by some portion of the civil population of a country to resist the legally established government or an occupying power and to disrupt civil order and stability. (JP 1-02)

safe area

A designated area in hostile territory that offers the evader or escapee a reasonable chance of avoiding capture and of surviving until he or she can be evacuated. (JP 1-02) In the context of unconventional warfare, a relatively inaccessible territory or innocent-appearing facility established by an organization for the purpose of conducting clandestine or covert activity in relative security. Also called a safe site. (FM 3-05.130)

Glossary

safe house
> An innocent-appearing house or premises established by an organization for the purpose of conducting clandestine or covert activity in relative security. (JP 1-02) Also called a safe site. (FM 3-05.130)

shadow government
> Governmental elements and activities performed by the irregular organization that will eventually take the place of the existing government. Members of the shadow government can be in any element of the irregular organization (underground, auxiliary, or guerrillas). (FM 3-05.130)

subversion
> Action designed to undermine the military, economic, psychological, or political strength or morale of a regime. See also **unconventional warfare.** (JP 1-02)

surrogate
> One who takes the place of or acts on behalf of another. (FM 3-05.130)

unconventional warfare
> A broad spectrum of military and paramilitary operations, normally of long duration, predominantly conducted through, with, or by indigenous or surrogate forces who are organized, trained, equipped, supported, and directed in varying degrees by an external source. It includes, but is not limited to, guerrilla warfare, subversion, sabotage, intelligence activities, and unconventional assisted recovery. (JP 1-02) Operations conducted by, with, or through irregular forces in support of a resistance movement, an insurgency, or conventional military operations. Also called **UW.** (FM 3-05.130)

unconventional warfare operational area
> A joint special operations area (JSOA) specifically designated for unconventional warfare operations. An unconventional warfare operational area is distinguished from other JSOAs by the intended involvement of non-DOD U.S. interagency, multinational, and/or nonstate partner elements, and the inherently political nature, typically protracted time frame, and usually discreet execution of UW. Also called **UWOA.** (FM 3-05.130)

underground
> The element of the irregular organization that conducts operations in areas normally denied to the auxiliary and the guerrilla force. (FM 3-05.130)

References

REQUIRED REFERENCES
These documents must be available to intended users of this publication.
 None

RELATED PUBLICATIONS
These documents contain relevant supplemental information.

ARMY PUBLICATIONS
AR 381-141, *(C) Intelligence Contingency Funds (ICF) (U)*, 16 January 2004
FM 1, *The Army*, 14 June 2005
FM 1-02, *Operational Terms and Graphics*, 21 September 2004
FM 2-0, *Intelligence*, 17 May 2004
FM 3-0, *Operations*, 27 February 2008
FM 3-05, *Army Special Operations Forces*, 20 September 2006
FM 3-05.20, *(C) Special Forces Operations (U)*, 10 October 2006
FM 3-05.30, *Psychological Operations*, 15 April 2005
FM 3-05.40, *Civil Affairs Operations*, 29 September 2006
FM 3-05.60, *Army Special Operations Forces Aviation Operations*, 30 October 2007
FM 3-05.120, *(S/NOFORN) Army Special Operations Forces Intelligence (U)*, 15 July 2007
FM 3-05.137, *Army Special Operations Forces Foreign Internal Defense*, 30 June 2008
FM 3-05.160, *Army Special Operations Forces Communications Systems Support,* 6 July 2006
FM 3-05.201, *(S/NOFORN) Special Forces Unconventional Warfare (U)*, 28 September 2007
FM 3-05.220, *(S/NOFORN) Special Forces Advanced Special Operations (U)*, *Volumes I and II*, 31 January 2007
FM 3-24, *Counterinsurgency*, 15 December 2006
FM 4-02.43, *Force Health Protection Support for Army Special Operations Forces*, 27 November 2006
FM 5-0, *Army Planning and Orders Production*, 20 January 2005
USASOC Directive 525-13, *(FOUO) Force Protection*, 1 October 1997

DEPARTMENT OF DEFENSE PUBLICATIONS
DOD Directive 3000.05, *Military Support for Stability, Security, Transition, and Reconstruction (SSTR) Operations*, 28 November 2005

JOINT PUBLICATIONS
Irregular Warfare (IW) Joint Operating Concept (JOC), Version 1.0, 11 September 2007
JP-1, *Doctrine for the Armed Forces of the United States*, 14 May 2007
JP 1-02, *Department of Defense Dictionary of Military and Associated Terms*, 12 April 2001
JP 2-0, *Joint Intelligence*, 22 June 2007
JP 2-01, *Joint and National Intelligence Support to Military Operations*, 7 October 2004
JP 3-0, *Joint Operations*, 17 September 2006
JP 3-05, *Doctrine for Joint Special Operations*, 17 December 2003
JP 3-13, *Information Operations*, 13 February 2006

References

JP 3-53, *Doctrine for Joint Psychological Operations*, 5 September 2003

JP 3-57, *Civil-Military Operations*, 8 July 2008

JP 5-0, *Joint Operation Planning*, 26 December 2006

Major Combat Operations Joint Operating Concept, Version 2.0, December 2006

OTHER PUBLICATIONS

AAA. The American Anthropological Association Statement on "Race." 17 May 1998 http://www.aaanet.org/stmts/racepp.htm

Arnold, M. *Culture and Anarchy*. Cambridge University Press: New York. 1869

Bendix, R. *Max Weber: An Intellectual Portrait*. University of California Press: Berkeley. 1977

Campbell, J. *The Masks of God*. Penguin: New York. 1968

Clausewitz, K. *On War*. Princeton University Press. 1989

Conboy, K. & Andradé, D. *Spies and Commandos: How America Lost the Secret War in North Vietnam*. University of Kansas Press: Lawrence, KS. 2000

Echevarria, A. *Fourth Generation War and Other Myths*. Strategic Studies Institute: Carlisle, PA. November 2005

Ferngren, G. (Ed) *Science and Religion: A Historical Introduction*. Johns Hopkins University Press: Baltimore. 2002

Fried, M. *The Notion of Tribe*. Cummings Publishing: Menlo Park, CA. 1975

Hammes, T.X. *The Sling and the Stone*. Zenith Press: St. Paul, MN. 2004

Jones, L., (Ed). *Encyclopedia of Religion*. 2nd ed. Macmillan Reference: New York. 2005

Mao Tse-tung. *Selected Military Writings of Mao Tse-tung*. Foreign Language Press: Peking. 1968

National Defense Strategy, March 2005

National Military Strategy, March 2005

National Security Strategy, March 2006

National Strategy for Combating Terrorism, February 2003

Pew Research Center. "Among Wealthy Nations US Stands Alone in its Embrace of Religion." 19 December 2002. http://people-press.org/reports/display.php3?ReportID=167

Qiao Liang and Wang Xiangsui. *Unrestricted Warfare*. PLA Literature and Arts Publishing House: Beijing. February 1999

Quadrennial Defense Review Report, February 2006

Reese, W. L. *Dictionary of Philosophy and Religion: Eastern and Western Thought*. Prometheus Books. 1996

Renan, E. "What is a Nation?" [Sorbonne Lecture]. 1882 http://www.ellopos.net/politics/eu_renan.html

Russell, B. *Wisdom of the West*. Crescent Publishers. 2 August 1989

Stalin, J. *Marxism and the National Question*. 1913 http://www.marxists.org/reference/archive/stalin/works/1913/03.htm

Sun Tzu. *The Art of War*. Griffith, S. (Trs.). Oxford University Press: London. 1976

Tolkien, J.R.R. *The Monsters and the Critics*. Harper Collins; New Ed edition. 1997

Tyler, E.B. *Primitive Culture*. John Murray: London. 1871

UNESCO. "Universal Declaration on Cultural Diversity." 2002 http://www.unesco.org/culture/pluralism/diversity/html_eng/Exhibition.shtml

USG. *An Overview of the United States Intelligence Community, Director of National Intelligence Handbook 07-0224*, Washington DC. 2007

USG. *CIA World Fact Book 2007*. March 2007. https://www.cia.gov/cia/publications/factbook

USG. "Revisions to the Standards for the Classification of Federal Data on Race and Ethnicity." Office of Management and Budget Directive 15, Federal Register Notice. 30 October 1997

USG. "Task Force Report on Coast Guard Roles and Missions." Washington DC. December 1999

USG. *The U.S. Department of State at Work*. Department of State Publication 11201, Washington DC. June 2005

USG. "U.S. Embassy in Iraq." Congressional Research Service, Library of Congress: Washington DC. 24 October 2006. http://fpc.state.gov/documents/organization/76927.pdf

USSOCOM Directive 10-1, *Terms of Reference for Component Commanders*, 19 November 2001

USSOCOM Directive 37-4, *(S/NOFORN) Confidential Military Purpose Funds (U)*, 14 April 2004

USSOCOM Directive 525-4, *(FOUO) Antiterrorism (U)*, 15 May 2005

SOURCES USED

These sources are used, quoted, or paraphrased in this publication. They were used for historical purposes only. Most of these references are available at the Combined Arms Research Library, Fort Leavenworth, Kansas, http://cgsc.leavenworth.army.mil/carl/index.asp.

FM 31-15, *Operations Against Irregular Forces*, May 1961 (obsolete)

FM 31-20, *Doctrine for Special Forces Operations*, April 1990 (obsolete)

FM 31-20, *Operations Against Guerrilla Forces*, October 1951 (obsolete)

FM 31-20, *Special Forces Group*, August 1955 (obsolete)

FM 31-20, *Special Forces Operational Techniques*, December 1965 (obsolete)

FM 31-20, *Special Forces Operational Techniques*, February 1971 (obsolete)

FM 31-20, *Special Forces Operations*, May 1958 (obsolete)

FM 31-21, *Guerrilla Warfare and Special Forces Operations*, May 1958 (obsolete)

FM 31-21, *Guerrilla Warfare and Special Forces Operations*, September 1961 (obsolete)

FM 31-21, *Organization and Conduct of Guerrilla Warfare*, October 1951 (obsolete)

FM 31-21, *Special Forces Operations*, June 1965 (obsolete)

FM 31-21, *Special Forces Operations*, February 1969 (obsolete)

FM 31-21, *Special Forces Operations*, December 1974 (obsolete)

FM 31-21A, *Special Forces Operations*, December 1974 (obsolete)

This page intentionally left blank.

Index

A
antiterrorism, 3-7, 4-4
area assessment, 4-5, 7-1, 7-2, 8-4, 8-7
area command, 4-3, 4-6, 4-10, 5-3, 5-4, 8-6, 8-8
area study, 4-5, 5-1, 7-1, 7-2, 8-7
Army National Guard, iv, 4-12, G-12, G-13, G-14
asymmetric, 1-1, 1-3, 1-4, 3-3, 3-6, 3-16, 3-19, 6-7, B-21, C-8, J-3
asymmetric threat, B-21
asymmetric warfare, 1-3, J-3, J-4
asymmetry, 7-10, J-4
auxiliary, 4-6, 4-7, 4-8, 5-6, 6-8, 6-9, 7-2, 8-5, 8-9, G-13

B
band, 8-4, H-1, H-10, H-11

C
cadre, 4-8, 4-9, 5-4, 5-5, 6-3 through 6-7, 7-10, C-9
Central Intelligence Agency (CIA), A-10, C-3, C-8, F-2, I-2, I-3
Civil Affairs (CA), 2-3, 2-7, 2-11, 2-12, 3-5, 3-6, 3-9, 3-10, 3-15, 3-16, 4-6, 4-10, 4-12, 4-13, 4-16, 5-2 through 5-4, 7-1 through 7-10, 8-3, 8-7, B-26, G-10, G-15
Civil Affairs operations (CAO), iv, 1-5, 3-18, 4-12, 4-15, 4-16, 7-1, 7-4 through 7-6, 7-8 through 7-10, 8-3
civilization, H-1, H-2, H-4, H-5, H-7, H-12
civil-military lines of operation, 7-2
civil-military operations (CMO), 1-5, 2-7, 3-18, 3-19, 4-10, 4-15, 5-6, 7-1, 7-3 through 7-9, B-18, B-25, B-26
clan, H-1, H-10
clandestine operations, 4-9, 5-5, C-3, J-2, J-3
combatant command (COCOM), 2-4, 2-5, 3-5, 3-10, B-25, C-4, C-5, C-9, C-10, G-1 through G-5, G-8, G-10
combatant commander (CCDR), 4-11, 8-4, G-2, G-4, G-6, G-7
communications support, 8-1, 8-3
confidential military purpose funds, 8-6
conventional warfare, 1-4, 1-5, 1-7, 2-10, 3-12, 3-19, 4-14, J-4
coordination, 2-1, 2-2, 2-5, 2-10, 2-11, 3-4, 3-5, 3-7, 3-15, 3-16, 4-4, 4-7, 4-12, 4-17, 5-7, 7-2 through 7-4, 7-7, 7-9, 8-2, 8-4, 8-5, A-2, A-11, B-18, B-20 through B-22, B-24 through B-26, C-1 through C-3, D-8, F-2, G-2, G-4, G-11
corporations, 2-7, 2-12, 3-17, 6-9, A-2 through A-4, B-14, B-16, D-1, D-3 through D-5
counterinsurgency (COIN), iv, 1-5, 2-1, 3-18, 3-19, 4-9, C-11, G-10, J-2, J-4
counterintelligence (CI), 1-5, 3-18, 4-7, 4-8, 7-1, 8-5, B-18, B-23 through B-26, C-3, C-6 through C-8, C-10, C-11, E-10, F-3
counterterrorism (CT), 1-3, 1-5, 2-9, 3-18, 3-19, C-2, C-5, C-7 through C-9, C-11, F-2, F-3, F-5, G-5, G-14
criminal, 1-5, 2-9, 3-3, 3-4, 3-6, 3-18, 4-4, A-2, A-5, C-7, F-3 through F-5
culture, 2-12, 3-1, 3-4, 3-11, 4-1, 6-5, B-5, B-13 through B-15, B-17, B-18, B-26, D-6, H-1 through H-6, H-8 through H-12, I-1

D
Defense Intelligence Agency (DIA), 8-2, C-4, C-5, C-10, G-4
defense support to public diplomacy, 2-2, 2-3, B-18, B-20, B-21, B-25, B-26
Department of Commerce (DOC), 2-6, 2-7, 2-11, 2-12, D-6
Department of Defense (DOD), 2-3, 2-10, 2-11, 3-2, 3-5, 3-7, 3-20, 4-1, 4-2, 4-12, 6-7, 6-10, 8-2, 8-5, 8-6, B-17, B-20, B-21, B-23 through B-26, C-4 through C-6, C-8, C-9, F-2, G-1, G-4, G-5, G-9, G-11, G-12, I-2, J-4
Department of Energy (DOE), C-5
Department of Homeland Security (DHS), 2-10, C-5, C-6, C-9, F-3, F-4, G-4, G-11, G-12
Department of Justice (DOJ), F-2, F-3
Department of State (DOS), 2-2, 2-3, 2-6 through 2-8, 2-11, 4-16, 6-10, A-11 through A-13, B-14, C-6, F-4, G-10
Department of the Treasury, 2-7, C-6, E-9
diplomatic, informational, military, and economic (DIME), 1-1, 2-1, 2-3, 4-11
diplomatic, informational, military, economic, financial, intelligence, and law enforcement (DIMEFIL), 1-1, 2-1, 2-3, 2-11, 2-12, 4-5, 4-17, 5-1
direct action (DA), 1-3, 3-11, 6-9, 8-10, G-14, J-3
Director of National Intelligence, C-1 through C-3, C-7, C-8
doctrine, iv, 1-3 through 1-5, 1-7, 2-1, 2-10, 3-1, 3-5, 3-7, 3-16, 8-3, C-8, D-3, G-4, G-11, G-15, J-2, J-3, J-4
Drug Enforcement Administration (DEA), 2-11, C-7, F-3, F-4

E
environment, A-1
 anarchic, A-1
 antiaccess, 3-3
 civil-military, 1-5, 7-2

Index

coastal, 5-2, E-7, F-4, G-12

complex, 2-2, 2-3, 2-7, 3-3 through 3-5, 3-12 through 3-14, 3-19, 4-2, 4-5, 4-17, 4-18, 5-1, 5-3, 5-4, 5-6, 7-6, 8-9, A-2, A-14, B-17, B-18, C-3, C-5, C-6, C-10, C-11, D-3, E-3, E-11

dynamic, 3-12, C-5, C-8, C-9

economic, 1-1, 1-2, 1-7, 1-8, 2-6 through 2-8, 2-11, 2-12, 3-1, 3-3, 3-9, 3-14, 3-16 through 3-20, 4-11, 4-14, 4-16, 4-18, 6-11, 7-1, 7-6, 7-8, A-1, A-2, A-4 through A-6, A-10 through A-12, B-4, B-9, B-16, B-17, C-4 through C-6, C-9, D-1 through D-3, D-5 through D-8, E-1, E-3, E-5, E-7 through E-10, F-4, G-12, H-5, H-9, H-10, J-1, J-2

financial, 1-1, 1-2, 1-5, 2-7, 2-8, 2-11, 2-12, 3-3, 3-18, 3-20, A-6, A-12, B-6, C-6, C-7, D-1, D-3, D-4, D-6, E-2, E-4, E-5, E-7 through E-11, F-1 through F-4, G-5, I-2, J-4

foreign, 1-3, 2-1, 2-2, 2-3, 2-8, 2-9, 2-11, 3-6 through 3-8, 3-11, 3-12, 3-15, 3-17, 3-19, 4-2, 4-14, 4-15, 4-17, 5-6, 7-10, 8-1 through 8-3, 8-5, 8-6, A-4, A-5, A-9 through A-13, B-9, B-13 through B-15, B-20, B-21, B-24, B-26, C-1, C-3 through C-11, D-1, D-2, D-4, D-6 through D-8, E-4 through E-6, E-8 through E-10, F-2 through F-5, G-1, G-2, G-8, G-10 through G-12

global, 1-5, 1-7, 2-1, 2-6, 2-8, 2-10, 2-11, 3-1 through 3-6, 3-12, 3-17, 3-20, 4-5, 4-9, 5-1, 6-8, A-2, A-3, A-6, A-8, A-11, A-12, B-8, B-16, B-20, C-5 through C-9, D-1, D-5, E-1, E-3, E-6 through E-9, E-11, F-1, F-3, G-1, G-5, G-7, G-10, G-13, G-14, H-4, H-5, I-3, J-3

hostile, 1-2, 1-7, 2-6, 3-4 through 3-7, 3-11, 3-13 through 3-15, 3-19, 3-20, 4-4, 4-6, 4-9, 4-10, 4-12, 4-13, 4-15, 4-16, 5-1, 5-4, 5-6, 7-8, 8-1, 8-3, 8-9, 8-10, B-16, B-17, B-26, D-5, H-7, J-1, J-2

human, iv, 2-1, 2-3, 2-5 through 2-12, 3-1, 3-10, 3-11, 4-15, 5-3, 5-4, 6-3, A-2 through A-5, A-8, A-9, A-11 through A-13, B-2, B-3, B-17, B-18, B-20, B-24, C-3, C-7, C-10, D-3, D-8, E-1, E-7, F-2, H-1, H-4 through H-6, H-9, H-10, H-12, H-13

information, iv, 1-2, 1-7, 2-1 through 2-12, 3-4, 3-6, 3-8, 3-16 through 3-18, 3-20, 4-5, 4-8, 4-12, 4-14, 4-16 through 4-18, 5-1 through 5-3, 6-3, 6-4, 6-6, 6-7, 6-9 through 6-11, 7-1, 7-2, 7-4 through 7-6, 7-8, 7-9, 8-1 through 8-3, 8-7, 8-8, A-1, A-2, A-12 through A-14, B-1 through B-5, B-8 through B-12, B-14 through B-26, C-1 through C-11, D-5 through D-7, E-10, E-11, F-1 through F-4, G-5, H-11

information-sharing, C-2

intelligence, 1-1, 1-2, 1-7, 2-3 through 2-9, 2-11, 3-3, 3-5, 3-6, 3-10, 3-13 through 3-15, 3-17, 3-19, 3-20, 4-4, 4-5, 4-7 through 4-10, 4-13, 4-14, 5-2 through 5-7, 6-5, 8-2, 8-4, 8-6 through 8-8, 8-10, A-1, B-18, B-19, B-22 through B-25, C-1 through C-10, D-7, E-10, E-11, F-3, F-4, G-9, I-1, I-2, J-2, J-3

international, iv, 1-1, 1-2, 2-1 through 2-3, 2-6 through 2-8, 2-12, 3-1 through 3-5, 3-11, 3-12, 3-15, 3-16, 3-18, 3-20, 4-1, 4-3, 4-7, 4-10, 4-17, 4-18, 5-7, 6-11, 7-3, 7-9, 7-10, 8-2, 8-3, A-1 through A-12, A-14, B-3, B-8, B-9, B-13 through B-16, B-24 through B-26, C-1, C-3, C-6 through C-9, D-1 through D-3, D-5 through D-8, E-4 through E-11, F-1 through F-5, G-2, G-12, H-6, J-4

law enforcement, 1-5, 3-18

marine, F-4, G-12

maritime, 2-10, 4-13, 6-11, 8-4, 8-5, 8-10, A-5, C-9, C-10, F-2, F-4, G-3 through G-5, G-9, G-12, I-2

natural, 1-1, 2-1, 2-6, 2-7, 3-8, 4-9, 5-4, 6-6, 7-2, 7-5, 7-8, A-1 through A-4, A-8, A-13, D-1, D-3, E-7, F-2, G-11, G-12, H-2, H-3, H-10, H-11

nonmilitary, 1-1, 2-1, 2-9, 2-12, 3-8, 4-3, 4-4, 4-10, 4-15, 5-1, 7-8, 8-3, B-15, B-16, J-4

open, 2-8, 6-6, A-6, B-11, B-15, B-26, C-3, E-8, H-8, H-10

operational, iv, 1-3 through 1-6, 1-8, 2-3, 2-5, 2-7, 2-8, 2-11, 3-3 through 3-10, 3-14 through 3-17, 3-19, 3-20, 4-2 through 4-5, 4-7, 4-13, 4-14, 4-16, 4-18, 5-1 through 5-5, 6-8, 6-9, 7-1 through 7-7, 7-9, 7-10, 8-1 through 8-3, 8-5, 8-8, 8-9, A-8, A-9, B-17, B-18, B-21 through B-26, C-2, C-5, C-7 through C-10, F-2, G-2 through G-10, I-1, I-2, I-3

peaceful, 1-1, 1-2, 2-6, 2-8, 2-10, 3-3, 3-13, 4-10, A-10, B-19

security, iv, 1-3, 1-5, 1-7, 2-2, 2-6 through 2-9, 3-1 through 3-7, 3-10, 3-13, 3-15, 3-16, 3-18, 4-4, 4-6, 4-8 through 4-11, 4-15, 4-17, 4-18, 5-3, 5-4, 5-6, 5-7, 6-1, 6-6, 6-9, 7-5 through 7-8, 7-10, 8-2, 8-5, 8-8, 8-9, A-3, A-10, A-12 through A-14, B-14, B-16 through B-21, B-23 through B-26, C-1 through C-9, D-8, E-3, E-9, E-10, F-2 through F-4, G-1, G-10 through G-12, G-14, H-2, I-2

sensitive, 1-2, 2-3 through 2-6, 3-4, 3-6, 3-11, 3-12, 3-14, 3-15, 4-10, 4-13, 5-2, 8-1, 8-3, 8-10, B-20, G-11, J-3 strategic, 1-4 through 1-7, 2-1, 2-2, 2-6 through 2-8, 2-10 through 2-12, 3-2, 3-4 through 3-17, 4-3, 4-6, 4-10 through 4-12, 4-18, 5-6, 6-8, 7-4, 8-1, 8-2, B-14 through B-16, B-19 through B-21, B-25, C-1, C-2, C-4, C-6, C-8, C-9, D-7, E-11, F-5, G-1, G-2, G-5, I-1, I-2, J-3, J-4

tactical, 2-7, 2-8, 3-8 through 3-10, 3-12, 3-15, 4-2, 4-3, 4-7, 4-9, 4-13, 4-16, 4-18, 5-2, 5-5, 6-4, 6-8, 6-9, 7-3, 7-4, 8-1, 8-2, 8-4, 8-5, 8-8, 8-10, B-14, B-21, B-23, C-9, C-10, G-5, G-6

unconventional warfare, iv, 1-2, 1-4, 1-8, 2-2, 2-3, 2-5, 2-6, 2-8 through 2-10, 3-4, 3-19, 4-1, 4-4, 4-7, 4-10, 4-17, 6-5, 7-2, 8-8, 8-10, I-1 through I-3, J-1

ethnicity, A-1, H-3, H-6, H-9

F

Federal Bureau of Investigation, 2-11, C-7, F-3

folklore, H-1, H-12

force health protection, 8-7

force protection, 3-10, 4-4, 5-5, 6-4, 7-1, 7-9, C-5

foreign humanitarian assistance, 3-19, 7-6

foreign internal defense (FID), 1-3, 1-5, 3-7, 3-18, 3-19, 4-9, 4-10, 5-7, 6-3, 6-10, 6-11, G-7, G-14

fourth-generation warfare, J-4

full-spectrum operations, 3-7, 3-8, C-11

G

geographic combatant commander (GCC), 2-1, 3-8, 3-10, 4-5, 8-4

globalization, 2-8, 3-1, A-1, A-2, B-5, D-1, D-5, D-6, F-3, H-3, H-5

guerrilla, 1-1 through 1-3, 3-9, 4-6 through 4-8, 4-10, 5-3, 5-4, 5-6, 6-1, 6-6, 7-1, 7-2, 8-5, 8-6, 8-8, 8-9, I-2, J-1 through J-3

base, 8-8

force, 4-7, 6-1, 8-6, 8-8, 8-9

warfare, 1-2 through 1-4

H

holistic, 1-7, 2-1, 3-20, 4-18, 5-6

hospitals and medical operations, 8-6

host nation (HN), 1-3, 2-2, 3-7, 4-10, 4-17, 5-7, 6-11, 7-4, 8-1, 8-2, B-14, E-6, G-2

human intelligence (HUMINT), 2-5, C-1, C-3, C-4, C-9 through C-11

I

indirect, 1-1, 1-4, 1-7, 2-8, 2-10, 2-12, 3-6 through 3-8, 3-11, 3-15, 3-18, 4-3, 4-11, 5-5, 6-6, 8-1, 8-10, D-3, J-3

information operations (IO), 1-5, 2-2, 2-3, 2-7, 3-13, 3-17 through 3-19, 4-7, 7-5, 8-4, B-1, B-16 through B-26, C-8, G-7, G-14

information providers, B-3

instruments of national power, iv, 1-1, 1-2, 2-1, 2-2, 2-6, 2-10 through 2-12, 3-8, 3-13, 4-11, 4-17, 4-18, A-1, A-10, B-2, C-2, G-2

diplomatic, 2-1

economic, 2-6

financial, 2-7, E-1

informational, 2-2, 2-3

intelligence, 2-3, 2-5, C-1

law enforcement, 2-8, 2-9, F-3

military, 1-1, 1-2, 2-10, G-2

insurgency, 1-1 through 1-3, 1-7, 1-8, 2-2, 2-6, 3-5, 3-19, 4-6 through 4-9, 4-18, 5-3, 5-4, 6-1, 6-2, 6-7 through 6-9, 6-11, 7-5, 7-8, C-6, I-1, J-1, J-3

insurgent, 1-3, 1-4, 2-5, 4-6, 4-8, 5-3, 5-6, 6-1, 6-3, 6-5, 6-9, 7-8, J-2, J-3

intelligence

community, 2-7 through 2-9, 2-11, 5-1, C-1 through C-9, E-10, F-2

contingency funds, 8-6,

intelligence preparation of the battlefield (IPB), 2-9, 4-16

intelligence preparation of the operational environment (IPOE), 4-5, 5-1

intelligence, surveillance, and reconnaissance, 2-5, C-4, C-8, C-9, G-7

interagency intelligence process, 2-4

intelligence community, C-9

intelligence contingency funds, 8-6

interagency, iv, 1-2, 2-1, 2-6, 2-8, 2-11, 2-12, 3-4 through 3-6, 3-8, 3-12, 3-15 through 3-20, 4-1, 4-2, 4-5, 4-11, 4-12, 4-14, 4-17, 4-18, 5-1, 5-2, 6-4, 7-7, 7-10, 8-1, 8-3, 8-5, 8-10, A-11, A-14, B-14, B-26, D-8, E-11, J-4

international

finance, E-4, E-5, E-7

law, A-2, A-3, H-6

organizations, A-5, A-6

trade, A-5, D-1

irregular

element, 4-3, 4-5, 4-9, 5-1

forces, 1-2, 1-3, 1-5, 1-7, 1-8, 2-3, 2-5, 3-5 through 3-12, 3-14, 3-15, 4-1, 4-3, 4-8 through 4-10, 4-12, 4-13, 4-16 through 4-18, 5-2, 5-5 through 5-7, 6-1 through 6-4, 6-10, 7-1, 7-3, 7-5, 7-8, 8-1, 8-6 through 8-10, J-1, J-2

organization, 4-2, 4-6 through 4-10, 4-15, 5-3 through 5-6, 6-8, 6-9, 8-8

warfare, iv, 1-3 through 1-8, 2-1, 3-12, 3-13, 3-17 through 3-20, 4-8, 4-9, J-4

J

Joint Chiefs of Staff (JCS), G-1, G-8, G-12

joint force commander (JFC), 2-3, 3-7, 3-8, 3-10, 3-13 through 3-17, 3-19, 3-20, 4-5, 4-12, 4-14, 4-17, 4-18, 5-1, 5-6, 8-10, A-13, B-21, B-22, B-25, G-2, G-7

joint operations, 2-4, 2-11, 3-2, 3-11, 3-12, B-18, B-25, C-1

joint special operations task force (JSOTF), 4-13, 4-14, 4-16, 7-4, 8-3, 8-5, 8-9

Index

joint task force (JTF), 2-3, 2-6, 2-7, 3-8, 3-11, 8-4, B-21, B-25, C-10
joint, interagency, intergovernmental, and multinational, 6-4, 6-5, 8-5

L

levels of war, B-18
logistics support, 7-5, 8-5, G-2, G-6

M

major combat operations (MCO), 1-5 through 1-7, 2-6, 3-12, 3-13, 3-16, 3-19, 3-20, 4-10, 5-6
mass base, 4-8, 5-5
media, 2-2, 2-11, 3-6, 3-17, 4-1, 4-15, 6-1, 6-3, 6-5, 6-6, 6-8, 6-9, 7-8, 8-4, A-2, B-1, B-3 through B-5, B-7 through B-13, B-15, B-21, B-25, H-3, J-4
military deception, 6-3, B-18, B-20 through B-22, B-24, B-25
multinational corporation, D-5, E-4, E-6
mythology, A-1, H-1, H-11, H-12

N

national defense strategy, 3-1, 3-2, 3-5
National Geospatial-Intelligence Agency (NGA), C-8, G-4
national military strategy (NMS), 3-2, 3-5, 3-14, C-10
National Reconnaissance Office, C-8
National Security Agency (NSA), 8-1, C-8, C-10
National Security Council (NSC), 2-1, 2-6, 3-1, C-1, C-3, G-1, G-2
national security strategy, 2-3, 3-4, 3-6, 3-11
nonstate actor, 1-4, 1-7, 1-8, 2-8, 2-12, 3-3 through 3-6, 3-19, 3-20, 4-4, 4-11 through 4-13, 4-15, 5-6, 8-5, A-8, A-10, E-4

O

Office of the Secretary of Defense (OSD), B-21, B-25

operations security (OPSEC), 4-4, 6-4, 6-9, 8-5, B-18, B-21 through B-25
other government agency (OGA), 4-16, 5-2, 5-7, 6-7, 8-7, 8-10
overt operations, 3-15, J-2

P

paramilitary forces, 1-3
paramilitary operations, 4-6, 5-4, J-3
pilot team, 4-5, 5-1, 5-2, 6-3, 7-2
political warfare, J-2
populace and resources control, 7-5
principles of war, 3-9
Psychological Operations, iv, 1-5, 2-3, 2-11, 3-5, 3-6, 3-9, 3-10, 3-12, 3-15, 3-16, 3-18, 3-19, 4-6 through 4-8, 4-10, 4-12 through 4-15, 5-2 through 5-4, 6-1 through 6-11, 8-3 through 8-5, B-16, B-18, B-21, B-24 through B-26, G-7, G-15, J-4
Psychological Operations acts, 6-2, 6-3
Psychological Operations assessment team, B-21
Psychological Operations group, 4-12, 8-3, G-15
public affairs, 2-2, 2-3, 6-10, B-14, B-18, B-20 through B-22, B-25, B-26
public diplomacy, 2-3, B-14, B-15, B-18, B-21, B-26

Q

Quadrennial Defense Review Report, 1-4

R

regular forces, 1-3, J-1
regulars, 1-1, 1-3
resistance forces, 4-10, 4-14, 4-16, 5-3, J-2
resistance movement, 1-2, 1-3, 1-8, 4-4, 4-6, 4-8, 4-15, 5-3, 5-4, 6-1, 6-3, 7-1, 7-2, I-1, J-1, J-3
rules of engagement (ROE), 3-11, 4-1 through 4-3

S

safe houses, 4-7, 4-8

Secretary of Defense (SecDef), 2-1, 2-10, 2-12, 3-5, 3-8, 3-14, 3-15, 4-5, 4-11, 4-12, 4-15, 6-1, 7-9, 8-6, C-4, C-5, G-1 through G-4, G-6, G-10
Secretary of State, A-10, B-14 through B-16, C-6, D-8, F-4
seven phases of UW, 7-1
shaping, 1-6, 2-3, 3-5, 3-12, 3-14, 4-5, 4-13, 4-16, 5-1, 7-5, B-11, D-8
Special Forces group (airborne), 8-3, G-14
Special Forces operational detachment A (SFODA), 2-11, 4-12 through 4-14, 5-2 through 5-4, 5-6, 8-7, 8-8
Special Forces operational detachment B (SFODB), 4-14
Special Operations Aviation Regiment (SOAR), 4-12, 4-13, 8-9, 8-10, G-15
special reconnaissance (SR), 1-3, 8-10, G-14
stability, security, transition, and reconstruction (SSTR) operations, 1-5 through 1-7, 3-12, 3-18, 3-19, 4-12
strategic communication, 1-5, 2-2, 3-18, B-2, B-20, B-21
subversion, 1-1, 1-2, 1-8, 3-17, 3-19, 4-7, 4-8, 4-10, 7-2, 7-8, J-1, J-2, J-3
surrogate, 1-3, 2-2, 3-9, 8-5, 8-10, J-3
Sustainment Brigade (Special Operations) (Airborne), 4-12, 8-4, 8-5, G-15

T

tactics, techniques, and procedures (TTP), iv, 3-5, 4-3, 4-4, 4-13, 5-1, 5-6, 7-8, G-4, J-4
theater special operations command (TSOC), 3-10, 4-5, 4-13, 4-14, 4-16, 5-2, 8-5
traditional warfare, 1-5, 1-8
transnational corporation, D-5, E-6
Treasury, 2-7, 2-8, C-6, E-9, E-10, E-11
tribes, 6-5, 8-7, A-1, B-17, H-9 through H-11

Index

U

unconventional assisted recovery, J-3

unconventional warfare (UW), iv, 1-2 through 1-5, 1-7, 2-1 through 2-3, 2-5 through 2-12, 3-1, 3-4 through 3-12, 3-14 through 3-16, 3-18 through 3-20, 4-1 through 4-6, 4-8 through 4-18, 5-1 through 5-7, 6-1 through 6-11, 7-1, 7-5, 7-7, 7-8, 7-10, 8-1 through 8-10, A-14, B-2, B-3, B-21 through B-26, G-14, H-1, I-1 through I-3, J-1 through J-4

   operational area, 1-4, 2-2, 2-3, 2-5 through 2-9, 2-11, 2-12, 3-9 through 3-12, 4-1, 4-3 through 4-6, 4-8 through 4-10, 4-12, 4-13, 4-15, 4-16, 4-18, 5-1 through 5-4, 5-6, 5-7, 6-4, 6-10, 7-2, 7-3, 7-5, 7-10, 8-2 through 8-10, H-1

underground, 4-6 through 4-8, 5-5, 5-6, 6-1, 6-5, 6-6, 6-8, 6-9, 8-5, J-1

unified action, 2-6, 3-16, G-1, G-2

United Nations (UN), 4-1, 4-10, 7-5, 7-9, 8-7, A-1 through A-4, A-6 through A-9, A-13, C-6, E-6, E-7, E-10, F-2, G-2, H-6, I-1

United States
   Army, 2-10, 3-5, C-11, G-5, G-9, G-11 through G-14, I-3
   Army John F. Kennedy Special Warfare Center and School, v, G-15
   Army Reserve, iv, 7-4, 7-7, 7-9, G-12, G-13
   Army Special Forces Command (Airborne), 4-12, G-14
   Army Special Operations Command (USASOC), 4-4, 4-12, 8-2, 8-5, G-13 through G-15, 1
   Coast Guard, 2-10, C-9, F-4, G-4, G-5, G-11, G-12
   foreign policy, 2-1
   Government (USG), 2-1 through 2-6, 2-8, 2-9, 2-11, 2-12, 3-1, 3-2, 3-5, 3-8, 3-11, 3-12, 3-14, 3-15, 4-1, 4-5, 4-9 through 4-11, 4-14, 4-16 through 4-18, 5-1, 5-6, 5-7, 6-6, 6-10, 7-4, 7-6, 7-10, 8-5, 8-6, A-11, B-2, B-14 through B-17, B-20, B-21, B-26, C-2, C-5 through C-10, D-3, D-6, E-4, E-5, E-9, E-10, F-3, F-4, G-2, G-4
   Information Agency, B-15
   Marine Corps (USMC), 2-10, C-10, G-5, G-10 through G-12
   Navy (USN), 2-10, 8-4, C-8 through C-10, G-4, G-5, G-7 through G-12
   Special Operations Command (USSOCOM), iv, 1-2, 3-5, 3-6, 4-4, 4-12, 8-1, 8-2, 8-6, G-1, G-3 through G-5, G-11, G-12

unrestricted warfare, 1-3, J-4

W

War on Terrorism (WOT), iv, 1-3, 3-2, 3-5 through 3-7, 3-19, 3-20, 8-2, C-9, E-5, F-5, J-4

warfighting, iv, 2-6, 2-10, 3-2, 3-4, 3-16, C-9, G-6

weapons of mass destruction (WMD), 3-1 through 3-3, 3-13, A-11, A-12, C-4, C-7, E-10, F-2

This page intentionally left blank.

FM 3-05.130
30 September 2008

By Order of the Secretary of the Army:

GEORGE W. CASEY, JR.
General, United States Army
Chief of Staff

Official:

JOYCE E. MORROW
Administrative Assistant to the
Secretary of the Army
0824601

DISTRIBUTION:

Active Army, Army National Guard, and U.S. Army Reserve: To be distributed in accordance with initial distribution number 115992, requirements for FM 3-05.130.

Printed in Great Britain
by Amazon